TOWARDS UTOPIA

TOWARDS UTOPIA
A Study of Brecht

KEITH A. DICKSON

CLARENDON PRESS · OXFORD
1978

Oxford University Press, Walton Street, Oxford OX2 6DP

OXFORD   LONDON   GLASGOW   NEW YORK
TORONTO   MELBOURNE   WELLINGTON   CAPE TOWN
IBADAN   NAIROBI   DAR ES SALAAM   LUSAKA
KUALA LUMPUR   SINGAPORE   JAKARTA   HONG KONG   TOKYO
DELHI   BOMBAY   CALCUTTA   MADRAS   KARACHI

British Library Cataloguing in Publication Data

Dickson, Keith Andrew
    Towards Utopia.
    1. Brecht, Bertolt—Criticism and interpretation
    I. Title
    832'.9'12   PT2603.R397Z/   77–30639
    ISBN 0–19–815750–9

*Printed in Great Britain by
Butler & Tanner Ltd, Frome and London*

Preface

NOT for nothing did Brecht call himself 'awkward'. There is general agreement about his stature as a writer but a very wide divergence of opinion as to what he is actually saying. Most publications on Brecht to date are divided into four mutually hostile camps, none of which does him full justice. Marxists have on the whole endeavoured to cash in on his universal popularity by displaying him as a plaster saint of Party orthodoxy or else they have condemned him as a dangerous heretic. Non-Marxists have mostly sought to differentiate between the poet and the propagandist or, more rarely, they have decried him as a subversive influence. The basic assumption of this present study is that the complete Brecht is inaccessible without a careful consideration of his political and philosophical views, but also that the critic who attempts to rank him alongside Johannes R. Becher as a superior kind of Party hack is equally incapable of evaluating his intellectual and artistic achievements. Again, criticism has tended to be too preoccupied with the gloomy picture of chaos and contradiction that emerges from his work to detect and analyse the political optimism that is its explicit or implicit corollary. This study seeks to demonstrate Brecht's belief in the perfectibility of human society, of which the classless Utopia is an attainable, though by no means inevitable, goal.

The first part of this analysis investigates the philosophical premises of Brecht's guarded optimism. It traces the continuity of thought that links the world of the apparent nihilist of the early twenties with that of the committed Marxist. To this end his developing conception of nature, man, society, and history is explored in depth. The second part shows how Brecht's work exposes the ideological superstructure of pre-revolutionary society, which obscures the road to Utopia by encouraging a stultifying apathy towards social problems or by diverting revolutionary zeal from its true objective. The final part examines the problem of literary form and shows how Brecht seeks to create new modes adequate to the expression of an activist interpretation of past and present and a utopian vision of the future.

Although the works that have made Brecht internationally famous are subjected to more or less detailed analysis this study of the utopian dimension of his thought also investigates works about which relatively little has so far been written, his poetry and fiction, for instance, his adaptations of *Antigone* and *Coriolanus*, and plays such as *Die Rundköpfe und die Spitzköpfe* and *Die Tage der Commune*. Although this method sometimes entails giving what may seem undue emphasis to works of less artistic merit it is hoped that a more comprehensive picture of Brecht will emerge as a result.

It is a commonplace of criticism that poetry is what gets lost in translation. If, as Lion Feuchtwanger maintains, Brecht is the greatest linguistic innovator writing in German this century, then clearly his poetry and even his prose will fare worse than most at the hands of the translator. For this reason all quotations from his creative works are here given in the original, so that even the reader with little German may be encouraged to try and catch some of the unique flavour of Brecht's language. Translations of passages marked with an asterisk are included in the Appendix on p. 310.

The manuscript was completed in the summer of 1975 but minor adjustments have been made in the light of subsequent research.

Warm thanks are due to the many colleagues whose expertise in contiguous fields of research brought valuable new insight, in particular to Mr. R. J. Beckley, Professor J. W. Bridge, Mr. F. D. Harvey, Dr. W. D. Hudson, Mr. J. R. P. McKenzie, Mr. I. R. D. Mathewson, Professor J. M. Ritchie, Mr. G. de Sainte Croix, Dr. D. Sedge, and Mr. H. W. Stubbs, but most of all to Professor W. E. Yates, whose rigorous scrutiny resulted in numerous changes in both form and substance; also to the editors of *Brecht Heute* and *Forum for Modern Language Studies* for permission to base two chapters on material first published in those journals; to the Bertolt-Brecht-Archiv, the British Library, the London School of Economics, and the university libraries of Exeter, Hull, London, and Frankfurt for their facilities; to

Mrs. Nancy Scattergood for secretarial assistance; to Dr. G. Opie for generous help with the proofs; and last, but by no means least, to several generations of students, without whose intervention this book would have been finished much sooner but would have been very different.

It is the author's pleasure to dedicate all royalties from this publication to Christian Aid, which tackles the fear and misery of the Third World in the same spirit, albeit with very different means, as the writer whose vision of a more just world is the subject of this book.

University of Exeter

Contents

Introduction

Die Kräfte waren gering. Das Ziel
Lag in großer Ferne
Es war deutlich sichtbar, wenn auch für mich
Kaum zu erreichen.
So verging meine Zeit
Die auf Erden mir gegeben war.*

(9:724)[1]

I T is not as a visionary that Brecht has made his international reputation, but as a satirist. As is so often the case with satirists, however, the world he condemns emerges much more vividly from his work than the Utopia by which he judged it, with the result that the utopian dimension of his writing has been largely overlooked, and the prophe the undoubtedly was has not infrequently been mistaken for a cynic.

Satire and utopianism are in fact correlatives. Although primarily concerned with the exposure of vice and folly, the satirist has usually sought to imply the possibility of reform. Thus Dryden maintained that 'the true end of satire is the amendment of vices',[2] Defoe that 'the end of satyr is Reformation',[3] and Swift, marginally less optimistic, that the satirist is inspired by 'a publick Spirit, prompting men of genius, to mend the world as far as they are able'.[4] The satirist's account of the present is orientated towards an ideal future from which the vice and folly he ridicules have been eradicated. As Schiller puts it in his classic comparison of 'naïve' and 'sentimental' literature: 'In satire actuality with all its deficiencies is confronted with the ideal as the supreme reality.'[5] Belief in the practicability of the ideal will vary in degree according to the

---

[1] Unless otherwise indicated, all references to Brecht's work are quoted from the twenty-volume Werkausgabe (*Gesammelte Werke*), first published by the Suhrkamp Verlag, Frankfurt, 1967, and reprinted here with their permission. The first figure refers to the volume, the second to the page. Translations are my own unlesss otherwise indicated.

[2] Quoted from A. Pollard, *Satire* (The Critical Idiom 7), 1970, p. 2.
[3] Ibid.   [4] Ibid., p. 73.
[5] *Werke* (Nationalausgabe), Weimar, 1943, ff. vol. 20 p. 442.

temperament of the individual satirist, and in any case he will not usually consider it his job to prescribe particular methods of achieving it. But belief in its desirability, together with a more or less malicious delight in undermining the complacency of those who settle for less, may be regarded as one of the satirist's main sources of inspiration, and certainly it was one of Brecht's.

The utopian is a satirist in disguise. His ideal commonwealth is an implicit criticism of his own society, the shortcomings of which can be measured against the standards of an imaginary world whose sole determinants are reason and good will. Thomas More, who introduced the word Utopia into the European vocabulary, encouraged the reader to compare his imaginary republic with Tudor England. Brecht himself once wrote: 'Thomas More described in his *Utopia* a country in which just conditions prevail—it was a very different country from the one in which he lived, but it bore a close resemblance, except for the conditions!' (18:232). The same might be said of the Land of the Houyhnhnms in Swift's *Gulliver's Travels*, of Butler's *Erewhon*, and countless other derivative utopias. As one historian of the genre puts it: 'The portrayal of an ideal commonwealth has a double function: it establishes a standard, a goal; and by virtue of its existence alone it casts a critical light on society as presently constituted.'[6] Social criticism is the common denominator of satire and utopian vision. 'Satire and utopia are not really separable,' concludes the same historian, 'the one a critique of the real world in the name of something better, the other a hopeful construct of a world that might be. The hope feeds the criticism, the criticism the hope.'[7]

Brecht uniquely combines the functions of satire and utopianism in his work. If the satirist is on the whole more vocal than the prophet, there are three main reasons. The first is rooted in Brecht's personal disposition as a writer, the second derives from his theory of literature, while the third is largely a matter of semantics.

Firstly, it must be admitted that Utopia is a dull place for poets, and there can be few who share the optimism of Fourier, who calculated that amongst Utopia's three billion inhabitants there would be thirty-seven million Homers and as many

[6] R. C. Elliott, *The Shape of Utopia*, Chicago and London, 1970, p. 22.
[7] Ibid., p. 24.

Molières. Writers almost invariably find the contradictions of the present world a much more rewarding subject than a future world in which the gulf between actuality and the ideal has been bridged. Brecht is no exception. No writer has taken a keener delight in the contradictory nature of reality than Brecht, who for this very reason, perhaps, found the dialectical philosophy of Hegel and Marx so congenial, and who rated the publication of Mao Tse-tung's book *On Contradiction* the outstanding literary event of 1954. Consequently, though he never lost faith in it as a political objective, he had little literary interest in a world from which all contradiction has been removed and where in consequence, as H. G. Wells once observed, 'that which is the blood and warmth and reality of life is largely absent'.[8] Its contours are plainly visible as a distant resolution of present discord, notably in the prologue of *Der kaukasische Kreidekreis*, in *Die Tage der Commune*, in *Coriolan*, and in some of the poetry; but it is significant that in the *Kreidekreis* it is Azdak's chaotic world that dominates our interest, not the idealized world of Georgian kolkhozniks, and that in both *Die Tage der Commune* and *Coriolan* the infant utopias are under siege. 'Our imagination of the good life', writes Robert Elliott, 'is as barren as our imagination of the bad is rich'[9] and, despite his political optimism, of no one is this truer than of Brecht.

Secondly, Brecht's theory of literature offers the writer every inducement to give free rein to his imagination of the bad. Brecht's art demands a dialectical response from reader and audience, who, instead of identifying with a mimetic simulation of reality, are expected to remain critically aloof from it, measuring its shortcomings against a viable alternative that is implied but not spelled out. As a rule, Brecht stubbornly refused to 'show us our tomorrow', as Andrei Zhdanov, Stalin's cultural executive, demanded of Socialist Realists.[10] It is perhaps as well that his unorthodox conception of socialist art led him in this direction, for the glimpses we have of a post-revolutionary world in his work do not make us regret that he usually sought his inspiration elsewhere. It seems as though Brecht accepted the paradox, that, although belief in a free society is what sustains his

[8] H. G. Wells, *A Modern Utopia*, 1905, p. 7.
[9] Elliott, op. cit., p. 120.
[10] A. Zhdanov, *On Literature, Music and Philosophy*, London, 1950, p. 16.

literary activity, it is impossible to depict the life led by free men within such a society. This is either because their energies will be devoted to the solution of tasks as yet unforeseeable, or because, as another unorthodox Communist has suspected, it is only in 'unperfect' societies that men develop their creative powers to the full and thus merit the poet's attention.[11]

The third reason for Brecht's relative neglect of Utopia is bound up with the traditional Marxist rejection of 'utopian', as opposed to 'scientific', socialism, despite the common historical background. Utopia has been defined as 'the secularization of the myth of the Golden Age'.[12] As Saint-Simon pointed out, secularization transposed the Golden Age from the past to the future, a feature it inherited from the millennialist tradition of the Church. In the eighteenth century the myth underwent a further change. More's enthusiastic traveller, Raphael Hythloday, discovered to his regret many things in his secularized New Jerusalem 'which I may rather wish for than hope for'.[13] But for the optimists of the French Enlightenment 'the infinite perfection of our species', foreseen by Condorcet, was much more than a chiliastic vision: it was a realizable goal. Though the moral utopias of Rousseau, the Jacobins, and Fourier differ considerably from the economic utopias of Condorcet, Turgot, and Saint-Simon, they all share a belief in the practicability of the utopian ideal, and some anticipate its immediate realization with the same fervid expectancy with which the early Christians awaited the dawn of the millennium. Their English counterpart, Robert Owen, himself a prosperous industrialist, wrote in 1817: 'Even now the time is near at hand . . . when swords shall be turned into ploughshares, and spears into pruning hooks—when every man shall sit under his own vine and his own fig-tree, and none shall make him afraid.'[14] The founding fathers of Orbiston, an industrial community inspired by Owen's ideals, expressed this millennial hope with even greater fervour

[11] M. Djilas, *The Unperfect Society*, 1969, p. 92.

[12] Elliott, p. 24.

[13] *Utopia*, pt. 2, Ch. IX.

[14] Quoted from James H. Treble, 'The Social and Economic Thought of Robert Owen', in *Robert Owen, Prince of Cotton Spinners*, ed. J. Butt, Newton Abbot, 1971, p. 31. Owen himself referred to this millennialist ideal as the 'New Religion', which would render all men 'rational, intelligent, wise, sincere and good' (*The Life of Robert Owen, written by Himself*, vol. I, 1857, p. 136).

in hymns such as the following, published in their official
journal:

> Ah! We shall see that glorious day,
> When, thron'd on Mercy's brow,
> The TRUTH shall rend that veil away
> Which blinds the nations now;
> When Earth no more with anxious fear
> In misery shall sigh;
> But pain shall cease—and every tear
> Be wip'd from every eye.[15]

Marx and Engels repeatedly acknowledge their indebtedness
to the earlier pioneers of a secular Utopia, but they entirely
reject their kind of prophecy on the grounds that it was not
rooted in the hard material facts of social reality, but represented merely another form of wishful thinking. They argue
that it offered an illusory palliative instead of an effective and
permanent remedy. *The Communist Manifesto* already warns
against false prophets and denounces Saint-Simon, Fourier
and Owen as 'critical-utopian' socialists, whose vision of social
justice was ultimately unrealizable because it fell short of a full-
scale revolution, of which the proletariat is the sole guarantor
and executive. Its joint authors object that in the minds of such
misguided idealists 'historically created conditions of emancipation' are ignored in favour of 'fantastic pictures of future
society'.[16] Above all, the utopians are accused of retarding the
revolutionary process of history by opposing political action,
because they were irrationally committed to a 'fanatical and
superstitious belief in the miraculous effects of their social
science'.[17] When Engels came to revise his *Anti-Dühring* as a
popular tract in 1880, he gave it the significant title *Die
Entwicklung des Sozialismus von der Utopie zur Wissenschaft* (the
standard English translation is entitled *Socialism, Utopian and
Scientific*). Engels again singles out Saint-Simon, Fourier and
Owen as examples of a reactionary brand of reformist socialism
that must give way to a truly scientific socialism. Scientific

---

[15] Ibid., p. 135.

[16] Karl Marx and Friedrich Engels, *Werke* (Institut für Marxismus–Leninismus
beim ZK der SED), Dietz Verlag, Berlin, 1956–68, vol. 4, p. 490. Unless otherwise
indicated, all references to Marx and Engels are quoted from this edition and the
translations are my own. Hereafter cited as Dietz.

[17] Ibid., p. 491.

socialism, though it never loses sight of its objective, does not attempt to foist its vision of the future upon the present by main force, but works constructively towards its Utopia by manipulating the empirically established laws of historical development. In *The German Ideology* Marx and Engels write: 'Communism is not for us a *state of affairs* that is to be established, an *ideal* to which reality will have to adjust itself. We call communism the *real* movement that abolishes the present state of affairs. The conditions of this movement result from the premisses now in existence.'[18]

In contrast to the utopians, Marx persistently refused to write 'recipes for the cookshops of the future'.[19] Both Marx and Engels proved in fact notoriously unreliable as prophets on the few occasions when they succumbed to the temptation. In 1850 Marx maintained that the discovery of gold in California would turn the Atlantic into an inland sea, and in 1888 Engels prophesied the subjugation of Canada by the United States within a decade, to say nothing of their chronologically and geographically inaccurate predictions of world revolution. Except for Engels's rather hazy notion of the 'withering away of the state' as the post-revolutionary prelude to full communism, neither the timing nor the nature of Utopia was the primary concern of the founders of scientific socialism. Instead of crystal-gazing, they devoted their energies to the empirical investigation of prevailing conditions and the practical problems of organization and propaganda.

So emphatic was their rejection of 'utopian' socialism that the very word fell into disrepute in Marxist usage. At the Soviet Writers' Congress of 1934 Zhdanov claimed that a vision of the Soviet future, to which loyal Soviet writers were committed, 'will not be utopian, since our tomorrow is being prepared by planned conscious work today'.[20] In the same spirit the glossary of a popular German edition of *Das Kapital* offers 'unrealizable' as a synonym for 'utopian'.

On the whole, orthodox Marxism in the twentieth century has dismissed the detailed prediction of all except the immediate future as wild and irrelevant speculation. The non-Marxist

---

[18] Dietz, vol. 3, p. 35.
[19] Quoted from D. McLellan, *The Thought of Karl Marx*, 1971, p. 216.
[20] Zhdanov, op. cit., p. 16.

world, on the other hand, has noted with alarm what happens to the ideal when a totalitarian state seeks to enforce its premature realization—one thinks of Zamyatin, Berdyayev, Koestler, Huxley, and Orwell. In the face of scepticism that spans the ideological frontiers the would-be utopian writer has had little encouragement. At the same time, Marxism has never retracted the claim advanced for it by its founder, that it is the 'solution of the riddle of history and knows itself to be this solution'.[21] In this spirit some of its more recent apologists, reacting against the dour pragmatism of the Stalinist era, have begun once more to articulate what Lenin calls 'the right to dream',[22] and, latterly, even the word 'Utopia' has reappeared in their writings as a symbol for an attainable social reality purged of the injustice that still vitiates it. Thus in 1969 Herbert Marcuse writes enthusiastically: 'Utopian possibilities are inherent in the technical and technological forces of advanced capitalism and socialism: the rational utilization of these forces on a global scale would terminate poverty and scarcity within a very foreseeable future',[23] though he hastens to add that only a radical transvaluation of values on both sides of the Iron Curtain will bring such a Utopia into being. Leszek Kołakowski, the intransigent intellectual rebel of a barely de-Stalinized Poland, is equally emphatic about the revolutionary's need to dream. He writes: 'The existence of a utopia as a utopia is the necessary prerequisite of its eventually ceasing to be a utopia'[24] and, more explicitly, 'goals unattainable now will never be reached unless they are articulated when they are still unattainable'.[25] His Yugoslav counterpart, Milovan Djilas, who has had more cause than most to decry the recidivism of the pseudosocialist camp, has called Utopia the 'inextinguishable primeval dream'[26] and claims that the 'hope for some future, insubstantial, dateless justice' was what sustained him for so many years in the notorious Sremska Mitrovica prison.[27]

The utopian motif in such recent Marxist writing does not indulge pipe-dreams of an impossible future, but discourages

---

[21] Dietz, Ergänzungsband 1 (*Ökonomisch-Philosophische Manuskripte*), p. 536.

[22] V. I. Lenin, *What is to be done?* Ch. 5B. (*Collected Works*, Moscow, 1960, ff., 5, p. 509).

[23] H. Marcuse, *An Essay on Liberation*, 1969, p. 4.

[24] L. Kołakowski, *Marxism and Beyond*, trans. J. Z. Peel, 1969, p. 91.

[25] Ibid., p. 90.   [26] Djilas, op. cit., p. 10.   [27] Ibid., p. 17.

complacency by pointing up the discrepancy between potential and achievement. The most vital notion that Marx inherited from Hegel was that the fundamental dialectic of history is a never-ending process. It can be retarded but never permanently arrested, and thus human society can never in fact attain that final state of perfection that we commonly associate with Thomas More's neologism. What the Marxist apocalypse predicts is something much more realistic than the roseate vision of the utopians, namely infinite progress towards an ever-receding goal. In his work on Ludwig Feuerbach, Engels writes:

> History can never reach a perfected termination in a perfect ideal condition of humanity . . . a perfect society, a perfect state are things that can only exist in imagination. On the contrary, all successive historical situations are only transitional stages in the endless course of development of human society from the lower to the higher. Each stage . . . must give way to a higher form that will also in its turn decay and perish.[28]

Even communism is not to be thought of as the definitive form of society. As early as 1844 Marx warned his disciples against the confusion of ends and means: 'Communism is the necessary form and the active principle of the immediate future, but communism is not itself the aim of human development or the final form of human society.'[29] Although society may resemble the ideal commonwealth more and more closely if it follows the route pioneered by scientific socialism, it can never be identified with it. Etymologically, Utopia is a non-place, and such it will remain since it will always represent a stage of development that society has not yet reached.

This is the sense in which the utopian image will be used throughout this present study. Brecht nowhere specifically mentions such passages as those quoted above, but his work as a whole reveals that this is how he came to understand historical development. He did not seriously envisage a state of absolute perfection as a realistic socio-political objective. But he did share the basically optimistic belief of the dialectical materialists, that human society is in a state of continuous flux, incessantly striving towards higher forms. The utopian dimension of

[28] Karl Marx and Friedrich Engels, *Selected Works*, Moscow, 1950, p. 328.
[29] Dietz, Ergänzungsband 1, p. 546.

Brecht's work functions as a social conscience, continually reminding society how far it still has to go.

This is most obviously true of Brecht's satirical depiction of capitalist society, but it may also be applied to the 'unperfect' societies behind the Iron Curtain, even if, for tactical reasons, Brecht's criticism of them is more discreet. The prologue of *Der kaukasische Kreidekreis* has often been an embarrassment to non-Marxist producers, not so much because it is dramatically less vivid than the rest of Brecht's work (which is true), but because it seems to identify the Soviet Union with Utopia, ignoring the purges, the show-trials and the labour camps that characterized Stalinist Russia. Reliable witnesses have testified to Brecht's condemnation of Stalinism, to which some of his own friends fell victim in the thirties, and it is at least arguable that his Soviet Utopia, like More's prototype, is an implicit criticism of Stalin's empire. The same argument applies to *Die Tage der Commune*, Brecht's last completed major work, written just before he decided to settle in East Berlin, and also to his adaptation of Shakespeare's *Coriolanus*, on which he was still working when he died. Marxist criticism has hailed both of these works as a vote of confidence in the German Democratic Republic. Yet this same self-willed Communist, who prided himself on being 'awkward' (*unbequem*), hung on to his Austrian passport and his Swiss bank account, continued to publish in the capitalist West, and even toyed with the idea of emigrating to China. Among his Buckow idylls he included a satirical poem ('Die Lösung') that openly derides the repressive attitude of the Pankow government after the abortive uprising of June 1953. If all this is an indication of Brecht's honest opinion, his sympathetic depiction of the ill-fated Paris Commune and of Rome's nascent democracy can be read as an implicit denunciation of all pseudo-socialist dystopias, including Walter Ulbricht's. At the same time, it is futile to read into such works a rejection of communism, as so many non-Marxist critics have done. If Brecht rejected the Pankow brand of socialism, it was not because it was too communist, but because, as one West German reviewer has observed, 'it was insufficiently creative, flexible, revolutionary, in other words, not communist enough'.[30]

Brecht's writing, whether in the satirical or the utopian mode,

[30] Ulrich Greiner, in the *Frankfurter Allgemeine Zeitung*, 10 Dec. 1971.

leaves no room for complacency. But neither does it leave room for despair. Its principal driving force, even in the earlier period, is his faith in the resilience and resourcefulness of men in their perpetual search for 'das Land, wo es besser zu leben ist' (8:217). All his most memorable figures, from the antisocial outcast, Baal, and the cowardly conformist, Kragler, to the wily and energetic opportunists, Azdak and Galilei, Mother Courage and Schweyk, are characterized by an unshakeable belief in man's inalienable right to happiness, even in the face of the most formidable opposition. Brecht's favourite mascot was a Chinese jade figurine, uncannily like Caspar Neher's idea of Baal, representing the indestructible God of Happiness. Brecht planned a play on the theme and gives an account of it in his retrospective interpretation of *Baal* in 1954. It was to have shown how men do everything in their power to destroy this god, but to no avail, and its moral was to have been that 'it is impossible to kill off entirely man's desire for happiness' (17:948). It is Brecht's passionate belief in this ineradicable human trait, tempered by a realistic awareness of the hazards to which it is exposed, that gives his brand of Marxism its peculiar accentuation, and his work as a whole its characteristic stamp. The possibility of progress towards Utopia is guaranteed by the mechanics of the historical dialectic and by the limitless energy of its personnel. The primary function of literature is to ensure that this progress is not impeded.

The editor of an anthology of communist classics has written of Karl Marx: 'He believed firmly in man's inherent rationalism and virtue, however much both might be crushed and distorted by the evils and irrationalities of society.'[31] Brecht could have wished for no fairer epitaph. The epitaph he actually proposed in one of his last poems, however, goes even further:

> Ich benötige keinen Grabstein, aber
> Wenn ihr einen für mich benötigt
> Wünschte ich, es stünde darauf:
> Er hat Vorschläge gemacht. Wir
> Haben sie angenommen.
> Durch eine solche Inschrift wären
> Wir alle geehrt.*
>
> (10:1029)

[31] A. P. Mendel (ed.), *Essential Works of Marxism*, 1965, intro., p. 1.

Here Brecht anticipates the success of his work as an instrument of social change in his own lifetime. More realistic, and on the whole more characteristic, is the elegy that rounds off the Svendborg cycle, 'An die Nachgeborenen'. It is dedicated to future generations that will have reaped the rewards of his bitter struggle in the dark ages before the Revolution:

> Das Ziel
> Lag in großer Ferne
> Es war deutlich sichtbar, wenn auch für mich
> Kaum zu erreichen.

$$(9:724)$$

The poet can see Utopia, but it is still a long way off. Although it may have seemed nearer in Buckow in the fifties than it had in Svendborg on the eve of the Second World War, it may be doubted whether the right to dream ever induced Brecht to believe that it was an immediate political objective. What seemed abundantly clear to him, however, was the road towards it, and the primary concern of his work is to urge his audience and his reader to take it while it is still accessible.

PART I:

ANALYSING REALITY

1. Nature

THE doctrine of nature that emerges from Brecht's work is closely related to his doctrine of man and his developing conception of society as a historical phenomenon. Taken in conjunction with these aspects of his thought, which later chapters will analyse in detail, his mature idea of nature forms the basis of his political optimism.

No one could have predicted this from Brecht's early work, however, in which the pessimistic tone predominates. The preoccupation with a desacralized natural order is so striking in his early work, particularly in his poetry, as to suggest that it was the principal cause of Brecht's pre-Marxist nihilism. The first of the prose psalms from the *Hauspostille* anthology states calmly and apparently without rancour: 'Über der Welt sind die Wolken, sie gehören zur Welt. Über den Wolken ist nichts' (8:241). Here, as in *Baal*, the sky demarcates a material cosmos that makes no transcendental sense to the pragmatist who maintained to the end of his life that the truth is concrete. The death of God had created for Brecht a metaphysical void, and nature, no longer 'der Gottheit lebendiges Kleid', emerges as a fundamentally hostile environment, at best coldly indifferent to human suffering.

Brecht instructs the reader of his *Hauspostille* to turn to certain of its poems 'during times when the raw forces of nature prevail' (8:169). If his early poetry is anything to go by these are frequent, for it reflects a chaotic world tyrannized by the storm, the shark, and the vulture, a world in which, despite their show of bravado and the temporary solace of opium and alcohol, the intrepid pioneers of Fort Donald, the reckless Vikings, pirates, and adventurers, Cortez's hapless *conquistadores*, and even the Soviet revolutionaries,[1] all succumb to the

---

[1] Brecht denied that he had the Russian Revolution in mind when he wrote 'Gesang des Soldaten der roten Armee' (which was omitted from editions of the *Hauspostille* after 1927), but Klaus Schuhmann, the most systematic Marxist

ruthless savagery of nature. There is a good deal more than
adolescent affectation in 'Das Lied vom Geierbaum', which the
typescript dates 1912 and in which birds of prey systematically
destroy a tree: it creates an archetypal image of nature's
senseless destructiveness. The sky appears as a protective womb
in the context of *Baal*, but it is unpredictable; it can be a
treacherous 'Haifischhimmel ... bös und gefräßig' (8:210),
and it may even cave in at any moment:

> Auch der Himmel bricht manchmal ein
> Indem Sterne auf die Erde fallen.
> Sie zerschlagen sie mit uns allen.
> Das kann morgen sein.*
>
> (8:89)

The corollary to this is the recurrent shipwreck-motif, which
indicates that even the boldest of us, 'Schlendernd durch Höllen
und gepeitscht durch Paradiese' (8:217), is no match for
nature's indiscriminate malice.

Even more desolate than the imagery of open hostility is that
of indifference. The forests in which the Fort Donald railway-
gang meets its doom in one of Brecht's earliest poems are 'ewig
und seelenlos' (8:13). The most characteristic epithet for the
sky is 'kalt', but it is also applied to the night, the wind, and the
forest, and seems to symbolize what is elsewhere explicitly
called 'die Kälte der Welt' (8:117). The most striking image
is found in the comic sonnet 'Kuh beim Fressen' (1925)—
perhaps a parody of Victor Hugo's 'La Vache' in which the
cow represents provident nature. Brecht's cow, though more
amenable than most of the creatures in his early poetry—it is
giving milk—demonstrates the sovereign indifference of nature
towards the human race with an unmistakable gesture:

> Und während sie sich noch mit Heu versieht
> Entnimmt ihr einer Milch, sie duldet's stumm
> daß seine Hand an ihrem Euter reißt.
>
> Sie kennt die Hand, sie schaut nicht einmal um
> Sie will nicht wissen, was mit ihr geschieht
> und nützt die Abendstimmung aus und scheißt.*
>
> (8:163)

---

interpreter of Brecht's poetry to date, refuses to take the denial seriously: see *Der Lyriker Bertolt Brecht, 1913–1933*, Berlin, 1964, p. 53.

In this relatively late poem nature still has the last word, which significantly rhymes with 'reißt', the rough action of the farmer's hand on the cow's udder. The context embraces a new theme: man exploiting nature for his own ends, but Brecht has little interest in it as yet. In the slightly later poem 'Von der Willfährigkeit der Natur' (1926) the moral neutrality of nature appears in a more serious light: elms bow to a furtive pederast, dust covers up a murderer's tracks, the wind muffles the shrieks of the drowning and rouses a syphilitic lecher by lifting a young girl's skirt.

In the face of this hostility and indifference, the poet experiences a sense of disillusionment and alienation. Like the ship on which Brecht's pirates go singing to their doom, 'Ihr Schiff, das keine Heimat hat' (8:224), man has no home, no natural refuge from the destructive forces of nature. A fragmentary poem of 1920 observes with envy how the trees shelter animals, despite the cruel wind that strips their branches: 'Wir sind sehr einsam, und es macht auch nichts' (8:62). Despite the show of retaliatory indifference, the alienation is keenly sensed and anticipates the later dream-poem ('Oft in der Nacht träume ich', written about 1926) in which the poet roams a nightmare world where no one needs the tables he makes, the fish-merchants speak Chinese, and someone else is wearing his clothes.

As a direct consequence of this alienation, much of Brecht's early poetry is concerned with the attempt to effect some kind of reconciliation with nature, however temporary. Two of his finest *Hauspostille* poems, 'Vom Klettern in Bäumen' and 'Vom Schwimmen in Seen und Flüssen' (1919), offer a partial reunification and refuge. Literally stripped of all connections with human society, the nude climber can become part of the tree and indulge the illusion of timelessness:

> Ihr sollt dem Baum so wie sein Wipfel sein:
> Seit hundert Jahren abends: er wiegt ihn.
> (8:209)

Similarly, the swimmer, a significant figure to whom the next chapter will return, can escape the normally hostile attentions of the wind 'Weil er ihn wohl für braunes Astwerk hält'. Pikes, the freshwater counterpart of the predatory sharks that infest

Brecht's sea-poetry, swim between his limbs and give him a temporary sense of oneness with nature ('ganz geeint'), as he lies there quietly, seemingly part of the river-bed—'als gehöre man einfach zu Schottermassen'—though the hypothetical subjunctive underscores the illusoriness of this self-identification with nature (8:210). Again, in the prose poem 'Vom Schiffsschaukeln' (1920) the ecstatic vocatives 'Schwester Luft, Schwester! Bruder Wind!' are a consciously romantic aberration, the temporary result of a mechanically induced vertigo, the cessation of which can be accurately predicted: 'Nachts um 11 Uhr', the moment the fairground closes (8:78). Brecht's avowed fondness for fairgrounds would doubtless encourage the Freudian analyst to identify the swing-boat in his poem as a thinly disguised symbol for sexual intercourse, and we are reminded that this was in fact Baal's favourite means of creating the illusion of security. It is, moreover, Baal who provides the clearest link between this theme and the nature-imagery, when in a moment of frustration he asks 'Warum kann man nicht mit den Pflanzen schlafen?' (1:29). The commonly assumed identification of Baal with Brecht is justified in this instance by the poems 'Von dem Gras und Pfefferminzkraut' and 'Die Geburt im Baum', both written the following year, where the poet claims to have committed incest with such improbable partners as stones and seaweed. This recurrent motif is clearly not a sign of sexual abnormality but of the thwarted desire for oneness with nature.

The only hope of union with nature lies in a return to the pre-natal oblivion, warmth, and security of the womb. In 'Ballade von den Abenteurern' the poet affects surprise that his homicidal adventurers ever left it for their treacherous seas of absinth:

> Warum seid ihr nicht im Schoß eurer Mütter geblieben
> Wo es stille war und man schlief und war da?
>
> (8:217)

The reader of Brecht's early poetry does not need to be a psycho-analyst in order to interpret the ship as a womb, water as birth, and travelling as a sublimated death-wish, for the three images constantly appear together in contexts where birth and death are thematically interlinked in a back-to-the-womb fantasy. One is advised, for instance, in 'Vom Schwimmen' to let oneself go and 'so tun / Als ob einen ein Weib trägt' (8:210).

Such an umbilical relationship with nature is, however, only a fleeting illusion in normal human experience and is only finally attained in death. In the famous *Hauspostille* ballad, Mazeppa, wildly out of control on his ghoulish ride strapped to a bolting horse, finds release only in death, when he is at last 'gerettet ins große Geborgen' (8:235). After life's fitful fever Ophelia too sleeps well in Baal's elegy 'Vom ertrunkenen Mädchen'. Commentators have paid too much attention to the theme of decay in this poem and too little to the serenity of its rhythm and to the ambiguity of its last line, in which Ophelia–Johanna undergoes her final metamorphosis: 'Dann ward sie Aas in Flüssen mit vielem Aas' (1:53; 8:252). Carrion is hardly a notion we associate with Shakespeare's 'melodious lay', nor with the countless imitations it has inspired, including Rimbaud's *Ophélie*. But Brecht praises carrion in a parody of Joachim Neander's famous hymn, 'Lobe den Herren', on the grounds that nature thrives on it ('Großer Dankchoral'). Is the drowned girl's final condition in Baal's poem not also enviable in its tranquillity? The prepositional phrase with which the poem closes indicates further that man's alienation from nature is overcome in death. She is, to quote Schuhmann's comment on another poem, 'absorbed into the metabolism of nature'.[2]

That for Brecht reunification with nature constitutes a fundamental problem is indicated by the persistence of the theme after his conversion to Marxism. Brecht based his remarkable 'Gleichnis des Buddha vom brennenden Haus' (1937) on a passage in Karl Gjellerup's novel *Der Pilger Kamanita* (1906), but the setting and phraseology have nothing in common with it, nor with the canonical *Majjhima Nikaya*, which contains two similar parables. Brecht's Buddha, somewhat incongruously yoked with Lenin as a political propagandist in the Svendborg chronicles, is asked by his disciples whether nirvana is comparable to 'dies Einssein mit allem Geschaffenen':

Wenn man im Wasser liegt, leichten Körpers, im Mittag
Ohne Gedanken fast, faul im Wasser liegt oder in Schlaf fällt

(9:665)

[2] Schuhmann, op. cit., p. 42, with reference to 'Das Schiff'.

In the event the question is dismissed as a theological abstraction, but the reappearance of the lazy bather establishes a thematic link between the anarchy of the *Hauspostille* and the political activism of the *Svendborger Gedichte*. It indicates that Brecht found in Marxism more than a political canalization of his anti-bourgeois sentiments, his pacifism, and his sympathy with the underdog. He found also an intellectually satisfying solution of his metaphysical dilemma. Marxism offered him a rational explanation of the alienation he had experienced, and simultaneously a method of overcoming it.

The poem 'Die Nachtlager' (1931) provides a pivotal image. Written five years after the decisive reading of *Das Kapital*, it encourages solidarity with New York's down-and-outs, whose temporary shelter from the wind and the snow leaves the social problem untouched:

> Einige Menschen haben ein Nachtlager
> Der Wind wird von ihnen eine Nacht lang abgehalten
> Der ihnen zugedachte Schnee fällt auf die Straße
> Aber die Welt wird dadurch nicht anders
> Die Beziehungen zwischen den Menschen bessern sich
>   dadurch nicht
> Das Zeitalter der Ausbeutung wird dadurch nicht verkürzt.*
>
> (8:374)

Nature remains potentially hostile until human relations are put on another footing.

It is for Brecht no longer nature itself that is the real menace, but society, which fails to provide adequate refuge. Human society is, as the central metaphor of the pre-Marxist play *Im Dickicht der Städte* had already indicated, a jungle, just as treacherous as that which destroyed the *conquistadores*. Friedrich Engels wrote in 1877: 'Socially active forces operate in exactly the same way as the forces of nature: blindly, violently, destructively, so long as we do not recognize them and take them into account.'[3] Such socially active forces may in fact appear a good deal worse. They make man as predatory as the shark, and more cunning—witness the celebrated opening lines of the *Dreigroschenoper*:

> Und der Haifisch, der hat Zähne
> Und die trägt er im Gesicht

[3] Dietz, vol. 20, p. 260.

Und Macheath, der hat ein Messer
Doch das Messer sieht man nicht.*
(2:395)

The idea appears momentarily in an early poem in which Brecht compares his contemporaries unfavourably with hurricanes ('Song zur Beruhigung mehrerer Männer'), anticipating the consciously political application of the same motif in *Mahagonny*:

Schlimm ist der Hurrikan
Schlimm ist der Taifun
Doch am schlimmsten ist der Mensch.
(2:526)

The image recurs in 'Der Taifun' (1941), in which Nazi 'pirates' make the typhoon seem the lesser evil, and by the same token, the children in 'Kinderkreuzzug', of the same date, perish in the bleak winter of 1939 only because Hitler's armies have invaded Poland.

The later plays draw freely on the same theme. When Grusche is crossing the dangerous ravine in *Der kaukasische Kreidekreis* a horrified bystander shouts to her above the wind that it is 2,000 feet deep. She replies: 'Aber diese Menschen sind schlimmer', referring to the pursuing soldiers (5:2043). In *Der gute Mensch von Sezuan* rain-clouds suggest to Wang, the water-bearer, the image of an udder ('Wolkeneuter'; 4:1527), which recalls the obliging cow in the sonnet, but he uses it in bitter irony: he depends for his precarious livelihood on the scarcity of water, and when it rains he is ruined. Although Wang is a most sympathetic character, his dream of bliss is a seven-year period of total drought when the inhabitants of Szechwan will grovel for his wares. These two examples reveal the full scope of the theme in Brecht's later work. Social chaos, which encourages man to exploit his fellow men, exposes him in turn to the hostility of nature, instead of enabling him to bring it under control. Furthermore, nature's potential benefits not only remain unexploited but are actually perverted into threats. Brecht's savage pun in his first 'Mahagonnygesang' indicates that the city, ostensibly the political animal's refuge from nature, is diseased:

Auf nach Mahagonny
Das Schiff wird losgeseilt

Die Zi-zi-zi-zi-zivilis
Die wird uns dort geheilt.*
(2:507; 8:244)

But there is no cure for it in Mahagonny, nor in the Berlin, Chicago, or London of Brecht's early plays, nor in any of Anna's seven cities in *Die sieben Todsünden*, nor in Szechwan. Small wonder that Brecht's early adventurers perished in search of 'das Land, wo es besser zu leben ist' (8:217).

It is easy to imagine the intellectual excitement Brecht must have felt during the honeymoon period of his espousal of Marxism, when he learned that man and nature are not mutually inimical components of the universe, but partners in a common evolutionary process. As early as 1844 Marx claimed that communism represents 'the *true* resolution of the conflict of man with nature and of man with man'.[4]

Marxist philosophy owes this idea of nature as a potential ally more specifically to Engels, who expounds it at length in his unfinished masterpiece *Dialektik der Natur*. A digest of this appears in his better-known polemic *Anti-Dühring* where he writes: 'The whole complex of conditions that surround man and that have so far dominated him now comes under the rule and control of men, inasmuch as they become masters of their own social organization.'[5] That Engels includes both nature and the social environment in this complex of conditions emerges from the resounding coda that he added to the popular abridgement of this work, *Socialism, Utopian and Scientific*, which culminates in the words: 'Men, at last masters of their own form of social organization, thereby become at one and the same time masters of nature and their own masters—free.'[6] Lenin, during the long gestation period of the Russian Revolution, cited this work with enthusiasm and reassured his disciples that a dialectical understanding of the universe made them *gospoda prirody* (Lords of Nature).[7] The renegade Trotsky, in an argument about ends and means that foreshadows Brecht's play *Die Maßnahme*, said that any action is justified 'if it leads to the increasing of the power of man over nature and to the abolition

[4] Marx–Engels, *Gesamtausgabe*, Berlin, 1927–35, vol. 1, pt. 3, p. 114.
[5] Dietz, vol. 20, p. 264.
[6] Ibid., vol. 19, p. 228.
[7] *Sochineniya*, Moscow, 1960, ff., vol. 13, p. 156.

of the power of man over man', and he equated this process with 'the liberation of mankind'.[8]

There is no need to document the emphasis Communism has always laid on the role of science and technology in the achievement of this end. Suffice it to quote from the Manifesto of the Communist Party of the U.S.S.R. issued in 1961:

> Communism insures the continuous development of social production and high labor productivity through rapid scientific and technological progress; it equips man with the best and most powerful machines, greatly increases his power over nature and enables him to control its elemental forces to an ever greater extent.[9]

It is thus no coincidence that Brecht's interest in science and technology dates more or less exclusively from his conversion. Lindbergh's heroic struggle 'gegen das Primitive', the ill-fated pioneer's defiance of gravity in 'Der Schneider von Ulm', and the revolutionary empiricism of Bacon and Galilei, can all be seen in this light. It is no use waiting in pious hope for Isaiah's age of gold 'when the wolf and lamb shall feed together'. It is man's historic mission to create it. In the first of the *Messingkauf* poems Brecht joyfully hails the New Age as a 'Zeit des Umbruchs und der großen Meisterung / Aller Natur' (9:761).

In the late twenties this mood induced Brecht to join the adherents of Neue Sachlichkeit in worshipping the machine in such poems as 'Sang der Maschinen', in which the sound of machinery ('die Muttersprache der Welt') replaces the wind in the maples (8:297–8); in 'Über das Frühjahr' spring is observed from a respectful distance, through the window of a railway carriage. There is in this latter poem a trace of nostalgia for 'Die Zeit der unaufhaltsam und heftig grünenden Bäume' (8:314), before the unseemly rush for oil, iron, and ammonia began. But there is no putting the clock back. It is through industry that science and technology bring nature under control.

Brecht was well aware that it is not sufficient to improve and extend industrial technology, since this will not of itself solve the basic antagonism between man and man. He satirizes such utopianism in the poem '700 Intellektuelle beten einen Öltank

---

[8] L. Trotsky, *The Basic Writings*, ed. I. Howe, 1964, p. 395.
[9] Quoted from *Essential Works of Marxism*, ed. A. P. Mendel, 1961, p. 420.

an' (1929), and a few years later the highly developed technology of the Third Reich provided ample confirmation of his scepticism.

Having accepted that Marxism offers the only genuinely scientific insight into the natural laws of society, it follows that the most urgent task is to restructure society in accordance with them. To support the Revolution and the Party that engineers it, is to achieve, in anticipation of ultimate mastery over nature, a dialectical oneness with it, of a kind entirely unknown to the early poetry, but rendered a good deal more intelligible in the light of it. I recall, not without sympathy, an attempt by one of my students to interpret the poem 'Vom Schwimmen' from memory. He made the acceptable point that in this poem Brecht 'implies the complete submission of the individual to a greater force outside himself'. Not remembering the date of the poem, however, the harassed examinee identified this greater force with the Communist Party, whilst the unification of the limbs in the water suggested socialist solidarity. Brecht was certainly not implying any such thing in 1919, but with a little misguided hindsight a pure nature-poem becomes a political cryptogram because the problem of nature and the problem of society are interrelated in Brecht's writing as a whole. Johannes Klein misses the point of Brecht's poetry when he argues that Brecht's feeling for nature seems incongruous in the work of a tough-minded Marxist.[10] Such a view ignores the fact that from Marxist classics Brecht learned to relate the two dialectically. Writing from an ideologically opposite standpoint Schuhmann makes a similar judgement: 'The struggle against the unleashed powers of nature was an illusory struggle, a substitute for the historically conditioned struggle against the exploiting class.'[11] But the activism of Brecht's middle period can be seen more meaningfully as a preoccupation with the problem of nature as Marx and Engels define it.

To be sure, nature in the Romantic sense is temporarily out of bounds for the propagandist, who has more urgent tasks in hand. Of the 46 poems from the *Hauspostille*, 29 deal with nature to a greater or lesser extent; of the 161 poems published in the *Gesammelte Werke* from the period 1926 to 1933, only 11 draw

[10] J. Klein, *Geschichte der deutschen Lyrik*, Wiesbaden, 1957, p. 855.
[11] Schuhmann, p. 189.

their themes and imagery from the world of nature, and of these only one fails to relate it to a social context, or make a political metaphor out of it, or dismiss it out of hand. The exception is 'Das Frühjahr', but even there, though 'das Neue' refers to the seasonal replenishment of nature, it tends to take on the political colour of its surroundings.

The Nazi crisis strengthened Brecht's resolve to abandon nature as a theme. It was, as one of the most famous of the poems of exile declares, a bad time for lyric poetry:

> Was sind das für Zeiten, wo
> Ein Gespräch über Bäume fast ein Verbrechen ist
> Weil es ein Schweigen über so viele Untaten einschließt!*
>
> (9:723)

The poet refuses to be distracted by the deceptive serenity of Svendborg and can still hear the cries of the Nazis' victims ('Über die Bezeichnung Emigranten'); spring in 1938 ('Frühling 1938') brought a freak snowstorm that matched the political climate and in 1940 it meant the breaking of the ice-floes and the threat of an invasion by sea ('1940'); he sees the lakes and woods of Finland and their rich harvest: 'Doch derer auch, die Korn und Milch nicht nährt' (9:822). Similarly, when Puntila, in a fine alcoholic frenzy, waxes lyrical about the beauty of Tavastland, Matti comments icily: 'Das Herz geht mir auf, wenn ich Ihre Wälder seh, Herr Puntila!' (4:1707). The barely audible stress on the possessive adjective explains why Brecht and Matti alike refuse to indulge in gratuitous lyricism. Until nature is freely available to all, the poet is not free to extol it.

After the Revolution, man and nature can at last enter into the fruitful partnership predicted by Engels's dithyrambic apocalypse. The finest expression of Brecht's faith in it is his Svendborg poem 'Die Teppichweber von Kujan-Bulak ehren Lenin' (1929), which describes the transformation of the environment by a poor weaving community in post-revolutionary Turkestan. Instead of a bust to Lenin they buy petrol, at the suggestion of a soldier in the Red Army, to clear the malarial swamps that threaten their already precarious existence. It is easy to deride Brecht's idealized picture of Soviet life, and it is only fair to point out that he based his poem on an ostensibly authentic account published in the *Frankfurter*

Zeitung on 10 October 1929. Brecht needed, and thought he had found, concrete evidence of the practicability of the new relationship between man and nature, and perhaps he took care not to look too closely at life in Soviet Russia lest it shatter the illusion. If reality did not justify the faith, so much the worse for reality!

Brecht found similar confirmation in a minor documentary novel of Socialist Realism describing work on the Volga–Don Dam project.[12] Inspired by it, his Buckow elegy 'Bei der Lektüre eines sowjetischen Buches' (1953) celebrates the taming of the river, which is described anthropomorphically in the style of the early poetry as 'zornerfüllt', 'erfinderisch', and 'teuflisch'; but the verb 'bezwingen' has a line to itself, which ushers in the concluding description of the irrigation of the barren Caspian plains and the bread it will provide (10:1014–1015). One of the dramatist Nikolai Pogodin's proletarian 'aristocrats', working on Stalin's White Sea Canal, exclaims: 'We laugh a fearful element to scorn, we lay our hand upon wild nature and say: You have sucked our blood long enough, you viper!'[13] Such is the heady optimism of the Socialist Realists as they responded in 1934 to the urgent call from Stalin and Zhdanov for a more constructive and positive *partiinost* (loyalty to the Party line). But Pogodin's rehabilitated criminal was addressing a post-revolutionary audience, for whom such defiance of nature is only meaningful within the context of total revolution. Only when the jungle of society has been tamed can the conquest of nature truly begin. In the same spirit Brecht writes of another river, in 'Lied der Ströme', one of his last poems:

> Wenn seine Herren verschwunden sind
> Zähmen wir ihn.

(10:1024)

It is social inequality that makes Old Man Mississippi into a permanent threat. When the slaves are their own masters, he will be transformed into their servant.

The emphasis here, as everywhere else in Brecht's work, is on

---

[12] The novel was *Utro velikoi stroiki* (*The Dawn of a Great Project*), by Anatoly Agranovski and Vasili Galaktionov (Moscow, 1952). The German translation was entitled *Ein Strom wird zum Meer*.

[13] N. Pogodin, *Aristokraty*, act III, sc. 5.

change. In a projected extension of *Dialektik der Natur* Engels wrote: 'But it is precisely *the changing of nature by men*, not nature as such by itself, that constitutes the most essential and most immediate basis of human thought'.[14] The mutability of things gave rise to a mixture of cynicism and regret in Brecht's early poetry—one recalls the evocative images of the cloud in 'Erinnerung an die Marie A.' and the passing cranes in 'Die Liebenden', but now it is precisely nature's capacity for change that solves the dilemma:

> Während so der Dinge Natur ihren Schrecken verloren
> Als sie den Ruf der Unänderbarkeit verlor . . .
>
> (10:895)

This is all of a piece with Brecht's dramatic theory, which aims above all to facilitate a critical attitude in Brecht's special sense of the term. One of the *Messingkauf* poems, entitled 'Über die kritische Haltung', offers examples of it:

> Die Regulierung eines Flusses
> Die Veredelung eines Obstbaumes
> Die Erziehung eines Menschen
> Der Umbau eines Staates
> Das sind Beispiele fruchtbarer Kritik.*
>
> (9:774)

and the imagery reappears in the *Kleines Organon für das Theater* (§ 22). Elsewhere Brecht describes the role of the spectator in Epic Theatre in commensurate terms: 'He is also received in the theatre as the great agent of change, capable of intervening in the processes of nature and society, no longer simply taking the world for granted, but mastering it' (15:302).

Once the possibility of fruitful intervention is accepted, the contemplation even of potentially destructive nature becomes a legitimate source of pleasure. In his *Kleines Organon* Brecht writes: 'Society can enjoy in all its glory even the river that threatens disaster when it bursts its banks, provided society is capable of mastering it, for then the river belongs to it' (16:673). Although in its context the errant river is a vivid symbol for the antisocial element in man, the statement may be taken literally, as 'Lied der Ströme' shows, and the notion behind it is again traceable to Engels: 'It is the difference between

[14] Dietz, vol. 20, p. 498.

the destructive force of electricity in the lightning of a storm and the harnessed electricity of the telegraph and the voltaic arc; the difference between the raging holocaust and fire working in the service of man.'[15]

Nature is domesticated and exploited by the Revolution, collaborating with man in 'das Werk der Verbesserung / Dieses Planeten für die gesamte lebende Menschheit', as Brecht wrote in a poem significantly entitled 'Keinen Gedanken verschwendet an das Unänderbare!' (8:392). In a later poem which expressly revokes the cynicism of the *Hauspostille*, we are challenged 'die Welt uns endlich häuslich einzurichten' (10:1032). The adverb 'häuslich' here explains Brecht's insistence on the house with its smoking chimney in the famous Buckow idyll, 'Der Rauch' (1953):

> Das kleine Haus unter Bäumen am See.
> Vom Dach steigt Rauch.
> Fehlte er
> Wie trostlos dann wären
> Haus, Bäume und See.*
>
> (10:1012)

A passage from Henri Lefèbvre's famous essay on Dialectical Materialism, written in 1938, reads like a commentary on this very poem:

> A tropical forest or a storm on the high seas are pure cosmic forces; man at their mercy is man impotent and isolated, outside nature because he is at the mercy of nature. But a humanized landscape—a house in that landscape built in an appropriate style—these show man within nature, reconciled with it precisely because he has appropriated it for his own use.[16]

It is the fruitful intervention of *homo faber* that not only domesticates nature but brings it to fulfilment.

In Brecht's later poetry the garden frequently replaces the jungle as a symbolic milieu in his private mythology. Here all is 'weise angelegt' ('Der Blumengarten', 10:1009), and methodically watered, pruned, and trimmed. Far from regarding nature as an inveterate enemy, man develops a protective

---

[15] Dietz, vol. 19, p. 223, and vol. 20, p. 261.
[16] H. Lefèbvre, *Le Matérialisme dialectique*, Paris, 1940. Quoted from the revised edition of 1949, p. 115.

attitude towards it—a theme rare in the early verse. During the period of exile Brecht describes in 'Frühling 1938' how he rushed out into the garden with his son one morning and covered a fruit-tree with a sack to protect it from a sudden snowstorm—a symbolic act of faith in a future that will survive the Nazis' barbarous millennium. As Schuhmann observes of another poem: 'The elemental force threatening man has become his helpless protégé.'[17]

The exploitation of the potentially fruitful earth is a theme that has its roots in Brecht's earliest attempts at lyric form. Whilst still at school he wrote 'Deutsches Frühlingsgebet', in which a peasant ignores the lark and the trees ('fröhlich und unnütz') and the background threat of war, and sees only the young corn on which his livelihood depends: the participial adjective 'grünend' occurs four times as a leitmotiv (8:5). On the other hand, the senile opium-smoker in 'Der Gesang aus der Opiumhöhle' asks:

> Wozu ewig Hirse säen in den
> Steinigen Boden, der sich niemals bessert
> Wenn doch keiner mehr den Tamarinden-
> baum, wenn ich gestorben, weiter wässert?*
> (8:91)

Like his Baal, he is 'antisocial in an antisocial society' (17:947). His counterpart in the dull but revealing poem 'Die Erziehung der Hirse' (1950) is Tschaganek Bersijew, who teaches the nomads of Kazakhstan to grow maize: 'So wie die Erde ist / Muß die Erde nicht bleiben' (10:982). In the line 'Tod den Faschisten! / Jätet das Unkraut aus!' (10:991) what elsewhere would be a hackneyed metaphor adumbrates the literal sense it will have later and suggests that the two processes are related methods of mastering the environment.

'Der große Oktober', written to celebrate the twentieth anniversary of the Bolshevik Revolution, represents a secularized hymn of thanksgiving, now that the Revolution has at last facilitated the just exploitation of nature:

> Noch die Ernte
> Ging in die Scheuern der Herren. Aber der Oktober
> Sah das Brot schon in den richtigen Händen!
> (9:676)

---

[17] Schuhmann, p. 96.

In the same way 'Mailied', written for children in 1950, secularizes the traditional May Day rites. It is now Labour Day and anticipates the fair distribution of the harvest, the symbolic first-fruits of post-war socialist endeavour:

> Grün sind die Fluren
> Die Fahne ist rot.
> Unser die Arbeit
> Unser das Brot!*
>
> (10:974)

The prayer of the anxious peasant in 'Deutsches Frühlingsgebet' has been answered three decades later in a way not dreamed of in the young Brecht's philosophy. Geared to the machinery of social revolution, nature has reverted to the provident Demeter of Arcadian myth. As the young convert had earlier put it in his famous appeal for revolutionary solidarity:

> Auf, ihr Völker dieser Erde!
> Einigt euch in diesem Sinn:
> Daß sie jetzt die eure werde
> Und die große Nährerin.*
>
> ('Solidaritätslied'; 8:369)

This explains why the fruit-tree becomes a dominant image of the later poetry and drama. The cherry-tree in Svendborg is akin to that which constitutes Lukullus' only mitigating circumstance before the just tribunal of the Underworld. The peach-trees in 'Augsburg', the apricot-trees in 'Frühling 1938', the raspberry-bushes in 'Glückliche Begegnung', even the luckless plum-tree in 'Der Pflaumenbaum', all betoken Brecht's philosophically orientated interest in what Walter Jens once termed 'the humanly domesticated'.[18] It can scarcely come as a surprise that Brecht's fruit-growing kolkhoz 'Rosa Luxemburg' wins its dispute against the dairymen in the controversial prologue of his *Kreidekreis*, though the latter will also get the land that makes for the best cheese in this socialized Eden.

There is no attempt to rescind the materialism of the early work. There is still nothing beyond the clouds, but there is a new will to civilize the refuge that remains:

> Außer diesem Stern, dachte ich, ist nichts und er
> Ist so verwüstet.

[18] W. Jens, Nachwort to Brecht's *Ausgewählte Gedichte* (edition suhrkamp 86), p. 85.

Er allein ist unsere Zuflucht und die
Sieht so aus.*

(10:959)

Nothing is more indicative of the fundamental change in Brecht's attitude to nature than the transmutation of the ship-image. In the *Hauspostille* it signified the doomed nonconformist and outcast. In 'Lied vom Glück', written about 1951, it has become the communist ship of state, safely piloted across chartered waters, whatever contrary winds may blow:

> Bewacht die Feuer im Kessel
> Steuert und rechnet gut
> Daß ihr durch alle die Stürme
> Kommt über alle die Flut!*

(10:997)

Whatever difficulties Brecht may have had in reconciling his own vision of Utopia with the Stalinist realities around him, he was apparently able to persuade himself that Ulbricht's leaky ship of state was at least sailing in the right direction.

The resultant sense of liberation in Brecht's later work, despite the manifold problems still facing world socialism, and despite periodic set-backs, is unmistakable. In the *Organon* Brecht declares that the transformation of nature is an 'act of liberation' and that his form of art communicates the pleasure it gives (16:687). In complete contrast to his former sense of alienation and reckless abandonment in the face of a hostile environment, in his last years Brecht can describe himself in 'Die Stimme des Oktobersturms' (1952) lying back in comfort—'bequem' has a line to itself—and hearing his own voice in the autumnal winds:

> Die Stimme des Oktobersturms
> Um das kleine Haus am Schilf
> Kommt mir ganz vor wie meine Stimme.
> Bequem
> Liege ich auf der Bettstatt und höre
> Über dem See und der Stadt
> Meine Stimme.*

(10:1003)

That quasi-Buddhistic 'Einssein mit allem Geschaffenen', which in Brecht's early work appears only as a fleeting illusion, is here represented as an accomplished fact.

Dialectically conceived, nature is no obstacle on the road to Brecht's Utopia. On the contrary, it is an essential precondition. By coming to terms with nature, socialist man makes that historic 'leap from the realm of necessity into the realm of freedom',[19] in which Engels saw the supreme achievement of the human race.

As the elegy 'Der Rauch' so clearly indicates, however, the problem of nature cannot be studied in isolation from the problem of man, whose environment it is and whose historical evolution constitutes an integral part of the natural order, and it is to these aspects of Brecht's analysis of reality that the following chapters will now turn.

[19] Dietz, vol. 19, p. 226, and vol. 20, p. 264.

2. Man and Society

(a) The Problem of Individualism

PIERRE Abraham's obituary epitomizes the attempt of so much Brecht criticism to pass off aggressive individualism as the lowest common denominator of his work: 'Brecht est né et reste, malgré tout ce qui a pu changer dans son entourage, un *anti*.'[1] On this reckoning the anti-bourgeois rebel of the twenties modulates effortlessly into the anti-Fascist campaigner of the thirties, the un-American Brecht of the forties, and even Ulbricht's 'awkward' court poet of the last period. A closer reading of Brecht's work indicates that this is only a superficial half-truth. The target of Brecht's aggression in the early work is not so much society, which cramps the individual's life-style. It is rather the individual himself, whose insistence on a unique identity makes society impossible. This reading transforms Brecht from an iconoclastic individualist into 'the apostle of a reaction against individualism', as one of his earliest American admirers observed.[2]

Brecht's amazing first play, *Baal*, provides a valuable clue to the Marxist-orientated conception of man that we find in his later work. Marxist critics have been understandably disconcerted by the conspicuously non-political nature of his early writing, and Brecht himself, looking back on *Baal* at the end of his career, said apologetically, 'I admit (and give fair warning): the play lacks wisdom' (17:948). Retrospectively he diagnosed Baal's condition as a social disease endemic in capitalism: 'He is antisocial, but in an antisocial society' (17:947). But the plain fact is that the play ignores society almost entirely and a self-centred individualist seems to dominate the stage from first to last. The original title, in which the proliferation of exclamation marks parodies the Expressionist style of its model

[1] P. Abraham, in *Europe*, Jan.–Feb. 1957, p. 8.
[2] H. R. Hays, 'The Poetry of Bertolt Brecht', *Poetry*, 67, 1945, p. 148.

(Hanns Johst's turgid play *Der Einsame*), even encourages this misinterpretation: *Baal frißt! Baal tanzt!! Baal verklärt sich!!!*

The first scene in all extant versions of the play shows Baal eating and drinking with complete indifference to his bourgeois admirers while they discuss modern poetry. In the kaleidoscopic series of loosely connected scenes that follow, Baal flouts every social convention. His prodigious sexual appetite, which makes him the male counterpart of Wedekind's Lulu, drives him to adultery, rape, seduction of minors (even two at a time), and homosexuality; he commits breach of contract and murder; he acknowledges no personal loyalties of any kind— even the tenderness he showed towards his mother in the early versions was later omitted. Like the fertility-god whose name he bears, he is the anarchical lord of life, brutal and destructive, beyond good and evil, a law unto himself. Other people are only a human sacrifice to his elemental lust. Small wonder if audiences have persistently seen in all this, as Brecht predicted, 'nothing more than the glorification of egotism' (17:947).

Herbert Jhering was the first to see more than this in the early Brecht. Writing of his adaptation of Marlowe's *Edward II* in 1923, he said that Brecht wrote for an age 'in which the greatness of the individual had in itself become questionable'.[3] Three years later Hugo von Hofmannsthal, once the protagonist of an ultra-sensitive individualism, showed similar insight in an astonishing curtain-raiser for the Viennese revival of *Baal*. Entitled *Das Theater des Neuen*, it takes the form of a dialogue between leading representatives of contemporary culture. At one point Egon Friedell, the cultural historian, attempts to persuade a sceptical Hermann Thimig that the present age needs to be redeemed from the curse of individualism, a product of the sixteenth century grown fat in the nineteenth. The actor Oskar Homolka (the most sensational of the early Baals) agrees with Friedell and declares that individuality is 'one of the arabesques that we have sloughed off'. Friedell continues: 'Oh yes, Thimig, I would go so far as to maintain that all the ominous events we have witnessed in Europe for the last twelve years are only a roundabout way of laying the worn-out concept of the European individual in the grave it has dug for itself.'[4] Friedell clearly

---

[3] H. Jhering, *Die Zwanziger Jahre*, Berlin, 1948, p. 166.

[4] Hugo von Hofmannsthal, *Lustpiele* (ed. H. Steiner), vol. 4, 1956, pp. 418–19.

dates the eclipse of individualism from the outbreak of the First World War. The massive destructiveness of that war and the chaos of abortive revolution and economic crisis that followed in its wake had shattered all faith in the value of the individual. Man, in the sense of a sovereign individual in the tradition of European Humanism, was dead, and Hofmannsthal saw that Brecht for one did not mourn his passing.

In the light of Hofmannsthal's prologue Baal's solipsism takes on a new meaning. It ceases to be wilful exhibitionism and becomes a desperate search for a new kind of identity, totally independent of the moribund society of which individualism was a decadent product. Baal's obsessive consumption of the sexual object is plainly not the result of glandular activity. What Baal is seeking is oblivion rather than sensation. When Baal advises his young friend Johannes to sleep with the girl he loves, he says: 'Wenn du sie beschlafen hast, ist sie vielleicht ein Haufen Fleisch, der kein Gesicht mehr hat' (1:11). The image of facelessness recurs in later versions of the play in Baal's Ophelia-poem (written 1920), where it symbolizes the same abandonment of individual identity:

Als ihr bleicher Leib im Wasser verfaulet war
Geschah es, sehr langsam, daß Gott sie allmählich vergaß:
Erst ihr Gesicht, dann die Hände und ganz zuletzt erst ihr Haar.
Dann ward sie Aas in Flüssen mit vielem Aas.*

(1:53)

Nature knows nothing of individuality and Baal emulates nature's sublime indifference by reducing all human relationships to physical contact. Pregnancy disgusts him not so much because it curtails his sexual activity but because it reminds him of personal ties which the animal in him has abjured, and the same notion probably underlies the homosexual motif, which links this play with *Leben Eduards des Zweiten von England* and *Im Dickicht der Städte*. Perhaps the most poignant expression of the idea is Baal's seemingly unmotivated outburst in an otherwise gentle scene with Sophie, in which he asks why one cannot sleep with plants (1:29). This would represent not only complete communion with nature, as the previous chapter showed, but also the depersonalization of the sexual experience. Even the common euphemism 'intercourse' implies a mutual relation which Baal categorically rejects, and it is perhaps for this reason that non-simultaneous orgasms are high on the list of favourite experiences ostensibly drawn up by Orge[5] (whom Baal, moreover, commends for spending part of his wedding-night in the lavatory).

Audiences have always been stunned by the flagrant carnality of the piece. Even after forty years Kenneth Tynan noted the bewilderment of a West End audience confronted by *Baal* for the first time, and commented: 'Firstnighters, as a group, do not like their noses rubbed in the fact of mortality; they prefer it to keep its distance and speak blank verse.'[6] It certainly does not keep its distance in *Baal*. It assaults the senses from beginning to end. Baal, to whom the whole universe is but the excrement of a dead God, tries to overcome what Hegel called 'the insignificance of finitude', by experiencing his mortality with greater intensity, but he can only do so at the expense of his individuality and his regard for it in others.

Herein lies the deeper significance of his name. The baalim of the fertile crescent were the natural enemies of Yahweh, the God of history, the Law, and the Covenant, and the God of individual responsibility. It was Yahweh, not Moloch or Ashtaroth, whose edicts began 'Thou shalt' and laid the moral foundations of Western civilization. Brecht's hero reverses Elijah's symbolic victory over the priests of Baal on Mount Carmel, and creates an amoral world of his own by renouncing his individual social identity once and for all. 'Ich ziehe mich noch in die Zehen zurück' (1:42) is Baal's own comic way of expressing his withdrawal. Whether or not it is true that Brecht, like his counterpart in Feuchtwanger's novel *Erfolg* (1922), wanted in vain to escape from his personality in order to be 'just one atom among many'[7] he grants this consummation to his first major character.

Baal's sensational life-style must be regarded as a warning rather than a model, since no society could ever be constructed in which such an anti-individualistic existence would not lead to self-destruction. Society necessarily involves personal

---

[5] In the *Hauspostille* poem 'Orges Wunschliste' (8:212).

[6] *Observer Review*, 10 Feb. 1963.

[7] Quoted from the translation by W. and E. Muir, *Success*, New York, 1930, p. 550.

relationships, and even Baal falls victim to petty jealousy when his lover Ekart is unfaithful. His sordid death in the forest indicates a tragic paradox. Baal seeks to overcome the alienation that stems from individuality and yet he dies in chilling isolation. Even the poor, with whom he had temporarily identified himself, spit in his face, and we are left with a sense of the futile expenditure of creative energy. Retrospectively we may argue with Brecht that society owes Baal a better outlet for his perverted talent. In its context Baal's renunciation of individual identity and the social obligations it entails is seen as a tragically impracticable attempt to solve the problem of alienation.

Though *Trommeln in der Nacht*, the first of Brecht's plays to be performed, won him the Kleist Prize for 1922 and was a box-office success, the older Brecht felt even more embarrassed by it than he did by *Baal*. He even thought of suppressing it after rereading it for the 1955 edition of his early plays. To pacify his Soviet admirers, who had conferred the Stalin Peace Prize upon him only the year before, he said he had known virtually nothing about the Bolshevik Revolution at the time and had consequently underrated the seriousness of its ill-fated German counterpart. The fact remains that the original title was *Spartakus*, and that its main character prefers a life of comfortable mediocrity with his shop-soiled bride to a hero's death on the barricades.

Marxist critics have bent over backwards to vindicate this renunciation of revolutionary commitment. Roman Szydłowski, one of Poland's two outstanding Brecht scholars, affects to see it as a landmark in the development of Brecht's 'dialectical' theatre: 'Kragler is incapable of evoking sympathy. He is a negative hero, awakening revulsion. The true heroes of the play are the revolutionary workers, whom Kragler has deserted. Brecht trusted the intelligence and critical thinking of the audience, their logic, moral sense and reason.'[8] Invoking the magic formula 'negation of the negation', Szydłowski argues that we are expected to reject Kragler and construct our own positive hero out of the ruins of the abortive uprising. This is a fair summary of Brecht's technique from the *Dreigroschenoper*

[8] R. Szydłowski, *Dramaturgia Bertolta Brechta*, Warsaw, 1965, p. 33.

onwards, but as a description of either the intention or the effect of *Trommeln in der Nacht* it is wide of the mark. Though Andreas Kragler is a far cry from the New Man of the Expressionist 'Heimkehrerstücke', Brecht's anti-hero ultimately wins the sympathy of the audience precisely because he accepts his lot and has no truck with the idealistic cliché-mongers on the barricades. 'Ich bin ein Schwein, und das Schwein geht heim' (1:123) is the ironical motto of the first of Brecht's long line of conformists. If a dialectical response to *Trommeln in der Nacht* is at all possible, it is not a rejection of Kragler's cowardice, it is the response facilitated by the line Galilei speaks after his cowardly recantation: 'Unglücklich das Land, das Helden nötig hat' (3:1329). Conformity seems to the young Brecht the only virtue that is not a dangerous illusion, for it at least guarantees survival.

Despite the superficial distinctions Andreas Kragler is blood-brother to Baal, for he too is the anti-individualist who finds security in anonymity, and in the renunciation of all ideals and personal relations. Even in his dealings with Anna it is the big, white bed that counts, not personal commitment to its occupant. Lacking Baal's superhuman energy he cannot defy the sordid world, but where he scores over him from a purely Darwinian point of view is in his capacity to meet it on its own terms. As Garga tells Shlink in the climactic scene of *Im Dickicht der Städte*: 'Es ist nicht wichtig, der Stärkere zu sein, sondern der Lebendige' (1:190). Kragler has no more illusions than Baal about his fellow men. The Murks and Balickes of his world feathered their nest at his expense in the war and he can expect no better deal from them now it is over. But in the long run it makes better sense to settle with them than to die building illusory utopias, whether according to Baal's or Rosa Luxemburg's blueprint.

Im Dickicht der Städte opens up another perspective. In 1924 the outraged Alfred Kerr wrote in his review of it: 'Enough of politeness. This is completely worthless rubbish. Completely worthless rubbish!'[9] What baffled Kerr and continues to baffle audiences is the total lack of motivation behind the savage

---

[9] Quoted from Dieter Schmidt, *Baal und der junge Brecht*, Stuttgart, 1966, p. 49.

conflict Brecht projected on the urban jungle of a pseudo-American megalopolis. The author expressly warned his audience not to look for a motive because there is none. They were merely to sit back and keep their eye on the finish, like spectators at a boxing-match—a favourite metaphor of Brecht's which prompted one producer to stage the whole play in a roped-off arena, with bells between the scenes.[10]

The finish reveals the defeated Shlink, a Malay timber-merchant and social outcast, hounded to death by the lynch-mob at the instigation of George Garga, once a meek junior librarian and now a human vampire. Garga spots that Shlink's unmotivated challenge was a perverted declaration of love, a desperate attempt to break out of the isolation of individualism:

Garga Jetzt, gegen Ende, verfallen Sie also der schwarzen Sucht des Planeten, Fühlung zu bekommen.
Shlink (*lächelnd*) Durch die Feindschaft?
Garga Durch die Feindschaft!

(1:186)

Even enmity is a desirable alternative to isolation. Shlink admits that Garga's diagnosis is accurate, but he argues that, whereas animals in the jungle establish real contact in their Darwinian struggle for survival, human beings never achieve it: 'Die unendliche Vereinzelung des Menschen macht eine Feindschaft zum unerreichbaren Ziel' (1:187). Another of the items on Orge's list of requests, 'mutual antagonisms' (8:212), is thus exposed as wishful thinking.

The very language with which individuals attempt to establish a meaningful relationship with each other is, paradoxically, proof of the unbridgeable gulf between them. 'Die Sprache reicht zur Verständigung nicht aus', claims Garga, and Shlink goes on to argue that even sexual intercourse, Baal's panacea for all metaphysical ills, is an illusory attempt to obscure the fact that real contact is impossible: 'Aber die Vereinigung der Organe ist die einzige, sie überbrückt nicht die Entzweiung der Sprache' (1:187). Martin Esslin has seen in this play a precursor of the Theatre of the Absurd,[11] and certainly the affinity is nowhere more uncannily close than in its critique

---

[10] Keith Hack's production at The Place in 1973.
[11] Martin Esslin, *Brecht: a Choice of Evils*, 1959, p. 15.

of language. It looks back to the 'deaf egotists exchanging monologues', as Marc Slonim so aptly describes Chekhov's characters[12]: one thinks of *The Three Sisters* where Andrei, the frustrated academic, can only talk openly with Ferapont because the latter is stone deaf, or of Solyony and Chebutykin who talk at cross purposes about onions and Caucasian meat-dishes because they are not really listening to each other. But *Im Dickicht der Städte* also looks forward to Beckett's metaphysical tramps, who establish rudimentary contact by abusing each other in simulated anger as they wait for Godot. The linguistic absurdity of plays in this tradition, in which Brecht's *Im Dickicht der Städte* forms an important link, reflects the existential absurdity of the individual. On this level the meaning of the play, despite its stylistic idiosyncrasies, is identical with that of *Baal* and *Trommeln in der Nacht*: individualism isolates.

The first signs of a solution to this dilemma occur in *Mann ist Mann*, the play Brecht began in 1921 and rewrote for the seventh time in 1926 on the eve of his conversion to Marxism. Here is yet another play which the older Brecht and his Marxist apologists found embarrassing. Szydłowski's otherwise leisurely biography, which devotes fourteen pages to *Eduard II*, allots a niggardly half-page to its discussion of *Mann ist Mann*, which is written off as 'decidedly pessimistic' and feebly excused on grounds of Brecht's ignorance of Marxism. The reason is clear enough. Where Kragler had betrayed the Revolution merely to save his own skin, Galy Gay gives whole-hearted support to his imperialistic exploiters. In the face of this even Szydłowski had not the nerve to speak of a negative hero who provokes our dialectical response. Ilya Fradkin, so far Brecht's most enthusiastic Soviet supporter, wrenches a moral from it by paraphrasing Brecht's title thus: 'The anti-humanist forces of bourgeois society and militarism depersonalize men to the point of total characterlessness and interchangeability'.[13] Ernst Schumacher draws elaborate parallels between Galy Gay, the dupe of British imperialism, and Hitler's short-sighted supporters in the years immediately following the première of Brecht's play; the storming of Sir El Dchowr is equated with

[12] M. Slonim, *An Outline of Russian Literature*, 1958, p. 176.
[13] Ilya Fradkin, *Bertolt Brecht: Put i metod*, Moscow, 1965, p. 92.

Dachau, Stalingrad, Oradour, Hiroshima, Korea, and Vietnam.[14]

This is all very well. Walter Tillemans made a morality play out of it on much the same lines for his Antwerp production of 1967, in which the soldiers wore the uniforms of American G.I.s in Vietnam, and the Royal Court Theatre, though less tendentious in its approach, gave a spirited performance in 1971 which suggested to one reviewer the caption 'Pop goes Imperialism'.[15] But none of this explains away the unmistakable sympathy evoked by the display of cowardly conformism, which links Galy Gay with Kragler. On revising this play for the 1955 edition, Brecht wrote: 'Here, too, I had a socially negative hero, who had been treated with a certain degree of sympathy' (17:951). He recalled that for the production of 1931 he had been obliged to omit the final section because he saw 'no possibility of giving a negative character to the growth of the hero within the collective', though he thought that a strong enough dose of 'Verfremdung' might now do the trick.

Widow Begbick offers the audience her own interpretation of the play during the entr'acte of this first full-scale essay in Epic Theatre. The version published in 1926 reads:

Herr Bertolt Brecht behauptet: Mann ist Mann.
Und das ist etwas, was jeder behaupten kann.
Aber Herr Bertolt Brecht beweist auch dann,
Daß man mit einem Menschen beliebig viel machen kann.
Hier wird heute abend ein Mensch wie ein Auto ummontiert,
Ohne daß er irgend etwas dabei verliert.
Dem Mann wird menschlich nähergetreten,
Er wird mit Nachdruck, ohne Verdruß gebeten,
Sich dem Laufe der Welt schon anzupassen
Und seinen Privatfisch schwimmen zu lassen.
Herr Bertolt Brecht hofft, Sie werden den Boden, auf dem Sie
  stehen,
Wie einen Schnee unter sich vergehen sehen
Und werden schon merken bei dem Packer Galy Gay,
Daß das Leben auf Erden gefährlich sei.[16]*

[14] Ernst Schumacher, *Die dramatischen Versuche Bertolt Brechts, 1918–1933*, Berlin, 1955, p. 111.
[15] Ronald Bryden, *Observer Review*, 3 Mar. 1971.
[16] Quoted from the original Propyläenverlag edition (Berlin, 1926), p. 62. Cf. *Gesammelte Werke*, 1:336–7.

On revising the play in 1954 Brecht tactfully inserted two additional couplets, which make it much easier to read a Marxist corollary into the text:

> Und wozu auch immer er umgebaut wird
> In ihm hat man sich nicht geirrt.
> Man kann, wenn wir nicht über ihn wachen
> Ihn uns über Nacht auch zum Schlächter machen.*
>
> (1:336)

But the 1926 version was by no means such an unambiguous condemnation of imperialism, to which Galy Gay, the most protean of all Brecht's characters, so profitably adapts himself. It was simply a comic revelation of the precariousness of human identity and the wisdom of renouncing it in the interests of survival. Galy Gay, the guileless packer of Kilkoa, sets out to buy a fish and ends up by capturing a fortress single-handed. The meek little man who cannot say no is brainwashed out of his individual identity by the soldiers and reassembled as a duplicate Jeraiah Jip, 'die menschliche Kampfmaschine' (1:376). Superficially, Fradkin's argument that this constitutes an attack on a system that destroys a man's individuality, seems cogent enough. But Widow Begbick insists that Galy Gay loses nothing in the process, and that she is at this point Brecht's *porte-parole* is indicated by the preface he wrote for the radio broadcast of his comedy in March 1927, in which he told listeners:

I suppose you will be telling yourselves it is rather regrettable that anyone should be tampered with in this way and simply forced to give up his precious ego, the only thing he possesses, as it were, but this is not the case. It is a comical matter. For the fact is, this Galy Gay is not the loser by it at all, on the contrary, he gains by the deal (17:978).

Galy Gay has in fact everything to gain by letting go of his 'Privatfisch' and succumbing to environmental pressure. Whether the actor chooses to project the imperturbable placidity of Hilmar Thate's Galy Gay at the Berliner Ensemble or the Schweykian opportunism of Henry Woolf's at the Royal Court, the role comes over as a tribute to man's capacity for survival, so long as he does not stand on his dignity as an individual. In the radio preface of 1927 Brecht rejected the interpretation of his hero as a spineless weakling: 'I suppose you are used to regarding a man who cannot say no as a weakling, but this Galy Gay is no weakling, on the contrary he is the strongest' (17:978). Brecht justified this unexpected reading with references to Galy Gay's renunciation of individuality: 'To be sure, he is only the strongest after he has ceased being a private individual, he only becomes strong as part of the mass.' The zeal of the communist neophyte shows through here, and for good measure he goes on to say that Galy Gay is only able to storm Sir El Dchowr because he expresses 'the absolute will of a mass of people'.

Brecht's retrospective interpretation is less spurious than it may seem, for the basic image goes back to the play's earliest origins. A note dated May 1921, which describes his embryonic piece as a 'monstrous mixture of tragedy and comedy', praises the durability of its ambiguous hero, 'who, because he lacks a centre, can endure any change, just as water flows into every kind of mould'. It concludes with a laconic synopsis:

> Here lives the donkey who is disposed to survive as a pig.
> The question is: does he then live?
> He is lived.
>
> (15:57)

The Expressionists would have linked this motif with the violent denunciation of capitalism, industrialism, and all that turns men into soulless appendages of the machine. One thinks of the dehumanized clerk in the second part of Kaiser's *Gas* trilogy, who defines himself solely in terms of his function: 'Ich bin Schreiber. Ich schreibe', or the mechanical figures in Karel Čapek's *R.U.R.*, which introduced the word *robot* into the vocabulary of modern technology. In *Mann ist Mann*, however, the argument stops well short of serious criticism and the overall motto seems to be rather what Garga's sister Marie says to Shlink in *Im Dickicht der Städte*: 'Ein Mensch hat viele Möglichkeiten, nicht?' (1:144).

The car-metaphor in Widow Begbick's curtain-speech is significant. (Brecht's lifelong enthusiasm for cars is well known and it seems appropriate that Feuchtwanger made his counterpart Pröckl a mechanic rather than a poet in his novel *Erfolg*.) Brecht was clearly influenced by the mechanistic psychology of

Behaviourism, according to which individual consciousness is a non-functional epiphenomenon. The disciples of Neue Sach-lichkeit hailed this school of thought with enthusiasm in Germany, and although Brecht satirized their extremism in his poem '700 Intellektuelle beten einen Öltank an', this was in 1929, when he had already consolidated his Marxist position. Until then he too had accepted the machine as a true image of the human condition and he did not as yet stop to ask to what use the machine was put.

L'homme machine learns the lesson of evolution in *Mann ist Mann* and adapts in order to survive. He becomes the acquiescent part of a larger mechanical whole, in this case the war-machine of a Kiplingesque imperialism. His transformation is complete and relatively painless. His identity card, according to Kalle (in the *Flüchtlingsgespräche*) the noblest part of man (14:1383), reads 'Jeraiah Jip', and Galy Gay has simply taken over where the original Jeraiah Jip left off. A man's a man, not in Burns's red-blooded sense but in the sense that he is conterminous with his social function and therefore replaceable. Anyone can be transformed into anyone else, given his social function, and to cling stubbornly to an inalienable identity under pressure is dangerous folly. Galy Gay himself, faced with the original Jeraiah Jip in the final scene, harangues his comrades: 'O ihr Knäblein, warum habt ihr mich statt Galy Gay damals nicht gleich noch Garniemand genannt? Das sind gefährliche Späße' (1:374). When Odysseus tells the outwitted Polyphemus that his name is Nobody it is only a taunt, but the anonymity of Galy Gay, as later that of Brecht's *alter ego* Herr Keuner (the word *Keiner* is pronounced thus in Brecht's native Swabia), is a more serious matter, for it is the individual's only protection against a hostile environment.

Galy Gay relates to Baal in his rejection of individualism and to Andreas Kragler in his refusal to play the hero. But in two respects he points forward to the later plays in a way that his predecessors do not. Firstly, he demonstrates the almost infinite resilience and adaptability of man. And secondly, he finds strength and protection by submitting to a suprapersonal collective will. Brecht's intensive study of Marxism in the early summer of 1926 enabled him to synthesize these two themes and solve to his own satisfaction the problem of individualism.

(*b*) *The Social Animal*

The cynical merchant in the later play *Die Maßnahme* asks: 'Was ist eigentlich ein Mensch?' (2:651). The answer in *Mann ist Mann* would appear to be that he is the random and unstable product of a changing environment. Since Brecht seems to have arrived more or less independently at this conception it is surprising how close he had come to the Marxist position without knowing it.

Marx takes to its logical, and at first sight unflattering, conclusion Aristotle's definition of man as the ζῷον πολιτικόν and he applies it to the problem of individualism: 'The individual *is* the *social being*', he wrote in an early work. In view of the charge commonly brought against him, that his philosophy is 'against the individual', it may be noted that even in this context he was careful to preface his definition with a caveat, all too often unheeded by his disciples: 'Above all there must be no attempt to define society as an abstraction over against the individual'.[17] Society must on no account be 'reified' (*verdinglicht*), i.e. treated as though it exists independently of the individuals who compose it. Thus, if it is true that the individual is exclusively defined in terms of society, it is equally true that society is defined in terms of the individual. 'Man is in the most literal sense a *zoon politikon*, not merely a social animal, but an animal that can develop into an individual only in society.'[18] It follows from this not that the individual does not count, but rather, as Brecht reminds the readers of his *Kleines Organon*, that 'the smallest social unit is not one individual but two individuals' (16:688).

This entirely reverses the way we have come to regard the individual in Western society since the Renaissance. Bereft of his autonomy, he can no longer be studied in isolation like a specimen under the biologist's microscope. Human nature as such no longer exists: 'Human nature is not an abstraction manifested in the separate individual. In its reality it is the total nexus of social relations.'[19] If the individual thinks of himself as a sovereign entity, independent of the society in

[17] Dietz, Ergänzungsband 1, p. 538.
[18] *Grundrisse der Kritik der politischen Ökonomie* (Rohentwurf), Dietz edn., 1953, p. 6.
[19] Dietz, vol. 3, p. 6.

which he lives, this is an illusion created by the uniquely human phenomenon of consciousness, which is in itself a product of social relations: 'It is not the consciousness of men that determines their being, but on the contrary their social being determines their consciousness.'[20] This very quotation passed almost verbatim into Brecht's notes on the opera *Aufstieg und Fall der Stadt Mahagonny*, in which Brecht for the first time essayed a comprehensive definition of Epic Theatre. Brecht attributes the maxim 'Thought determines existence' to the conventional forms of dramatic art, while claiming that Epic Theatre adopts as its motto the Marxist axiom 'Social existence determines thought' (17:1010).

As early as 1922 Brecht had praised Bavaria's comic genius, Karl Valentin, for eschewing 'cheap psychologisms' in his sketches (15:39), and if after his study of Marxism he still consistently refused to apply the principles of depth psychology to characterization it was not because, as Gerhard Szczesny has suggested,[21] he was an emotional Peter Pan who never outgrew the adolescent fear of selfhood, but rather because he had become convinced that a study of the individual's private inner world tells us nothing significant about him. 'We must not start with the individual but work towards him', wrote Brecht in the *Organon* (16:682) and in 1954 at a rehearsal of *Der kaukasische Kreidekreis* he put it even more drastically: 'One should never take the personality of a character as a starting-point, for man has no character.'[22]

This deterministic psychology is by no means pessimistic. If human nature turns out to be nothing other than the 'nexus of social relations', then although the individual's identity is a good deal more precarious than is commonly supposed, his potential for development is commensurately greater. Brecht once remarked in a rehearsal that character is not like an ineradicable stain of grease in a pair of trousers,[23] and in the *Organon* he writes: 'There is a lot in a man and a lot can be

[20] Dietz, vol. 13, p. 9.

[21] G. Szczesny, *Das Leben des Galilei und der Fall Bertolt Brecht*, Frankfurt, 1966, pp. 80 ff.

[22] Quoted from *Materialien zu 'Der kaukasische Kreidekreis'*, ed. W. Hecht, Frankfurt, 1966, p. 72.

[23] H. J. Bunge, 'Brecht probiert', *Sinn und Form*, Sonderband Brecht, 1957, p. 324.

made of him. He does not have to remain as he is; he must be considered not only in the light of what he is but in the light of what he might be' (16:682).

The notion of change is fundamental to Brecht's conception of Epic Theatre. The *Mahagonny* notes posit 'unchangeable man' as the dominant theme of classical theatre, whereas Epic Theatre works from a conception of man as a being who is capable of both undergoing change and bringing it about ('der veränderliche und verändernde Mensch') (see p. 235). If a man is as adaptable as Galy Gay, then he is not permanently trapped within his alienated individuality. He can change the world into the kind of environment that fosters the growth of an entirely new form of personality.

(c) *The Individual and the Collective*

Even before that distant goal is achieved the social animal finds his greatest self-fulfilment as an integral part of a larger organism. Here is another aspect of the problem of individualism that links the nihilistic world of the early Brecht with the Utopia of the committed Communist.

In *Mann ist Mann* Widow Begbick expresses Galy Gay's renunciation of individuality by means of a vivid metaphor. She says the hero is requested to adapt to the way of the world 'und seinen Privatfisch schwimmen zu lassen' (1:336). The image of the swimmer in Brecht's work is found as early as 1919 in the poem mentioned in the previous chapter, 'Vom Schwimmen in Seen und Flüssen', in which the poet's ideal self, despite the title, is not a swimmer at all, but a drifter. He allows the current to bear him along so that he becomes temporarily integrated into the natural process:

> Natürlich muß man auf dem Rücken liegen
> So wie gewöhnlich. Und sich treiben lassen.
> Man muß nicht schwimmen, nein, nur so tun, als
> Gehöre man einfach zu Schottermassen.
> Man soll den Himmel anschaun und so tun
> Als ob einen ein Weib trägt, und es stimmt.
> Ganz ohne großen Umtrieb, wie der liebe Gott tut
> Wenn er am Abend noch in seinen Flüssen schwimmt.*
>
> (8.210)

The anonymity of the prescription with the repetitive use of the indefinite pronoun (*man muß . . . als gehöre man . . . man soll*) not only reflects the breviary's avowed practicality, but also forms a link with the anti-individualist theme of the early plays.

Martin Esslin, in support of his interpretation of Brecht in terms of a head-versus-heart dichotomy, sees the drifter as a symbol of man in the grip of uncontrollable passion.[24] He seems to miss the rare sense of harmony and repose that the image evokes. Both here and in Baal's Ophelia-poem the idea of floating anonymously with the prevailing current is presented as a desirable alternative to the conflict caused by individual self-assertion.

Brecht's use of the imagery of swimmer and current is one of the many aspects of his early work that explain why he later found Marxism intellectually and emotionally satisfying. The conception of history as a strong current flowing in a predetermined direction has frequently been denounced as a revisionist heresy by the orthodox Marxist, because it encourages a fundamentally un-Marxist objectivism. But it is a persistent image in Marxist writing for all that. Marx uses it himself in the epilogue to *Das Kapital*.[25] In his essay *Socialism, Utopian and Scientific* Engels cites Heraclitus, in whose famous dictum 'All is flow' he discerns a 'primitive, naïve but intrinsically correct conception of the world' inasmuch as 'everything is fluid, constantly changing, constantly coming into being and passing away'.[26] Trotsky uses the image to illustrate his conception of the 'rhythm of history', maintaining that revolutionaries 'know how to swim against the stream in the deep conviction that the new historic flood will carry them to the other shore'.[27] In the 1931 version of *Mann ist Mann* Widow Begbick follows up her famous interlude with a song entitled 'Das Lied vom Fluß der Dinge', and thereafter the image crops up again and again in Brecht's writings but is always related to Dialectical Materialism, which Brecht defined as 'the doctrine of the flow of things' (18:237).

At first sight the river-image hardly seems conducive to the expression of an activist philosophy. Brecht first reveals its Marxist dimension in the didactic play *Die Horatier und die*

[24] Esslin, op. cit., p. 216.
[26] Ibid., vol. 20, p. 20.
[25] Dietz, vol. 23, p. 28.
[27] *Basic Writings*, p. 395.

Kuriatier (written for children in 1934), which might well have been based on Bacon's dictum: *Natura vincitur parendo*. It contains an episode in which the Horatian warrior learns to use the strong current of a river to supplement his flagging strength in a life-and-death struggle with the enemy. His raft carries him like a battering-ram into the enemy ranks and he inflicts a crushing defeat. If this variation of the image is applied to the historical process it will be seen that it advocates a policy of conquest by submission. Since, however, as Trotsky's metaphor indicates, the prevailing current will not necessarily remain the strongest, it becomes imperative to discover how to identify the right current before submitting to it. Brecht found in Dialectical Materialism a systematic method for tackling the problem.

The picture which emerges from Marx's analysis of historical development is that of a continuous flux, not, however, in the sense of a simple linear development, but of a complex pattern of evolution through contradiction. Although Marx claimed to have stood Hegel on his head by substituting hard economic realities for Hegel's metaphysical Idea, he adopted his dialectical system of analysis. The Hegelian triad—thesis–antithesis–synthesis—became for the young Marx a description of revolution. The state of society at any given time (thesis) contains the seeds of its own destruction (antithesis) which leads to social upheaval until a new order emerges from the clash of opposing forces (synthesis). Marx thought that this dialectic operated in accordance with determinable laws, analogous to Newton's laws of motion. To understand and learn to control these laws constitutes the final phase of man's 'prehistoric' evolution as a social animal. This will enable him to 'overthrow all conditions in which man is a humiliated, enslaved, deserted, and despicable being'.[28]

How clearly Brecht grasped the full significance of all this on his first contact with the Marxist classics it is hard to say, but it must have become clear to him that the metaphysical problem of alienation, which had preoccupied him in the period from *Baal* to *Mann ist Mann*, was solved once he had accepted that it was rooted in concrete but alterable social relations. Instead of remaining in a state of perpetual and fruitless conflict with the environment, the individual can

[28] Dietz, vol. 1, p. 385.

locate and reinforce the historical process destined to change it, and so emancipate his highest potential. As a member of a suprapersonal collective Galy Gay attains a novel sense of fulfilment inaccessible to him as a private individual. From a Marxist point of view his mistake (and Brecht's at the time) is in failing to recognize that the will of this collective is at loggerheads with what Lenin liked to call the 'will of history'. That particular current was not the 'new historic flood'. Though it is hardly a valid interpretation of the play as it stood in 1926, Brecht's own verdict on it thirty years later is revealing: 'The problem of the play is the spurious, inferior collective (that of the "gang") and its seductive power, the same collective that Hitler and his sponsors were recruiting in those very years, exploiting the indeterminate longing of the petty bourgeoisie for the workers' historically mature and genuine social collective' (17:951). It was with this 'genuine collective' that Brecht now confronted the individual in much of his work after 1926.

Class becomes the shibboleth of Brecht's revolutionary phase: '*Class* is a concept in which many individuals are comprehended and thus eliminated *qua* individuals' (16:615). The revolutionary working class with its 'historic mission' now assumes the same role in Brecht's thinking as the lakes and rivers in 'Vom Schwimmen', the tree in 'Vom Klettern', and the womb in the 'Ballade von den Abenteurern', all of which offered the individual a temporary refuge from alienation. It differs from these, however, in the permanence of its guarantee.

Although *Der Ozeanflug* has nothing to do with class as such, Brecht's Lindbergh is the first hero of the new order. Originally entitled *Der Lindberghflug*, this experimental work was first performed at the Baden-Baden Music Festival of 1929, by which time, however, Brecht had already renamed it *Der Flug der Lindberghs* to avoid any suggestion of hero-worship. Perhaps inspired by the generous tribute Lindbergh paid to his team of collaborators in his published memoirs (significantly entitled *We*) Brecht pluralized the role and made the collective Lindberghs sing:

> Sieben Männer haben meinen Apparat gebaut in San Diego
> Oftmals 24 Stunden ohne Pause
> Aus ein paar Metern Stahlrohr.

Was sie gemacht haben, das muß mir reichen
Sie haben gearbeitet, ich
Arbeite weiter, ich bin nicht allein, wir sind
Acht, die hier fliegen.*

(2:571)

When Brecht later learned that the real Lindbergh had expressed sympathy with the Nazi cause he must have felt that
history had endorsed his deep-seated mistrust of the individual.
At any rate, when the Süddeutscher Rundfunk asked permission
to broadcast the work in December 1949, Brecht insisted on
changing the title again, this time to *Der Ozeanflug*, and
Lindbergh's name was deleted altogether from the text. 'Mein
Name tut nichts zur Sache' (2:568) proclaims the new chorus,
thus completing the process of symbolic collectivization begun
during Brecht's spate of enthusiasm for his new faith.

In the austere companion piece, *Das Badener Lehrstück vom
Einverständnis*, the argument is carried a step further. The
chorus calls upon the fallen heroes to renounce their individuality and their imagined right to privileged treatment, until all
except one are able to declare in unison: 'Wir sind niemand'
(2:604). The exception is Charles Nungesser, named after a
French aviator who died in an attempt to cross the Atlantic a
fortnight before Lindbergh's successful flight in May 1927. Like
Icarus, Brecht's pioneer has overreached himself, but he dies
unlamented because he clings stubbornly to his heroic identity.
Unlike the others, who are now 'einverstanden mit dem Fluß
der Dinge' (2:610), he leaves the scene alone and unrepentant
and is ritually excommunicated by the chorus.

In the operatic diptych *Der Jasager/Der Neinsager* the young
hero of the first piece follows the example of Nungesser's
comrades and acquiesces in his elimination in the interests of
the group. Brecht had originally adapted a Japanese noh play,
Taniko, which Elisabeth Hauptmann had translated for him
from Arthur Waley's popular collection. Though this first
version had modernized the setting, its young hero offers himself as a sacrifice on no more plausible grounds than his Asiatic
model, namely out of respect for a time-honoured tradition.
When it was performed at the Karl-Marx-Schule in Berlin-
Neukölln in 1930, shortly after the première, the audience was
asked for its comments and several of them faulted Brecht's

logic. Even a ten-year-old thought the hero's self-sacrifice insufficiently motivated. Brecht accepted their criticism and rewrote the piece as *Der Neinsager*, in which the boy now refuses to die on the grounds that the circumstances do not justify his sacrifice. A new plot was constructed under the old title *Der Jasager*, in which the hero consents to his death because his illness jeopardizes the success of a medical expedition on which the welfare of a whole community depends. All extant versions of the play begin with a line which reveals the origin of Brecht's mistake: 'Wichtig zu lernen vor allem ist Einverständnis'. The renunciation of individuality had assumed such cardinal importance in Brecht's thinking that he failed to notice that the abstract doctrine of acquiescence was barely distinguishable from the blind obedience demanded from the yes-men of Nazism during the same period.

Roman Szydłowski equates Brecht's obsession with sacrifice and acquiescence with the 'leftism' that Lenin once diagnosed as the children's disease of communism. According to him Brecht as an enthusiastic convert 'donned the ascetic's penitential hair-shirt and renounced the many achievements of his earlier work'.[29] But Brecht had not renounced the early work at all. The epic form is radical, even by comparison with the sensational *Dreigroschenoper*, but the theme of sacrifice is a logical extension of the anti-individualism of his early drama and poetry. Gerhard Szczesny in his biased attack on Brecht stresses the connection as follows: 'His conversion from the anarchistic priest of Baal to the rigoristic pedagogue did not in the final analysis constitute a contradiction: both attitudes deny the human individual.'[30] This is a bad misreading of Marxism, which aims at a social form 'in which individuality, far from being eliminated, becomes a more significant factor than in any previous form of society',[31] as one recent Marxist humanist has put it. Szczesny's remark does, however, underline the continuity in Brecht's thinking.

In the period of the Lehrstücke Brecht is not concerned with the nature and function of post-revolutionary individuality, but with the question of subordinating it to class-interests in the current struggle. The most complex of the Lehrstücke and

[29] Szydłowski, p. 105.   [30] Szczesny, op. cit., p. 100.
[31] Helmut Fleischer, *Marxismus und Geschichte*, Frankfurt, 1969, p. 100.

Brecht's starkest play, *Die Maßnahme*, was, for Communists, alarmingly frank about the cost of commitment. Four communist agitators have returned from an abortive mission in Mukden and are summoned before a special Party tribunal to justify the liquidation of a comrade. They demonstrate how they had all renounced their individual identity when their mission began, donning symbolic masks—a device that Brecht took over from the Japanese noh play—in a scene ominously entitled 'Auslöschung' ('Obliteration'). As he distributed the masks the local Party organizer had said:

Dann seid ihr nicht mehr ihr selber, du nicht mehr Karl Schmitt aus Berlin, du nicht mehr Anna Kjersk aus Kasan und du nicht mehr Peter Sawitsch aus Moskau, sondern allesamt ohne Namen und Mutter, leere Blätter, auf welche die Revolution ihre Anweisung schreibt.*

(2:637).

Again the motif of acquiescence, but this time the ideological context is unambiguous: the agitators are 'einverstanden mit dem Vormarsch der proletarischen Massen aller Länder, ja sagend zur Revolutionierung der Welt'. Their headstrong young comrade had also sacrificed his individual identity to a suprapersonal cause that promises the abolition of injustice. But his impulsive nature had proved a constant threat to their mission. Instead of infiltrating unobtrusively in accordance with the Party directive, he had laid down stones for the barge-hauliers when they slipped in the mud, attacked a policeman for harassing the textile-workers, and angrily denounced a rich tycoon as a heartless exploiter. Assuming the role of the dead comrade, one of the demonstrators shows how he had forsworn his allegiance, removing his mask and thus revealing his individual identity. The four agitators comment in unison:

> Und wir sahen hin, und in der Dämmerung
> Sahen wir sein nacktes Gesicht
> Menschlich, offen und arglos. Er hatte
> Die Maske zerrissen.
>
> (2:658)

He had then consented to his death, and his identity was permanently obliterated in quicklime.

It is tempting to see in this solution a prophetic description of the fate that overtook countless thousands of 'individualists' under Stalin. Probably this is why the Left has reacted so strongly against the play. Alfred Kurella, who saw the première in Berlin in 1930, wrote it off at once as a 'typically petty-bourgeois intellectualistic work' on the grounds of its idealistic presentation of the conflict of feeling with reason.[32] Szydłowski rejects it on the grounds that it advocates an abstraction as the highest good, 'the altar on which sacrifices are senselessly and needlessly laid'.[33] Fradkin for his part dismisses Brecht's 'faith in the abstract-rationalist geometry of revolutionary morality'[34] as a travesty of Marxism.

It must be admitted that the motivation of the young agent's death, like that of his counterpart in the first version of *Der Jasager*, is threadbare in the extreme. This in itself suggests that Brecht was at this stage more interested in dramatizing the idea of redemption through sacrifice than in providing cogent reasons for it, and it was almost certainly his realization of this that later made him refuse permission for the play to be performed. Yet Marxist criticism entirely overlooks the sympathy that Brecht evokes for his young 'Gefühlssozialist', which gives the play a genuinely tragic dimension. Brecht could see clearly enough at the time that without passionate concern for the victims of injustice there will be no revolution. Yet without the strict subordination of the individual to a suprapersonal discipline, the Revolution will remain a pious hope. That the surviving agitators are not themselves bloodless robots is emphasized by the fact that they all take it in turns to impersonate their dead comrade, and thus they all readily identify with him in declaring 'Mein Herz schlägt für die Revolution' and 'Ich glaube an die Menschheit' (2:634). The essential difference is that, whereas he endangers the mission with his spontaneous demonstration of sympathy, they have learned to canalize it into organized revolutionary activity.

In *Die Maßnahme* Brecht has dramatized the tragic dilemma facing every revolutionary, who must be prepared, while he is fighting for a more human world, to make the supreme sacrifice of 'all dem, was den Menschen rund macht und

[32] A. Kurella, 'Ein Versuch mit nicht ganz tauglichen Mitteln', *Literatur der Weltrevolution*, Moscow, 1931, no. 4, p. 103.
[33] Szydłowski, p. 116.   [34] Fradkin, op. cit., p. 100.

menschlich', as Brecht put it in a poem a few years later (9:519). His agitators cut the same tragic figure as the one described by Bakunin and Nechayev in their *Catechism of a Revolutionary*: 'The revolutionary is a doomed man. He has no personal interests, no affairs, sentiments, attachments, property, not even a name of his own . . . All the tender, softening sentiments of kinship, friendship, love, gratitude, and even honour itself, must be snuffed out in him by the one cold passion of the revolutionary cause.'[35] Lenin rejected this as the portrait of a fanatical terrorist but he admitted that 'absolute submission to a single will, for the purpose of achieving success in work, organized on the pattern of large machine industry, is unquestionably necessary'.[36]

It is in this connection that Brecht's depiction of the Communist Party in *Die Maßnahme* is particularly revealing. Neither here nor anywhere else does his notion of it resemble Lenin's paramilitary élite, which owed much more to Lenin's Narodnik predecessors than to Marx and Engels and gradually, especially later under Stalin, transformed the dictatorship of the proletariat into the dictatorship of the Party. It is still a matter of dispute whether Brecht ever joined the German Communist Party, but it seems highly improbable and in any case largely irrelevant since Brecht evinced surprisingly little interest in practical politics. Be that as it may, in his literary writings the Party embodies the idea of a collective will, in which the individual finds legitimate self-expression and salvation. One of the interpolated songs, entitled 'Lob der Partei', begins:

Der Einzelne hat zwei Augen
Die Partei hat tausend Augen.
Die Partei sieht sieben Staaten
Der Einzelne sieht eine Stadt.
Der Einzelne hat seine Stunde
Aber die Partei hat viele Stunden.
Der Einzelne kann vernichtet werden
Aber die Partei kann nicht vernichtet werden
Denn sie ist der Vortrupp der Massen
Und führt ihren Kampf

[35] Quoted from G. S. Counts and N. Lodge, *The Country of the Blind*, Boston, 1949, p. 12.
[36] *Sochineniya*, vol. 15, p. 218.

T U—C

Mit den Methoden der Klassiker, welche geschöpft sind
Aus der Kenntnis der Wirklichkeit.*

(2:657)

Although the Party is here pointedly contrasted with the individual, there is ideally no conflict between the two since the Party is the expression of all individuals united by a common purpose. As a collective force it sees more than the individual and is not subject to the limitations of time and space, but it is not independent of him. In the dialogue immediately preceding the song the errant comrade asks: 'Wer aber ist die Partei?' and he receives the reply:

Wir sind sie.
Du und ich und ihr—wir alle.
In deinem Anzug steckt sie, Genosse, und denkt in deinem Kopf
Wo ich wohne, ist ihr Haus, und wo du angegriffen wirst, da
    kämpft sie.*

This idea became a leitmotiv of Brecht's work. Geneviève, the idealistic young schoolmistress in *Die Tage der Commune*, tells the disillusioned Jean on the very threshold of defeat that the Communards are learning from their experience. Jean asks what good this knowledge will do them when they are dead, and Geneviève replies: 'Ich spreche nicht von dir und mir, ich sagte "wir". Wir, das sind mehr als ich und du' (5:2189). In a late poem we read: 'Genossen, laßt uns nicht ICH sagen' (10:964), and another advocates 'ein friedlich WIR' (10:1020).

Brecht appears to have regarded the political realization of this ideal as a remote eschatological event and there is little evidence that he considered the First German Workers' and Peasants' State to be anything more than a tentative step in the right direction. But he had already found one restricted sphere in which a partial realization was attainable as a paradigm of the political future. Brecht wrote: 'The act of artistic creation has become a collective process' (17:1215), and it was in allegiance to this principle that he had relegated his own name from the traditional place of honour in the first theatre programme for the *Dreigroschenoper*, where he appears together with five collaborators, despite the fact that it was indisputably Brecht who was the talk of the town. Throughout his life Brecht preferred to work out his ideas, especially theatrical ideas, in

close co-operation with fellow writers such as Lion Feuchtwanger and Hella Wuolijoki, co-producers such as Hardt and
Burri, stage-designers such as Caspar Neher and Teo Otto,
actors such as Charles Laughton and Ernst Busch, and of course
an impressive succession of composers: Kurt Weill, Paul
Hindemith, Hanns Eisler, and Paul Dessau. During the final
period at the Berliner Ensemble the testimony of countless
visitors and fellow workers suggests he came very close to the
ideal of an artistic democracy, which only lapsed occasionally
into enlightened dictatorship because of the respect he inspired
in others. Konstantin Fedin, accustomed to a very different
artistic climate in Russia, described the Ensemble as an 'arena
of collaboration' and was amazed to find that even the scene-
shifters were given a say in the production.[37] Just eleven days
before he died Brecht wrote the following note for the Ensemble's projected London visit: 'It must be observed that
many artists are at work here, forming a collective (ensemble),
the aim of which is to communicate stories, ideas, works of art,
to the audience in a joint endeavour' (17:1296). Within the
privileged seclusion of his own theatre Brecht had, it seems,
found a practical fulfilment of his desire to sublimate the
individualistic I in a collectively productive We. Moreover, in
Brecht's private Utopia the individual was by no means dra-
gooned into mindless conformity, but rather enabled to
contribute his uniqueness to a common fund of creative thought.

Brecht bequeathed to posterity the formidable task of translating this symbolic commonwealth of talent into political and
social reality, but there can be no doubt that he believed it
possible. Beyond the Revolution man would come of age as a
social animal and create just such a commonwealth, in which,
to use one of the *Manifesto*'s most eloquent phrases, 'the free
development of each is the condition for the free development
of all'.

[37] K. Fedin, 'Vyechny Iskatel', *Literaturnaya Gazeta*, 17 Aug. 1956.

3. The Historical Perspective

Introduction

BRECHT'S profound interest in history is a by-product of his interest in Marxism and there is little evidence of it in what he wrote before 1926. The early poetry revels in exotic décor and violent action, but even if historical adventurers such as Cortez and Alexander put in a brief appearance, its themes and characters are largely timeless. The early plays have near-contemporary and largely fictitious backgrounds, the only apparent exception being the adaptation of *Edward II*, but even here, despite the (mostly invented) dates in the projected scene-headings, Brecht showed less respect than Marlowe for historical authenticity. If he began to take a lively interest in history after 1926 the reason for this is to be sought in the nature of the world-view to which he had been converted.

Marxism is essentially an interpretation of history. The true father of Marxism is not Ricardo or Malthus, who provided its economic basic, nor Babeuf, whose rudimentary socialism proclaimed that the aim of society is happiness and that happiness consists in equality. It is rather Hegel, whose dialectical method enabled Marx to make a diagnostic study of all previous forms of society and from them evolve a blueprint for a rationally and scientifically constructed Utopia. In his English preface to *The Communist Manifesto*, and with the heady confidence inspired by nearly half a century of revolutionary socialism, Engels prophesied that Marx was destined to do for history what Darwin had done for biology. Engels was right. The development of civilization over the last hundred years bears eloquent testimony to the transforming power of ideas that looked to history for their ultimate sanction.

For this reason Brecht the Marxist is concerned to turn his

readers and audiences into serious students of history. In a fine cycle of poems entitled *1940* there is one in which the poet considers his young son's question, whether he should bother learning history. He is momentarily tempted as an exile-weary father to indulge a cynical despair:

Wozu, möchte ich sagen. Lerne du deinen Kopf in die Erde stecken
Da wirst du vielleicht übrigbleiben.

But Brecht's Marxist-orientated reading of history allows no room for the philosophy of the ostrich, and history takes pride of place in his recommended trivium in an age when Nazi ideology was busy distorting history for its own ends:

Ja lerne Mathematik, sage ich
Lerne Französisch, lerne Geschichte!
(9:818)

One of the most fitting tributes to Brecht is a bronze statue and plaque by Werner Stötzer, which were unveiled in the forecourt of the Deutsche Staatsbibliothek in Berlin in October 1961, to commemorate the library's tercentenary. To the right of the path leading up to the main entrance stands a pensive worker, book in hand. He is looking across the path to a plaque, which shows a symbolic cross-section of history from the semi-legendary fall of Atlantis to the victories of Frederick the Great. The reliefs are accompanied by the text of Brecht's poem 'Fragen eines lesenden Arbeiters'. This poem asks who built the fabulous cities of Thebes, Babylon, and Lima, the Great Wall of China, and the triumphal arches of Rome. Were palaces the only buildings in Byzantium? Did Alexander and Caesar, Philip of Spain and Frederick the Great make their conquests single-handed?

Jede Seite ein Sieg.
Wer kochte den Siegesschmaus?
Alle zehn Jahre ein großer Mann.
Wer bezahlte die Spesen?*
(9:656–7)

The proletarian reader has a vested interest in the answers to these questions, which in turn lead to the question raised in the poem 'Solidaritätslied':

> Wessen Morgen ist der Morgen?
> Wessen Welt ist die Welt?
>
> (8:370)

All Brecht's work from 1926 onwards is an attempt to provide the kind of insight into the social mechanism of history that makes the Marxist answer to this question the most convincing.

Reduced to its simplest terms the Marxist answer is based on the hypothesis that man and his milieu coexist in a dialectical relationship. Man is a product of his social environment. This in turn is his own product, though he is temporarily alienated from it and will remain alienated from it until revolution finally emancipates him. The impressive facts and figures Marx so laboriously excavated from the British Museum were used to substantiate his claim that the dialectical law of history still operates today and, once grasped, can be used to reconstruct human society in a way which brings the environment permanently under control.

The realization of man's latent potential was for Brecht, as for Marx, the only legitimate end-product of historical research: 'The conception of man as a variable of the environment, the environment as a variable of man, that is to say the reduction of the environment to relations between men, is the product of a new mode of thinking: historical thinking' (16:628). This form of historical thinking demands much more than the pedantic accumulation of authentic historical detail. As one Marxist critic has observed: 'What matters is not the authenticity of the historically documented event, but the historicity of the thought-content.'[1] One of Brecht's poems for children, 'Der Schneider von Ulm', is 'authenticated' in apparently the same way as the fictitious events of *Eduard II* by means of a sub-title: 'Ulm 1592'. In the style of a popular ballad the poem describes an abortive attempt to defy the law of gravity with the aid of artificial wings. The historical tailor of Ulm, whose exploits became proverbial in Brecht's native Swabia, was Albrecht Berblinger, an ingenious amateur mechanic, who

---

[1] H. Kaufmann, *Bertolt Brecht: Geschichtsdrama und Parabelstück*, Berlin, 1962, p. 184.

invented and tested an unsuccessful kind of glider in 1811. Brecht's fictitious date raises the eccentric artisan to the level of a pioneer and martyr of scientific progress, by ranking him alongside Brecht's other heroes, Giordano Bruno, Francis Bacon, and Galileo Galilei, in the Age of Discovery. The tailor's inglorious end seems to justify the scepticism of the Bishop, who concludes the poem with a solemn prediction that man will never learn to fly. Within the context of the poem the tailor's folly constitutes a form of the heresy for which Giordano Bruno was arrested in the same year, and of which Galileo also stood accused at his trial. The tailor's death is ostensibly a divine judgement on him for flouting an infrangible law of nature. Yet the reactionary Establishment does not really have the last word. Hans Mayer describes a seminar in which students were asked to write a critique of this poem from memory. Several of them mentioned the 'stanza' in which the Bishop is proved wrong.[2] Though there is no such stanza in the text of the poem, the reader superimposes on it a corollary based on his knowledge of modern aviation. This vindicates the tailor's defiance of ossified beliefs, just as a knowledge of refrigeration and atomic physics puts the death of Bacon (in *Das Experiment*) and Galilei's recantation, respectively, into a new historical perspective.

Brecht's ballad emphasizes a basic characteristic of all his mature writing, the real centre of gravity of which is shifted, by means of an implied antithesis, from within the work itself to the world of present social reality. This is what Brecht understood by the term 'Historisierung', which he offered as a synonym for 'Verfremdung' (15:302). In one of his appendices to the *Messingkauf* he wrote: 'In the process of historicization one particular social system is examined from the point of view of another social system. The development of history provides the perspective' (16:653). The present is weighed and found wanting by a pointed comparison with the past, real in such works as *Die Geschäfte des Herrn Julius Caesar* and *Leben des Galilei*, imaginary in *Der kaukasische Kreidekreis* and *Coriolan*.

For Brecht, then, the study of history is not, as with Sir Walter Scott or Alexandre Dumas, a form of escapism, but a treatment of urgent contemporary problems. The distancing

[2] Hans Mayer, *Anmerkungen zu Brecht*, Frankfurt, 1965, p. 46.

effect achieved by geographical and historical transposition—
an essential function of *Verfremdung*—throws contemporary
reality into sharper relief. 'The spectator no longer takes refuge
from the present in history,' wrote Brecht in the *Messingkauf*,
'the present becomes history' (16:610).

But Brecht goes further than this. He follows Marx in urging
that historical analysis is not only a means of understanding
the present in terms of the past, but an instrument for changing
it. The epitaph on Karl Marx's tomb in Highgate Cemetery
epitomizes the practical purpose his historical thinking was
intended to serve: 'The philosophers have only interpreted the
world in various ways: the point, however, is to change it.' It
was not Marx's intention to offer an alternative interpretation
of reality, differing from others merely in the degree of empiricism, but to precipitate a cataclysmic struggle in which the
lessons of history, once learned, would assure the victory of a
class that had nothing but its chains to lose. It is not the past
historic that dominates the grammar of Marxist historiography,
but the imperative, and it is characteristic that *The Communist
Manifesto*, which begins with a potted social history of Europe,
ends with a strident call to arms.

In *Die Maßnahme* one of the choruses addressed to the
audience culminates in the line 'Ändere die Welt: sie braucht
es!' (2:652). Though seldom expressed as starkly as this, the
same political imperative characterizes all Brecht's later work.
Only a couple of years before his death, in a statement intended
to supplement the points he had made about *Verfremdung* in
his *Kleines Organon für das Theater*, Brecht wrote that the only
legitimate aim of theatre is to bring society to 'regard its condition as historical and improvable' (16:706). In their context
the words 'historical' and 'improvable' are virtually interchangeable, indicating that for Brecht history is a function of
social change.

At this point it is appropriate to emphasize how much closer
to Marx Brecht stands than the official apologists of Soviet
Marxism, whose philosophical and aesthetic values were
dogmatically codified by Stalin during Brecht's lifetime. It was
convenient for a dictator to deify history as an inscrutable higher
will that could only be propitiated by the rites he prescribed as
its high priest. At times Marx himself inclined to blur the

important distinction between a law and a trend, and an empirical statement about the way things are and the conditions under which they might be otherwise took on the aura of apocalyptic prediction. The suggestion that history is an autonomous mechanism is unmistakable, for instance, in the following passage: 'In the social production of their life men enter into particular, necessary production-relations, which are independent of their will and correspond to a particular stage of development of their productive forces.'[3] There is, however, no warrant for a mechanistic interpretation of history within the context of Marx's work as a whole. If there were it would make nonsense of Communism's urgent call for active intervention. To set about organizing a revolution that is the inevitable outcome of independent economic processes would, as Rudolf Stammler once suggested, be rather like forming an Astronomical Society for the purpose of obtaining an eclipse.

Though Lenin spoke darkly of the will of history and Trotsky of its rhythm, Marx himself repeatedly warned that men are the 'authors and actors' of their own history. 'History does nothing,' he asserted in a striking passage in *The Holy Family*, 'it does not possess immense riches, it does not fight battles. It is man, alive and real, who does all this, possesses things and fights. It is not "history" that uses man as a means to an end, as if it were an individual in its own right. History is nothing but the activity of man in pursuit of his ends.'[4] In the light of such passages as this the inadequacy of the term 'historical determinism', commonly used to describe Marx's philosophical system, is obvious and it has led one writer to propose the term 'anthropological interpretation of history' instead.[5]

This is not to say that history is the anarchical free-for-all proclaimed by the voluntaristic interpretation which has largely dominated Western thought since the eighteenth century. 'Men make their own history,' wrote Marx as a corrective to this view, 'but they do not make it just as they please; they do not make it under circumstances chosen by themselves, but under circumstances directly encountered, given, and transmitted from the past.'[6] The point of Marx's specific form of

---

[3] Dietz, vol. 13, p. 8.   [4] Ibid., vol. 2, p. 98.
[5] Erich Fromm, *Marx's Concept of Man*, New York, 1961, p. 13.
[6] Dietz, vol. 8, p. 115.

determinism is that men can learn to change the circumstances and make history according to their own will.

Marx believed that such freedom is the goal of history, but since history is only the activity of men in pursuit of their ends there is no built-in guarantee that this goal will ever be reached. As one Marxist puts it: 'History is not progress towards a higher degree of humanity and freedom, but the increasing possibility of such progress.'[7] Such an interpretation of Marxism leaves plenty of scope for the evangelist, for whom the message of social salvation is an urgent kerygma without which the goal of history may never be attained, despite the increasing likelihood. For Brecht, who defines his form of mimesis as the 'depiction of reality for the purpose of influencing reality' (16:717), the function of artistic communication is to demonstrate the dialectical nature of historical reality so persuasively that the addressee will demand the right to make his own history instead of being made by it.

This is true of all Brecht's writings but it is particularly applicable to those with historical themes, since these represent at one and the same time a new reckoning with the past and an activistic interpretation of the present. In the ensuing sections four of Brecht's major works are examined, each of which reveals different aspects of his historical optimism, but which all affirm the belief that man is capable of transforming himself from the object of history into its subject, and so performing what Engels described as 'the leap from the realm of necessity into the realm of freedom'.[8]

Die Geschäfte des Herrn Julius Caesar

Brecht, who proudly maintained that Latin had been his strong subject at school and who retained a keen interest in the world of classical antiquity, was particularly fascinated by the figure of Julius Caesar. He had been impressed by Erich Engel's production of Shakespeare's *Coriolanus* in 1925 and a few years later he was discussing with Erwin Piscator and Fritz Sternberg the possibility of staging *Julius Caesar* along similar lines. Nothing came of this, but in the winter of 1937–8 he began

[7] H. Fleischer, *Marxismus und Geschichte*, Frankfurt, 1969, p. 95.
[8] Dietz, vol. 19, p. 226 and vol. 20, p. 264.

toying with the idea of a play of his own on the life of Caesar and embarked on a programme of extensive research into the historical background. Discouraged mainly by the unwieldy nature of the material, he was soon thinking rather of a historical novel. His novel was never completed, but the four parts published posthumously in 1957 constitute about two-thirds of the work as Brecht envisaged it.

Political events in Germany gave the Caesar-theme a topical appeal for the anti-Nazi diaspora. It is no coincidence that Alfred Neumann published a novel in 1934 with the title *Der neue Cäsar* and Brecht's friend and collaborator, Lion Feuchtwanger, one in 1936 entitled *Der falsche Nero*. Not only had Caesar and his heirs bequeathed to the Kaisers and the Tsars their imperial title, but as prototypes of the dictator offered ample scope for allegorical exposures of Hitler's tyranny. Moreover, the Nazi ideologues had grafted their own version of the racial myth on that of Mussolini's Fascisti—who had taken their very name from the traditional insignia of the Roman lictor—and they looked to Caesar as a model of Aryan superiority. In Brecht's own private collection of newspaper cuttings there is an article from the *Völkischer Beobachter* in which a photograph of Caesar's bust is accompanied by the following description, under the rubric 'Europas Schicksalskampf im Osten': 'The long slender skull of the proud Roman, whose facial expression shows resolute energy, coolly calculating intellect, and a subtle hint of contempt for his fellow men, reveals typical features of the Nordic race.'[9]

Small wonder if in his novel Brecht was tempted here and there to accentuate the parallels between the Senate and the Reichstag, the Catilinarian conspiracy and the German Left, the parts played by the middle classes in the establishment of the respective dictatorships, and above all Caesar's resemblance to Hitler as the strong man carried to power by an economic crisis. One example for many illustrates Brecht's method. History records that combustible material was found in the possession of Cethegus, Catiline's accomplice, at the time of the putsch. Brecht works this incident into his novel, but in his version of the incident the incriminating evidence has been deliberately planted on Cethegus, and Clodius later uses it to

9 Bertolt-Brecht-Archiv 187/115.

blackmail Crassus into financing Caesar's career. In its context this inevitably evokes memories of the burning of the Reichstag and the subsequent purge of the German Left that made Hitler's dictatorship virtually unassailable.

Brecht was aiming at something much more ambitious than a thinly veiled allegory, however, for, as he told Karl Korsch at the time, the difference in historical background made a strictly allegorical approach impossible.[10] Brecht's fragmentary comedy, *Aus nichts wird nichts*, written 1929–30, before Hitler's rise to power, contains a song in which the name of Caesar is a transparent metaphor for all rulers, irrespective of the historical circumstances:

> Seht, wie er aufsteigt! Er kommt
> Unaufhaltsam, in den Händen die Sonne.
> Jetzt steigt er herauf
> Er heißt: der Cäsar!*

The second strophe begins similarly but changes the tense and generalizes Caesar's historical role:

> Seht, wie er aufstieg! Er kam
> Unaufhaltsam, in den Händen die Sonne.
> Oft stieg er herauf
> Er hieß immer anders.*
>
> (7:2961)

It was in this spirit that Brecht embarked on his Caesar-novel. An unpublished note reads: 'The novel depicts the foundation of an empire and the establishment of a dictatorship, incidentally on a strictly historical basis, the whole thing is not a disguised biography of Hitler or Mussolini.'[11]

The four extant books contain a wealth of authentic detail, for which Brecht consulted Plutarch and Suetonius, as well as other ancient sources and numerous modern historians. An unpublished note states: 'I read these books simply because I wanted to disclose the business affairs of the ruling classes at the time of the first great dictatorship, that is, with a mischievous eye! Decoding the history books is no easy job.'[12] Brecht's copious notes have been preserved and include monetary

---

[10] See Wolfdietrich Rasch, 'Brechts Marxistischer Lehrer', *Merkur*, 17, 1963, p. 1000.

[11] Brecht-Archiv, 348/07.   [12] Ibid., 188/41.

tables, economic statistics, maps, and biographical details. Much of this found its way into the novel and builds up into a persuasive pattern of well-documented fact. Some fifty historical characters put in at least a brief appearance, together with a large number of imaginary extras: bankers, jobbers and speculators at one end of the plebeian scale, tradesmen, artisans and soldiers at the other, and slaves as the anonymous but indispensable manpower of all ancient society. The geography of the Mediterranean world, the topography of Rome, and the technicalities of Roman civic and military institutions are all well represented, and great care is taken over the dating of events.

Thornton Wilder warned the readers of his own Caesar-novel *The Ides of March* (1948), that 'historical reconstruction was not one of its primary aims'. Although in most respects Brecht's novel is characterized by a much higher degree of historical authenticity, it might well have been prefaced by a similar caveat. Ilya Fradkin notes Brecht's 'modernization of the details' with alarm: 'Brecht has written a novel and not a piece of scientific research; the reader who counts on finding a historically accurate picture of the Rome of this period will be on the wrong track, and it will not lead him to a sound understanding either of Roman history or of the meaning and significance of Brecht's novel.'[13] In the main Brecht restricts his use of poetic licence to encouraging the reader to feel that his principal task is not to study the mechanism of Roman society as such, but to compare it with his own.

Brecht's novel is well spiced with anachronisms, though they are largely terminological. The English term 'City' is used throughout the book to link the world of the plebeian speculator of ancient Rome with modern capitalism. Others include clubs and Junkers, trusts and monopolies, the Chamber of Commerce and the Corn Exchange, and there are modern clichés such as *kapitalstark*, *unfair*, *Realpolitik*, *Börsenkrach*, and *Zeit ist Geld*. But this never develops into the wholesale and grotesquely comic anachronism of, say, Max Frisch's play *Die chinesische Mauer* (1946), in which an ancient Chinese emperor is taught the theory of relativity. Brecht expressly criticized Feuchtwanger for imitating Mommsen's anachronistic terms *Staatsanwalt* and

[13] Fradkin, *Bertolt Brecht: Put i metod*, pp. 153 f.

General to represent the Roman offices of *praetor* and *legatus*, on the grounds that the widely differing historical circumstances invalidate such crude equivalents, despite their obvious useful- ness as 'alienation-effects' (15:364–5). The elaborate machinery of a boom-and-bust economy, with its export trusts, its stocks and shares, cheques and credit notes, the slum landlordism of Crassus, and Cato's filibustering, all this underscores for the modern reader basic similarities between the two cultures. Despite the acknowledged differences they operate in accord- ance with the same dialectical laws which the Marxist sees at work in all societies at all times. Fradkin warns against taking Brecht's reconstruction too literally:

> Over Caesar's shoulder Brecht sees the dictators and politicians of our own time. It is as though the author were saying to the reader: I relay the facts faithfully, but it is my undisputed right as a novelist to conjecture the real state of affairs behind the scenes; and the important thing is not how authentic is the explanation of this or that specific motive or action of Caesar's, but that in principle an explanation of the behaviour of dictators, generals, politicians, and other such 'great men' of an exploiter-society, is not to be sought where the myth-makers of bourgeois historiography and the creators of the authorized heroic legends see it, but in the sphere of class struggle and the carefully concealed material interests of the ruling classes.[14]

Brecht's novel takes as its basic premiss the axiom with which *The Communist Manifesto* begins: 'The history of all hitherto existing society is the history of class struggles.' The class struggle in Republican Rome from the time of the Gracchi until the establishment of Caesar's dictatorship is represented as a complex process. In the foreground there is the struggle for supremacy between a predominantly landowning senatorial oligarchy and the wealthier section of the equestrian order, which was beginning towards the end of the second century to amass fortunes out of tax-farming, speculation, banking, and commerce. The City is seen as the creation of the Gracchi in the sense that it was their political agitation that gave the more ambitious *equites* their opening. In the wake of this 'democratic' revolution, which even Sulla's dictatorship failed to curb, Pompey emerges as the unwitting tool of capitalist speculators

---

[14] Op. cit., p. 154.

who hope he will secure them lucrative concessions in Asia. The Catilinarian conspiracy is engineered by the City in order to blackmail Pompey into a more amenable attitude, but the ruse misfires when the putsch threatens to wreck the Constitution, in which the City, despite its manifold differences with the Senate, has a vested interest. After Pompey has outlived his usefulness Caesar is the City's next protégé, and although Brecht's novel stops well short of the Civil War, it is clear from Brecht's notes on the relevant chapter that this was to have been depicted as the decisive show-down between Senate and City, assuring the latter its lasting supremacy.

Such in broad outline is the astonishing picture of the Roman Revolution that emerges from Brecht's novel. One Marxist interpreter, though critical of his occasional lapses into anachronism, makes the rash claim that Brecht has 'succeeded in recreating historical reality towards the end of the Roman Republic'.[15] But Brecht's fanciful reading of the Republican era is quite unacceptable as serious historiography. For one thing, Brecht confuses political and economic struggle, a misreading for which Marx himself, despite his impressive knowledge of the ancient world, was perhaps partly at fault.[16] Subsequent scholarship has established beyond reasonable doubt that the *equites* belonged to essentially the same class of wealthy Junkers as the senatorial aristocracy and were not by any means so irreconcilably at loggerheads with the conservative oligarchy.[17] Like George Thomson, who invented an emergent class of merchants to explain the growth of Athenian democracy, Brecht attributes far too much significance to the scope of trade, commerce, and merchant banking in Republican Rome. Consequently, he defines the Roman Revolution exclusively in terms of a nascent capitalism, though Marx himself reproved Mommsen for applying this term to the very differently structured economy of ancient Rome.[18]

[15] H. Dahlke, *Cäsar bei Brecht: eine vergleichende Betrachtung*, Berlin, 1968, p. 196.
[16] Cf. Marx's letter to Engels of 8 Mar. 1855.
[17] See esp. P. A. Brunt, 'The Equites in the Late Republic', in *The Crisis of the Roman Republic*, ed. R. Seager, Cambridge and New York, 1969, pp. 83–115; there are more detailed accounts with similar conclusions in E. Badian, *Publicans and Sinners*, Dunedin, 1972, and C. Nicolet, *L'Ordre équestre à l'époque républicaine*, i, Paris, 1966. (I am indebted to Mr. Geoffrey de Sainte-Croix of the University of Oxford for drawing my attention to these publications.)
[18] It may be noted, however, that the far from tendentious Matthias Gelzer,

Some of these distortions are doubtless due to Brecht's concern to make his Republican Rome resemble Weimar Germany more closely than the facts warrant. Above all, however, the novel represents an attempt to break down the reader's conditioned response to tradition. Even if Brecht had lived long enough to take stock of subsequent research, he might well have thought that his misrepresentation of the class struggle of ancient Rome ultimately affects the underlying purpose of the novel as little as his casual anachronisms.

The other aspect of the class struggle depicted in the novel is one about which there is probably now little disagreement. The real losers in the struggle between the factions of ancient Rome were the property-less plebs, the peasantry, the urban proletariat, and the slaves, at whose expense the exploiters on both sides of the political fence lined their pockets. All these sections of the community must have been adversely affected by the influx of cheap slave-labour from the new provinces, and it is to these anonymous victims of history that Brecht's imaginative reconstruction is dedicated. It answers the question raised in the poem 'Fragen eines lesenden Arbeiters', in which Caesar's achievements are also the subject of sceptical inquiry: 'Wer bezahlte die Spesen?' It reads between the lines of recorded history and exposes the contrast between the extravagant luxury of the minority and the appalling squalor in which the vast majority of the Roman population lived. In one passage of unusually graphic description, Caesar's slave-secretary, Rarus, recalls the splendour of Pompey's triumph after his resounding victories in Asia: the crown jewels of Mithridates, a gaming-table, thirty-five crowns, and three statues, all of solid gold, are paraded through the stinking, narrow streets of ancient Rome. The slave's unconscious *Verfremdung* of Pompey's achievement culminates in the description of a legionary snatching up an old shirt that had been knocked off a washing-line by the gigantic tablets on which Pompey's campaigns were commemorated. The shirt had fallen on top of one of the golden idols. 'Das ist was *er* erbeutet', a bystander had muttered at the time (14:1355). As the unseen chorus sings at the end of *Mutter Courage*: 'Der

---

writing three years after Brecht's death, refers to the *equites* as Rome's 'capitalist bourgeoisie' (*Caesar, Politician and Statesman*, trans. P. Needham, Oxford, 1968, p. 18).

g'meine Mann hat kein Gewinn' (4:1438). By means of such interpolations Brecht has sought to remedy the 'almost total lack of annals of the poor', noted by one textbook written while Brecht was still at school.[19]

If the picture of poverty and exploitation, bribery and corruption, hypocrisy and violence that Brecht pieced together from his patient researches is plausible enough, his presentation of Caesar is a different matter. Caesar is another of the long line of Brecht's heroes from his Eduard II to his Coriolan, whose historical reputation, so often enhanced by literary tradition, is systematically demythologized. The debunking of Caesar as soldier[20] and statesman differs, however, in one essential particular. Brecht's novel not only cuts Caesar down to size, but also exposes the process by which the traditional myth of his greatness was engendered. Mummlius Spicer, the shrewd banker who has risen to prosperity by financing Caesar's career, observes candidly of the official histories of his day: 'Da sie von uns geschrieben sind, konnten wir natürlich unsere Anschauung der Dinge zur Geltung bringen' (14:1191). This interpretation of traditional historiography is clearly based on Marx's famous statement: 'The ideas of the ruling classes are, in every age, the ruling ideas.'[21]

The main body of the novel explores Caesar's career through the eyes of his secretary, whose journal is the subject of hard bargaining in Book I between Spicer, who has acquired it as Caesar's agent, and an anonymous young historian who records the interview at first hand. He arrives at Spicer's comfortable villa in the Campagna in the hope of finding new material for his projected biography of Caesar. He has been brought up on the same 'authorized legends' that later passed via Plutarch and Suetonius into our own textbooks and literary tradition:

Der große Caius Julius Caesar ... hatte ein neues Zeitalter eingeleitet. Vor ihm war Rom eine große Stadt mit einigen zerstreuten Kolonien gewesen. Erst er hatte das Imperium gegründet. Er hatte

[19] W. E. Heitland, *A Short History of the Roman Republic*, Cambridge, 1911, p. 139.

[20] The penultimate book of Brecht's novel was to have dealt with the Gallic War. In one fragmentary section Caesar, preoccupied by the Egyptian cotton-boom, forgets the name of his great adversary, Vercingetorix (Brecht-Archiv, 188/44).

[21] Dietz, vol. 3, p. 46.

die Gesetze kodifiziert, das Münzwesen reformiert, sogar den Kalender den wissenschaftlichen Erkenntnissen angepaßt. Seine Feldzüge in Gallien, welche die römischen Feldzeichen bis ins ferne Britannien trugen, hatten dem Handel und der Zivilisation einen neuen Kontinent eröffnet. Sein Standbild stand unter denen der Götter, nach ihm nannten sich Städte und ein Jahresmonat, und die Monarchen fügten seinen erlauchten Namen zu den ihrigen zu. Die römische Geschichte hatte ihren Alexander bekommen.* (14:1176)

This account was compiled, detail for detail, from the records of the ancient chroniclers. The ancient world deified Caesar during his own lifetime. Starting perhaps with Dante, who located Caesar's murderers alongside Judas Iscariot in his *Inferno*, modern opinion down to the present day has been hardly less flattering. Theodor Mommsen called him 'the sole creative genius produced by Rome, and the last produced by the ancient world',[22] and Matthias Gelzer, probably Caesar's most reliable modern biographer, writes that 'demonic genius raised Caesar ... in every respect above all his contemporaries'.[23] As another historian puts it: 'Opinion has varied widely as to Caesar's character, but his greatness has never been denied.'[24] Never, that is, until Brecht. It is precisely the image of the deified colossus that Brecht seeks to undermine.

The process of demythologization begins with the young historian's encounter with Spicer, the banker, Afranius Carbo, a lawyer and business man, and an anonymous veteran of Caesar's campaigns in Gaul. At every turn the narrator finds his quest for the 'real' Caesar frustrated by the apparently cynical distortions of the great dictator's former acquaintances. In the eyes of Spicer and Carbo the great Caesar was a bankrupt libertine who owed his achievements to his almost arbitrary adoption by big business, and the legionary only saw Caesar twice in ten years. Later in the novel, Vastius Alder, a jaundiced elderly poet, regrets that the only theme in Caesar's life worthy of literature is his assassination, which alone has 'patina'. He comments ironically: 'Für die Dichtung ist der Mann, von dem wir sprechen, etwas, in das Brutus sein Schwert steckte'

---

[22] T. Mommsen, *The History of Rome*, trans. W. P. Dickson, 1901, vol. 5, p. 305.
[23] Gelzer, op. cit., p. 331.
[24] F. B. Marsh, *A History of the Roman World from 146 to 30 B.C.*, 1935, p. 255.

(14:1328), which is, of course, the focal point of Shakespeare's dramatization.

Spicer's account of young Caesar's capture by Cilician pirates typifies Brecht's method.[25] The historical Caesar appears to have handled the matter with astonishing sang-froid. He devoted himself to sport and literature, treated his captors in a cavalier fashion, said the ransom they were demanding was too low, and promised that he would crucify them as soon as he was set free, as indeed he did. This incident is still widely cited as an instance of Caesar's wit and daring. Gelzer, for instance, sees in it 'evidence of his limitless audacity and self-confidence',[26] and a more popular biography records that Caesar 'responded to this deadly danger with the fantastic, almost feverish courage which later made him the idol of his soldiers'.[27] Spicer gets the young historian to recite the anecdote and his version tallies almost verbatim with the account given by Plutarch. Then his host reveals the less flattering truth behind the legend. According to his version (for which, it is hardly necessary to add, there is not a scrap of documentary support) the pirates were in reality Asiatic slave-traders, whose commercial interests were beginning to conflict with those of their Roman competitors; Caesar was personally involved in the slave-trade and the twenty talents' ransom was actually the compensation demanded by his Asiatic rivals for poaching on their preserves; Caesar succeeded in raising fifty talents, pocketed the difference, and then silenced his competitors before they could let out the secret. As for Caesar's famous sense of humour, Spicer remarks 'Er hatte nicht für einen Aß Humor. Er hatte aber Unternehmungsgeist' (1190).

Similarly, Caesar's courageous refusal to divorce his first wife and the eloquent oration he later delivered at her funeral, are reinterpreted as the outcome of self-interest and bribery. Spicer meets his visitor's objection that Caesar was after all a loving father of six, with the comment: 'Er liebte gerade damals. Einen syrischen Freigelassenen' (1185). True, Caesar's sexual behaviour did at times shock even Rome's notoriously

---

[25] Cf. Klaus-Detlef Müller, *Die Funktion der Geschichte im Werk Bertolt Brechts*, Tübingen, 1967, pp. 117 ff.

[26] Gelzer, p. 24, though the author admits that the incident 'lent itself to embellishment'.

[27] Alfred Duggan, *Julius Caesar*, 1955, p. 44.

permissive society. Suetonius, who has a penchant for scurrilous detail, gleefully relays the elder Curio's libellous *bon mot* that Caesar was 'every woman's man and every man's woman',[28] but he does so to show that his hero was only human after all, and not to undermine his prestige. Brecht's indignant young historian leaves in a huff after his first interview with Spicer, remarking: 'Die menschliche Unfähigkeit, Größe da zu sehen, wo sie ist, schien mir lästiger denn je' (1199).

Spicer's revision of Caesar's traditional image serves as an introduction to the Caesar of Rarus' private journal. Here Brecht avails himself of a well-worn comic device which relies for its effect on the truth of the old saying that no man is a hero to his valet. As Spicer hands over the precious manuscripts from which his visitor expects so much, he warns him: 'Erwarten Sie nicht, darin Heldentaten im alten Stil zu finden, aber wenn Sie mit offenen Augen lesen, werden Sie vielleicht einige Hinweise darauf entdecken, wie Diktaturen errichtet und Imperien gegründet werden' (1207). This warning proves amply justified, for the young historian finds in Rarus' journal no material for his projected biography.

Caesar emerges from the journal as a licentious and un-principled careerist. He sells his talents to anyone who can afford to finance his expensive tastes and it is with some justification that Fulvia, a fashionable courtesan, compares his conduct with her own.[29] At no point does he successfully take the initiative. When he attempts to do so by speculating in real estate during the Catiline crisis, it is disastrous since he entirely misjudges the complex political situation. At the end of the second book Rarus makes the following ironical assessment: 'Eines jedenfalls hat dieses halbe Jahr bewiesen: ein Politiker großen Formats ist C. nicht und wird es nie sein. Bei all seinen glänzenden Fähigkeiten! Was Rom mehr denn je braucht, der starke Mann, der unbeirrbar seinen Weg geht und der Welt seinen Willen aufzwingt, eine große Idee verwirklichend, ist er nicht. Er hat weder den Charakter dazu noch die Idee. Er macht Politik, weil ihm sonst nichts übrigbleibt. Er ist aber

---

[28] Suetonius, *De Vita Caesarum*, Ch. 72.

[29] 14:1228–9; cf. an unpublished fragment in the Brecht-Archiv: 'caesar wird nun wechselseitig gekauft, er hält sich für den einsatz ebenso bereit wie die pro-stituierte fulvia' (188/12).

keine Führernatur. Ich sehe schwarz in unsere Zukunft'*
(1309).

In the *Dreigroschenroman* Hale, misquoting Clausewitz, defines
the politics of the bourgeois era as the 'continuation of business
by other means' (13:916).[30] Rarus notes that the triumphal
procession requested by Caesar to mark his success as proconsul
in Spain will be difficult to stage-manage, since the trophies he
has brought back with him are not ivory chamber-pots but lead-
mine concessions (14:1356). Caesar's policy, far from appearing
ludicrous in the eyes of Spicer and Carbo, is regarded as an
exemplary realism, hence the ironical title of the fourth book,
'Klassische Verwaltung einer Provinz'. Spicer remarks that
generals of the senatorial party used to boast that the grass
ceased to grow where their legions had trod, but such a policy
had killed the goose that lays the golden eggs: 'Jeder Sieg des
Heeres war eine Niederlage der City' (1181). Caesar showed
what a province was really worth by way of commercial
exploitation. The failure to see the progressive nature of this
trend is anachronistically described by Carbo as a lack of
historical sense (1400). Behind this remark is the Marxist
conviction that the bourgeois revolution represents partial
progress, as Brecht stressed in a letter to Korsch.[31] The City
has played off Pompey against Catiline but cannot afford to let
either of them make the running. When they have served their
turn they are both dropped, and this gives Caesar his big chance.

Caesar thinks he is using the City to further his private
ambitions, whereas in reality it is Caesar who is being used. He
occupies the same position in the historical process as Brecht's
other Hitler-figures, Iberin and Arturo Ui. He is merely an
expendable tool in the hands of wily speculators who operate
behind the scenes and have therefore never found their way
into the history-books. To them Caesar is a cipher and is
referred to as 'C.' throughout. By implication any other cipher
might have done just as well. As Brecht put it in an article
for the *Berliner Börsen-Courier* in 1929: 'the "heroes" vary with
the different phases, they are interchangeable' (15:197). In
the poem 'Eine Voraussage', written at the beginning of the
Hitler era, Brecht describes Hitler as 'der Hanswurst, den die

---

[30] Cf. 14:1487 and 17:1138.
[31] Rasch, op. cit., p. 1001 (see p. 66 n. 10).

Kohlenbarone / In unserm Lande den Führer spielen lassen' (9:544). The social forces have undergone fundamental changes in the two thousand years that separate the two dictatorships, but not the way in which they operate. Caesar's sponsors wield the real power in Brecht's Rome, men such as his fictitious banker Afranius Cullo, 'dem vielleicht größten Finanzier der City, dessen Name beinahe nie genannt wird' (1298). Caesar himself is as insubstantial as a shadow-puppet and in this respect he resembles the Wagnerian Hitler who appears in the final scene of the Berliner Ensemble's production of Brecht's *Schweyk im Zweiten Weltkrieg* as a gigantic but impotent shadow.

In this way Brecht seeks to correct what Georgi Plekhanov calls the optical illusion of history,[32] whereby the real motivating forces are obscured behind illustrious and seemingly autonomous personalities. Plekhanov's essay on the role of the personality in history, written at the turn of the century, presents an uncompromisingly monistic view, maintaining, for instance, that the history of France would not have been substantially different if Napoleon had been killed at the Battle of Arcole, and that even in the realm of art the Renaissance would have developed along much the same lines if Raphael, Michelangelo, and Leonardo da Vinci had all died prematurely. For Plekhanov, much more emphatically than for Marx, history is exclusively the product of conditioning social factors. 'The personal characteristics of the individual', he wrote, 'are only a "factor" of social development when, where, and inasmuch as social conditions permit them.'[33] As Brecht's Aufidius puts it, in a passage from *Coriolan* that is decidedly more Plekhanovist than Shakespearian in tone: 'unser Wert hängt ab von dem Gebrauch / Den unsre Zeit macht von uns' (6:2480).

The surprising effect of Brecht's Plekhanovist reinterpretation of Caesar's era is to rank Caesar alongside the proletariat and slaves of Rome as one who is exploited by others. At the end the reader is left with the impression of a mediocre dilettante who is no freer than his secretary to determine his own fate, much less that of the Roman Empire.

The monistic theory has often been criticized, even by Marxists, some of whom claim that there is no warrant for it

[32] G. Plekhanov, *Izbrannye filosofskie proizvedeniya*, ii, Moscow, 1956, p. 3.
[33] Ibid., p. 28.

in the writings of Marx and Engels. Marx did, however, agree with Helvetius that if a given historical epoch needs leaders it invents them,[34] and Engels in one of his last letters specifically mentions Caesar as one of those leaders precipitated by historical crises. He claims that if Caesar had been suppressed some other figure would have fulfilled his role in history.[35] The objections to this view are obvious enough. The very history of Communism seems to refute it. There is very little in Marx that cannot be traced back to his predecessors—Babeuf, Fourier, and Saint-Simon; Kant, Hegel, and Feuerbach; Adam Smith and David Ricardo—but it took the genius of Marx to fuse their ideas into a revolutionary concept that has changed the history of the world. It is equally difficult to believe that Soviet Russia would be the same today without the contributions of Lenin and Stalin.

It is one thing to explain by what conflux of circumstances a man is carried to greatness, and quite another to maintain that he got there without any conscious assertion of those unique qualities with which nature has endowed him. In the case of Caesar a non-Marxist historian can say of him that he 'merely gave effect to causes long at work', but this does not prevent him from rating Caesar at the same time as 'one of the greatest men known to us in the history of the world'.[36] Historical greatness is the joint product of chance and genius. In his classic study M. M. Bober writes: 'History is the record of the interaction of many-faceted human nature with the many-sided environment. In this interaction the behaviour of man is not tropismic but is informed with intelligence, purpose, and the inclination to change and improve.'[37] Surveying Caesar's many-faceted nature, one of Brecht's own sources, Theodor Mommsen, wrote: 'Gifts such as these could not fail to produce a statesman.'[38] In denying Caesar these gifts, Brecht fails to explain one essential fact about him that demands an explanation. Why was it Julius Caesar rather than any other Roman who conquered Gaul, defeated Pompey, reorganized Roman

[34] Dietz, vol. 7, p. 63.
[35] Letter to W. Borgius, 1 Jan. 1894 (Dietz, vol. 39, p. 207).
[36] Heitland, op. cit., pp. 472–3.
[37] M. M. Bober, *Karl Marx's Interpretation of History*, Harvard, 1955, pp. 371–2.
[38] Mommsen, op. cit., p. 308.

society, laid the foundations of the Empire, and cast the mould that still largely contains the Mediterranean world?

Brecht's failure to provide this explanation is partly due to his more or less monistic view of history and partly to his instinctive aversion to all conventional forms of heroism. But another motive was also at work. Like Marx himself, Brecht writes both as a historian and as a moralist. The conclusion we are invited to draw from his account of the age of Caesar is that if Rome's oppressed multitudes had begun to ask the kind of questions raised by the pensive worker in 'Fragen eines lesenden Arbeiters', the history of Rome, and indeed of Western civilization as a whole, might have been very different.

Between the lines of Brecht's novel is the unwritten history of missed opportunities. Had the lower orders seized their chance at the time of the Catilinarian conspiracy—Brecht noted that even Mommsen called its supporters the Communists of ancient Rome—they might have set up the world's first workers' democracy overnight. The illusory greatness of Caesar, or for that matter of Cicero, Pompey, Crassus, and the rest, need not have stood in their way, since the latter were like themselves only cogs in a machine. Carbo, the successful tycoon and lawyer, is expressing a dangerous half-truth when he says to the young historian:

Und ich höre, daß Sie von der richtigen Seite herangehen an ihr Thema. *Der Gedanke des Imperiums! Die Demokratie! Die Ideen des Fortschritts!* Endlich ein auf wissenschaftlicher Grundlage geschriebenes Buch, das der kleine Mann lesen kann *und* der Mann der City. Sein Sieg, ihr Sieg! Fakten!* (14: 1199).

If the young scholar were to have used Rarus' memoirs as the basis for an economic history of Caesar's era it would have pioneered a wholly new method of historiography. But it would have had to show that the victory of the City, implemented by Caesar, is not synonymous with the victory of the little man. His victory would have meant the overthrow of the system that had precipitated the struggle between City and Senate in the first place.

In the event the little man failed to see his opportunity. When he wrote his Caesar-novel Brecht was concerned to prevent history from repeating itself, as the development of the Third

Reich was beginning to suggest it might. *Die Geschäfte des Herrn Julius Caesar* was written in an age of fanatical mythography. Speaking of Nazi historians an unpublished fragment explicitly denounced 'the fatalism that emanates from their works like the stench of rotting flesh'.[39] In the novel Brecht counters myth with myth. History itself may not have resembled either of them very closely, but Brecht's at least offered hope to the victims of a seemingly unassailable tyranny. Brecht follows Marx in rejecting any interpretation of reality which denies that collectively men are potentially free to make their own history.

Leben des Galilei ·

Leben des Galilei is unique amongst Brecht's plays in that it adopts a famous historical figure as its central character. Moreover, despite the narrative chorus and the projected documentation, the pioneer of Epic Theatre was himself embarrassed by its more or less conventional structure, which he labelled retrograde and 'opportunistic'.[40]

This was not so much a concession to commercial theatre as a reflection of Brecht's attitude to his historical material. He had a horror of 'historical "corn"' (17:1125), but he was concerned to do justice to the known facts of a complex and critical period of history. Although he completed the first draft of his play in three weeks in November 1938 his preliminary research had been just as thorough as with the Caesar-novel. He is known to have studied Erich Wohlwill's voluminous monograph, works by the astronomers Henri Mineur, Jeans, and Eddington, as well as those of Galileo, Francis Bacon, and Montaigne, and he consulted an eminent physicist, Christian Møller, in Copenhagen.

It is not difficult to see what attracted Brecht to the life and times of the apostle of the scientific method. He doubtless saw resemblances between the historical Galileo and himself. Both were essentially teachers who found in witty dialogue an ideal

---

[39] 'Aber desto entsetzlicher wird der fatalismus, der ihren werken entströmt wie ein fauliger geruch' (Brecht-Archiv, 187/47).

[40] *Arbeitsjournal* (entry for 25 Feb. 1939), i, Frankfurt, 1973, p. 40.

form of instruction; both were at one and the same time hard-boiled rationalists and sensuous men of the flesh; both experienced a head-on collision with the established order and yet both thought discretion the better part of valour. A reviewer of the German première in 1955 was hardly exaggerating when he called Brecht's Galilei[41] a self-portrait of the author.[42] At the same time Brecht was fascinated by the dramatic confrontation between two irreconcilable ideologies: on one side of the arena the rigid dogmatism of the Peripatetics, since Aquinas the authorized spokesmen of the Church on all scientific matters, and on the other the new scientific world-view, which subjected all preconceived notions to critical inquiry and experiment.

In Brecht's form of historiography, however, immediate social relevance is always the primary consideration. There were for Brecht in 1938 two important links between the Galilean era and his own time. Firstly, Galileo, as the prototype of the modern intellectual, set an example of courage and determination to the enslaved intelligentsia of the Third Reich, many of whom had brought German science into disrepute by selling out to the new regime. Writing at the same time as Brecht, a very different interpreter deduced a similar moral from the story of Galileo: 'If we feel ourselves to be members of the species Homo sapiens and believe that wider and deeper knowledge will make us more truly men, we must resist to the last the insidious progress of government by lies, even though like Galileo di Galilei we go down before it.'[43] The 1938 version of Brecht's play incorporates one of his favourite Keuner-anecdotes. Galilei tells his assistants how a Cretan philosopher (Keunos!) served the agent of a repressive regime for seven years without replying to his question: 'Wirst du mir dienen?' On the death of the agent the wily philosopher removed the body, fumigated and redecorated the house, and then said at last with a sigh of relief: 'Nein.'[44] Although Brecht told the

---

[41] Brecht follows the German convention in referring to Galileo di Galilei by his second name. It will be convenient in this study to distinguish between Brecht's character and his historical counterpart by calling the former Galilei and the latter Galileo.

[42] Gerhard Schön in the *Stuttgarter Zeitung*, 20 Apr. 1955.

[43] F. Sherwood Taylor, *Galileo and the Freedom of Thought*, 1938, p. ix.

[44] Ernst Schumacher, *Drama und Geschichte: Bertolt Brechts 'Leben des Galilei' und andere Stücke*, Berlin, 1968, p. 24.

Danish press at the time that the play was not specifically written as anti-Nazi propaganda,[45] the Keunos-anecdote may be taken as representative of its topical bias.

There is, however, a much more important link. If ours is the scientific age, as Brecht insisted, Galileo was its most outstanding pioneer. His achievement is unthinkable without Copernicus, who had formulated his theory of a heliocentric universe a full twenty years before Galileo was born. But it was Galileo who drew the consequences. It was one thing to contemplate the revolutionary new idea as a mathematical construct, but quite another to observe it through a telescope. In the controversial *Dialogo* Salviati declares, 'We are concerned with the real universe, not with a paper one', and in the final version of Brecht's play his counterpart says to Sagredo: 'Der Kopernikus, vergiß das nicht, hat verlangt, daß sie seinen Zahlen glauben, aber ich verlange nur, daß sie ihren Augen glauben.'[46] The lunar mountains, the four satellites of Jupiter, the phases of Venus, and the rotating sunspots were manifestly there, whether or not they squared with Aristotle and Ptolemy. 'Und das', as Andrea says in his quaintly anglicized German, 'ist ein Fakt' (3:1237, 1277). Johannes Kepler wrote to Galileo on 13 October 1597, with the advice: 'Have faith and go forward'.[47] Galileo did, and this is what makes him on any reading a hero of science. This is the Galileo to whom an apocryphal tradition going back to the year of his death attributed the words, supposedly uttered under the very nose of the Inquisition, *Eppur si muove*. Significantly, this legend furnished the title of the first draft of Brecht's play: *Die Erde bewegt sich.*[48]

This Galileo is largely identical with the standard Marxist interpretation. The *Great Soviet Encyclopedia* hails Galileo as 'one of those men of science who have known how to break down the

[45] See Helge Hultberg, *Die ästhetischen Anschauungen Bertolt Brechts*, Copenhagen, 1962, p. 205.

[46] 3:1260. For convenience of reference all quotations will be taken from the text of the Suhrkamp Werkausgabe even when the unpublished earlier version is under discussion, unless there is a substantial discrepancy.

[47] *Opere*, ed. A. Favaro, 1890, vol. x, p. 70. The translations are my own unless otherwise indicated.

[48] Brecht-Archiv, 143/1–140. Only three scenes have so far been published: in Schumacher, *Drama und Geschichte*, pp. 20 ff. (extracts) and Szczesny, *Das Leben des Galilei*, pp. 103 ff. (in full). Textual differences in other scenes are in fact relatively few and insignificant.

old and create the new, whatever the obstacles'. Leonardo Olschki, whose book, *Galilei und seine Zeit*, Brecht possessed, winds up his impressive study of the period with a resounding peroration which aptly characterizes the Galileo in whom Brecht believed in 1938: 'He was the first model of the moral courage that overcomes the dread of profound mysteries and has recognized in the discovered truth the object of adoration and the goal of infinite striving.'[49]

Giorgio de Santillana describes the show-down between Galileo and the Inquisition as 'a vast conflict of world views, of whose implications the principals themselves could not be fully aware'.[50] In order to articulate the events of the Galilean era Brecht vouchsafes to Galilei and his opponents an anachronistic insight. The historical Galileo would certainly have been bewildered to learn how his literary double seriously envisages mankind entering in its diary for 10 January 1610 the words: 'Heaven abolished' (3:1250). Urban VIII would have been equally amazed to learn that it was he, and not Voltaire, who invented the *bon mot:* 'If God did not exist it would be necessary to invent him' (3:1290). But this is not a question of the wilful distortion of history, but of 'X-raying' it, as Brecht later said of his adaptation of *Coriolanus* (16:888). In addition, some events were clearly edited with a view to their theatrical effectiveness. Brecht's Galilei discovers all the moons of Jupiter at a sitting, plans his observations of the moon's surface while the duped Signoria of Venice is still mouthing platitudes about his 'invention' of the telescope, and his serious study of floating bodies and sunspots is post-dated by a good decade to highlight the effect of Cardinal Barberini's accession to the Throne of St. Peter. But all this is no more than an accentuation of the central conflict.

Brecht was concerned to underscore the unique feature of Galileo's revolution, which was that he mooted areas of knowledge in which the Church was not the competent authority. In his celebrated letter to the Grand Duchess Cristina in 1615 Galileo wrote of the Church's pretensions to infallibility in science: 'Why, this would be as if an absolute despot, being neither a physician nor an architect, but knowing himself free

---

[49] L. Olschki, *Galilei und seine Zeit*, Halle, 1927, p. 471.
[50] G. de Santillana, *The Crime of Galileo*, 1958, p. 137.

to command, should undertake to administer medicines and erect buildings according to his whim—at grave peril of his poor patients' lives and the speedy collapse of his edifices.'[51] He concedes to the Supreme Pontiff absolute authority in matters of faith, but argues that 'It is not in the power of any created being to make things true or false, for this belongs to their own nature and to the fact.'[52] Brecht catches the gist of this passage in his hero's pithy aphorism: 'Die Winkelsumme im Dreieck kann nicht nach den Bedürfnissen der Kurie abgeändert werden' (3:1297). No one who reads Galileo's story is likely to feel the surprise he expressed himself when he found his *Dialogo* on the Index in 1632, where it in fact remained for two hundred years. It was not until 1964 that Galileo was officially rehabilitated by a Church whose power he had so seriously undermined.

Brecht deliberately evaded the strictly theological issues raised by the Galilean dispute. In his notes on the play in 1939 he quite correctly maintains: 'It corresponds to the historical truth that the Galilei of the play never turns directly against the Church. There is no statement of Galileo's to support such an interpretation' (17:1110). Not only did the historical Galileo not attack the Church, but, if a more intelligent man than Roberto Bellarmino had been in charge of his case in 1616, he might well have become one of its most vigorous apologists. He had been a novice of the Jesuit Order and retained a lively interest in theology. He was deeply concerned by the discrepancy between what Scripture had to say about cosmogony and what Nature herself seemed to be saying. The biblical account of how Joshua commanded the sun to stop was keenly debated at the time, and not least by Galileo himself. He was sure that the Copernican doctrine would not contradict Scripture, properly understood. In a letter to his pupil Benedetto Castelli —perhaps the model for Brecht's Andrea—he expressly states the view that Scripture is infallible, but not its interpreters. Again, in his letter to the Grand Duchess, Galileo says that Scripture often speaks figuratively, and that interpretation is a matter of distinguishing image from fact. In Galileo's own day there were such far-sighted interpreters as Cardinal Baronius,

[51] Quoted from S. Drake, *Discoveries and Opinions of Galileo*, New York, 1957, p. 193.
[52] Ibid., p. 210.

who declared that 'the intention of the Holy Ghost is to teach us how one goes to Heaven, and not how Heaven goes'.[53] It was to such percipient minds that Galileo addressed his own revolutionary theology. Brecht touches on this in Scene 7 where he makes an exasperated Galilei say to Barberini and Bellarmin: 'Aber, meine Herren, schließlich kann der Mensch nicht nur die Bewegungen der Gestirne falsch auffassen, sondern auch die Bibel! (3:1288). Nevertheless, by and large, Brecht is content to show that Galileo's discoveries pioneered an essentially materialistic conception of reality, and their theological implications pass unnoticed.

This omission causes one serious defect in Brecht's account of the scientific revolution. His Galilei is made the unambiguous representative of the scientific world-view, opposed by an obsolescent dogmatism. In actual fact the conflict between the sacred and the secular was by no means so clear-cut. Sherwood Taylor writes of the historical Galileo: 'The conflict between the cause of scientific truth and the right of the Church to dictate its members' beliefs raged in his heart, no less than in the world outside.'[54] Even a Marxist feels that Brecht did less than justice to a complex historical situation: 'Brecht secularized, profaned the historical conflict between faith and knowledge, in which Galileo was so violently involved, thereby robbing his subjective decision of its individual tragedy'.[55]

Brecht's over-simplified polarization was the result of his desire to treat the Church exclusively as a temporal institution, the ruling class of seventeenth-century Italy. In his notes Brecht wrote: 'In this play the Church, even where it opposes free research, functions simply as authority. Since science was a branch of theology it is a spiritual authority, the final arbiter in scientific matters. But it is also a secular authority, the final arbiter in political matters' (17:1110). The minor clergy is intended to represent a cross-section of the civil service, and Brecht suggested that the aged cardinal in Scene 6 should resemble nothing so much as a die-hard Tory or a Louisiana Democrat (17:1132). In point of fact Brecht has been more lenient towards the clergy than might have been expected. The

[53] Quoted from S. Drake, *Galileo's 'Dialogue'*, Univ. of California, 1953, p. 186.
[54] Sherwood Taylor, op. cit., p. 156.
[55] Schumacher, *Drama und Geschichte*, p. 66.

bigotry of low-comedy characters such as Tommaso Caccini, who preached a sermon in Florence in 1614 on the text 'Ye Galileans, why stand ye gazing up into heaven?', or Horatio Grassi, whose speculations on the comets of 1618 Galileo refuted with such an unnecessary *tour de force*, or the opinionated wits who comprised the League of Pigeons: all this is condensed by Brecht into one burst of satirical merriment in Scene 6, where prelates reel about the stage in derision of Galilei's moving earth, until they are silenced by Christopher Clavius's laconic (and authentic) 'Es stimmt' (3:1282). Moreover, their prejudice and rancour are offset by the sympathetic portrait of Fulganzio, the Little Monk, whose inner conflict between obedience to the Church and obedience to the evidence of his own senses was very much the experience of the thinking Church as a whole.

The principal luminaries of the Church also get away lightly. Roberto Bellarmino struck his less generous contemporaries as a 'sophisticated dunderhead', a 'petulant railer', and a 'reptile with hooked teeth',[56] but posterity has been kinder and he was eventually canonized for his more saintly qualities in 1930. Brecht inclines to this more indulgent reading, despite the fact that Bellarmino had been responsible for the condemnation of Giordano Bruno in 1600 and also for the notorious injunction that enabled the Inquisition to engineer Galileo's downfall. Marxist historians unanimously follow Wohlwill in condemning the injunction as a forgery. Brecht skilfully dramatizes the injunction by having Bellarmino recite it to Galilei during the battle of proverbs in the presence of recording clerks, but there is no mention of a subsequent tampering with the text. Brecht explained in his notes that he was not interested in the purely legalistic side of the controversy (17:1111). He was after much bigger game. The Church must be condemned as a powerful instrument of class domination, not as a devious petty bureaucracy.

Francesco Barberini, a fellow member of the Accademia dei Lincei, was kindly disposed towards Galileo, and the rash optimism Brecht's hero experiences when he hears that Barberini has been elected Pope is an imaginative dramatization of historical fact. But Cardinal Barberini, amateur scientist, and

[56] De Santillana, op. cit., pp. 75, 79.

Pope Urban VIII, managing director of a global enterprise, were two entirely different characters, as the historical Galileo soon found to his cost. No part of Brecht's play reflects historical truth more faithfully than the impressive scene in which the new Pope dons his elaborate vestments and reviews the political pressures that force him to override his personal sympathy for Galilei: the disastrous course of the Thirty Years War, the struggle with Spain and the Holy Roman Empire, the bargain with the Swedes. Brecht said he had ignored Urban's personal grudge against Galileo (17:1111). He was alluding to the latter's tactless description of the Pope's 'scurrilous fooleries', as Salviati described them in the *Dialogo* to Simplicio, a not over-intelligent Aristotelian.[57] Actually, Brecht makes Urban specifically refer to the matter during the investment scene. 'Das ist allerdings eine Unverschämtheit', he says when he hears of it from the Inquisitor (3:1324), but Brecht was careful to subordinate the private grudge to strictly socio-political considerations.

Brecht's unexpectedly generous treatment of the Church is all of a piece with his reduction of the historical crisis to an ideological upheaval which might have resulted in social revolution. To this end Brecht updates Galileo's rationalism so that it can be seen more clearly as a major contribution to the secularization of thought which reached its climax with Marx and Engels. All that Galileo wrote bears witness to his 'inexhaustible faith in man's capacity to understand',[58] but Brecht deliberately makes his hero sound as though he is quoting baron d'Holbach or Ludwig Feuerbach when he exclaims 'Ich glaube an die Vernunft' (3:1287). This relates him audibly to the conceptual world of his philosophical heirs.

Brecht's Galilei sees the chief function of his research in the submission of all natural phenomena to sceptical inquiry. Brecht, who wrote a poem entitled 'Lob des Zweifels', insisted in rehearsals that the punch line of *Leben des Galilei* was the hero's statement: 'Meine Absicht ist nicht, zu beweisen, daß ich recht habe, sondern: herauszufinden, ob' (3:1311). For the pre-Galilean thinker doubt had been synonymous with heresy. For Brecht's Galilei it is the essence of life itself, and conversely for Urban VIII its universal acceptance would herald the end of his temporal power.

[57] De Santillana, op. cit., p. 320.   [58] Ibid., p. 112.

Scientifically controlled doubt will dispel the 'Perlmutter-dunst von Aberglauben' (1340), which makes ignorant peasants try to scare off the plague with rattles, cast horoscopes, or believe that witches fly around on broomsticks. Brecht's hero is very much concerned with the enlightenment of the common man. It was natural for Brecht to exaggerate Galileo's insistence on writing in his vigorous Tuscan vernacular instead of the elegant but esoteric Latin of the Scholastic cliques. The historical Galileo explained his reasons for this in a letter to Paolo Gualdo in 1612, in which he said that many potential students were put off science because the dog Latin in which it was written made them suppose it consisted of impenetrable mysteries: 'Whereas I want them to realize that nature, having given them eyes to see her works, just as well as the sons of gentlemen, has also given them the wits to grasp and understand them.'[59] Brecht dramatized this attitude in Scene 4 of the final version. Brecht's Aristotelian philosopher commences an arid disputation in Latin, but is interrupted in full spate by Galilei, who objects that his lens-polisher will not be able to follow the argument (3: 1266).

Brecht makes Galilei claim that in his day astronomy reached the market-place (1241). The historical Galileo had no intention of reaching peasants and fishwives with his astronomy, merely of breaking the monopoly of an exclusive coterie. Still, such foreshortening is not a serious misrepresentation of the historical process, since universal access to knowledge was an indirect consequence of Galileo's secularization of thought. But even in the earlier versions Brecht went much further than this. The carnival scene *à la* Breughel has a historical basis[60] and in this sense it is true to say that astronomy reached the market-place. But Brecht gives it a characteristic bias that takes it well beyond the known facts. The ballad-singer of the 1938 version demonstrates that since the sun no longer revolves around the earth, the whole accepted order of society will be turned upside down. The builder will keep his building for himself and the wood-chopper will burn his own fuel, whereas:

> Die Fürsten müssen sich die Stiefel schmieren
> Der Kaiser backt sich selber sein Brot

[59] *Opere*, xi, p. 327.
[60] Schumacher, *Drama und Geschichte*, p. 50 (and n. 12, p. 394).

> Die Soldaten gehen auf der Straße spazieren
> Und horchen auf kein Gebot.[61]*

Urban VIII thinks it merely bad taste to write in the idiom of
fishwives and wool-merchants, but the Inquisitor sees much
more disturbing social implications. If the common man gets
his hands on the new science he may start asking awkward
questions. As the prelate puts it in Scene 6, 'Da ist kein Unter-
schied mehr zwischen Oben und Unten' (3:1280). The historical
Galileo was aware of the fact that his findings revolution-
ized much more than astronomy, and that they undermined
the flattering anthropocentricity of medieval philosophy. Indeed, they anticipated the desacralized universe we now in-
habit, in which uncertainty has been raised to a scientific
principle.

Nevertheless, Brecht's conclusions are quite unhistorical. He
imputes to Galileo's contemporaries the capacity to view the
topsy-turvy Copernican macrocosm as a working model of
their own social microcosm. Like Schiller's Grand Inquisitor in
Don Carlos, Brecht's senile cardinal in Scene 6 is on the verge of
collapse and actually faints just a few moments too soon to hear
confirmation that the moribund order he represents has been
shaken to its foundations. His last speech defiantly supports the
old cosmology: 'Ich bin nicht irgendein Wesen auf irgendeinem
Gestirnchen, das für kurze Zeit irgendwo kreist. Ich gehe auf
einer festen Erde, in sicherem Schritt, sie ruht, sie ist der
Mittelpunkt des Alls, ich bin im Mittelpunkt, und das Auge des
Schöpfers ruht auf mir und auf mir allein. Um mich kreisen,
fixiert an acht kristallene Schalen, die Fixsterne und die
gewaltige Sonne, die geschaffen ist, meine Umgebung zu
beleuchten. Und auch mich, damit Gott mich sieht'* (3:1282).
At first sight the cardinal's dread is of an existential nature, like
that of the Little Monk's Campagna peasants, who, without a
divinely appointed order, will begin to say: 'Kein Sinn liegt in
unserm Elend, Hunger ist eben Nichtgegessenhaben, keine
Kraftprobe; Anstrengung ist eben Sichbücken und Schleppen,
kein Verdienst'* (1295). It is Galilei himself who shows there is
more to it: 'Ihre Campagnabauern bezahlen die Kriege, die der
Stellvertreter des milden Jesus in Spanien und Deutschland

---

[61] Schumacher, op. cit., p. 27; Szczesny, *Das Leben des Galilei*, p. 115.

führt. Warum stellt er die Erde in den Mittelpunkt des Universums? Damit der Stuhl Petri im Mittelpunkt der Erde stehen kann!'* (ibid.) Divine patience must give way to divine wrath and the oppressed must rise against their oppressors, just as Galilei has reversed the accepted order of things in the universe at large.

There is no warrant for this interpretation in the history of the Galilean era and once more it is a question of arguing that social revolution was an indirect consequence of the Copernican revolution of ideas. Brecht has again X-rayed history, showing the barely discernible shifts of a particular age writ large against the teleological movement of history towards a secular Utopia. Such is the broader significance of Brecht's original Galilei as a hero of science.

To be sure his heroism is of a characteristically Brechtian stamp. It is that of the anti-hero who sees no virtue in martyrdom. Galilei needs freedom to pursue his research, but he also needs to make a living from a profession in which only immediate utility pays a reasonable dividend. This is the Galilei who dupes the Venetian Signoria into granting him an extra 500 scudi a year for his plagiarized telescope and writes a servile letter—Brecht took it almost verbatim from Wohlwill—to Cosimo II of Tuscany in order to cash in on his new 'Medicean stars'. And it is the same Galilei who recants when threatened with torture and excommunication. There is no point in roasting merely to provide story-book heroics. This Galilei could have said with Kragler, the first of Brecht's anti-heroes, 'Ich bin ein Schwein, und das Schwein geht heim', and with Azdak, one of the last, 'Ich mach keinem den Helden'. Thus the moral of the first version was not Andrea's taunt 'Unglücklich das Land, das keine Helden hat!', but Galilei's own dialectical rejoinder which survived all revisions: 'Unglücklich das Land, das Helden nötig hat' (3:1329). But Galilei is a hero after all. Under the eyes of the Inquisition he completes his *Discorsi*, the climax of his life's work. In the final scene we see that Andrea has learned more from his teacher than scientific truth. He has overcome one of the five difficulties outlined by Brecht in his famous essay of the same period,[62] by learning how

---

[62] 'Fünf Schwierigkeiten beim Schreiben der Wahrheit' (18:222–39).

to get the truth into the right hands. The real cloak-and-dagger story of the way in which the *Discorsi* reached the libraries of Europe is more complex than Brecht's, but in its essentials it illustrates the same triumph of guile.

Brecht's work on the Galileo theme antedates, if only by a few weeks, the sensational success of Hahn and Strassmann in splitting the atom in December 1938. Five years later Brecht was working on his American version of the play in collaboration with Charles Laughton in Hollywood. With the Laughton of *Mutiny on the Bounty* and *The Private Life of Henry VIII* in the title role and taking an active part in the business of translating Brecht's text, there were bound to be some major shifts of emphasis. Sure enough, Brecht's American Galileo emerged from the rehearsals robuster, earthier, less of a martyr-hero, and more of a sly opportunist than before. But it was on 6 August 1945, when the new version was already well advanced, that the greatest single influence was brought to bear on Brecht's conception of the play. At 8.15 that morning, Japanese time, an American B-29 dropped the first atomic bomb on the totally unprepared city of Hiroshima. Sixty thousand civilians were killed outright, another 100,000 seriously injured. With that single tragic event the Age of Science passed into its most problematical phase.

Brecht reports that the average American was stunned into silence by the news, despite the fact that it spelled the end of the war in the Far East. Brecht's comment on it in his preface to the American edition is now proverbial: 'Overnight the biography of the founder of modern physics read differently' (17:1106). The Hiroshima catastrophe put an entirely new construction on Galileo's recantation, which suddenly seemed to both Brecht and Laughton less like a crafty manœuvre and much more like a shameful sell-out to unscrupulous reactionary forces. The hero of science had become the social traitor, whose discoveries led not only to the Industrial Revolution but also to the atomic bomb, and his recantation now represented the 'original sin of modern science' (17:1109).

The major shift in emphasis in the American version necessitated fundamental textual changes. The most significant of these occurs in the scene where Andrea visits Galilei some years after his recantation. The new Galilei denounces himself, in a manner suspiciously like that of the Radeks and Bukharins in Stalin's famous show trials. He confesses that he handed over his research to the ruling authorities, to use, or not to use at all, or to misuse, just as they saw fit. He declares that the only legitimate goal of science is the alleviation of human misery and he admits to having lost sight of this goal through sheer cowardice. He denies that he founded a new kind of ethic, as Andrea (and the earlier Brecht) had generously supposed, formally recanting merely in order to continue the struggle underground. His profoundest regret is that his example will have prevented the development of a kind of Hippocratic oath for all scientists. Instead he has paved the way, he says, for a race of ingenious pigmies, whose present jubilation over any new discovery will one day be echoed by a universal cry of horror—a rather painfully transparent prophecy. This new Galilei still agrees with the first that a new age has dawned, but his cowardly recantation has made it infinitely more difficult to discern in it the contours of a scientific Utopia.

Historically, this astonishing interpretation rests solely on the temporary paralysis of scientific research after Galileo's trial. Brecht said to Ekkehard Schall, acting the part of Andrea in a late rehearsal of the penultimate scene with the Ensemble: 'Science is ruined, the Church is sitting on it with its fat behind.'[63] It is true that a profound despair speaks to us from Benedetto Castelli's letters, and Milton, who visited Galileo personally in · his Arcetri retreat in 1638, wrote in his *Areopagitica* that what Italian scientists produced after Galileo's recantation was nothing but 'flattery and fustian'. Descartes temporarily abandoned his treatise *Le Monde*. But by now the prophet's mantle had passed into the hands of Protestant scholars, and it can be confidently maintained that the great pioneer's recantation in no way retarded the development of science. The real reason for the stagnation of Italian science is one no Marxist can concede and that is simply that its Castellis and Scheiners were not Newtons and Bradleys.

Brecht would doubtless have thought this objection irrelevant, since he was out to establish that Galileo's recantation had stifled the revolutionary potential of science, rather than

[63] *Materialien zu Brechts 'Leben des Galilei'*, ed. W. Hecht, Frankfurt, 1963, p. 141.

merely its factual content. Brecht never denied Galileo's signal contribution to the Industrial Revolution, but he qualified it with the serious charge of treason, saying that Galileo was 'in a certain sense its technical creator and its social traitor' (17:1133) and thus at one and the same time 'a promoter of science and a social criminal'.[64]

Quite apart from the question of the validity of this accusation, it reveals a curious inconsistency in Brecht's own thinking. Elsewhere, as we noted in the previous chapter, Brecht's view of history is virtually monistic. Yet suddenly Brecht requires a scapegoat for the failure of science to create a social ethic that would have made Hiroshima unthinkable, and instead of merely representing a scientific trend, as he had done in the first version, Galilei is now made individually responsible for the whole subsequent course of history and in particular for the development of thermonuclear energy as a threat to civilization. It seems that Brecht was aware of this inconsistency, for he went to some lengths to invent a socio-economic substructure which is in such a state of ferment that, but for his cowardly recantation, his hero might have been the catalyst of a major social revolution in seventeenth-century Italy. The new Galilei is made to confess to Andrea: 'Unter diesen ganz besonderen Umständen hätte die Standhaftigkeit *eines* Mannes große Erschütterungen hervorrufen können' (3:1341).

In view of the gravity of Brecht's indictment of the historical Galileo it must be stressed that this revolutionary ferment has no documentary basis of any kind.[65] I argued earlier that the muted references to it in the first version were relatively harmless since they could be interpreted in a broadly symbolic way. But in the later revisions Brecht renders himself guilty of a gross distortion of historical fact. It is hardly playing fair with a historical character to invent a social revolution and then blame him for betraying it. Yet this is exactly what Brecht has done. To the role of the Little Monk Brecht now adds Ludovico Marsili, who is not only an amateur scientist but a harassed landowner, who expressly rejects Galilei's doctrine because of the dangerous effect it would have on his tenants. Another new

---

[64] *Materialien*, p. 106.
[65] Ernst Schumacher (p. 170 ff.) shows convincingly that the political backwardness of the Italian bourgeoisie at the time of Galileo made revolution inconceivable.

figure, Vanni, an iron-founder, who represents Italy's nascent capitalism, urges Galilei to hold out against the Inquisition because the new age needs a leader, and he claims that Galilei has more powerful backing than he thinks. Brecht also rewrote the carnival-scene, in which the ballad-singer, who is now described as half-starved, offers much more trenchant social criticism. His ballad includes a new stanza in which the heliocentric universe is specifically related to the established order of society with its rigid hierarchy 'on earth as it is in heaven'. The Copernican revolution is represented as follows:

> Auf stund der Doktor Galilei
> (Schmiß die Bibel weg, zückte sein Fernrohr, warf
>   einen Blick auf das Universum)
> Und sprach zur Sonn: Bleib stehn!
> Es soll jetzt die creatio dei
> Mal andersrum sich drehn.
> Jetzt soll sich mal die Herrin, he!
> Um ihre Dienstmagd drehn.*
>
>   (3:1313)

A new refrain asks the question: 'Wer wär nicht auch mal gern sein eigner Herr und Meister?' These characters represent the 'Volk', which Brecht now claims replaces Galilei as the real hero of the play (17:1109).

Galilei's alleged crime is that he has known the truth and suppressed it, and the new Galilei stands condemned out of the mouth of the old: 'Wer die Wahrheit nicht weiß, der ist bloß ein Dummkopf. Aber wer sie weiß und sie eine Lüge nennt, der ist ein Verbrecher!' (3:1300), words that Andrea quotes to him verbatim after the recantation (1326).

Brecht knew how badly the public would take his new Galilei. He also knew that even as he stood there was enough of a hero left in him to win over audiences. Accordingly, Brecht played his meanest trick on his historical model by falsifying ✓ his private life as well, in order to make him 'more negative as a human being'[66] and thus elicit a more critical response from the audience.

There had been little enough of Galileo's private life in the first version. There was no mention of his affair with Marina Gamba, nor of the chaotic domestic circumstances that made

[66] *Materialien*, p. 117.

him the victim of sponging relatives, nor of the tender relationship between Galileo and his eldest daughter who took the veil. Brecht had invented a completely different daughter for him, the personification of filial piety like her historical namesake, but with high hopes of marrying Galilei's rich pupil, Ludovico Marsili. One of the three scenes to be radically reorientated is the present Scene 9, which originally showed how Virginia broke off her engagement to Ludovico because of the pusillanimity he revealed when her father resumed his controversial study of the sunspots. In the later versions it is Galilei who sends him packing, whilst Virginia is off stage trying on her wedding-dress. When she returns Ludovico has already gone. Virginia faints and Andrea and Fulganzio move to her aid, but Galilei simply turns back to his instruments with the words: 'Ich muß es wissen' (3:1312). The audience is bound to agree with Frau Sarti when she says to Galilei: 'du hast kein Recht, auf dem Glück deiner Tochter herumzutrampeln mit deinen großen Füßen!' (3: 1308), especially when it becomes clear that he did so merely to indulge a private passion and not primarily in the interests of science. At a rehearsal Brecht said bluntly to Regine Lutz, the Virginia of his intended Berlin production, that Galilei had deprived her of a life of her own.[67] This unfavourable impression is accentuated in the penultimate scene, in which we see Galilei gorging himself on roast goose and indulging in irony at Virginia's expense as he dictates a servile letter to the Archbishop.

It is fascinating to observe what a major shift in emphasis, with minimal textual changes, the important motif of Galilei's hedonism underwent. The extraordinary vitality of the historical Galileo was well dramatized in the 1938 draft. In the first scene, which remained unchanged in the later versions, the Zurich audience saw a corpulent Galilei stripped to the waist, enjoying his morning tub and his glass of milk, simultaneously initiating his landlady's young son in the delights of the new science. Anyone who saw Hans-Dieter Zeidler play Puntila and Galilei in a single season under Harry Buckwitz in Frankfurt, or Ernst Busch as Galilei and Azdak at the Berliner Ensemble, will certainly have recognized the family likeness in a dynasty of hedonists that can be traced back to Baal and forwards to Don

[67] *Materialien*, p. 117.

Juan. But there is an essential difference between Galilei and the others. His intense love of physical sensation is all of a piece with his hunger for knowledge and his passion for sharing it with others. This was in fact a dominant trait in the character of the historical Galileo, who in the *Dialogo* described his *alter ego*, Filippo Salviati, as 'a sublime wit that fed not more hungrily upon any pleasure than on elevated speculation'. 'As a confirmed materialist,' wrote Brecht of his main character, 'he insists on physical pleasures. He would not actually drink whilst working, but the important thing is, he *works* in a sensual way' (17:1127). In the play he makes Barberini say of him: 'Er denkt aus Sinnlichkeit' (3:1324), and it is this knowledge which makes him so sure that Galilei's temperament is not the stuff of which great martyrs are made.

This trait constitutes the 'Grundgestus' of the final version. In discussing with Sagredo his straitened circumstances as an underpaid Venetian academic, Galilei says: 'ich esse gern anständig. Bei gutem Essen fällt mir am meisten ein' (3:1253). Although this motif was present from the start it was accentuated in the later versions, partly no doubt under the influence of Laughton, who had a flair for expressing character physically. In the pivotal scene Galilei pauses in the middle of his work on floating bodies and sunspots to praise the wine he is drinking: 'Er hat kleine Schatten in sich. Und er ist beinahe süß, läßt es aber bei dem "beinahe" bewenden.—Andrea, räum das Zeug weg, Eis, Schaff und Nadel.—Ich schätze die Tröstungen des Fleisches. Ich habe keine Geduld mit den feigen Seelen, die dann von Schwächen sprechen. Ich sage: Genießen ist eine Leistung'* (3:1306). A little later in the same scene, Ludovico, describing the tricky situation on his estates, accuses Galilei of eating olives without a thought for such things. His choice of words ('geistesabwesend') causes Galilei to remark: 'Junger Mann, ich esse meine Oliven nicht geistesabwesend' (3:1309). At first sight a merely Falstaffian touch, but it is essentially the same hedonistic trait which brings him to recant, not in order to win time, but from fear of pain. He becomes in the eyes of his assistants an irresponsible gourmet: 'Weinschlauch! Schneckenfresser!' shouts Andrea as Galilei returns from the hall of abjuration. When Andrea revisits him he is no longer planning the clandestine dissemination of his research. Working or eating, he is simply indulging a bad habit. Vanity alone prompts him to hand over his illicit copy of the *Discorsi*, which thus reach the world by the sheerest fluke. When we last see this new Galilei he is settling down to his roast goose.

Brecht's denigration of his hero is even more strongly worded in his notes and conversations. At a rehearsal early in 1956 he said to Regine Lutz: 'The thing is just this—he is an incorrigible glutton. He overeats, he's earthy, sinful and carnal.'[68] Although Brecht is here trying to see him through Virginia's eyes it must be remembered that this particular Virginia is his own creation. Brecht had to work hard on his historical model in order to delineate the social traitor. As Brecht noted himself: 'That is one of the great difficulties: getting the criminal out of the hero. Nevertheless, he is a hero—and nevertheless he becomes a criminal.'[69]

The problem was to prevent the audience from seeing in the modified Galilei what Brecht himself had seen and admired in his historical counterpart ten years earlier. Without the same intense vitality that leads him to prefer the comforts of the flesh neither the real Galileo nor Brecht's would have made any of his sensational discoveries in the first place. The crowning irony of Brecht's work on this theme, which extended over two decades, is that in practice the historical Galileo, hero of science and a fascinating personality in his own right, wins hands down over the traitor and coward Brecht had tried so hard to make of him. Ernst Busch was persuaded to adopt the new line of characterization for the Berlin production, but it clearly went against the grain,[70] and even the Ensemble's audiences, faced with a production on which Brecht had lavished over 120 hours of intensive rehearsal to within four days of his death, saw much more of the hero than the villain in his refurbished Galilei.

It is the very ambivalence of the main character that gives *Leben des Galilei* at one and the same time its powerful theatrical appeal and its subtlety as a work of art, albeit at the expense of its credibility as a historical essay. Brecht made it difficult, but not impossible, for the audience to feel that this Galilei is

[68] *Materialien*, p. 119.
[69] Ibid., p. 121. [70] Ibid., p. 122.

ultimately saying exactly what his historical model said in a letter to Fabri de Peiresc two years after his recantation: 'I have committed no crime.' Few are convinced by Brecht's argument that at critical points in the development of society it may be a crime to be incorrigibly human.

Mutter Courage und ihre Kinder

Brecht began working on the idea for a play on the subject of the Thirty Years War in 1939, just as C. V. Wedgwood was completing her own scholarly study of the same historical phenomenon. In her foreword to the 1949 reprint she wrote of her book: 'It was written . . . under the advancing shadow of the Second World War, and it may be that the apprehension of those years can be felt vibrating from time to time in its pages.' Brecht might well have said the same of his own account. Throughout the thirties he had turned out one work after another denouncing the German variant of Fascism, showing that its pernicious *Weltanschauung* leads inevitably to war. In the autumn of 1939, with Austria, Czechoslovakia, and Poland already under the Nazi yoke, it was all too clear that Hitler's foreign policy was about to plunge Europe into war on an unprecedented scale. Although theoretically the First World War might have furnished a more vivid illustration of Brecht's point, he was doubtless aware that it was still much too close to attempt an objective assessment. The Thirty Years War, the nearest thing to a world war before 1914, facilitated a more dispassionate analysis in that spirit of 'smoking observation' that Brecht sought to foster in his form of theatre.[71]

'The Thirty Years War', Brecht wrote in his notes on the play, 'was one of the first large-scale wars that capitalism brought upon Europe.'[72] For him war belonged to that same process of economic exploitation that allegedly characterizes all class-based society, 'the continuation of business by other means' (17:1138). This explains why, although all histories of the Thirty Years War to date have ranked it amongst the most fanatical religious wars in history, Brecht exonerates religion

[71] 'Die Haltung des Rauchend-Beobachtens' (17:992).
[72] *Materialien zu 'Mutter Courage und ihre Kinder'*, ed. W. Hecht, Frankfurt, 1964, p. 92.

from any part in the conflict of interests. In Scene 3 Mother Courage, who exploits both sides without compunction, offers her assessment of the war to the cook and the chaplain: 'Wenn man die Großkopfigen reden hört, führens die Krieg nur aus Gottesfurcht und für alles, was gut und schön ist. Aber wenn man genauer hinsieht, sinds nicht so blöd, sondern führn die Krieg für Gewinn. Und anders würden die kleinen Leut wie ich auch nicht mitmachen'* (4:1375). Mother Courage does not know the whole truth about this war, but she is certainly at this point articulating Brecht's Marxist attitude.

The elimination of the religious motive is an exaggeration rather than a falsification. It is true that Frederick V wrote in 1619: 'My only end is to serve God and His Church',[73] but it is equally true that James I said, 'I mean to make use of all religions to compass my ends'.[74] Even of Gustavus Adolphus, the most devout of the Protestant princes, it has been said, 'He was in sober fact the protagonist of Swedish expansion on German soil'.[75] Other assessments of his role have been more generous, but it is a fact that the God of all the combatants in this unusually sordid imbroglio became conveniently identified with dynastic interests, territorial greed, and sheer egomania. Of Gustavus, for instance, another historian writes: 'In point of fact both the political and religious aims were inseparably connected in the King's mind . . . His political enemies were at the same time his religious enemies; it was the religious differences which gave the political differences such a keen edge and such deeper significance.'[76] As for the troopers, their motives were still less idealistic, most armies being 'a mere collection of mercenaries without religion, without pity and without remorse'.[77] At any rate there is no room in Brecht's chronicle for discussion of a complex religious conflict that involved not only Protestants and Catholics, but also Jesuits, Capuchins, and Utraquists on the one side and Lutherans and Calvinists on the other. For Brecht this was all a matter of the ideological superstructure of history, not its actual driving force.

Brecht's historical researches appear to have been, as usual,

---

[73] C. V. Wedgwood, *The Thirty Years War*, 1956, p. 98.
[74] Ibid., p. 190.   [75] Ibid., p. 281.
[76] Georg Winter, *Geschichte des Dreißigjährigen Krieges*, Berlin, 1893, p. 349.
[77] S. R. Gardiner, *The Thirty Years' War*, 1874, p. 205.

conscientious, and since he aimed neither at allegory nor at a tale of private woe, the seemingly arbitrary limits he has imposed on his account of the Thirty Years War invite careful attention. A comprehensive study of the war would necessarily involve an analysis of the European situation prior to the outbreak of hostilities. The mutual antagonism of Habsburg and Bourbon, the Dutch problem, the emergent sense of national identity in Bohemia and Hungary, the rivalry of Denmark and Sweden, the formation of League and Union: all this and more is what sparked off the conflagration. Even if Brecht had begun his survey in 1618 he might reasonably have been expected to allude to the Bohemian crisis, the division into two main power blocs, the dashing of Protestant hopes at White Hill and the ensuing stalemate.

Brecht ignores all this. The first scene is set in a remote province in Sweden, where, as the recruiting-sergeant complains, there has been no war for years, and where men are in consequence happy but undisciplined. Sweden was more heavily committed than most countries after 1630 but it remained one of the few European countries the war never reached. The year too is interesting. After six years of bitter fighting 1624 was more a year of respite than of war, following Frederick's enforced armistice with Ferdinand. But it was not without importance. It was the year of Mansfeld's visit to London to drum up recruits and subsidies—to the nearest month contemporary with Brecht's opening scene; it was a year of tension in Austria as anxious eyes were kept on the precarious balance of power in Bohemia; Urban VIII, newly elected, was making his anti-Habsburg policies felt, thus providing moral support for the foxy antics of Richelieu, another newcomer to the power game in 1624; John George of Saxony recognized Maxmilian's Electorate in the interest of German solidarity; it was also the year of Wallenstein's spectacular land-grab in Bohemia. Any of these incidents might have introduced Brecht's anatomy of the war, but he turns instead to peaceful Dalarne, almost as far from the nerve-centre of the war as he could have got, and ignored by all the standard histories. It is a historical fact that a three-year truce, a temporary breathing space in the protracted dynastic struggle of the Vasas, was nearing its end. This was followed by four years of intensive

campaigning, during which Gustavus, obsessed with the dream
of the Baltic as a 'Swedish lake', secured a valuable foothold on
the Continent and muzzled the Habsburg's faithful watchdog,
Sigismund III. Gustavus's contemporaries saw little significance in his invasion of the Continent at the time and were
obliged to look up Sweden in their atlases, while for the Emperor
it was 'halt a Kriegel mehr'.[78] Gustavus had in fact only been
biding his time until Germany would be forced to accept his
offer of intervention. All this is indisputably history, but it
seems to belong to a different chapter. Few histories of the war
can afford to trace so remote a connection between a recruiting-
campaign in Dalarne and the war in Germany, let alone follow
the fortunes of Gustavus in Poland as Brecht does in the second,
third, and fourth scenes of his play.

The new perspective created by Brecht's opening gambit
suggests that sooner or later war affects the whole world and
directly or indirectly finds its way into the remotest valleys.
Perhaps Brecht had Sweden's traditional neutrality in mind,
for in such a war as this no country is truly neutral, and even if
armed conflict never reaches its borders, its manpower and its
economy will not be immune for long. The most important
effect of Brecht's opening, however, is the implication that the
familiar division into 'periods', 'phases', and 'spheres of influence' is a mere textbook convenience which has little to do
with the reality of war. S. R. Gardiner notes that 1648 marks the
end simultaneously of the Thirty Years War of Germany and
the Eighty Years War of the Netherlands, whereas 'for France
1648 is hardly a date at all',[79] since peace in one quarter for her
merely meant she could devote greater energy to the continuing
conflict with Spain. If at times even the historian admits that
wars are blurred at the edges, for Brecht it is an axiom that
affects the very structure of his play.

Towards the middle of the piece, and with no attempt at
continuity, Brecht's own history of the war and that of the
traditional historian momentarily overlap. We are made eye-
witnesses of the sack of Magdeburg, the most sensational atrocity
of the whole war, for which, Schiller said, 'history has no
language and poetry no brush'.[80] But Brecht's scene is in a

---

[78] Winter, op. cit., p. 339.   [79] Gardiner, op. cit., p. 216.
[80] Schiller, *Geschichte des Dreißigjährigen Kriegs*, Säkularausgabe, xv, p. 182.

very low key. We remain on the periphery of the event, seeing only its impact on the lives of Mother Courage and Kattrin, nor is there any indication of the criminal blundering that led to it or of the reprisals that followed. Again, we watch troops dodge the funeral of Tilly, who had been mortally wounded in a skirmish with the Swedes near Ingolstadt. It is emphasized that his death will not alter the course of the war in the slightest. When Mother Courage asks the chaplain anxiously whether this means the end of the war (and thus her financial ruin) he replies cynically, and entirely in the spirit of Brecht's own attitude to heroism: 'Weil der Feldhauptmann hin ist? Sein Sie nicht kindisch. Solche finden sich ein Dutzend, Helden gibts immer' (4:1401). Similarly, we almost encroach upon the 'real' scene of the war again after the Battle of Lützen, which must on any reckoning be accounted one of its major events. Even Ferdinand is said to have grieved over the death of his most formidable and chivalrous adversary, but no tears are shed for Gustavus in Brecht's play. His death causes only a temporary 'outbreak of peace', as Mother Courage describes it, during which the impetuous Eilif faces a firing-squad for committing an offence that only a few scenes earlier had been rewarded as an act of heroism. After passing thus close to the centre of gravity of the war we leave it again and move into its 'last phase', as the historians usually call it, with no explanation of the shift of emphasis from the Sweden–Habsburg axis to the predominantly Bourbon–Habsburg conflict, which can be dated roughly from the arrival in Brussels of the French declaration of war on Spain in May 1635. The action of the play passes on into war-torn Saxony where the Imperial Army mounts an unsuccessful attempt to storm Halle, which changed hands so many times that historians do not bother to keep the score. This insignificant Protestant victory costs only one life, but Brecht includes it in his survey of the war because it is the life of Mother Courage's last remaining child.

The last three scenes reflect faithfully the growing sense of confusion and despair, which drained the war of whatever idealism and sense of purpose it may once have had for at least some of the contestants. Mother Courage comments on the appalling results of famine and pestilence, those seasoned camp-followers of both armies, which culminated in reliably documented outbreaks of cannibalism. 'The war reveals a spectacle of purposelessness and hopelessness,' writes one historian of this phase, 'a general fatalism and cynicism in wickedness seem to deepen as the war drags its interminable length.'[81] Brecht's army cook says simply: 'Die Welt stirbt aus' (4:1423), and this is very much the impression left by the last few scenes of the play. At the end of the last scene, with Mother Courage now bereft of all her children, it still seems as though the war has a long life ahead of it, as the chaplain cynically predicted a few years earlier (4:1402), and the armies march on. The final chorus prophesies that the war will last a hundred years. That the prophecy is wrong by exactly eighty-eight years is not the point, for war in Brecht's sense is continuous, an ineluctable condition of pre-revolutionary society. By choosing this particularly degrading, destructive, and protracted war as the subject of his play, and by readjusting the historical focus, Brecht has succeeded in suggesting a war that has no geographical boundaries and no clearly definable beginning and end. It bursts the artificial limits imposed on it by the historian, reaching right down to our own century and beyond.

Brecht's second major reinterpretation affects the characters and it parallels the method he adopted for the novel on Caesar. The period of the Thirty Years War was not in any case particularly rich in attractive personalities. Neither the military exploits of its Mansfelds and Torstenssons nor the statesmanship of its Eggenbergs and Oñates offer much scope to a dramatist, to say nothing of the weathercock politics of the aristocracy. But few students of the period have failed to respond to the energetic Gustavus Adolphus, the inscrutable Wallenstein, the dashing duc d'Enghien, or even the dogged Tilly. Brecht is one of the few. After providing the historical framework of the first four scenes, *il re d'oro* dies unsung in a laconic sub-title to Scene 8; Oxenstjerna, his aide and successor, is reduced to a synoptic heading in the first scene; Wallenstein is not so much as mentioned. No historically authenticated character is in fact allowed on the stage. The historian's heroes are kept in the wings and the stage is dominated by a resourceful camp-follower and her children, a cynical padre, a scoundrelly cook, a whore, and an amorphous mass of anonymous peasants and troopers.

[81] David Ogg, *Europe in the 17th Century*, rev. edn., 1954, p. 167.

Brecht's Lukullus is amazed to find in the Underworld that nobody has heard of him. His military successors are threatened with the same fate in *Mutter Courage*. Off stage in Scene 6 we hear a roll of drums and the strains of a funeral march as the hero of Magdeburg is borne by his more conscientious followers to his grave. On stage, Mother Courage is making an inventory of the wares with which she seeks to wrest a living for her children from the chaos and destruction of the war, and says all in one breath: 'Schad um den Feldhauptmann—zweiund-zwanzig Paar von die Socken—, daß er gefalln ist, heißt es, war ein Unglücksfall' (4:1399–1400). Not hers to sit upon the ground and tell sad stories of the death of kings, or their generals, but to see that the raw materials of war are still intact. At the end of the same scene, when Kattrin, already handicapped by a war-experience in her childhood, returns after a brutal assault has been made on her, the padre, hearing the artillery honour the dead general, mutters reverently: 'Das ist ein historischer Augenblick.' Mother Courage replies: 'Mir ist ein historischer Augenblick, daß sie meiner Tochter übers Aug geschlagen haben' (4:1408), and for the first and only time in the play she curses war.

The fluctuating fortunes of the common man, of whom the orthodox political historian has so little to say, are for Brecht the real stuff of history. History faintly recalls a nameless peasant who exclaimed, 'I was born in war. I have no home, no country and no friends, war is all my wealth and now whither shall I go?'[82] Here is the historical counterpart of Mother Courage as she appears in the final scene, though Brecht's character is less querulous about it as she straps herself to the wagon and moves on despite everything. Or again: 'The young girl, who in better times would have passed on to a life of honourable wedlock with some youth who had been the companion of her childhood in the sports around the village fountain, had turned aside, for very starvation, to a life of shame in the train of one or other of the armies by which her home had been made desolate.'[83] This is almost detail for detail the story of Yvette Pottier. For the historian such things can be nothing but a brief illustration, a deviation from his main purpose, in pursuit of which the suffering of the anonymous masses remains

[82] Wedgwood, op. cit., p. 505.   [83] Gardiner, p. 213.

largely statistical. He may supply facts and figures, historical maps, graphs showing population-losses and the like, but these do not amount to the reality of suffering. Aware of the inadequacy of his medium in this respect, Gardiner asks at one point, 'How is it possible to bring such scenes before our eyes in their ghastly reality?'[84] It is precisely to this question that Brecht as a dramatist has an answer unique to his craft, and what has been said of Fontane as a historical novelist is equally true of Brecht: 'He has written the history which the historians cannot remember.'[85]

Brecht's worm's-eye view does much more, however, than dramatize the sufferings of the poor at the expense of the historian's heroes. It is bifocal. Not only are some of the outstanding events of the war discussed in the course of the dialogue. They also appear in the projected synopses, which often pin them down to a specific date and location, in the manner Brecht had pioneered in his adaptation of Marlowe's *Edward II*. These projections contribute towards a radical *Verfremdung* of history which is now seen as the repercussion of world-historical events on the lives of a representative cross-section of the unremembered masses. Conversely, their unrecorded exploits are transformed into events of historical moment. Before the Magdeburg scene the projected text reads:

Zwei Jahre sind vergangen. Der Krieg überzieht immer weitere Gebiete. Auf rastlosen Fahrten durchquert der kleine Wagen der Courage Polen, Mähren, Bayern, Italien und wieder Bayern. 1631. Tillys Sieg bei Magdeburg kostet Mutter Courage vier Offiziershemden.*

(4:1396)

In the version first performed in Zurich in 1941, Mother Courage grudgingly sacrifices the shirts for bandages; in the revised version written for Berlin eight years later they are removed on the sly by Kattrin, but either way textbook history has undergone an alienation-effect. The fall of Magdeburg is said to have cost some 25,000 citizens their lives: it costs Mother Courage four shirts, despite the fact that she is on the

---

[84] Gardiner, p. 183.
[85] H. B. Garland, 'Theodor Fontane', in *German Men of Letters*, ed. A. Natan, 1961, p. 222.

winning side. As she has said earlier, victory and defeat are equally expensive for the little man (4:1379).

There is an additional interest in this particular caption in that it shows that the play offers more than sympathy with the underdog. The underdog is also criticized for his passivity and for his stubborn and unrealistic belief in his ability to exploit the historical situation to his own ends.

The soldiers in Brecht's play are largely passive, but this does not make them the innocent victims of circumstance. Mother Courage gives an ironical account of their passivity, in which Brecht's philosophy of history transforms persiflage into serious criticism:

Mir tut so ein Feldhauptmann oder Kaiser leid, er hat sich vielleicht gedacht, er tut was übriges und was, wovon die Leute reden, noch in künftigen Zeiten, und kriegt ein Standbild, zum Beispiel er erobert die Welt, das ist ein großes Ziel für einen Feldhauptmann, er weiß es nicht besser. Kurz, er rackert sich ab, und dann scheiterts am gemeinen Volk, was vielleicht ein Krug Bier will und ein bissel Gesellschaft, nix Höheres. Die schönsten Plän sind schon zuschanden geworden durch die Kleinlichkeit von denen, wo sie ausführen sollten, denn die Kaiser selber können ja nix machen, sie sind angewiesen auf die Unterstützung von ihre Soldaten und dem Volk, wo sie grad sind, hab ich recht?* (4:1400–1).

In *Schweyk im Zweiten Weltkrieg* Hitler's grandiose plans for world domination founder on the pusillanimity of the Schweyks in his millennial empire. At the end of Scene 8 of *Mutter Courage* the heroine sings another strophe of her theme song, the second quatrain of which says of war:

> Von Blei allein kann er nicht leben
> Von Pulver nicht, er braucht auch Leut!
> Müßts euch zum Regiment begeben
> Sonst steht er um! So kommt noch heut.*
> (4:1421)

Eric Bentley's translation of the last line[86] recalls Kitchener's famous recruiting-poster of the First World War. The unspoken corollary is that if the soldiers refuse to rally round the warmongers, there will be no war. This endorses the ironical impression the audience receives from the foreshortening effect

---

[86] In Bertolt Brecht, *Plays*, vol. ii, 1962, p. 66: 'If it's to last, this war needs you!'

of the first scene, that the Thirty Years War cannot begin again at all without Eilif.

The complicity of Mother Courage herself is much more active. The war did not catch her unawares. In the first scene not the least of the many ironies created by the unusual choice of location is that Mother Courage, who says she cannot afford to wait for the war to reach Bamberg, her home town, has traversed the whole of Europe in search of business. A situation created by the war at many removes is there as the play begins, and into this situation rolls the covered wagon of a small-time opportunist. Even the death of the horse did not deter her and, significantly, when we first see her wagon it is drawn by her two strapping sons. The Berliner Ensemble's official programme shows a picture of this wagon and on the opposite page there is a photograph of its modern counterpart with the caption: '1933–1945. Railroad trucks of the American Standard Oil Company, whose profits in peacetime (1939) amounted to $55,800,000, in wartime (1945) $100,400,000, i.e. almost double.' Fair comment. But Brecht's potent symbol, which dominates the stage from beginning to end, expresses more than this over-explicit programme-note. It demonstrates Anna Fierling's tragic dual function in the play: that of a mother, for whom the wagon is a mobile home, and that of a profiteer, for whom it is a valuable investment. Brecht wrote of his heroine: 'Mother Courage . . . recognizes, in common with her friends and guests and just about everyone else, the purely commercial nature of war: that is precisely what attracts her. She believes in war to the very end' (17:1150). In one of her songs, in a strophe written specially by Brecht for the Berlin production in a vain attempt to inhibit the sympathy Therese Giehse's Mother Courage had elicited in Zurich, she sings: 'Der Krieg ist nix als die Geschäfte / Und statt mit Käse ists mit Blei' (4:1409).

If audiences stubbornly continue to admire this attitude despite the changes Brecht made in the text, it is not, as he seems to have thought, that they fail to see in her a 'hyena of the battlefield', as the padre calls her (4:1414). It is rather that they see and admire the selfless motive behind her brazen attempt to beat the capitalist warmongers at their own game: 'Auf was ich aus bin, ist, mich und meine Kinder durchbringen mit meinem Wagen' (4:1406). This is what she tragically fails to do.

She arrives in Dalarne to make money and protect her children from the war: she makes half a guilder and loses a son. She sacrifices all her children to an inexorable Moloch, each one the price of a commercial enterprise: Schweizerkas because she haggles too long over his ransom, and Kattrin because she is too preoccupied with a fluctuating market to keep her out of harm's way during a crisis. She retains the courage that earned her her nickname, but also her blind obstinacy in thinking she can turn the war-game to her advantage. What she fails to grasp is, as the chaplain picturesquely puts it, that anyone who wants to breakfast with the Devil needs a long spoon (4:1414). Someone is certainly making a fortune out of this war, but it is demonstrably not Mother Courage, whose wagon gets steadily more dilapidated.

But Mother Courage's assessment of the war is at least partially right. It is man-made, not the work of fate or what insurance policies still quaintly call an act of God. Brecht specifically warned against any fatalistic interpretation of history: '*Historical conditions* may not be conceived . . . as inscrutable forces . . .: they are created and maintained by man' (16:679). This is where Anna Fierling differs so strikingly from Maurya in John Synge's *Riders to the Sea*, the play to which both *Die Gewehre der Frau Carrar* and *Mutter Courage* were a kind of 'counter-project' (*Gegenentwurf*), to use a term Brecht coined later.[87] The sea destroys Maurya's children, whereas Eilif, Schweizerkas, and Kattrin are the victims of a man-made conflict to which their own mother contributes more than most.

Despite Brecht's warning there is a strong sense of fatality in the play, and critics persisted in speaking of it as a Niobe tragedy. This is because within the historical limits of the Thirty Years War Mother Courage has no viable alternative. Collectively men are seen to be the executors of their own doom and the whole course of history is determined by their action or inaction. The opportunities presented to them for turning it to their own advantage, however, are brief and rare. In 1688, 1789, 1871, and 1917 their chance will come in one place or another, but in the meantime there is little they can do. Anna Fierling can either wait passively for the war to destroy her and her children, as it destroys the citizens of Magdeburg, or she can

[87] *Gesammelte Werke*, 5, Anmerkung 2.

harness her wagon to it in a vain attempt to exploit the exploiter. Tragically, she services the machinery of destruction.

To the consternation of Friedrich Wolf, who mildly rebuked Brecht in an interview for not making her see the error of her ways,[88] Mother Courage learns nothing from her tragic experience, no more, Brecht said, than a guinea-pig learns from the experiment of which it is part (17:1150). Brecht was too much of a realist to play at make-believe with history. Like Tolstoy, whose realism he guardedly admired, Brecht can stand far enough back from the historical process to see that it is men who make it, but he can see just as clearly as the great Russian realist that whilst they are making it they are 'the involuntary tools of history, performing a task which is concealed from them, although comprehensible to us'.[89] If there is anagnorisis in *Mutter Courage* it does not take place on-stage, as in the Aristotelian tradition, but in the auditorium of Brecht's Epic Theatre. It is not Mother Courage as a tragic character, but those who study her fate, who must be taught to see how history works.

Nothing distinguishes Brecht's method as a historical dramatist so sharply from that of more conventional Communist writers as this aspect of *Mutter Courage*, quite apart from the wide divergence of theatrical techniques. Marxism is committed to the dogma of historical optimism, and its literature, according to the prescription in the *Great Soviet Encyclopedia*, must be imbued with its 'life-asserting force, consciously reflecting the inevitability of victory of the new over the old, the revolutionary over the reactionary'.[90] J. R. Becher, the poet laureate of orthodox German Communism, rounds off his *Winterschlacht* (one of the few non-Brecht plays adopted by the Berliner Ensemble) with a rousing apotheosis of the Red Army, in which he had himself fought against his own countrymen during the war:

> Zum Sieg der deutschen Freiheit beigetragen
> Hat auch *die* Schlacht

---

[88] The interview was published under the title 'Formprobleme des Theaters aus neuem Inhalt' (17:1142–7).

[89] R. F. Christian, *Tolstoy's 'War and Peace'. A Study*, 1962, p. 93.

[90] The phrase (*zhizneutverzhdayushchaya sila*) occurs in both the *Malaya* and *Bolshaya sovyetskaya entsiklopediya* in the articles on Socialist Realism.

concludes one of its officers. The Stalingrad disaster becomes retrospectively a victory for German freedom since it heralds the end of Nazi tyranny. The Red Army as *deus ex machina* represents the victorious life-asserting force of the Revolution, in the face of which Hitler's reactionary regime is inevitably doomed.

Brecht was no less committed than Becher to the dogma of historical optimism, but the lesson he hoped his audiences would learn from *Mutter Courage* is much more subtle than anything in Becher's pious doggerel. The life-asserting force in this play is not that of triumphant socialism, of which there is not the faintest hint. It is to be found in the reactionary figure of Mother Courage, whose indomitable will to survive is prone to tragic error but is the real guarantee of ultimate victory. Brecht's chronicle from the Thirty Years War teaches that man will make history 'under conditions of his own choosing', to use Marx's famous phrase,[91] only when he has learned from bitter experience to harness to his own needs Anna Fierling's stubborn courage, her protective instinct, and her mis-spent energy.

Die Tage der Commune

Brecht's last historical work has been unjustly neglected. The pundits of Socialist Realism wrote off *Die Tage der Commune* as defeatist and 'objectivist'[92] which means that it lacks the glossy heroics and revolutionary romanticism demanded by the disciples of Zhdanov. The West, on the other hand, has been puzzled by the apparently un-Brechtian design of the piece: no sign of the alienation-effect apart from two choral interludes delivered in the style of agitprop audience-rousers. Yet a Polish critic was hardly going too far in describing *Die Tage der Commune* as 'Brecht's political last will and testament',[93] and certainly it is Brecht's most elaborate attempt to document the revolutionary mechanics of history.

Like *Mutter Courage*, *Die Tage der Commune* also constitutes a 'counter-project'. It was an attempt to correct the historical perspective suggested by the play *Nederlaget (The Defeat)*, written in 1933 by the Norwegian Communist, Nordahl Grieg.

[91] See above, p. 63 and n. 6.
[92] See J. Rühle, *Theater und Revolution*, Munich, 1963, p. 186.
[93] Szydłowski, *Dramaturgia Bertolta Brechta*, p. 311.

Grieg's play was doubtless brought to Brecht's attention by his companion-in-exile, Margarete Steffin, whose translation appeared posthumously in 1947. Brecht's radical reworking was begun in 1948 at a time when he was still trying to make what Martin Esslin calls his 'choice of evils'. It was banned by the S.E.D. in 1951, and Brecht never lived to see its première, which took place in November 1956 in Chemnitz. Though it was published in the *Versuche* in 1957, it was not until 1962 that the Berliner Ensemble adopted it in a production by Manfred Wekwerth, in which the Parisian barricades were intended to suggest the recently erected Berlin Wall.

The choice of subject-matter is hardly surprising, though it is interesting that both Grieg and Brecht preferred to show the Revolution in defeat, unlike their Soviet counterparts, who still monotonously extol the triumphs of 1917. Frank Jellinek in his pre-war study of the Commune writes: 'The Commune made grave revolutionary errors. Those errors have actually been more fertile for future revolutionaries than the Communards' limited successes.'[94] Their abortive uprising served Lenin as a dummy run for the Bolshevik Revolution, the success of which was at least in part due to the fact that he had learned the lessons of the Commune. But the Commune also made a more positive contribution to the history of Communism. Less than a month after the event Karl Marx, whose initial response had been lukewarm, was hailing it as 'a new beginning of world-historical importance',[95] and Engels maintained that if we want to know what the dictatorship of the proletariat looks like in practice we need only look to the Paris Commune.[96] In 1968 the streets of Paris again rang with cries of 'Vive la Commune' from revolutionary students, and a visit to the Mur des Fédérés, where the besieged Communards made their last stand, is still an obligatory pilgrimage for every pious socialist.

Though *Die Tage der Commune* is not a particularly long play Brecht has compressed into its twenty-one loosely integrated scenes a wealth of authentic detail. His research was again thorough: among his sources were Prosper Lissagaray's invaluable eyewitness account of the uprising, the Commune's own *Journal officiel*, Marx's *Civil War in France*, and Hermann

[94] F. Jellinek, *The Paris Commune 1871*, 1937, p. 16.
[95] Dietz, vol. 33, p. 209.   [96] Ibid., vol. 22, p. 199.

Duncker's collection of original documents. He showed greater respect for authenticity than in the case of the novel on Caesar and *Leben des Galilei,* and there was no need for the bifocal effect of *Mutter Courage,* since here was one of those rare moments in history when the proverbial little man was demonstrably making his own history.

Brecht's drama of the Commune preserves the main outline of the political crisis: from the collapse of Trochu's Government of National Defence, as a result of which the National Guard found itself master of Paris, through the hectic period of indecision and utopian planning, the heroic defence of the Commune's infant democracy, and on to the bitter end at the barricades. Brecht telescopes and edits some of the now legendary events of *l'année terrible,* but in general the Marxist critic, Hans Kaufmann, is right when he says Brecht has not falsified the record for propaganda purposes.[97]

Die Tage der Commune is perhaps the only work of Brecht's that could be termed 'epic' in that peculiarly Anglo-American sense of a large-scale historical canvas. Ample street-scenes, which reveal the views of the populace, the presentation of a petition signed by 552 women from one *quartier,* reports on the increasing chaos within the National Guard, sessions of the Commune incorporating extracts from the *Journal officiel* almost verbatim, the return of soldiers from the front and from Versailles with the latest news, the appearance of news-vendors who punctuate the action with other impressions and rumours from outside, and on the plane of international statesmanship the scenes with Thiers, Favre, and Bismarck: all this contributes to the panoramic breadth of an impressive historical mosaic.

Brecht's treatment of the Commune's personnel is characteristic. There are fifty specified roles, nine of which are historically authentic, but Brecht avoids making any of them into a story-book hero or heroine of the barricades. Grieg had made Louis-Nathaniel Rossel, the Communards' most able tactician, into a critic of their military incompetence, but Brecht relegates him to a passing reference in a speech of Delescluze. This revaluation typifies Brecht's method. Heroes such as Dombrowski and Wroblewski are passed over in favour of representatives of the anonymous masses, such as 'Papa', Coco and Jean, and the

[97] H. Kaufmann, *Bertolt Brecht: Geschichtsdrama und Parabelstück,* Berlin, 1962, p. 52.

Commune's legendary heroines such as Louise Michel and Elizabeth Dimitrieff are replaced by unprepossessing figures such as Madame Cabet, Geneviève Guéricault, and Babette.

Of the historically authentic characters whom Brecht brought into sharper focus, Eugène Varlin was an obvious choice. An ex-bookbinder of peasant stock, he was a member of the anti-Jacobin International and many of the Commune's most forthright measures were due to his energy and enthusiasm. Yet he appears in only six scenes and, though the most vocal of the historical figures, has a smaller share of the dialogue than Geneviève and less than half that of 'Papa'. He authentically represents the Marxist Left in the play, proclaiming the Commune's revolutionary principles and putting forward the motions that became its most progressive decrees. Brecht's only serious departure from the facts is that he makes him one of the 'hawks' of the Commune, whereas the historical Varlin, realizing that the revolution was premature, opposed the plan to march on Versailles. Brecht's motive was presumably to give added weight to the extremist camp without suggesting reckless fanaticism.

Charles Delescluze was another attractive candidate. A Jacobin republican at heart, he enthusiastically espoused the Commune, and although years of hardship and imprisonment had made him almost incapable of coherent speech, he delivered several rousing addresses, took over the supreme military command after the resignation of Rossel, and died bravely at the barricades. Grieg made much of this colourful figure, yet in Brecht's version he appears in only one scene, in which he chairs the debate between the moderates and the extremists and appropriately announces the decision of the Commune in favour of the former, to which historically he himself had belonged. Of the others, Gabriel Ranvier, who had been a member of the Committee of Public Safety but was otherwise a very minor figure, is given a handful of lines by Brecht as a representative but not too extreme militant. Charles Beslay, whom the *Dictionnaire de la Commune* described as 'an innocuous deputy with little hair and less eloquence', plays the same disastrously conciliatory role in Brecht's play as he did in history.

This leaves only Raoul Rigault, the self-styled Saint-Just

of the Commune, who wielded more actual power than any other single Communard. Even Marxists still rate him as a dangerous fanatic, and Grieg allots him a major role as an almost demonically inspired terrorist. He has been compared with Beria and Eichmann as a coolly professional killer.[98] Brecht makes nothing of his potential as villain of the piece, and although he concedes him a political role second only to that of Varlin, it is solely as a reasonable supporter of the militant faction. His notorious henchman, Theophile Ferré, is not even mentioned. In this way Brecht reduces the alleged atrocities to sporadic and untypical outbreaks of violence.

Brecht's handling of his historical personnel reveals one of the major shifts of emphasis in his adaptation of Grieg. The Norwegian Communist emphasized one of the Commune's most palpable failings: its lack of effective leadership. Had there been a Lenin in Paris on 18 March 1871 the history of Europe might have taken a very different course. Accordingly, Grieg depicted the main political figures of the Commune as a motley assortment of well-meaning but incompetent greenhorns. Certainly the eighty-one good men who met for the first time in the Hôtel de Ville on 29 March were no match for the wily Thiers. Francis Jourde spoke for all of them when he said: 'We were very embarrassed by our authority.' Yet though Brecht does not deny their weaknesses he does not over-emphasize them, and accordingly he gives the political executives of the Commune a good deal less limelight than he might otherwise have done. The whole point of his interpretation of the Commune is that its unique strength lay in its being a spontaneous uprising without leaders of the traditional stamp. The Central Committee's final pre-election address called upon the citizenry to choose 'men of sincere convictions, men of the people, resolute, active, with clear judgment and an acknowledged honesty'.[99] This is exactly how Brecht has presented them, simply as the executors of the collective will of the people. Revolution and government are not in Brecht's Commune the responsibility of a dedicated élite but of the whole people, to whom the elected representatives are immediately answerable. This interpretation is corroborated by the available

[98] A. Horne, *The Terrible Year*, 1971, p. 134.
[99] S. Edwards, *The Paris Commune 1871*, London, 1971, p. 278.

historical evidence, such as the decision taken in the Eighteenth Arrondissement, to hold daily meetings between citizens and delegates, the explanation for which appeared on a poster on 5 May: 'Those elected by the people have the duty of keeping in constant touch with their electors in order to give account of the mandate they have received and to submit themselves to questions.'[100] The increasing severity of the siege seems to have put an end to this scheme, but full participatory democracy has perhaps never seemed such a reality as it did in Paris during the spring of 1871.

This explains why the fictitious figure of Pierre Langevin occupies such a key position in *Die Tage der Commune*. Next to 'Papa', Langevin's role is the most generous and he figures in no less than eight of the scenes, appearing more often than any other character except Geneviève. He is obviously intended to represent the typical Communard. A moderate at first, later inclining towards a tougher policy when he realizes that the Commune is the victim of its own generosity, he supports the policy of free speech and secularization (historically almost the only issue on which all the Delegates were agreed) and initiates the inexperienced Geneviève in the difficulties of revolution on a shoe-string budget. As the brother of the poor seamstress, Madame Cabet, and uncle of Jean, an unemployed engine-driver, he appears in the street-scenes as well as the sessions of the Commune, and in the penultimate scene it is he who brings the doomed defenders news of battle. There is nothing even remotely heroic about this man. Quietly effective, shrewd, sensible of the Commune's tragic shortcomings, unassumingly idealistic, his main function is to serve as a link between the citizenry and its elected representatives. Thus in the important Scene 4, in which the Central Committee meets for the first time since its seizure of power, Langevin relays news of the policy debate to 'Papa', who is standing on the steps outside.

By reducing the stature of the historical Communards Brecht has not only written a play without a hero in the manner of Gerhart Hauptmann's *Die Weber*; he has sought to convey, if not quite the reality, then at least the spirit of the Commune, by obliterating the distinction between the rulers and the ruled. Even Stalin in his first full-length pamphlet quoted with

[100] Edwards, op. cit., p. 278.

approval Arthur Arnould's claim that in the Paris Commune 'the people were the rulers, the only rulers'.[101] In this spirit Brecht has dramatized the short-lived dictatorship of the proletariat. The *vox populi* forms the ground swell of the whole drama, and in several scenes the views of the populace and its elected representatives are orchestrated almost in the manner of a classical chorus. The six Commune scenes are generously punctuated by anonymous comments reflecting a broad spectrum of opinion, and in Scenes 4 and 7 they constitute almost a third of the total dialogue.

'Papa' is the chief representative of the important group of citizens whose individual fates register the repercussions at street level of the world-historical events of which Paris was the focal point for ten momentous weeks. A builder and a member of the National Guard, he is represented as a typical patriot in the war against Prussia, and in the chaotic interregnum that followed it as an agitator for the overthrow of Trochu's 'Government of National Defection'. After the seizure of power he shows himself a militant, demanding the march on Versailles and the execution of all spies and traitors. But there is something of the visionary in him as well, and characteristically the last time we see him he is still defending the barricade in the Place Pigalle, seemingly indestructible as the end approaches. Representing the opposite extreme, Madame Cabet, who pleads for non-violence and successfully intercedes for Geneviève's fiancé, is shot down by the Versaillais in the penultimate scene. Geneviève occupies a middle position between the two. She too pleads against bloodshed in her first scene as the Communards seize power. As an educational idealist she is put in charge of the Ministry of Education and winces at the enormity of the task, which has to be tackled without previous experience, without knowledge of the educational set-up in Paris, and above all without financial backing. Yet in the critical scene in which her fiancé turns up as a spy for Thiers, having been released from a Prussian prisoner-of-war camp after the deal with Favre, she coldly rejects him and consents to his execution. The characteristic strength and weakness of the Commune's leaders are thus matched by qualities amongst the ordinary citizens. In this

[101] R. Payne, *The Rise and Fall of Stalin*, 1966, p. 110.

way the citizens as a body are shown to be responsible for both the success and the failure of the Commune.

Brecht is the successor of Hauptmann in creating a play that not only dispenses with heroes but also with plot. Even Grieg was at pains to construct a plot that allows for psychological realism in the delineation of characters such as Rigault, for whom terror is an end in itself, or Madame Thiers, who derides her husband's sterility, or Lucien and Pauline, lovers who find time to philosophize on life and death as the Versaillais move in for the kill. Brecht courageously abandons even these vestiges of traditional plot. The characters' private lives are strictly subordinated to their historical relevance. 'We ought not to introduce even the love-theme,' wrote Brecht, 'unless it has a bearing on the political events.'[102] Jean Cabet's flirtation with Babette illustrates to some extent the call for sexual promiscuity by such extremists as Rigault, and the theme of Babette's pregnancy is introduced to motivate her interest in the Commune's political future. Jean curses the women, especially Babette, for talking about the future so much, but Geneviève whispers to him: 'She has to, Jean' (5:2184). Paradoxically, it is for this very reason that Babette mans the barricade. Similarly, François's shyly affectionate attitude towards Geneviève provides a contrast with her fiancé, Guy Suitry, who sees in her only a means of escape from his predicament. Geneviève's rejection of him (admittedly one of Brecht's least endearing scenes) is heartless rather than tragic, but it points to a moral dilemma affecting the Commune as a whole, forced into callousness in the interests of self-preservation.

The events involving the Faure brothers reach out to the political scene beyond. François is a student of physics. Madame Cabet, his landlady, has pawned his microscope and textbooks in his absence in order to pay her rent. His brother Philippe leaves Paris for Versailles in order to earn enough money in the regular army to redeem the pledges. When the Commune issues its decrees remitting rents and debts and authorizing the free return of pledges at the Mont-de-Piété, all is well and Philippe returns, incidentally providing inside information about the atmosphere at Versailles. He deserts them shortly

---

[102] Brecht-Archiv, 1081/43–4. Quoted from Kaufmann, p. 63.

before the end, in Jean's eyes a louse, for the more tolerant François 'kein besonders mutiger Mensch, da er nicht denken gelernt hat' (5:2184). There is just enough characterization in these figures to make them credible against their historical background, but no more.

To these real and fictitious characters Brecht follows Grieg in adding Adolphe Thiers, the Chief Executive of the National Assembly, whom Marx called 'that monstrous gnome'.[103] As a historian in his own right, Thiers, unlike the inexperienced Communards, was well aware of the necessity of profiting from the lessons of history. Born just after the Great Revolution and having lived through two others, he was determined to ensure that a fourth was not debited to his account. Brecht's caricature of him—he plans the downfall of the Commune as a servant runs his bath and he foams at the mouth at the receipt of bad news—is hardly just to this unsympathetic but shrewd statesman, with his passion for statistics, his impressive self-confidence, and what a less biased historian calls his 'luminous intelligence'.[104] The same may be said of Bismarck: Brecht shows the Iron Chancellor debating the release of prisoners of war with Jules Favre as he listens to his favourite *prima donna* at the Frankfurt Opera. The collusion between the two is authentic, however, and the scene dramatizes a situation satirized often enough by contemporary cartoonists, one of whom showed the two of them squatting round a cooking-pot as Paris stews in its own juice.[105] Thiers's abstemiousness (we first see him drinking milk to preserve his health for the good of France) and Bismarck's fondness for opera both suggest parallels with a more recent dictator. In the Berliner Ensemble production, following up a suggestion of Brecht's, the same actor, Martin Flörchinger, played the parts of Thiers and Bismarck, which underscored the fact that during this historical crisis national differences were discreetly forgotten. Brecht emphasizes Bismarck's domestic difficulties with a clamorous Left, led by Liebknecht and Bebel. (The latter's congratulatory speech is read verbatim to the Commune by Delescluze in Scene 10.)

Despite the caricature the function of these statesmen and

[103] Dietz, vol. 17, p. 322.
[104] F. H. Brabant, *The Beginnings of the Third Republic*, 1940, p. 25.
[105] Horne, op cit., p. 139.

their underlings is serious. In Scene 6 'Papa' and Jean scoff at what they think is Langevin's exaggerated notion of the power of these political giants, and they perform a satirical charade. But while they joke, what historians of the Right called 'l'armée de l'ordre'—Brecht makes both Bismarck and Thiers repeatedly use the word 'Ordnung'—is gathering for a savage onslaught on their newly won citadel. Not for nothing is Thiers given the last word in the play. As the aristocracy and wealthy bourgeoisie watch the death-agonies of Paris through their opera-glasses—a scene inspired by a metaphor in Marx's own account—Thiers says triumphantly: 'Frankreich, das ist—Sie, Mesdames et Messieurs' (5:2192). The ruling classes have reasserted their power.

For the previous seventy-two days, however, Bismarck and Thiers had lost control of history, and the 'vile multitude', as Thiers termed the Parisian populace, controlled the destiny of France. One of the most striking features of the Commune is the exhilaration that accompanied their short-lived victory. This was for them more than a civil war, it was Armageddon. A stirring poster displayed on 5 April by the Central Committee typifies their mood:

Citizens of Paris, we are back to the great days of sublime heroism and supreme virtue . . . Workers, do not be deceived: this is the final struggle, that of parasitism against labour, exploitation against production. If you are fed up of vegetating in ignorance and of wallowing in misery; if you want your children to be men getting the profit of their own labour, and not a sort of animal trained for the workshops or the battlefield, sweating themselves to make the fortunes of an exploiter or spilling their blood for a despot; if you no longer want your daughters, whom you cannot bring up and look after as you would like, to become objects of pleasure for the arms of that aristocrat, money; if you want an end to poverty forcing men to join the police and women the ranks of prostitution; finally, workers, if you want the reign of justice, be intelligent and arise! And with your strong hands bring down vile reaction to be trodden under your feet![106]

It has been argued often enough that the Commune 'had nothing to do with Communism',[107] that it was 'by no means entirely an anti-capitalist revolution',[108] and that it was 'only

---

[106] Edwards, op. cit., pp. 220–1.   [107] Horne, p. 112.
[108] Edwards, p. 252.

partially proletarian and only secondarily socialist'.[109] Even Marx, ten years after the event, conceded that 'the majority of the Commune was in no way socialist, nor could it be'.[110] Nevertheless, in his *Civil War in France* he called it 'the glorious harbinger of a new society'[111] and this was how the Commune saw itself. In its famous Proclamation of 19 April it jubilantly hailed 'a new political era, experimental, positive, scientific'.

The Commune did not have enough time to achieve much in the way of practical legislation, but the little it did enact indicates that its claim was not much exaggerated. The repeal of the repressive Rent Act, the remission of debts, the prohibition of the sale of pawns, the declaration of the principle of free education, the secularization of the schools, the abolition of night-work in the bakeries, and the tentative move towards egalitarianism in pay: these were all measures that received massive support. Nor were they merely the result of the progressive thinking of a handful of radicals. On 10 May Villiers de l'Isle-Adam wrote in *Le Tribun du peuple:* 'A whole population is discussing serious matters, and for the first time workers can be heard exchanging their views on problems which until now have been broached only by philosophers . . . a new century has just dawned.'[112]

It is this dawning of a new era that Brecht sought to dramatize in *Die Tage der Commune,* not the academic issue of the Commune's socialist orthodoxy or the lessons to be learned from its failure. The giddy state of excitement that enveloped Paris from that first radiant Sunday morning is admirably conveyed by Scene 6, the longest in the play. The citizens celebrate the birth of a millennial Utopia. It begins with François exclaiming: 'Das ist die Commune, das ist die Wissenschaft, das neue Jahrtausend, Paris hat sich dafür entschieden', and more poetically Geneviève calls it 'den Anbruch der Morgenröte' (5:2143). It is 'Papa', however, who best expresses the popular apotheosis of the Commune in a speech based on a lyrical passage from Marx's *Civil War in France:* 'Das ist die erste Nacht der Geschichte, Freunde, in der dieses Paris keinen Mord, keinen Raub, keinen frechen Betrug und

---

[109] E. S. Mason, *The Paris Commune*, New York, 1930, p. 321.
[110] In his letter to D. Nieuwenhuis, 22 Feb. 1881 (Dietz, vol. 35, p. 160).
[111] Dietz, vol. 17, p. 362.   [112] Edwards, p. 283.

keine Schändung haben wird. Zum erstenmal sind seine Straßen sicher, es braucht keine Polizei. Denn die Bankiers und die kleinen Diebe, die Steuereintreiber und die Fabrikanten, die Minister, die Kokotten und die Geistlichkeit sind nach Versailles ausgewandert: die Stadt ist bewohnbar'* (5:2150). The complementary scene in the Hôtel de Ville, immediately following, reflects the same mood at executive level as the Delegates assemble in front of slogans (based on an election manifesto of the Eleventh Arrondissement, which Brecht found in Duncker's collection); they proclaim the right to live, the freedom of the individual, freedom of conscience, of the press and of association, and universal suffrage. In order to stress that this is an expression of the popular will, Brecht links it with the scene in which Langevin completes Geneviève's political initiation with the warning: 'Erwartet nicht mehr von der Commune als von euch selber' (5:2158).

Despite the authenticity of the details it is clear that Brecht's dramatization is orientated towards the future rather than the past. Brecht's ill-fated idealists anticipate a Utopia for which history was by no means ready in 1871. Hans Kaufmann, so far the only critic to rank *Die Tage der Commune* amongst Brecht's major dramas, writes: 'In *Die Tage der Commune* we see the world which begins beyond the antagonistic class-conflicts as a practical reality, built into the plot within the present tragedy.'[113] *Die Tage der Commune*, like the prologue of *Der kaukasische Kreidekreis* and the closing scenes of *Coriolan*, shows the goal of history itself rather than merely a link in the chain. In the spirit of Zhdanov's celebrated address to the Soviet Writers' Congress of 1934, Brecht, for once, enables us to 'see our tomorrow'[114] as he himself envisaged it.

This is not to deny a tragic element in *Die Tage der Commune*, but it is essentially an 'optimistic tragedy' after the manner of Vsevolod Vishnevski. Its mood is very different from that of *Die Maßnahme* or *Die heilige Johanna der Schlachthöfe*. The Young Comrade retards the process of world revolution by succumbing to an instinctive sympathy for the immediate plight of the downtrodden, and Johanna frustrates a crucial strike because she sees violence as an evil irreconcilably at odds with her urge to love. The same tragic dilemma reappears in *Die Tage der*

---

[113] Kaufmann, p. 92.   [114] See above, p. 3 and n. 10.

Commune but it is in an entirely new key. Even Grieg treated the theme very liberally by making Rigault the villain without whose satanic gifts the hero is lost. We have already seen how Brecht cuts Rigault down to size. His view, shared by Varlin, Ranvier, and eventually by Langevin, is 'terror versus terror' (5:2179) and this view is echoed by 'Papa', Coco, and many of the citizens, But it is the slogan 'socialism marches without bayonets' (5:2165) which reflects the majority view nevertheless. In particular it is Geneviève and Madame Cabet who articulate what Lenin called the Commune's 'excessive magnanimity',[115] At the end of Scene 4 Geneviève exclaims idealistically: 'Es wird eine neue Zeit sein und es wird kein Blutbad gewesen sein' (5:2137).

This raises the issue which cost the Commune much sympathy at the time and provided Thiers with invaluable propaganda. On the morning of 18 March an enraged mob lynched the unpopular generals, Lecomte and Thomas. Though the majority of its members were undoubtedly shocked by an atrocity committed in the name of their revolution, the Commune failed to dissociate itself from it. Since this was not a direct result of the Commune's policy Brecht rightly reduces it to the merest footnote. The same may be said perhaps of the execution of Archbishop Darboy, whom the Communards had hoped to exchange for the captured Blanqui—a serious tactical blunder worth two army corps to Versailles, according to Thiers. The execution of the Archbishop, together with some seventy other hostages by Rigault and Ferré, took place during the final desperate phase of the battle, most of Rigault's other prisoners, some 400 in all, having been released soon after their arrest. Compared with the many thousands of Communards massacred after the fall of the last barricade—20,000 is now regarded as a conservative estimate—the Commune's acts of violence pale into insignificance and Brecht justifiably extenuates their enormity, while at the same time showing much more restraint than Grieg in his depiction of the brutality of the Versaillais. Other excesses such as the lynching of police spies by the mob and the demolition of the Vendôme Column are accorded their proper rating as the rowdyism of extremists whom neither the Central Committee nor the Commune itself

[115] Lenin, 'Lessons of the Commune', *Collected Works*, 13, p. 476.

ever quite managed to control. Brecht concedes just one moment of tragic pathos when Rigault, asked if he denies that
violence is degrading, replies simply: 'No, I do not deny it'
(5:2180). But as Langevin puts it to Geneviève in the previous
scene: 'in diesem Kampf gibt es nur blutbefleckte Hände oder
abgehauene Hände' (5:2174), and the lack of compunction
showed by Geneviève when she betrays her fiancé reveals
that Brecht did not intend to develop it into a major tragic
theme.

There is much more emphasis on a related problem, the
Communards' incurable respect for legality. At the time it
seemed otherwise. The historical Rigault, when questioned by
a citizen about the legality of his dismissal of an official,
replied: 'I am not making legality; I am making a revolution'[116]
and Élie Reclus asked on the day of the Commune elections,
'What does legality mean at a time of revolution?'[117] These
revolutionaries had absorbed the spirit of Marx's famous
dictum: 'Violence is the obstetrician of every old society
pregnant with a new one.'[118] But such extremists were a
minority in the Paris Commune, as is shown by the two issues
to which Brecht, like Grieg, devotes the most space: the
failure to march on Versailles and the failure to seize the
Bank of France.

Marxists unanimously follow Marx himself in condemning
these fatal weaknesses. Not only did the Central Committee
let some 20,000 troops of the line leave Paris on 18 March,
but it failed to strike at Thiers before he had time to reassemble
his demoralized forces and make the bargain with Bismarck.
Brecht authentically depicts his Communards debating the
issue of school meals while Thiers is preparing his attack.
Again, Beslay was duped by the marquis de Plœuc into believing that the seizure of the Bank of France would bring
about a catastrophic devaluation of the franc. Consequently,
the Communards were ill equipped either to fight their campaign or to implement their reforms.

All of the Commune's faults could have been remedied in
time, but as Marx wrote in his account of it, 'Time was not

[116] A. Castelot, *Paris, the Turbulent City*, 1962, p. 319.
[117] Edwards, p. 157.
[118] *Das Kapital*, ed, B. Kautsky, Leipzig, 1929, vol. i, p. 384.

allowed to the Commune'.[119] This motif appears in Brecht's play in the form of a resigned comment from Langevin as he reviews the Commune's noble but ineffectual principles: 'Wenn wir Zeit gehabt hätten! Aber das Volk hat nie mehr als eine Stunde. Wehe, wenn es dann nicht schlagfertig, mit allen Waffen gerüstet, dasteht' (5:2173). Brecht has here revived the tragic theme of Ferdinand Lassalle's play *Franz von Sickingen* (1859), so keenly debated by Marx and Engels: the seemingly inevitable conflict between revolutionary fervour and practical know-how.

Brecht wisely avoided what must have been a very real temptation, to turn this genuinely historical play into a Lehrstück. Friedrich Wolf's revolutionary drama *Die Matrosen von Cattaro* (1930) closes with the sentenced rebel, Franz Rasch, saluting the Red Flag as it is hauled down by the reactionary forces, and exclaiming: 'Comrades, do it better next time!' In the same spirit Grieg's Lucien cries out: 'Next time we must win. Win! Win!', as the last barricade falls to the strains of Beethoven's Ninth. This note of perfervid didacticism is almost entirely lacking in *Die Tage der Commune*, and the only thing a would-be revolutionary can profitably learn from it is the callousness of histroy on its circuitous route to Utopia.

At the same time, the element of hope is an important ingredient. At the final session of the Commune Delescluze says simply: 'Sollte, Bürger, es unseren Feinden gelingen, Paris in ein Grab zu verwandeln, so wird es jedenfalls niemals ein Grab unserer Ideen werden' (5:2176). To emphasize the principle of hope—one of several traits that links Brecht's utopian brand of Marxism with that of Ernst Bloch—Brecht introduces one of his favourite symbols. As the besieged Communards prepare for their last stand on Easter Sunday (in reality it was Whitsun), the resurrection of their ideals is hinted at by Madame Cabet's refusal to let the others cut down an apple-tree to improve the barricade. In the penultimate scene there is no Beethoven and no impassioned rhetoric, but the stage-direction ends with the sentence: 'Der Apfelbaum steht in voller Blüte' (5:2189). Hans Kaufmann, who has no hesitation in calling Brecht's last major play a tragedy, rightly qualifies the term by describing it as a tragedy in which the

---

[119] Dietz, vol. 17, p. 348.

supersession of the tragic is an integral part of the action.[120] For Brecht, as for Bloch, hope and defiance have pre-empted the function of pity and fear in this new kind of optimistic tragedy.

Brecht's assessment of the doomed revolutionaries tallies with that of a subsequent chronicler: 'The legend is greater than the actual event and its failure more important than anything moderation could have gained, for without such "failures" all vision would be lost.'[121] Brecht has dramatized this vision and his tribute to the martyrs of the Paris Commune endorses Auguste Renoir's eloquent epitaph: 'They were madmen, but they had in them that little flame that never dies.'[122] *Die Tage der Commune* offers no guarantee that history will redeem their sacrifice, but it offers hope.

[120] Kaufmann, p. 95.　　　　[121] Edwards, pp. 365–6.
[122] A. Horne, *The Fall of Paris*, 1965, p. 432.

PART II:

EXPOSING THE SUPERSTRUCTURE

1. Introduction

THE notion of economic determinism underlies all Marx's ideas about man and society. Production-relations were for him what the Absolute Idea had been for Hegel, the demiurge of history. On this reading of social evolution mind is essentially a derivative of matter: 'It is not the consciousness of men that determines their being, but, on the contrary, their social being determines their consciousness.'[1] At any point in history the economic substructure evolves a more or less elaborate ideological superstructure, which both reflects and protects it. Since the ruling class controls the intellectual as well as the economic means of production it follows that the dominant ideas of any era are 'nothing but the ideal expression of the dominant material relations', as Marx wrote as early as 1845 in *The German Ideology*.[2] In short: 'The ideas of the ruling class are in every age the ruling ideas.'[3] The very fact that the class origin of such ideas is not grasped even by their creators gives them a relative autonomy which can seriously impede the dialectical progress of history. Thus, although all radical change in society must begin with its economic substructure, a criticism of the ideological superstructure is also imperative in order to break down conditioned responses that inhibit the revolutionary will.

Brecht was no economist and in any case literature is hardly the best vehicle for economic analysis, whereas the social and political institutions that Marx identified as the ideological superstructure have always been the raw material of literature. Since literature itself is an integral part of the superstructure there is even a certain poetic justice in using it to expose the class basis of ideas for which it is usually an unconscious apology.

One of the Keuner-anecdotes takes the form of a parable that reveals Brecht's critical methods in miniature. Asked by

[1] Dietz, vol. 13, p. 9. [2] Ibid., vol. 3, p. 46. [3] Ibid.

his landlady's daughter whether sharks would be nicer to the little fishes if they were human beings, Herr K. assures her that they would. The sharks would see conscientiously to the social welfare of the little fishes on the grounds that a happy fish tastes better than a miserable one; in the schools the little fish would learn in their geography lessons how to locate the sharks so that they could be eaten; moral education would impress upon them the beauty and grandeur of self-sacrifice, encouraging the belief that a better future depends on obedience and that wars against the little fish of other sharks are a sacred obligation; art would show the beauty of sharks' teeth and the theatre would portray heroism so convincingly that the spectators would swim blissfully into the jaws of the sharks; religion would teach that a little fish is only really happy in the belly of a shark; finally, the sharks would encourage social inequality, giving some of the little fishes positions of authority over the others. 'In short,' concludes the parable, 'civilization and culture would really only begin to exist in the sea, if the sharks were human beings' (12:396).

Brecht's work as a whole follows the pattern of this parable, which omits only the law in its satirical survey of a class-based superstructure. In the chapters to follow, Brecht's interest in four dominant aspects of the superstructure will be analysed in detail: religion and the related issue of morality; law, which raises the question of justice in an unjust society; political ideology, of which Brecht saw the paradigm in Fascism; and literature, which involves an evaluation of the classical tradition. Not only do these four areas reflect major preoccupations of society during what Marx called its 'prehistoric'[4] phase, but they are held largely responsible for concealing the need for revolution. By showing what he regarded as their true relation to the vested interests of the ruling class Brecht sought to clear away the ideological debris that obscures the road to Utopia.

[4] Dietz, vol. 13, p. 9.

2. Religion

An official statement issued by the Soviet Communist Party bluntly declares 'the untenability of religious beliefs', echoing the belligerent atheism of *The Communist Manifesto*, which repudiated 'all religion and all morality'. As early as 1841 the young Marx had already adopted the Promethean motto 'I hate all the gods'. 'It raises that cry', he had written of his philosophy, 'against all the gods of heaven and earth that do not recognize man's consciousness as the supreme Deity.'[1] He later went so far as to insist that the proper starting-point for all criticism is the criticism of religion.[2]

It is therefore not surprising that Brecht analysed the role it played as an integral part of the social superstructure. But his almost obsessive preoccupation with religion, which antedates by a full decade his conversion to Marxism, indicates a personal involvement of great intensity. Eric Bentley was hardly exaggerating when he claimed it was a subject Brecht could not keep away from for more than a few pages at a time.[3]

Nearly all Brecht's biographers cite his laconic reply to the questionnaire circulated by *Die Dame* for its issue of October 1928. Asked to state the greatest single influence on his work he wrote: 'Sie werden lachen: die Bibel.' Nor does his writing before and after that date suggest that his reply was flippant. His very first play, completed when he was only fifteen, was an adaptation of the Judith story and entitled *Die Bibel*; his first anthology, *Die Hauspostille*, was originally printed on Bible paper and contains parodies of the Psalms and the Protestant hymn; the hymn form reappears in the *Dreigroschenoper* and in the *Hitler-Choräle*, whilst the language of *Das Badener Lehrstück vom Einverständnis* suggests a Jesuit *exercitium*; *Mutter Courage*, set against a background of the bloodiest religious war in history, bristles

---

[1] Dietz, Ergänzungsband 1, p. 262.
[2] Ibid., p. 378.
[3] E. Bentley, *Seven Plays by Bertolt Brecht*, New York, 1961, p. xl.

with quotations from religious literature; Galilei and Barberini rag each other with biblical proverbs. Similarly, biblical themes and allusions abound. The Christmas-theme appears several times in the early poetry; Galy Gay denies his wife and Mother Courage her son three times, Shlink and Macheath are both betrayed and arrested on a Thursday evening, and the latter, on reducing the police chief to tears, comments: 'Den Trick habe ich aus der Bibel' (2:446); Puntila boasts he could walk on a lake of brandy, and Johanna drives the profiteers from the Salvation Army headquarters with her banner; Azdak is dressed in a robe by soldiers, mocked, and beaten, and the way he addresses an old peasant woman in the language of the Annunciation has been aptly described as 'a strange translation from religious into human terms, which still has an atmosphere of genuine devoutness'.[4] The list could be extended almost indefinitely.

To some extent this reflects the early influence on Brecht of his Protestant mother, who seems to have awakened in him a profound admiration for the powerful language and imagery of the Lutheran Bible. In his essay 'Über reimlose Lyrik mit unregelmäßigen Rhythmen' he describes its prosody as 'gestisch'[5] and admits to imitating it. In most cases, however, there is much more than linguistic imitation involved, rather what Hans Mayer calls 'umfunktionierte Theologie'.[6] Brecht uses the language and imagery of the religion into which he was born in order to expose its inadequacy as a practical philosophy. This is true even of his work prior to 1926, but it was the study of Marxism that gave the scepticism of his youth a new impetus and a new perspective.

Both the politically orientated anticlericalism of the French rationalists and the anti-supranaturalism of the age of science are discernible in the Marxist critique of religion. Despite the furore it caused at the time the scientistic approach has worn less well, though the cruder kind of Communist propaganda still cashes in on it. In Brecht it finds its most naïve expression in the didactic cantata *Der Ozeanflug*, in which the intrepid pioneer, Lindbergh, defines God as the product of pre-

---

[4] Ronald Gray, *Brecht*, Edinburgh, 1961, p. 110.
[5] See below, p. 290 f., n. 8.
[6] Hans Mayer, *Bertolt Brecht und die Tradition*, Pfullingen, 1961, p. 47.

scientific ignorance and exults in his expulsion by modern technology:

> Unter den schärferen Mikroskopen
> Fällt er.
> Es vertreiben ihn die verbesserten Apparate aus der Luft.
>
> (2:577)

Marxist critics were themselves not slow to refute such a simplistic form of atheism. After all, even St. Jerome, writing in the fourth century, had rejected a literalistic interpretation of the Bible's spatial metaphors as a philosophical absurdity. The idea recurs in subtler form when Brecht's Galilei, giddy with the success of his new telescope, formally announces the abolition of Heaven (3:1260). On the whole, as we saw in an earlier chapter, Brecht was not interested in the theology of the Galilean era; but his play does assume that science will supersede theology as a means of understanding reality. In a sense he was right. If it is true that the astronomer Laplace told Napoleon he had no need of God to explain natural phenomena, he spoke for modern science as a whole. At the same time, a cautious Marxist warns against 'the smug illusion that good scientific propaganda will make it possible to do away with religion'.[7] And for their part theologians, even in Brecht's lifetime, had already stopped looking for God in the interstices of human knowledge and located him exactly where Brecht's Galilei does: 'In uns oder nirgends!' (3:1255).

The survival of the atheism of the Philosophes in Marxist thinking is much more interesting and had a profounder influence on Brecht's work. In *Le Christianisme dévoilé* (1756) baron d'Holbach wrote: 'Religion is the art of making men drunk with ecstasy in order to divert their attention from the evils heaped upon them here below by those who govern them.'[8] It was this same collusion between religion and reactionary politics, historically the result of Constantine's adoption of Christianity as the state religion, that provoked Marx's famous description of religion as the opium of the people and Lenin's talk of 'spiritual gin'. Augustine's skilful manipulation of Pauline theology to justify slavery and Thomas Aquinas's

---

[7] Roger Garaudy, *From Anathema to Dialogue*, trans. L. O'Neill, 1967, p. 92.
[8] *Textes Choisis*, Paris, 1957, vol. i, p. 131.

defence of serfdom in feudal Europe are among the grosser consequences of Constantinianism emphasized by Marx and Engels. Lenin, writing against the background of an extremely reactionary Russian Orthodox Church, summed up the case against religion by saying: 'Every defence or justification of the idea of God, even the most refined, the best-intentioned, is a justification of reaction.'[9]

There is of course another side to the coin, as Marx and Engels, who distinguished more carefully than Lenin between religion and its abuse, were well aware. Engels described early Christianity as one of the most revolutionary factors in the history of the human mind and saw its direct historical descendants in such figures as Thomas Münzer, whose followers in the Peasants' War marched under the slogan 'Lord uphold Thy divine justice'. In the same spirit a modern Marxist writes: 'The thesis that religion always and everywhere turns men away from action is in flagrant contradiction to the facts of history.'[10] Nevertheless, the point made by the early Marxists and reiterated by Brecht is that the Church has repeatedly sold out Christian principle to the Establishment and in so doing it has seriously retarded the progress of history.

Brecht's most aggressive treatment of the theme is the description of Fewcoombey's apocalyptic dream in the *Dreigroschenroman*, in which Christ is found guilty of aiding and abetting capitalism with his parable of the talents. This cannot be taken seriously as biblical exegesis, but it illustrates vividly enough the Marxist critique of Constantinianism. The motif crops up again and again in Brecht's writings. In the children's ballad 'Der Schneider von Ulm' it is almost inevitably a bishop who derides the foolhardy pioneer's attempt to transcend his divinely appointed limits; in the story *Das Experiment* it is a curate who cuffs the stable-boy for learning to read during matins; in *Die heilige Johanna der Schlachthöfe* it is the Salvationist Snyder who instructs the poor that God will compensate them in the next world for the miseries they endure in this, and in *Puntila* the pastor regrets that they now seem to doubt this. In a poem significantly entitled 'Über den bürgerlichen Gottesglauben' an imaginary congregation attri-

[9] Letter to Gorki, Nov. 1913 (*Collected Works*, 35, p. 128).
[10] Roger Garaudy, *Marxism in the 20th Century*, trans. R. Hague, 1970, p. 87.

butes social inequality to the inscrutable wisdom of God, while 'Lob des Zweifels' explicitly contests the belief that a leaky roof is a divine dispensation. The deeper social implications of religious scepticism are discussed in the scene from *Leben des Galilei* in which the sympathetic Little Monk asks the founder of modern physics how he can countenance the despair of the poor Campagna peasants whom the new astronomy has cheated of their compensatory heaven. The unspoken corollary is that if religion condones their misery, then the peasants must learn to reject its illusory consolation and demand their compensation now.

Brecht's bitter indictment of a Church that has failed its mission and capitulated in the face of human misery occurs in a poem written about 1931, 'Die drei Soldaten', in which God is put against a wall and shot for failing to come to the aid of the poor. Two years later the Nazi era began, and the gloomy record of the German Churches under Hitler did little to correct Brecht's one-sided impression of organized religion as a massive confidence trick. The moving papal encyclical 'With Burning Sorrow' and the heroic rearguard action of Pastor Niemöller's Bekennende Kirche came too late to put a spoke in Hitler's wheel. In the meantime Bishop Müller's 'Deutsche Christen' contrived to reconcile the Gospel with the new ideology, even though Bormann publicly announced that they were irreconcilable. In the scene 'Bergpredigt' in *Furcht und Elend* the chaplain cuts a poor figure as he self-consciously attempts this same reconciliation of opposites at the deathbed of a despairing believer. When Brecht's Schweyk is asked if he is a German Christian he replies disarmingly: 'Nein, ein gewöhnlicher' (5:1982). But the *Kriegsfibel* contains the most caustic variation of the theme. Beneath a photograph of the victorious Falangist general, Juan Yagile, kneeling before the altar at a celebratory mass, is the virulent caption: 'Gott ist ein Faschist.'[11]

Quite apart from its political exploitation, the other-worldliness of so much traditional Christian thought was anathema to the sensualist in Brecht, who in one of his first poems extolled tobacco and brandy as sacraments and in one of his last listed showers and comfortable shoes among his priorities

[11] *Kriegsfibel*, Berlin, 1955, p. 5.

(8:261; 10:1022). Max Frisch, who was struck by Brecht's resemblance to a Jesuit seminarist, aptly characterized the essential difference between the 'religious 'attitude and Brecht's when he wrote; 'Christians concentrate on the next life, Brecht on this.'[12] Brecht was clearly expressing his own belief when he made his earliest Baal say to the prison chaplain: 'Ich glaube an kein Fortleben und bin aufs Hiesige angewiesen',[13] and the final poem in his 'devil's breviary' warns against the fallacy of supraterrestrial hope:

> Laßt euch nicht verführen
> Zu Fron und Ausgezehr!
> Was kann euch Angst noch rühren?
> Ihr sterbt mit allen Tieren
> Und es kommt nichts nachher.*
>
> (8:260)

A full-blooded 'Diesseitigkeit' is the most dynamic and the most human trait of all Brecht's favourite characters, from Baal, who says that so long as wine exists the existence of God is an irrelevant abstraction, to Galilei, who recants because his wine and his roast goose are ultimately more important to him than the future of science. A transcendental God, whether or not he is a Fascist, is simply irrelevant to their needs.

It is quite possible that the cynicism of Brecht's early work was, in Martin Esslin's words, 'the mask of one whose faith has been shattered'.[14] What shattered his faith and impelled him to find an effective surrogate was not so much that he found religion intellectually unsatisfactory as that it seemed irrelevant. Mother Courage, endeavouring to get the chaplain to chop firewood, counters his excuse that his job is the care of souls with the words: 'Ich hab aber keine Seel. Dagegen brauch ich Brennholz' (4:1404). Beneath the persiflage is Brecht's most serious criticism of the religious attitude: it fails to meet real human need.

Brecht's first play, *Die Bibel*, is set against a background of the religious wars of the Netherlands in the sixteenth century. The commander of the besieging Catholic forces offers to spare the town from plunder if a virgin will offer herself to him.

---

[12] Max Frisch, *Tagebuch 1946–49*, Frankfurt, 1971, p. 288.
[13] See D. Schmidt, *'Baal': Drei Fassungen*, Frankfurt, 1968, p. 55.
[14] *Brecht: a Choice of Evils*, p. 7.

An aged Protestant is scandalized when his own granddaughter, who says simply: 'Deine Bibel ist kalt', accepts the challenge (7:3032). To the old man her soul is worth more than a thousand lives, but she takes the doctrine of the neighbour literally and sacrifices herself for him. By contrast with her father and brother, who egg her on to save their own skins, her response is felt as truly religious in the sense of the verse: 'Greater love hath no man than this, that he lay down his life for his friends.' Twenty years later Brecht was writing *Mutter Courage*. In the penultimate scene the city of Halle is threatened with destruction and the instinctive reaction of the pious peasants is to pray. Kattrin, on the other hand, translates her concern for the innocent children of Halle into action. She mounts the roof, draws up the ladder after her, and beats her drum. In a comparable situation in *Die Gewehre der Frau Carrar* the prayers of the Spanish peasants are drowned by the artillery of the victorious Nationalists. Prayer, as the most intimate expression of the religious attitude, is seen in all cases as an impotent substitute for action.

Brecht seems to have been conscious of the fact that his own brand of atheism was directed not against religion as such but against its misguided apologists. Discussing the heroine of *Die heilige Johanna der Schlachthöfe*, he commented: 'It will be seen ... that she is not speaking of God at all, but of talking *about* God ...' (17:1021). In *Die Mutter* there is an interesting scene in which Pelagea Wlassowa encounters the stodgy orthodoxy of a landlady who is full of pious quotations but nevertheless evicts a tenant who cannot pay the rent. The latter asks despairingly: 'In der Bibel steht ganz deutlich: Liebe deinen Nächsten. Warum werfen Sie mich da auf die Straße?' (2:884) The padre in *Die Gewehre der Frau Carrar* defends his pacifist attitude by citing the commandment 'Thou shalt not kill', but Pedro insists that if he renders a man about to be shot incapable of self-defence, then he is himself guilty of his death. Such passages demonstrate the truth of Jacques Maritain's assertion that Marxist atheism is largely the product of 'a Christian world unfaithful to its own principles'.[15]

Karl Thieme discerned 'basic Christian truth'[16] in the angry

[15] J. Maritain, *True Humanism*, 1938, p. 33.
[16] K. Thieme, 'Des Teufels Gebetsbuch', *Hochland*, 29, 1931–2, p. 411.

young Brecht of the *Hauspostille* and certainly there is more than modish cynicism in such a poem as 'Hymne an Gott', which concludes as follows:

> Viele sagen, du bist nicht und das sei besser so.
> Aber wie kann das nicht sein, das so betrügen kann?
> Wo so viel leben von dir und anders nicht sterben konnten—
> Sag mir, was heißt das dagegen—daß du nicht bist?*
>
> (8:54)

In the face of human need atheism is not enough. Marx followed Feuerbach in rejecting any kind of atheism that was merely lack of faith, defining socialism as 'positive human consciousness'.[17] Brecht demands the same positivism. Of his adaptation of *Don Juan* he wrote: 'Don Juan is not an atheist in the progressive sense. His unbelief is not combative, demanding human intervention. It is simply lack of faith. There is no alternative conviction here, just no conviction at all' (17:1258). If mere lack of faith characterizes Brecht's earliest writing, he later replaced it with the conviction that man is the creator of his own destiny. As Marx put it: 'The criticism of religion ends with the doctrine that man is the highest being for man.'[18]

The most positive contribution made by Marx and Engels to the analysis of religion consisted in the study of its origins. Instead of dismissing it as a combination of pre-scientific superstition and reactionary bluff, they asked the supremely important question: To what human need is religion a response? In the wake of Hegel and Feuerbach they came to see religion, and in particular the doctrine of God and salvation, as the exteriorization of human need. 'The existence of religion', wrote Marx in *The Jewish Question*, 'is the existence of a deficiency.'[19] Both Marx and Engels noted that primitive Christianity postulated the absolute equality of all men before God, but they held that this passion for justice, inherited from Judaism, was 'celestialized' (*verhimmelt*) by later adherents who sought their Utopia in the next world instead of in this. On the same argument the doctrine of atonement is a mystical solution of the problem of alienation. The solution was illusory from

---

[17] Dietz, Ergänzungsband I, p. 546. [18] Ibid., p. 385.
[19] Ibid., p. 352.

their point of view, but the problem was real enough. Religion was not only the opium of the people but also 'the soul of soulless conditions' and 'the sigh of the oppressed',[20] not only a palliative of human suffering but also a protest against it.

This is the linchpin of Marxist humanism, which proclaims the autonomy of man and in place of a chiliastic vision of equality in the hereafter posits a realizable Utopia in the world of social reality. In 1969 Roger Garaudy, despite his sympathy with the religious viewpoint, was still confidently claiming that 'Marxism can integrate all the human aspirations which are to be found, in a mysterious form, among believers.'[21] It is in this sense (and in this sense only) that Brecht can be described as a religious writer. He demands that society should dispel religious illusions by eradicating the need for them. His *alter ego*, Herr Keuner, was once asked if he thought there was a God, to which he replied that if the answer would affect the questioner's attitude, then it proved he still needed a God (12:380). Brecht did not need one. He found in Marxist humanism the only adequate response to human need.

Two of Brecht's best-known works are exclusively concerned with the humanist critique of religion. The first of these is Brecht's updated version of the St. Joan story, *Die heilige Johanna der Schlachthöfe*, a large-scale parody of Schiller set against a background of the Depression in Sinclair's Chicago. Like his ambiguous villain, Pierpont Mauler, Brecht had been impressed by the active concern of the Salvation Army for the world's down-and-outs, combining soup-kitchen charity with a gospel of personal salvation. His Johanna Dark, lieutenant of the Black Straw Hats, exemplifies this selfless evangelism. Her opening speech is a fervent declaration of solidarity with the 'entmenschte Menschheit' of the poor, whose last hope in a doomed world is God.

Johanna's philanthropy is inspired by the purest motives. She thinks only of the spiritual welfare of the downtrodden. She is appalled that they should prefer soup to salvation, but when she hears of a man accidentally processed as canned meat and then sees his widow grovelling to the foreman of his factory for free meals, she begins to see that the material needs of the oppressed must first be met before her gospel can make sense.

---

[20] Ibid., p. 378.   [21] Garaudy, *Marxism in the 20th Century*, p. 115.

Despite the warning of her comrades not to dabble in worldly affairs Johanna meets the tycoons on their own territory and pleads with them to reconcile service to the customer with service to the neighbour, but her plea falls on deaf ears. The canned-meat king, Pierpont Mauler, is shrewd enough to see that the only effective alternative to the kind of economic first aid attempted by charity is a drastic revision of the entire social system, but this he claims would militate against her interests as well as his own, since it would render not only capitalism, but also God, redundant. Such an overhaul would, moreover, entail a revolutionary new conception of man for which Johanna is by no means prepared.

After being dismissed from the Black Hats for spreading subversive ideas, Johanna throws in her lot with the Communists, who at least offer a practical solution of the problem of social injustice. Her duties as a greenhorn propagandist conflict, however, with her religious ideals and she is responsible for the failure of the general strike. Too late Johanna realizes that compassion for the poor under present conditions necessarily involves violence: 'Es hilft nur Gewalt, wo Gewalt herrscht' (2:783). Her God of love seems incongruous in a world of hatred. When she faces her formidable adversary for the last time he has already bribed the local organizer of the Black Hats to serve up pro-capitalist apologetics along with the soup and pious saws. His generously subsidized religion will continue to classify social chaos as an inexplicable natural phenomenon like the rain. Johanna, dying of pneumonia contracted while living amongst the poor, denounces the salvationist gospel of deferred justice and demands that the world be changed at once. The scene culminates in a bitter rejection of God as an impotent bystander:

> Darum, wer unten sagt, daß es einen Gott gibt
> Und ist keiner sichtbar
> Und kann sein unsichtbar und hülfe ihnen doch
> Den soll man mit dem Kopf auf das Pflaster schlagen
> Bis er verreckt ist.*
>
> (782)

The Establishment, preferring a saint to a revolutionary, attempts to drown her despairing cry with hymns of praise, and the roseate glow that accompanies Schiller's Johanna to her heroic death also ironically floods Brecht's epic stage.

One important motif, not fully developed in *Die heilige Johanna*, is the transvaluation of ethics that results from the abandonment of the religious premiss. In her final speech Johanna renounces the religious postulate of individual goodness and demands instead a social order that facilitates it:

> Sorgt doch, daß ihr die Welt verlassend
> Nicht nur gut wart, sondern verlaßt
> Eine gute Welt!
>
> (780)

After an incubation period of ten years this theme reappears as the pivotal issue of one of Brecht's finest plays. *Der gute Mensch von Sezuan*, at the beginning of which three gods are investigating the rumour that it is impossible to be good and survive in a world of poverty and hardship. Their terms of reference are: 'die Welt kann bleiben, wie sie ist, wenn genügend gute Menschen gefunden werden, die ein menschenwürdiges Dasein leben können' (4:1492). Their investigations in the poverty-stricken province of Szechwan appear to substantiate the rumour until they come across Shen Te, who is reputedly a model of kindliness and self-sacrifice and is known locally as the Angel of the Suburbs. And yet even she has had to resort to prostitution to survive. The thousand dollars with which the gods reward her hospitality are intended to enable this virtuous woman to lead 'ein menschenwürdiges Dasein' and thus fulfil the conditions of the decree. When the tobacco-shop Shen Te buys with the money is invaded by an army of parasites and creditors, however, her natural impulse is to shelter the parasites and pay off the creditors, which would reduce her once again to penury. She finds herself obliged to impersonate a ruthless cousin, Shui Ta, who promptly evicts the insurgents. His invention was only intended as a temporary stopgap and the gods do not judge it too harshly, but Shen Te finds that she needs her heartless cousin more and more often in order to reconcile her impulsive generosity with the interests of self-preservation. The Shen Te component of Brecht's schizoid heroine becomes almost completely absorbed into Shui Ta, who is eventually accused of her murder. At the trial Shen Te reveals her true identity to the gods and pleads extenuating circumstances:

> Euer einstiger Befehl
> Gut zu sein und doch zu leben
> Zerriß mich wie ein Blitz in zwei Hälften.
>
> (4:1603)

The split personality is one of Brecht's favourite dramatic devices,[22] though he was not even remotely interested in abnormal psychology. As with Anna, the heroine of *Die sieben Todsünden*, and Puntila, Shen Te's schizophrenia can be readily diagnosed as a social disease of capitalism, the internal contradictions of which force the individual to adopt two mutually antagonistic attitudes. Shen Te's case is, however, more serious, since it raises an existential problem not found elsewhere in Brecht in such painful intensity. Both Anna and Puntila find their instincts at loggerheads with their reason, but in neither case is there a moral issue, much less a religious issue, involved. In Shen Te's case the 'temptation to goodness', which links her with Grusche Vachnadze, is a natural impulse that enjoys divine sanction. 'Wie angenehm ist es doch, freundlich zu sein!' she exclaims to the audience (4:1570). 'Zu schenken war mir eine Wollust,' she pleads at her trial, 'Ein glückliches Gesicht / Und ich ging wie auf Wolken' (1604). But social conditions and the predatory habits they have engendered in her fellow men have made her goodness impracticable. As soon as she becomes pregnant her mother-instinct, like that of Mother Courage, prompts her to obey the law of the jungle. Her child shall not rummage the dustbins of Szechwan for food like that of Lin To, the carpenter she herself has ruined:

> Was ich gelernt in der Gosse, meiner Schule
> Durch Faustschlag und Betrug, jetzt
> Soll es dir dienen, Sohn, zu dir
> Will ich gut sein und Tiger und wildes Tier
> Zu allen andern, wenn's sein muß.*
>
> (1573)

As the custodians of a supranatural order Brecht's imaginary gods have a vested interest in Shen Te's altruism. If men try

---

[22] Cf. W. H. Sokel, 'Brecht's split characters and his sense of the tragic', in *Brecht: a Collection of Critical Essays*, ed. P. Demetz, Englewood Cliffs, 1962, p. 127 ff.

hard enough, their goodness will compensate for the evil in the world and then the Herculean task of transforming it will not be necessary. Brecht's parable shows that individual goodness is not only inadequate to deal with the evil in the world but, in extreme cases, suicidal. Though she no more sees a way out of her dilemma than Mother Courage, Shen Te is forced to recognize the existential paradox and tells the gods: 'Etwas muß falsch sein an eurer Welt' (1603). But the gods refuse to accept the unpalatable truth that their world is uninhabitable. Like Johanna's angry denunciation, Shen Te's despairing cry for help is swamped by an operatic finale, and Brecht's gods, a parody of the classical *deus ex machina*, retire on a timely pink cloud to well-deserved oblivion.

The Epilogue, apologizing for this untidy end, characteristically leaves the audience with the responsibility for finding an effective solution of Shen Te's problem:

> Soll es ein andrer Mensch sein? Oder eine andre Welt?
> Vielleicht nur andere Götter? Oder keine?
>
> (1607)

The theological dimension of the work is indicated by the choice offered in the last line. Atheism would remove the ultimate sanction for Shen Te's goodness, but it would not solve her dilemma, since her goodness is a powerful emotional impulse, not conventional piety. Alternatively, the god of almost any historical religion could put up a better performance than Brecht's incompetent trinity. But the Christian imagery of the Cross teaches that neither an omnipotent God nor a moral superman are any guarantee of survival. There remains only the possibility of a new world. The defeatism of the spongers, who say 'Wir können die Welt nicht ändern' (1537), is implicitly rejected by the Epilogue, the ostensibly open ending of which is transparent bluff.

The Revolution will change the world. But will it solve Shen Te's dilemma? It has been argued that Brecht's ending is more open than he knew because, although revolution would eliminate many of the stresses which make Shen Te's dilemma so painful, it would still leave the basic conflict between altruism and self-interest unsolved.[23] The point is

---

[23] Cf. V. Klotz, *Bertolt Brecht: Versuch über das Werk*, Darmstadt, 1957, p. 23.

that Brecht's implied solution is much more radical than it seems at first sight. There is an alternative Epilogue which ends with the couplet:

> Kein größeres Glück gibt es auf Erden nun
> Als gut sein dürfen und Gutes tun.
>
> (4:Anm. 2)

This Epilogue demands a Utopia in which Shen Te will be able to indulge her altruistic impulse without having to retire periodically behind the mask of a ruthless exploiter. But in the Utopia demanded by the Epilogue of the definitive version of the play, Shen Te will no longer experience such an altruistic impulse because the injustice to which it was a response will have been abolished. Earlier in the play Wang submitted that the gods might alleviate human distress by demanding less: reasonableness instead of justice, for instance, good will instead of love, and decorum instead of honour. The gods are the first to see that this is asking for more, not less. Only a radical transformation of society would make these concessions workable, and such a transformation would in turn render the gods themselves redundant, as Pierpont Mauler told Johanna. Mother Courage argues that if generals knew their job there would be no need for heroes. By implication the ideal community is not one where saints and heroes abound, but one where they are an anachronism.

Until such a community is a political reality, however, there remains the question of the morality incumbent upon those who pave the way for it. It has often been alleged that Marxism is fundamentally amoral, but in fact it has geared the moral idealism of religion to its own needs. Communism demands the same selfless devotion as Christianity and it too has inspired martyrs who sacrificed self-interest to the needs of their neighbour. The essential difference is that whereas the Christian Gospel identifies every fellow creature with the neighbour-in-Christ, the Communist derives his morality from the needs of the revolutionary class alone. In the interests of this class all petty-bourgeois squeamishness must be abandoned and Lenin's 'sea of blood' may have to be crossed on the way to the 'truly human morality' demanded by Engels.[24]

[24] Dietz, vol. 20, p. 88.

On occasions the old idealism may conflict with the new, as it does tragically in *Die Maßnahme* where the Young Comrade's instinctive response to human need undermines the strategy of the omniscient Party. In his case compassion has not been fully canalized into productive revolutionary activity. As the Chorus puts it in that play: 'Wer für den Kommunismus kämpft, hat von allen Tugenden nur eine: daß er für den Kommunismus kämpft' (2:638). The end that justifies the means is not now the will of God, but the will of history. Once this will has been enacted, the prehistory of the human race, as Marx called it,[25] will have come to an end and so will the new morality that made it possible. The word virtue will disappear from the vocabulary of Utopia.

The roots of Brecht's optimism are to be sought not so much in the Marxist doctrine of God as in the Marxist doctrine of man. In effect Marxism revived the Pelagian heresy, which rejected the concept of original sin. Marx seems, like Rousseau and Fourier, to have believed that evil is essentially a product of the social environment. This was basically the message Brecht intended to penetrate the apparent cynicism of the *Dreigroschenoper*:

> Wir wären gut—anstatt so roh
> Doch die Verhältnisse, sie sind nicht so.
> (2:432)

Shen Te claims that it is evil, not good, that requires an unnatural effort:

> Den Mitmenschen zu treten
> Ist es nicht anstrengend? Die Stirnader
> Schwillt ihnen an, vor Mühe, gierig zu sein.
> (4:1570)

The Japanese mask on the wall of Brecht's study offered the same optimistic reading of human nature:

> An meiner Wand hängt ein japanisches Holzwerk
> Maske eines bösen Dämons, bemalt mit Goldlack.
> Mitfühlend sehe ich
> Die geschwollenen Stirnadern, andeutend
> Wie anstrengend es ist, böse zu sein.*
> (10:850)

[25] Ibid., vol. 13, p. 9.

It is here that Christianity and Marxism ultimately part company and not on the question of the existence of God. If the doctrine of original sin is more than a theological abstraction and expresses a basic fact of human nature, then the harmony of Brecht's Utopia will be perpetually jeopardized by the very fact that its citizens are autonomous human beings. After all, even on Brecht's reckoning, under identical conditions of hardship men react as differently as Wang and Sun, Shen Te and Frau Shin. There is no guarantee that such differences will disappear with the advent of a completely egalitarian society and no sign as yet that such a society stops every man desiring more than his fair share. True, the Communist experiment is still in its infancy, and Brecht would doubtless have argued that greed and the lust for power are a moribund survival from capitalism, but the history of Communism to date has demonstrated that revolutionary idealism can rapidly degenerate into anything from bureaucratic pettiness to wilful despotism. The interesting case of post-revolutionary Poland, where the Church, contrary to all expectation, has actually gained ground, suggests that this may well be the inalienable function of religion within Communism, not to retard the progress of revolution, but on the contrary to prevent the evil in man from corrupting it. At all events Brecht's heady optimism blinded him to the need for any such safeguard and his personal blueprint for Utopia makes no allowance for a Church.

It is tempting to speculate whether Brecht, with his undeniable interest in religion, would have welcomed the recent dialogue between Marxism and Christianity, described by a leading Marxist as a 'noble rivalry in the human contest'[26] and by a leading Churchman as a 'fruitful conflict'.[27] Brecht did not live to see this surprising development. The primary task as he saw it was not to reconcile religion with dialectical materialism, but to develop human society in such a way as to make religion superfluous.

[26] Garaudy, *From Anathema to Dialogue*, p. 76.
[27] J. B. Metz, quoted in ibid., p. 109.

3. Law

BRECHT's predilection for courtroom scenes has often been noted with interest. *Die Maßnahme* and most of *Das Verhör des Lukullus* take the form of a tribunal; trials form the climactic scenes of *Die Ausnahme und die Regel, Der gute Mensch von Sezuan,* and *Der kaukasische Kreidekreis,* and figure prominently in *Mahagonny, Die Rundköpfe und die Spitzköpfe, Arturo Ui, Furcht und Elend des Dritten Reiches,* and *Der Prozeß der Jeanne d'Arc zu Rouen 1431;* imaginary trials take place in *Mann ist Mann, Der Dreigroschenroman,* and *Puntila.* Moreover, Sergei Tretyakov tells us that in the early thirties Brecht planned to dramatize a whole series of famous historical trials, including those of Socrates, Karl Marx, and George Grosz.[1]

To some extent, no doubt, the dramatic cut-and-thrust of forensic dialogue inspired the playwright's interest in legal procedure. Shakespeare's *Merchant of Venice,* Kleist's *Der zerbrochene Krug,* and Shaw's *Saint Joan* had already demonstrated the theatrical potential of courtroom drama. But in Brecht's case there is much more at stake than dramatic excitement. Indeed, his courtroom settings can more appropriately be ranked amongst the epic features of his theatre, since the reconstruction of past events by witnesses and their interrogators automatically divests them of their dramatic immediacy and thus furnishes a ready-made alienation-effect. The real attraction of the courtroom for Brecht was that it provided a symbolic backdrop for a kind of *Weltgericht* in which pre-revolutionary society is weighed and found wanting.

This theme had been adumbrated by the *Hauspostille* ballad 'Von der Kindesmörderin Marie Farrar' (1922), the very diction of which satirizes legal jargon. The girl is found guilty of infanticide and sentenced to death, but the poet demands her posthumous rehabilitation and by implication

---

[1] S. Tretyakov, 'Bert Brecht', *Internationale Literatur,* May 1937, p. 60 ff; reprinted in *Brecht: a Collection of Critical Essays,* ed. Demetz, p. 16 ff.

condemns the harsh world into which she and her child were born. But apart from this poem and the marginal exception of the comic trial-scene in *Mann ist Mann*, the theme plays little part in Brecht's early work. His later work, on the other hand, reveals an interest in the subject almost as obsessive as his interest in religion, and this is essentially a by-product of his study of Marx, who claimed that criticism of the one leads logically to a criticism of the other.[2]

Neither Marx nor Engels developed a philosophy of law in the strictest sense, but their entire work is sustained by a passion for justice. One legal historian writes:' From the Communist Manifesto to the programs of the Internationals, the work of Marx and Engels is founded upon a fervent desire for true law which fully realizes justice as an ideal concept. Their faith in the possibility of such a definitive realization of justice is the very core of their philosophy of law.'[3] That the author of 'Marie Farrar' would find this faith congenial was a foregone conclusion, but it is not merely the Marxist passion for justice that has passed into Brecht's work. Its insistence on the contradiction between justice and legality in all pre-revolutionary society powerfully influenced him.

Marx and Engels, rejecting Hegel's idealization of law as the embodiment of human freedom, saw it as an essential component of the repressive social superstructure, the function of which is to blunt men's awareness of the basic injustice of society and so to safeguard the economic interests of its ruling class. In the *Manifesto* there is only a passing reference to law, which is subsumed under the general notion of the state as 'the executive committee of the bourgeoisie'.[4] Bukharin and Preobrazhensky's *ABC of Communism* is more explicit and ranks 'bourgeois justice' amongst the 'various institutions of bourgeois society which serve to oppress and deceive the working masses',[5] and in the same spirit the *Great Soviet Encyclopedia* defines it as 'the will of the ruling class translated into statutory form'. This radically positivist notion

[2] Dietz, vol. 1, p. 379.

[3] C. J. Friedrich, *The Philosophy of Law in Historical Perspective*, Univ. of Chicago, 1958, p. 153.

[4] Dietz, vol. 4, p. 164.

[5] N. Bukharin and E. Preobrazhensky, *The ABC of Communism*, trans. E. and C. Paul, 1969, p. 271.

of law is based on its persistent association with the defence of property rights in legal theory from the Scholastics onwards. John Locke, for instance, defined political power as 'a right of making laws, with penalties of death and consequently all lesser penalties for the regulating and preserving of property'.[6] This explains why only a man of property had the right to vote until well into the nineteenth century. In no respect did Marx make a more radical break with tradition. Proudhon's maxim, 'La propriété, c'est le vol', became an integral part of his social philosophy.

A basic principle of law, which Marx, whose grandfather was a rabbi, would have been the last to dispute, is enshrined in the Jewish Torah: 'Ye shall not respect persons in judgement: but ye shall hear the small as well as the great' (Deut. 1:17). Its secular counterpart is the Platonic axiom: 'Injustice arises when equals are treated unequally and also when unequals are treated equally.'[7] Marx's basic contention was that bourgeois society, by perpetuating the unjust distribution of wealth, alienates the exploited from their rights and thus contradicts the notion of justice as the exclusion of arbitrariness. Since the legal system of any society is designed to preserve it, it follows that in pre-revolutionary society legality and justice are mutually exclusive.

The close association of the judicial system with the economic interests of the ruling class is a constantly recurring theme in Brecht's writing after 1926. In the *Dreigroschenoper*, Peachum, who exploits the limited philanthropy of his fellow citizens, insists on the legality of his business and complains when Brown, as chief of police, fails to protect it: 'Wir halten uns doch alle an das Gesetz! Das Gesetz ist einzig und allein gemacht zur Ausbeutung derer, die es nicht verstehen oder die es aus nackter Not nicht befolgen können. Und wer von dieser Ausbeutung seinen Brocken abbekommen will, muß sich streng an das Gesetz halten'* (2:463). *Aufstieg und Fall der Stadt Mahagonny* depicts the collusion between law and capital in even more lurid terms. Paul Ackermann is sentenced to death for debt by his own creditors, a *reductio ad absurdum* of the idea

---

[6] Locke, *Two Treatises of Civil Government*, Bk. II, Ch. 1 (Everyman edn., p. 118).
[7] Plato, *Laws*, vi, para. 757.

of justification by property, and a cryptic scene-heading reminds the audience that the lawcourts of Mahagonny are no worse than those elsewhere. After such comic distortion it is no surprise for the reader to learn that Carbo, the shrewd lawyer in *Die Geschäfte des Herrn Julius Caesar*, is managing director of a big combine.

Personal experience seemed to endorse Brecht's view. In the summer of 1930 he lost his rather quixotic suit against the Nero Film Company for breach of contract over Pabst's projected film version of the *Dreigroschenoper*. Having refused a handsome out-of-court settlement of 25,000 marks, which with some justification he interpreted as hush-money, Brecht made the best of a bad job and documented the case at some length as a 'sociological experiment' (18:139–209). He claimed to have proved that the court exclusively protects the vested interests of capital and that it could not find in his favour because this would contradict its function within capitalist society. Actually the acrimonious essay fails to prove anything very much except Brecht's understandable chagrin, but its significance within his work as a whole is clear enough. The case provided an object-lesson on the conspiracy between capital and law, and thus on the relationship between the economic substructure of bourgeois society and its ideological superstructure.

Again, as in the case against religion, the development of German society after the advent of National Socialism seemed to Brecht a further corroboration of the theory. From the Marxist point of view Article 109 of the Weimar Constitution, guaranteeing 'equality before the law', was meaningless in the context of a capitalist society where exploitation is legitimized, and the servile attitude of the legal profession in the Third Reich merely endorsed a *Gleichschaltung* that was already an accomplished fact. The care with which Hitler cultivated the myth of a legal revolution is an indication of the importance attached to the role of law in Nazi Germany, though it was conceived in terms of the most cynical legal positivism. The emergency powers assumed by the Chancellor under Article 48 and their consolidation by the Enabling Act in March 1933 were the legal foundation of Hitler's dictatorship. The legal profession itself put up little resistance to the gross perversion of justice that followed. Already in April 1933 a Civil Service

Act had purged it of anti-Nazi elements and after the appointment of a fanatical Party man, Hans Frank, as Commissioner of Justice, the reduction of the law to a tool of the New Order was all but complete. Judges were required to belong to the League of National Socialist German Jurists. The regular Reichsgericht, though retaining a measure of independence of which a few liberally minded lawyers made good use, was subordinated to a Sondergericht, which tried political offences, and to the notorious Volksgerichtshof. There was no jury and no right of appeal, and on the rare occasions when they failed to reach a verdict acceptable to the Party, as in the case of Martin Niemöller, the S.S. stood by as a state within the state with its own coercive machinery. It was thus completely logical for Göring to claim on 12 July 1934 that 'the law and the will of the Führer are one', and in fact the very next day Hitler appointed himself 'oberster Gerichtsherr' of the German nation. In 1936 Hans Frank spelled out the legal significance of this to a convention of lawyers, who were warned: 'There is in Germany today only one authority, and that is the authority of the Führer.'[8] When another susceptible Chancellor claimed to embody the law, he was using a mere figure of speech, but it was a political reality of Hitler's regime, which was consequently, as one historian puts it, legal but not legitimate.[9] Nazi Germany ignored Augustine's maxim that an unjust law is no law at all, and the inevitable result, as exemplified by the pernicious Nuremberg Laws of 1935, was the complete divorce of legality and justice.

Brecht's most direct treatment of the Nazi attitude to law is in *Furcht und Elend des Dritten Reiches*, the longest scene of which, significantly entitled 'Rechtsfindung', exposes the spinelessness of the legal profession, whose motto is quoted in the introductory jingle: 'Recht ist, was dem deutschen Volke nützt.' Only slightly less direct is the parodistic reconstruction of the Reichstag fire trial in *Arturo Ui*. Brecht's court is in fact a much more submissive tool of the new regime than its historical counterpart. There is no evidence that in reality star witnesses were beaten up as they are in Brecht's account, and certainly

---

[8] W. L. Shirer, *The Rise and Fall of the Third Reich*, Pan Books edn., 1964, p. 343.

[9] Friedrich, op. cit., p. 202.

the Dutch half-wit, van der Lubbe, was not drugged like Fish into a helpless stupor by the Nazis under the judge's very nose. Brecht's satire reflects the grosser abuses of the law after the constitution of the Volksgerichtshof and Sondergericht, and perhaps this explains why Brecht omits any reference to the courageous performance of Georgi Dimitrov, the Bulgarian Communist whose acquittal infuriated the Nazi Party. The deeper implications of the parody are revealed by Ui himself who indicates that the proper function of the law under a dictatorship is to legitimize the crimes of the regime:

> Hab ich den Richter nicht in meiner Tasche
> Indem er was von mir in seiner hat
> Bin ich ganz rechtlos. Jeder kleine Schutzmann
> Schießt mich, brech ich in eine Bank, halt tot.*
>
> (4:1741)

More obliquely, but perhaps more effectively, the relationship between the vested interests of the regime and its legal machinery is dramatized in *Die Rundköpfe und die Spitzköpfe*. Iberin's provisional dictatorship is given the same semblance of legality as Hitler's in order to win popular support. At a point when the offensive against the Red Sickle is going badly the Inspector declares that the people's 'natural sense of justice' has replaced the pedantic codification of the law. The principle of equality before the law is abandoned in the interests of racial ideology, but only to camouflage economic inequality, in which the regime, as the executive committee of the ruling class, has a vested interest. Accordingly, when Callas's demand for a remission of arrears on his extortionate rent finds popular approval, Iberin, knocking over a chair in his haste, personally replaces the judge and deftly converts the charge to one of racial degradation. When the case is retried the courtroom is noticeably more plush, and the judge, in a new robe, smokes a fat cigar. Moreover, once the civil war is over, Iberin reasserts the inviolability of property as a sacred Tschuchian principle and demands the restoration of the horses Callas confiscated from his landlord. 'Nicht gegen Eigentum erging mein Urteil,' declares Iberin, 'nur gegen seinen Mißbrauch' (3:992), and he hypocritically reaffirms the principle of equality before the law. Since the legal machinery of Yahoo survives Iberin's dictatorship intact, this work demonstrates more clearly than any other the Marxist view that a Fascist regime's jurisdiction differs in degree but not in kind from that of a liberal democracy. In both instances social injustice is given the full sanction of the law.

This theme had in fact already been elaborated in the didactic play *Die Ausnahme und die Regel* (1930). The basic class division of capitalism is represented here by the ruthless merchant, Karl Langmann, and his Chinese coolie. In an attempt to steal a march on his competitors the merchant crosses the desert with reckless haste. Running out of water, he misinterprets the coolie's offer of a drink as an attack and shoots him dead. His trial is intended as a working model of capitalist justice. The judge, whose pompous diction parodies legal jargon, rules that the merchant shot the coolie in self-defence. Although the merchant's brutality towards the coolie is established, it is seen as an extenuating circumstance, since it explains why the merchant expected the coolie to take advantage of him. Moreover, the coolie's death has cost the merchant his contract. The defendant is acquitted, and even his victim's widow is not granted compensation. Whether such a verdict would ever be reached by a properly constituted court in a capitalist democracy is beside the point. The parable seeks to demonstrate in grotesquely exaggerated form that the law is an instrument of class domination.

At first sight Brecht's satire invites comparison with plays such as Galsworthy's *The Silver Box*, the moral of which appears to be the same, namely that there is one law for the rich and another for the poor. In Galsworthy's play a poor man, taking advantage of a drunken prodigal, steals a silver snuffbox and is subsequently sentenced to imprisonment in a dramatic trial-scene. The young rake, who in his cups has also stolen a handbag, gets off scot-free because he has the right contacts. 'It's 'is *money* what got '*im* off', shouts the accused and his last word is '*Justice!*' Like Brecht, Galsworthy demands reform. But it could be achieved by ensuring that the law as it stands is put into effect without partiality, whereas in Brecht's parable the best that such limited reform could hope to achieve is that the widow would receive compensation. The basic class antagonism, which is the real cause of the coolie's death, would be left unaffected. When Brecht's players finally turn to the audience and exclaim:

> Und wo ihr den Mißbrauch erkannt habt
> Da schafft Abhilfe!
>
> (2:822)

they are calling for nothing short of a full-scale revolution.

The 'right to revolution', as Engels termed it, emerges in fact as the 'only real "historic right"'[10] of the oppressed proletariat on a Marxist reading of social justice. History is the supreme court by which standards of justice are themselves judged. Marx himself used the image of history as a judge and the proletariat as the instrument by which its sentence is carried out.[11] This explains why Brecht makes 'Papa' in *Die Tage der Commune* reject Langevin's plea that Lecomte should be handed over to the law, with the words 'Wir sind die Justiz' (5:2129), and demands the execution of the Versailles general. The only difference between this kind of summary justice and lynch-law is that in its revolutionary context it is held to represent the will of the people. In this way the conception of law as the general will, introduced by Rousseau and elaborated by Kant, undergoes a new and radical development. The Marxist regards only the will of the proletariat as the legitimate general will, and it follows that the interests of the proletariat alone determine the nature of true law.

Brecht dramatized this notion in his play for radio, *Das Verhör des Lukullus* (1939). In this symbolic tribunal the vested class-interests of the judges in *Mahagonny*, *Die Ausnahme und die Regel*, *Die Rundköpfe und die Spitzköpfe*, and *Arturo Ui* have been reversed. The dead Roman general is judged in the Underworld by a peasant, a slave, a fishwife, a baker, and a courtesan. His exploits, which include the conquest of fifty-three cities and the capture of seven Asiatic kings, are condemned as negative contributions to history, since they only benefited the rich at the expense of the poor on both sides.

Brecht seems to have toyed with the idea of a sequel to *Die Ausnahme und die Regel* in which the whole case is retried by a Soviet court, which, like that of the Underworld in *Lukullus*, would be founded solely on the historic right of the

---

[10] Dietz, vol. 22, p. 524.   [11] Ibid., vol. 12, p. 4.

proletariat as a revolutionary class.[12] It is probably as well that the sequel remained unwritten, but the same basic idea forms the framework of Brecht's most controversial play, *Die Maßnahme*. It is Brecht's only attempt to dramatize legal proceedings outside the jurisdiction of a class society in the world of historical reality. The Soviet tribunal which judges the four agents is not portrayed as an institution working according to strictly codified rules—in which respect the Soviet legal system still in no way differs from that of any other country—but rather as a sympathetic council. It endorses the agitators' liquidation of a colleague as a tactical expedient. It has been pointed out often enough that the necessity of the measure adopted is far from proven, that the case is hardly a representative one, and that neither the Party nor its legal representatives function in this way. The contrast with Stalin's show-trials springs readily to mind. But such criticism misses Brecht's point, that all actions must ultimately be judged in the light of world revolution, which is the only historically sanctioned right.

There remains the question as to what will happen to the law when the Revolution is finally accomplished. Engels at least had no doubts on this score. Like religion, it will wither away, together with the rest of the apparatus of state. An idealistic Soviet jurist, Yevgeny Pashukanis, was still confidently predicting this after the October Revolution, and if he was silenced by Stalin it was only because the doctrine of socialism-in-one-country was held to justify the retention of the coercive legal apparatus. Theoretically, the notion of the redundancy of law under full Communism is still orthodox Marxist doctrine. As Confucius, another of Brecht's favourite philosophers, cannily put it: 'The main thing is to see to it that there are no lawsuits',[13] and if there are no lawcourts in Utopia it will be because there are no cases to try. According to the *ABC of Communism* lawcourts will simply become 'organs for the expression of public opinion' and assume 'a purely moral significance'.[14] It may be recalled that Swift's Houyhnhnms had no word for law in their language and were horrified by Gulliver's account of English legal practice, since in their view

[12] Brecht-Archiv, 323/2.
[13] *The Wisdom of Confucius*, ed. Lin Yutang, New York, 1938, p. 198.
[14] p. 277.

'reason alone is sufficient to govern a rational creature'.[15] This idealized notion of civilized behaviour in a truly human community recurs in one of Lenin's most inspiring passages. In *State and Revolution*, written on the very eve of the Revolution itself, he prophesied: 'People will gradually become accustomed to the observance of elementary rules of living together . . . to their observance without force, without compulsion, without subordination, without that special apparatus for compulsion which is called the state.'[16]

Only once did Brecht attempt to deal with this aspect of the Marxist apocalypse, but he did so in a work that combines consummate craftsmanship and popular appeal to such a degree that it accentuates the utopian bias of his work as a whole.

Der kaukasische Kreidekreis was inspired by two versions of a legend whose dominant theme is justice. Klabund's free adaptation of Li Hsing-dao's thirteenth-century *Chalk Circle*, produced with spectacular success by Max Reinhardt in Berlin in 1925, ends with the edifying couplet:

> Gerechtigkeit, sie sei dein höchstes Ziel
> Denn also lehrt's des Kreidekreises Spiel.*

In the play the case of the disputed child is tried twice. A corrupt judge is bribed by the false mother into awarding her custody of the child, which secures her claim on the property of her mandarin husband. The case is retried by the new Emperor, whom the heroine, ex-prostitute Haitang, has known and loved as Prince Pao. He finds in favour of the real mother, Haitang, ostensibly because the test of the circle proves her motherhood, but actually because he already knows the truth, since he is the child's father himself! Here legality and justice are assumed to be identical, and only the corruption of the judiciary gives rise to injustice. The fairy-tale ending is a symbolic celebration of the pre-established harmony of the world, which the wickedness of men has only temporarily disrupted. Basically similar is the biblical version (1 Kgs. 3:16-28) in which Solomon likewise determines the real mother by applying an equally spectacular test. Like Li Hsing-dao's Emperor, Solomon is both ideal ruler and ideal judge, and thus

---

[15] *Gulliver's Travels*, pt. IV, Ch. 7.   [16] *Collected Works*, 25, p. 462.

the full coercive power of the state can be invoked to safeguard justice. In this case divine sanction guarantees the absolute identity of natural and positive law, and since the latter is likewise administered by an incorruptible judge, there is no miscarriage of justice.

Brecht's ingenious adaptation of the legend draws on both versions, but the theme of justice is completely transformed. Brecht retains the two litigants, the disputed child, and the decisive test of the chalk circle. From Klabund Brecht further borrowed the idea of a corrupt judge and the inheritance which the false claimant stands to gain from the suit. The most striking departure from either of the versions is that Brecht's corrupt judge awards the child to the false mother, and thereby paradoxically upholds justice by abusing the law.

Legality and justice, far from coinciding, do not even overlap in the medieval Georgia (Grusinia) of Brecht's drama. The Marxist notion of law as the handmaid of exploitation is everywhere in evidence. No sooner has he come to power than Prince Kazbeki seeks to appoint his nephew in place of the unfortunate Illo Orbeliani, hanged by the rebellious carpet-weavers during the recent putsch. 'Wir brauchen Frieden', he says, 'Und Gerechtigkeit' (5:2073–4), which is transparently a demand that the law guarantee the immunity of his regime. Again, when Natella Abaschwili brings her action against Grusche, the two sycophantic lawyers receive a handsome fee for their eloquence, and the less intelligent of the two lets out the secret by revealing that they will forfeit it if Natella loses her inheritance. Thus, when Azdak shamelessly receives bribes in court, saying 'Ich nehme', as though this were a traditional forensic formula, Brecht is not satirizing corruption. Although Azdak, the most brazen of Brecht's many opportunists, lines his own pocket while the going is good, his characteristic gesture also exposes the interdependence of property and law. Azdak feigns annoyance when Grusche fails to offer a bribe: 'Ganz richtig. Von euch Hungerleidern krieg ich nichts, da könnt ich verhungern. Ihr wollt eine Gerechtigkeit, aber wollt ihr zahlen? Wenn ihr zum Fleischer geht, wißt ihr, daß ihr zahlen müßt, aber zum Richter geht ihr wie zum Leichenschmaus'* (5:2099). The juxtaposition of meat and justice speaks for itself.

Azdak's inspired buffoonery when the soldiers put him through his paces prior to his appointment does much more than prove that the law is an ass. It is also an ingeniously disguised form of social criticism. In his assumed role as the Grand Duke he submits that it was only Georgia that lost the war, not its profiteers, who in fact made a fortune out of munitions and supplies. The charge of misconduct of the war is thus unfounded and a court of law would have to reject it. The fact that no such case is ever brought before the real courts of Georgia in itself implies that the sole function of legal institutions in pre-revolutionary society is to protect its ruling class.

The six cases which Azdak judges himself on stage reveal not only his unique combination of self-interest, sympathy for the underdog, wit, and cunning, but also the fact that only an outrageous abuse of the law can fulfil the demands of justice. In the four hilarious cases that precede Grusche's, Azdak, as a revolutionary *manqué*, brings in verdicts which could never be upheld by a conscientious magistrate and which are nevertheless felt by the audience to be just. A doctor, who has treated a poor patient free of charge, is acquitted, despite his professional incompetence, and his former benefactor, whose health has been undermined by this unwarranted generosity, is fined for bringing the action in the first place. A blackmailer is convicted, but half his fee finds its way into Azdak's pocket because the victim wishes to remain anonymous. A landlord's action against his stable-boy on a charge of raping his daughter-in-law is dismissed after Azdak has seen how she sways her hips, and she is convicted of assault with a dangerous weapon! Lastly, a poor widow is acquitted of the charge of receiving stolen goods and her rich accusers are fined for impiety. By Azdak's logic it is a miracle if the poor receive help, so there is good reason to accept the widow's naïve supposition that it was Saint Banditus and not the notorious brigand Irakli who was her benefactor. Since all these cases are wildly improbable, to say the least, it is irrelevant to ask how a conventional court would have dealt with them. The main point is that Azdak relies on his own horse-sense to dispense rough justice, and not on the codified statutes of the law, on which he symbolically sits throughout every session. Consequently, Azdak's verdicts are just, but illegal. As the Chorus puts it, he breaks the law like bread to feed the poor (2086).

The climax of Azdak's brief career is the case of Natella Abaschwili, wife of the assassinated governor of Nukha, versus Grusche Vachnadze, the kitchen-maid who rescued Natella's child during the putsch and brought it up as her own son.

Brecht has often been criticized for the clumsy structure of this play with its two quite different and largely independent plots, for which their fictitious author, Arkadi Tscheidse, even apologizes in the prologue: 'Es sind eigentlich zwei Geschichten' (2007). But the rigid compartmentalization of the two simultaneous actions is a necessary and effective dramatic device. Brecht's aim is to convince the audience of the legitimacy of Grusche's claim in the last scene by demonstrating the heroism, dogged determination and self-sacrifice that made her the 'real' mother of the abandoned child. In this way the audience is predisposed to accept Azdak's verdict. Solomon's judgement in the biblical story is felt as just, not so much because his ruse reveals the natural mother, but because 'her bowels yearned upon her son'. In Brecht's version the natural mother was busy salvaging her dresses when danger threatened and it was Grusche who succumbed to the terrible temptation to goodness. Natella reclaims Michel, not, as her glib barrister maintains, because blood is thicker than water, but because he is the guarantor of her property rights. Azdak, 'the good, bad judge' whose position is already threatened by the restitution of the *ancien régime*, performs his last paradoxical act of illegal justice. The test of the circle gives Grusche the right to keep the child, and the 'accidental' divorce of Grusche and Jussup completes Azdak's contemptuous travesty of the law.

The fairy-tale atmosphere of the piece has disturbed many audiences but is entirely functional. Improbable coincidences engineer the conventional happy ending. Grusche's case is tried by the only magistrate in all Georgia who could conceivably find in her favour, and it is his last case. He was all but lynched by the troops and owes his unexpected reprieve to the fact that in a fit of momentary compassion he had saved the life of the Grand Duke, who turns up again at the end in the nick of time. In other words, justice was the merest fluke.

As in Brecht's Mongolia (*Die Ausnahme und die Regel*), so also in his Georgia the exception proves the rule.

This seemingly pessimistic implication has misled some interpreters into seeing the whole play as an inverted expression of the inescapable brutality of human existence, in which happiness and humanity, justice and love, are dependent on the quirks of fortune. One English commentator, for instance, insists that the *Kreidekreis* 'is not sustained by a faith in the possibility of transforming the world through the revolution of the proletariat'.[17] Such a reading entirely ignores the prologue, which is an integral part of the play.

Nowhere is the epic dimension of Brecht's theatre of more significance than in the *Kreidekreis* and its prologue. The story we watch unfold is not that of Grusche and Azdak, but that of Arkadi Tscheidse and his amateur troupe, who re-enact the legend. Beneath the masks and exaggerated make-up of the peasants and soldiers, princes and officials of ancient Grusinia, are their descendants, the Georgian kolkhozniks of the prologue, who, having just expelled the Nazi usurpers from their native soil, stage this historical pageant to reinforce their claim on the disputed valley.

It has frequently been maintained that the moral spoken by the ballad-singer at the end has no connection with the rest of the play, and that the prologue, which the West German press denounced as 'bolshevistic wrapping',[18] is therefore entirely irrelevant. Producers, embarrassed by the low key in which the prologue is written, have not infrequently made this the excuse to omit it in performance, thereby distorting the meaning of the play as a whole and leaving the final lines almost meaningless:

> Ihr aber, ihr Zuhörer der Geschichte vom Kreidekreis
> Nehmt zur Kenntnis die Meinung der Alten:
> Daß da gehören soll, was da ist, denen, die für es gut sind, also
> Die Kinder den Mütterlichen, damit sie gedeihen
> Die Wagen den guten Fahrern, damit gut gefahren wird
> Und das Tal den Bewässerern, damit es Frucht bringt.*
>
> (5:2105)

The chief objection seems to be that the child is lumped

---

[17] W. A. J. Steer, 'The thematic unity of Brecht's *Der kaukasische Kreidekreis*" *German Life & Letters*, 21, 1967–8, p. 10.

[18] *Materialien zu 'Der kaukasische Kreidekreis'*, ed. Hecht, Frankfurt, 1966, p. 144.

together with tractors and valleys and thus robbed of its individual humanity, whereas in fact it is Natella who treats the child as a means to an end and Grusche who loves it for its own sake. In this way Grusche is genuinely more 'useful' to the child, but it is a bad misreading of the play to conclude that Brecht reduces mother love to a kind of fertilizer.

Such a fallacy is really the child of another, namely that the legend of Azdak and Grusche is an endeavour to 'articulate, explore and thus resolve a case of social conflict', as George Steiner writes.[19] One of the most comical misconstructions is that of the Soviet critic Ilya Fradkin, who objected that in Soviet Russia agricultural disputes are not settled by ballad-singers, but by the appropriate government office, in this case the *sel'khozartel*.[20] In point of fact the dispute over the valley has already been settled to the satisfaction of all parties, not by the ballad-singer, and still less by the agricultural expert, who merely chairs the debate. The issue is decided by the collective farm-workers themselves in a spirited, but friendly and rational discussion.

The goat-breeders had been driven out of their valley by the German invader and returned to find their fellow partisans, members of a fruit-growing collective, not only in possession of the valley but with elaborate plans for the construction of a reservoir to render the whole area more productive. The under-standable resentment of the original inhabitants gives way to persuasive reasoning. When one of the dairymen, significantly an older man, produces a piece of cheese made elsewhere and indignantly demands their opinion of it, he is amazed to discover that it meets with unanimous approval. In an earlier version of the scene the cheese was produced in the original valley and proved the quality of the pasture. The change in the text indicates Brecht's purpose more clearly. Good cheese can be produced elsewhere, whereas a good reservoir can only be constructed here owing to the lie of the land. The dairymen cede their land, and the story of Azdak and Grusche is not so much an argument as a ritual celebration of the triumph of reason over chaos.

---

[19] George Steiner, *Language and Silence*, 1967, p. 191.
[20] I. Fradkin, 'Bertolt Brecht: khudozhnik mysli', *Teatr*, Moscow, 1956, no. 1, p. 153.

Brecht was so convinced of the necessity of the prologue, which he claimed was the starting point of his dramatization and not a pious afterthought, that he renumbered the scenes, and 'Der Streit um das Tal' is now Scene 1 of the published text. The real link between the play and its framework is not the theme of utility but that of justice. Whereas in medieval Grusinia justice was dependent on chance and chicanery in open defiance of the law, in modern Georgia it is the natural result of living together in a society where reason and good will are its permanent guarantee. A vestige of atavistic legalism, based on an anachronistic conception of property, still clings to the arguments of the dairymen, one of whom says: 'Nach dem Gesetz gehört uns das Tal.' But this is a throw-back and is readily countered by his opposite number who replies: 'Die Gesetze müssen in jedem Fall überprüft werden, ob sie noch stimmen' (2003). Grusche no longer needs Azdak. In the world of the prologue, as the Polish critic Szydłowski puts it, 'the temptation to goodness is victorious under conditions of socialism'.[21] History has transcended Azdak's legendary golden age, 'almost of justice' as the ballad-singer ironically dubs it. Justice is not now the exception but the rule.

Ilya Fradkin, now more generous than he dared to be twenty years before, rightly calls Brecht's prologue 'the apotheosis of socialist humanism'.[22] But it is clear from his argument that his enthusiasm for it has less to do with Brecht's apocalyptic conception of justice than with the Socialist Realist style he adopted for it on the one hand, and its apparent tribute to Soviet society on the other. This raises the question as to whether Brecht really believed that his prologue offered an authentic picture of contemporary Soviet life. It is after all well known how Stalin settled agricultural disputes, which on his own reckoning cost some ten million recalcitrant peasants their lives. There is only hearsay to support the view that Brecht was highly critical of developments in the Soviet Union under Stalin, and there is the ring of truth about the apocryphal story according to which he refused to join Ulbricht and Becher in exile there because he could not get any sugar for his coffee. Brecht's honest opinion will probably never be known, but it seems very

[21] *Dramaturgia Bertolta Brechta*, p. 267.
[22] Fradkin, *Bertolt Brecht: Put i metod*, p. 184.

unlikely that he identified his Georgia with any political reality. It is ultimately as symbolic as his Mahagonny and Chicago, Kilkoa and Szechwan. Whereas these stood for any pre-revolutionary society, the Georgia of his *Kreidekreis* prologue is a symbol of that infant Utopia that lies beyond revolution and has even superseded the dictatorship of the proletariat. The distant future goal prophesied by the poem 'An die Nachgeborenen' is vividly envisaged as a political reality of the present.

Although Brecht was no more given to crystal-gazing than Marx, the *Kreidekreis* and its prologue give the clearest image of the Utopia in which he believed. Its citizens are, in Cicero's famous phrase, 'born for justice' and their motto is identical with that of the Justinian Code: *honeste vivere, neminem laedere, suum cuique tribuere*, only there is now no need for law to enforce it. Hegel recounts the story of a Pythagorean philosopher who, asked by a father how he might best educate his son, replied: 'By making him the citizen of a state with good laws.'[23] Ostensibly this is the function of laws in socialist countries today and Meyer's *Neues Lexikon*, tactfully omitting any reference to their withering away, defines them as 'precepts of socialist morality'. Brecht's utopians have transcended this stage. They have already become accustomed to the elementary rules of living together, of which Lenin speaks, and therefore no longer need laws.

[23] Hegel, *Philosophie des Rechts*, para. 153 (*Werke*, Berlin, 1832, ff., vol. 8, p. 214).

4. Political Ideology: Fascism

Introduction

THE history of Germany after 1928 is responsible for the fact that Brecht's analysis of the dominant role played by political ideology within the superstructure of society is almost exclusively restricted to the German variant of Fascism.

Brecht's basic attitude towards National Socialism was predictable. He had been No. 5 on its secret blacklist since before the Munich Putsch, apparently for his vilification of the German soldier in his 'Legende vom toten Soldaten'. He went into exile the day after the Reichstag fire and did not return for fifteen years to a country which, despite his avowed internationalism, was the only place in the world where he ever really felt at home.

Only rarely does Brecht's work during this unhappy period betray feelings of despair. He never lost faith in his Utopia, since for him the triumph of Fascism was only a temporary retardation of history's progress towards its ultimate objective. Nevertheless, the reign of terror, which Hitler boasted would last a thousand years, constituted a very serious set-back and Brecht devoted himself energetically to the campaign against it. From 1933 onwards he published prolifically in London, Paris, Prague, Copenhagen, Amsterdam, and Moscow, wherever a German-speaking readership could still be reached, and nearly everything he wrote during that period can be classified under the rubric *in tyrannos*.

The intellectual component of Brecht's anti-Fascist attitude is clear. The veneer of socialism on the Nazi programme, though taken seriously by the Strasser brothers, Röhm, and even Goebbels in the early days, was never intended as more than an electioneering stunt by Hitler, who despised all forms

of socialism. Marxism especially he regarded as a Jewish conspiracy and in any case it contradicted what he called the
'aristocratic principle of nature',[1] the right of the strong to
rule the weak. By the same reasoning, democracy was arrant
nonsense to Hitler, who followed Mussolini in regarding the
masses as a gullible mob, incapable of independent political
judgement.

Fascism was, moreover, a fundamentally irrational philosophy and its leaders made no secret of their contempt for
reason. Mussolini's Fascisti had marched under the slogan
credere, ubbidire, combattere, and National Socialism in its turn
demanded blind obedience to the will of the Führer, not
reasoned commitment. The frantic efforts of its ideologues to
deduce Aryan supremacy from the anatomy of the foot, or to
prove that Jesus was not a Jew, were only a pseudo-intellectual
smoke-screen. Alfred Rosenberg was ironically right in calling
it the Myth of the Twentieth Century, impervious to reason
and unassailable because it would 'create facts'.[2]

Galilei speaks for Brecht when he tells Sagredo: 'Ich glaube
an den Menschen, und das heißt, ich glaube an seine Vernunft'
(3:1256). Brecht saw in Fascism the very antipathy of the cool,
rational 'Haltung des Rauchend-Beobachtens' (17:992) his
Epic Theatre sought to stimulate, and he claimed later that it
was Fascism's 'grotesque emphasis on the emotional' (15:242)
that led him to overstress somewhat the rational element in his
own form of theatre. Perhaps it is only a coincidence that
Hitler adored and Brecht loathed the music of Wagner, but
certainly Brecht equated it with all he most bitterly opposed
in the traditional theatre and which he saw translated into
the politics of National Socialism: the massive assault on the
emotions and the inducement of a kind of hypnotic trance in the
audience. Indeed, the elaborately staged mass meetings of the
Nazi Party with their noisy rhetoric induced exactly that
hypnotic empathy against which Brecht inveighed so often in
his theoretical writings on theatre. One eyewitness speaks of
the 'atmosphere of religious frenzy and devotion'[3] when Hitler
delivered his impassioned speeches, and another said of them:

---

[1] *Mein Kampf*, Munich, 1936, p. 69.
[2] A. Rosenberg, *Der Mythus des 20. Jahrhunderts*, Munich, 1930, p. 700.
[3] F. L. Carsten, *The Rise of Fascism*, 1967, p. 231.

'never do they make the listener reflect or exert his critical faculty'.[4] Brecht analyses this political stagecraft in one of the *Messingkauf* dialogues, entitled 'Über die Theatralik des Faschismus' (16:558 ff.). Brecht's spokesman, Karl, describes the lighting, the background music, the singing, and the surprise effects that were all part of the Nazis' stock-in-trade, and recalls how Hitler took lessons in posture and elocution from a professional Munich actor, a motif that later found its way into *Arturo Ui*.

Finally, the Nazis' institutionalization of violence, a dominant trait in Fascist thinking since Georges Sorel, and their glorification of war, were anathema to the pacifist in Brecht. Mussolini had declared: 'War brings up to their highest tension all human energies and puts the stamp of nobility on the peoples who have the courage to meet it.'[5] Such a statement was nonsensical cant to the poet who had written 'Legende vom toten Soldaten' at the beginning of his career and at the end of it was even to fall foul of Ulbricht's censors because the unqualified pacifism of *Die Verurteilung des Lukullus* failed to allow for the holy war against capitalism. True, Brecht had written fashionable jingoistic verse himself at school, and the familiar anecdote of his allegedly traumatic experience as a medical orderly loses some of its force when we learn that he worked in a V.D. ward, but the pacifist, even at times quietist, streak in his writing is quite unmistakable nevertheless. This is not to deny that Brecht enjoyed conflict. Doubtless he found dialectical materialism so congenial not least because it interpreted reality in terms of conflict. But this conflict was not an end in itself. It was directed towards the ultimate liberation of men's energies for the task of domesticating their environment.

On all counts Fascism as a political ideology conflicted with Brecht's deepest convictions about the nature of man and society. His personal anti-Nazi campaign, however, was severely handicapped by his unquestioning acceptance of the orthodox Marxist interpretation of Fascism. At the risk of splitting the anti-Nazi opposition at a time when unity of purpose was of the essence, Brecht unreservedly presented Fascism as a virulent mutation of capitalism.

[4] Ernst Nolte, *Three Faces of Fascism*, trans. L. Vennewitz, 1965, p. 292.
[5] Quoted from the article on Fascism in the *Encyclopaedia Britannica*.

In his speech to the Seventh Congress of the International in 1935, Georgi Dimitrov, who himself only narrowly escaped the Nazis' anti-Communist witch-hunt, defined Fascism as 'the most vicious offensive of capital against the working masses'. The 1961 Manifesto of the Communist Party of the U.S.S.R. still interprets it in the same light as an 'open terroristic dictatorship of the most reactionary, most chauvinistic and most imperialist elements of finance capital' and insists that its sole aim was 'to divert the proletariat and its allies from the class struggle'.[6] This tallies exactly with Brecht's own definition in his essay 'Fünf Schwierigkeiten beim Schreiben der Wahrheit': 'Fascism is a historical phase which capitalism has entered, and thus it constitutes something new and at the same time something old. Capitalism exists in Fascist countries only in the form of Fascism, and *Fascism can only be fought as capitalism, in its most naked, brazen, oppressive and treacherous form*' (18:226–7). He goes on to say that the only appreciable difference is that under non-Fascist forms of capitalism the butchers wash their hands before bringing in the meat. Thus for Brecht the Hitler era was not a separate historical phenomenon. Fascism was merely an extension of the historical class struggle to which all Brecht's writing had been devoted since 1926. Brecht's Hitler is of the same lineage as Mackie Messer and Pierpont Mauler.

The ensuing sections focus on those of Brecht's plays which specifically attempt to analyse the origins and effects of German Fascism and at the same time predict its inevitable collapse.

Die Rundköpfe und die Spitzköpfe

Die Rundköpfe und die Spitzköpfe began as a free adaptation of Shakespeare's *Measure for Measure*, which Brecht was to have produced for Ludwig Berger at the Berliner Volksbühne in November 1931.

It is not immediately obvious why Brecht should have been attracted to Shakespeare's melodrama, which is dominated by the sort of psychological conflict that did not interest Brecht in the slightest. In *Measure for Measure* the main characters are a pious novice, who can only save her brother at the expense of her chastity, and a tyrannical Puritan, who succumbs to the

[6] Quoted from A. P. Mendel, *Essential Works of Marxism*, 1965, pp. 412–13.

very temptation for which he has condemned another man to death. And the moral of this most moral of Shakespeare's plays is that justice must be tempered with mercy, since even rulers are only human. There does not seem much for the ardent anti-Fascist campaigner in that.

Brecht regarded *Measure for Measure* as Shakespeare's most progressive play, however. The real point of Shakespeare's ingenious reworking of George Whetstone's arid sermon is that public and private morality are inextricably interwoven, and if *Coriolanus* is the most political of Shakespeare's tragedies, *Measure for Measure* is his most politically orientated comedy. The ineffectual Duke of Vienna abdicates temporarily in favour of his 'outward-sainted deputy', Angelo, whom power corrupts. Brecht saw more than most when he summed up the political gist of the play with the words: 'It demands of those in high places that they apply to others the same measure by which they themselves would be measured.'[7] He had only to replace psychological with socio-economic factors for Shakespeare's romance to illustrate the Marxist theory of economic determinism. The final collapse of the Weimar Republic gave Brecht new ideas and he rewrote his adaptation several times. In exile he revised it yet again and the finished product is many removes from Shakespeare.

The theme of justice links Shakespeare's comedy with Brecht's final adaptation, and many of the original characters are still recognizable, but their motivation is drastically altered. Emanuele (the new Claudio) is no longer simply afraid of death, but eager to preserve his estates from impending revolution, and the chaste Isabella yields to the ultimatum because she will otherwise be pauperized by her brother's death; Nanna takes her place because Isabella can afford to buy her indemnity. Similarly, whereas Shakespeare's over-indulgent Duke abdicates temporarily because gross sexual licence has undermined Vienna's morale, Brecht's Vice-Regent reluctantly hands over to a detested fanatic because of a severe economic crisis. If he has no more difficulty than his model in resuming office once his deputy's brutal interregnum has put the Establishment back on its feet, this is because he has the backing of

---

[7] Brecht-Archiv, 268/81.

five powerful landowners, whose wealth is the real power behind the political façade.

On this parable Brecht superimposed allegorical features in order to accommodate contemporary political developments in Germany. President Hindenburg's vested interests in the Junker estates gave the Vice-Regent his new profile; Missena, though his name recalls the Secretary of State, Otto von Meissner, represents Franz von Papen, on whose advice Hitler was invited to form a cabinet; above all, Hitler contributed to the characterization of Iberin his middle-class origins, his racial ideology, and his bogus appeal for moral idealism. Of Yahoo's political institutions the Huas (Hutabschlägerstaffel) represent Hitler's private army of thugs, the Sickle corresponds to the German Communist Party, and the Roundheads (Tschuchen) and Peakheads (Tschichen) to the Aryans and Jews; even the conflict with Russia is adumbrated by the forecast of a campaign against the Squareheads in search of new markets. Although Shakespeare's Austria is transferred to a vaguely Latin-American Yahoo (originally Peru), the events are set against a recognizably modern background so that the repercussions of the Wall Street crisis in Germany can be more effectively suggested. Yahoo's problems are essentially those of an expanding agrarian economy with its roots in a still predominantly feudal society, but the parallels with Weimar Germany are close enough to be effective.

The most striking allegorization is the transformation of Shakespeare's fallen angel into a caricature of Hitler. Here an important distinction must be made between the Angelo Iberin of the final draft and the Tomaso Angelas of the earlier version, published in the *Versuche* under the title *Die Spitzköpfe und die Rundköpfe*. The role of Angelas is appreciably longer than that of his Shakespearian counterpart, which indicates the degree of importance Brecht was then prepared to concede to Germany's evil genius. Angelas is a fanatical ideologue, inspired by a vision of a morally superior nation, untainted by the present spirit of materialism which he attributes to the subversive influence of the Peakheads. If Isabella is right in surmising that a 'due sincerity' governed Angelo's deeds before he met her, then Shakespeare's 'man of stricture and firm abstinence'—one notes the convenient resemblance to Hitler—is not so far removed from Brecht's Angelas. Indeed, so sincere is Angelas's perverted idealism that when he faces Isabella with the familiar ultimatum, he is only putting her to the test. He seems genuinely horrified to discover that it is a Roundhead who is prepared to sell herself and that her father puts the material problem of the rent before his daughter's honour. Angelas seems to be expressing an honest conviction when he says: 'Das wirtschaftliche Denken ist der Tod jedes völkischen Idealismus'.[8] With his warped form of puritanism he even outdoes his Shakespearian model, and at the end there is an aura of almost tragic grandeur about him as he witnesses a return to moral anarchy, shattering his dream of empire in a nobler world of racial purity. In a scene remarkably prophetic of Hitler's petulant outbursts in the last days of the war, the crazed visionary feels betrayed and deserted: 'Ich bin in eine Falle gelockt! Man hat mich hier verschoben! Was ich wollt, war anderes.'[9] The Big Five, whose unwitting puppet he has been all along, mock his adolescent idealism and unworldliness, leaving him no choice but to back down when the Vice-Regent returns. Ordered to abandon his racial propaganda once it has outlived its usefulness, he replies meekly: 'Jawohl, mein Fürst!'

Although Iberin also capitulates he cuts a very different figure. Brecht had in the meantime revised his assessment of Hitler's political role and now had second thoughts about presenting him as a tragically deluded fanatic, manipulated by others. In the revision he reduced the role of the dictator to less than half the number of lines and we are left with a much more willing tool of the *ancien régime*. Iberin still occasionally seems to be taken in by his own cant, but we are left in little doubt that he knows his place. It is the initial failure of the government to suppress the peasants' revolt that compels him to adopt diversionary tactics. Brecht introduced the epic device of newsflashes into the trial-scene and Iberin keeps a wary eye on them before formulating his racial theory. If Callas, as a representative smallholder, can be made to swallow the racial myth, then Emanuele de Guzman will stand in the dock not as an exploiting landowner, but as a racial enemy. The restitution of Callas's honour will cost the state nothing, whereas the remission of extortionate rents would lead to revolution. At the re-trial,

[8] *Versuche* 17, Heft 8, Frankfurt, 1959, p. 315.　　　[9] Ibid., p. 363.

when the internally divided Sickle has been defeated, there is no longer any need to exploit racial prejudice. Callas is severely reprimanded and the horses he had seized are returned to de Guzman's estate. What really divides the inhabitants of Yahoo is once again social status, not the shape of the head.

Three fallacies vitiate the interpretation of Fascism offered in this interesting play. Firstly, the implication that Hitler was a mere tool in the hands of industrial tycoons. No historian would deny the role of industry and capital in Hitler's dramatic rise to power. Hjalmar Schacht told the Nuremberg jury how in January 1933 he had personally collected 3 million marks at a meeting of leading industrialists, amongst them Krupp, Thyssen, Schnitzler, Vögler, and Bosch, to finance Hitler's election campaign. They had been panicked by fear of a Bolshevik revolution into backing a right-wing dictatorship, like very many of the seventeen million voters who endorsed it two months later. But once it became a political reality, those who had paid the piper no longer called the tune. There is nothing to suggest that Hitler was either their dupe or their compliant executive, and many, like Thyssen, lived to regret the pact they had made with the devil.

The second fallacy is the supposition that Hitler's dictatorship was only an emergency measure to save monopoly capitalism from the consequences of its inner contradiction, and that as soon as the threat from the Left had been averted, Hitler would meekly step down to make way for the old firm. In the event it was not the democratic-republican forces of Germany that ousted Hitler from the Chancellery, but the combined armies of a dozen countries after six years of total war. There was no political machinery left by which the dictator could have been removed internally, and even the ill-fated bomb-plotters discovered few chinks in his armour. Until recently Marxists have persistently ignored Engels's teaching about the 'relative autonomy' of the superstructure, which makes far more sense of Hitler's dictatorship than the dogma of economic determinism.

This criticism applies also to the third, and worst, fallacy on which Brecht's play is based. Brecht uncritically accepted the orthodox Marxist view that what the *ABC of Communism* calls 'vestiges of intertribal enmity' are deliberately inflamed by capitalism as a diversionary ruse: 'The bourgeoisies of all countries, especially of late, join in the cry, "Down with the Jews!" The aim of this is to switch off the class struggle of the workers against their capitalist oppressors, into a struggle between nationalities.'[10] These words were written by Preobrazhensky during the October Revolution, many years before the history of Soviet–Jewish relations showed that racism is a phenomenon that cuts across the ideological frontiers. Brecht had less excuse. He ignored the vital psychological factors behind Fascism, which in almost every country where it flourished evolved a pernicious form of racial prejudice. Western psychologists have persuasively interpreted this as a by-product of the 'authoritarian syndrome', writ large in the form of a nationalized inferiority complex. The origins of Hitler's own rabid anti-Semitism are still obscure, though multiracial Vienna was a notorious breeding-ground for it. But whatever sparked it off, it already reached a grand climax of vindictive illogicality in *Mein Kampf*, which was written in 1924 and sold a million copies in Hitler's first year of office. Its enthusiastic reception shows that it met a genuine psychological need for a scapegoat that can be blamed for both personal and national shortcomings.

There are, it is true, passages in *Mein Kampf* that seem to support Brecht's argument. Hitler wrote, for instance, that it is part of the art of leadership to be able to 'focus the attention of a whole nation against a single enemy'.[11] What makes history so much more complex than the Marxist will have it, is that Hitler, like Brecht's Angelas, was the victim of his own propaganda. A master of what George Orwell calls 'double-think', he was quite capable of identifying both Marxism and capitalism with the international 'Jewish conspiracy'. Nothing less than full conviction fires the virulent rhetoric of *Mein Kampf*, and the same is true of most Nazi writing from the pseudo-philosophical ranting of H. S. Chamberlain and Alfred Rosenberg down to the pathological obscenity of Julius Streicher's *Stürmer*. These demagogues really believed that race was 'the key problem of world history', as the *Völkischer Beobachter* maintained in a pre-war leader.[12] The fact that the sheer intensity of

[10] *The ABC of Communism*, p. 245.   [11] *Mein Kampf*, p. 129.
[12] *Der völkische Beobachter*, 9 Aug. 1935.

their faith converted millions was an essential part of the German tragedy, but any attempt to pass it off as an electioneering stunt leaves far too much unexplained.

But Brecht went even further. In the final scene of the play rich members of both races celebrate the restoration of law and order, hence the punning sub-title: 'Reich und reich gesellt sich gern'. The defeated revolutionaries, regardless of the shape of their heads, share a common gallows in an orgy of retribution. Ironically, the later version, written at a time when the truth about the concentration camps was beginning to leak out, contains a hint of the final solution. One of Iberin's men parrots an official slogan: 'Ausrottung der Spitzköpfe, wo immer sie nisten!' (3:929). The difference between Iberin and Hitler in this respect is that the latter meant exactly what he said. How Brecht managed to square his interpretation retrospectively with the evidence of Auschwitz, whose gas chambers and incinerators made no distinction between rich and poor, and, worse still, how in defiance of the facts he could continue to believe that rich Jews themselves condoned the Nazi policy of genocide, remains an enigma.

It is of course easy to be wise after the event, and Brecht's political short-sightedness was largely the result of premature judgement. But when we find that he was prepared to rewrite such a trifle as *Der Flug der Lindberghs* twenty years after its première in order to correct the historical perspective, but that he was unprepared to retract or even qualify the serious misinterpretation of Fascism in this play, he can fairly be accused either of political immaturity or of excessive 'Parteitreue'. Despite its literary merits no work of Brecht's demonstrates his limitations as a political thinker more clearly than *Die Rundköpfe und die Spitzköpfe*.

Der aufhaltsame Aufstieg des Arturo Ui

Brecht's 'historical gangster show' was written in Finland in 1941 with one eye on the commercial prospects in America. This partly explains why the resistible rise of Adolf Hitler is mounted, in the style of a Heartfield photomontage, on an imaginary framework of the Al Capone era in Chicago. The assassination of Ernst Röhm is allegorically depicted in terms of

Al Capone's liquidation of some of his lieutenants in 1929, and the Dollfuss incident incorporates details of the murder of O'Bannion, whose funeral Capone attended in person.

Brecht's choice of metaphor was inspired by the surfeit of gangster films he had seen on his first visit to America in 1935, and he knew it was a risk. Cinema-goers are prone to idolize the criminal, provided his crime is on a grand scale and committed with skill and daring. Yet it was precisely Hitler's reputation as a sublime criminal that Brecht sought to demythologize. As he points out in his notes on the play, the perpetrators of great political crimes are by no means the same thing as great political criminals, and he wrote *Arturo Ui* to undermine 'the customary and dangerous respect for great killers' (17:1179). This explains why Brecht draws no direct parallel between Hitler and the notorious Al Capone himself, compared with whom Arturo Ui is a third-rate hoodlum, hoisted to power by sheer good luck. In the third scene Ragg taunts Ui with the rumour that Givola has been to Capone in search of a job, and this is intended to give the audience the real measure of a down-at-heel rowdy whose talent does not match his ambition. As with Caesar and Iberin, Brecht again seeks to persuade us that the dictator's greatness is an optical illusion created by his backers, who themselves shun the limelight in their own interests.

Literary parody adds a third dimension which serves the same purpose. Hitler's celebrated oratory is less awe-inspiring when we see Ui acquire it from an out-of-work actor by learning Mark Antony's funeral speech. Ui's Faustian courtship of Betty Dullfeet, his brazen seduction of her over her husband's coffin in the manner of Richard III, and the incongruous classical blank verse (which links this play with *Die heilige Johanna*), all expose Hitler–Ui as an attitudinizing sham. This double montage gives Brecht's chronicle all the piquancy of a well-drawn political cartoon.

Beneath the slapstick the remaining figures of the allegory are immediately identifiable. Hermann Göring, the vain, coarse, and ambitious Reichsmarschall, is represented by Emanuele Giri, who after each murder flagrantly sports his victim's hat; Joseph Goebbels, Hitler's propaganda genius, whose Mephistophelean limp was a gift for cartoonists, reappears as a rather subdued Giuseppe Givola; Ernesto Roma is Ernst Röhm, the homosexual vulgarian and chief executive of Hitler's early strong-arm tactics, though Brecht ignores his sexual aberrations as an irrelevance; Gregor Strasser, chief representative of the spurious Nazi Left, is perhaps less easily recognizable in the minor figure of Tedd Ragg. Mayor Dogsborough is easily decoded as Hindenburg, tottering symbol of the Weimar Constitution, and Clark, the Trust's enterprising errand-boy, as the opportunistic Papen. The cast-list is completed by Hindenburg's son Oskar and the half-witted Dutch arsonist Marinus van der Lubbe, in the respective guises of young Dogsborough, who parrots everything his father says, and the gibbering Fish, who has to suffer the consequences for the burning of Hook's warehouse.

Martin Esslin has found the allegory laboured,[13] and Ronald Gray thinks it flippant,[14] but Brecht's prologue insists it was 'strictly realistic' (4:1723). Brecht was not simply debunking the Great Dictator through ridicule, like Charlie Chaplin, but seeking to expose the historical forces that brought him to power. In order to achieve this he had to preserve the main historical parallels at the risk of straining the gangster-metaphor beyond the point of credibility. Esslin's objection that Brecht knew nothing about Chicago recalls the old complaint about Shakespeare giving Bohemia a coastline. Brecht's real scene is Germany and even in exile he knew plenty about that.

The main contours of the Nazi era are anticipated by the fairground-barker in the prologue. The side-show extravaganza presents a potted history of Germany from the 'Osthilfe' scandal to the annexation of Austria, punctuated by fifteen news-flashes projected on a special screen between the scenes.

The decay of the Weimar Republic in the twenties is telescoped into the first five scenes, which satirize Hindenburg's involvement in the 'Osthilfe' scandal. It seems unfortunate that Brecht devotes over a third of the play to what was historically a very minor incident. It is true that the senile President accepted from the Junker lobby a generous donation of land at Neudeck in East Prussia, which enabled him to see Schleicher's 'agrarian Bolshevism' in a less favourable light. It is also true that the Nazis later added 4,000 tax-free acres to it for

---

[13] Esslin, *Brecht: A Choice of Evils*, p. 269.   [14] Gray, *Brecht*, p. 94.

Chronological Table

<table>
<tr><td>Historical Events</td><td>Arturo Ui</td></tr>
<tr><td>

1929 The Wall Street crash has serious repercussions in Germany.

1930 Brüning appointed Chancellor. He invokes Article 48 of the Constitution and overrules the Reichstag.
Over 4,000,000 unemployed.

1931 Hitler forms the Harzburg Front with Hugenberg's Nationalists.
Over 5,000,000 unemployed.

1932 Hindenburg re-elected President. Hitler polls over 13,000,000 votes.
6,000,000 unemployed.
First Papen, then Schleicher succeed the moderate Brüning.

1933 Papen intercedes with Hindenburg for Hitler, who is then appointed Chancellor (30 Jan.).
Reichstag fire (27 Feb.).
Suspension of Constitution.
Nazis receive 44 per cent of votes in Reichstag elections (5 Mar.).
Enabling Law (23 Mar.).
German re-occupation of the Rhineland.

1934 Murder of Ernst Röhm and other S.A. leaders (30 June).
Death of Hindenburg (2 Aug.).
Hitler appoints himself 'Führer und Reichskanzler'.

1935 Murder of Austrian Chancellor, Dollfuss, by Nazis (25 July).

1938 Hitler interviews Schuschnigg at the Berghof (12 Feb.).
Anschluss (13 Mar.).

1939 Invasion of Czechoslovakia (15 Mar.).
Non-aggression pact with U.S.S.R. (23 Aug.).
Invasion of Poland (1 Sept.).
Declaration of war on Germany by Britain and France (3 Sept.).

</td><td>

1. The Trust panics. Desperate measures are needed to solve the economic crisis.
2. Dogsborough is persuaded to buy a shipyard from the Trust at a give-away price.
3. Arturo Ui is down on his luck, but news of Dogsborough's purchase gives him ideas.
4. Dogsborough regrets the deal and rejects Ui's offer of 'protection' but is alarmed by the rumour of an official inquiry.
5. Ui defends Dogsborough at the inquiry. A star witness is murdered.

6. Ui takes elocution lessons from an out-of-work actor.
7. Ui's offer of protection, reinforced by the burning of a warehouse, is accepted by the greengrocers of Chicago.

8. The warehouse fire trial. A key witness is beaten up. Fish is sentenced and Ui's gang acquitted.

9. Dogsborough writes his penitent testament, in which Ui is condemned.
10. Givola doctors the testament. Gang rivalry breaks out. Roma is accused of irresponsible terrorism. Ui plans the take-over of Cicero.
11. Roma is shot in a garage by Givola on Ui's instructions.
12. In Cicero Ui declares his honourable intentions towards Dullfeet and his wife Betty.
13. At Dullfeet's funeral Ui courts his widow's favour.
14. Roma's ghost prophesies Ui's downfall.
15. Under armed escort Ui addresses the greengrocers of Cicero: 'Tomorrow the world!'

</td></tr>
</table>

services rendered. Brecht overrates this as a pivotal event, typifying Hitler's handling of a glorified protection-racket. But it serves to stress the important role of opportunism in Hitler's career. On hearing from Bowl how Dogsborough had accepted the Trust's transparent bribe, a hitherto lethargic Ui exclaims 'Now I smell business!' Hitler's virtuoso manipulation of the complex political situation, his sense of timing, and his uncannily reliable amateur psychology still baffle his biographers.

Research has largely substantiated the popular rumour on which Brecht draws for his depiction of the Reichstag fire, namely that the Nazis themselves were responsible for it. The left-wing scapegoat, the concealed petrol drums, even the convenient contiguity of Göring's palace are all featured in Brecht's allegory. The aftermath is equally authentic. The public is intimidated into accepting an armed dictatorship as the price of an illusory restoration of law and order. On the very day Brecht left for Prague Hitler's emergency decree, ironically entitled 'For the Protection of the People and the State', suspended indefinitely the constitutional rights of all citizens. Less than a month later the Enabling Act set the official seal on Hitler's dictatorship.

The vexed question of Hindenburg's testament is also effectively incorporated into Brecht's parable. Dogsborough's posthumous denunciation of Ui represents the presumed gist of the elusive document Papen later claimed to have drafted. It probably recommended a return to constitutional monarchy, whereas the doctored version Hitler issued to the press endorsed his fusion of the offices of President and Chancellor. This fraud removed the last constitutional brake on Hitler's dictatorship, just as it gives Ui a free hand to 'protect' the cauliflower-dealers.

The most ingenious piece of compressed allegorization is the breathless sequence of scenes that takes the plot from the murder of Roma to the deal with Cicero. Historically there was no immediate link between the liquidation of Röhm's private army and the annexation of Austria. Röhm envisaged a second revolution which would install his S.A. as the armed élite of the Third Reich. Brecht retains the motif of discontent, even reproducing the authentic accusation that Hitler was betraying the Nazi Left. It was not, however, as Brecht's parable implies, commerce and industry that Hitler in the first instance sought to appease in murdering his old comrade-in-arms. It was rather the Reichswehr, whose tacit assent to Hitler's dictatorship, one of the many important factors that Brecht ignores, was jeopardized by Röhm's uncontrollable rabble. Moreover, both Hitler and the S.S. were genuinely alarmed by the growing independence of the S.A. Nor does Brecht include Papen's ill-timed but courageous anti-Nazi speech in Marburg (17 June 1934), which probably more than anything else induced Hitler to move against Röhm before he lost his own grip on the revolution. This omission again has the distorting effect of making the tycoons bear the sole responsibility for Röhm's murder, which historically must be seen as part of Hitler's personal strategy in a complex struggle for power involving the army, the trade unions, the popular vote, and the middle-class demand for a stable but respectable regime, as well as the always uncertain backing of industry.

The link with the *Anschluss*, though inauthentic, is a more justifiable foreshortening. The murder of Dullfeet follows hard on the assassination of Roma, and indeed only a few weeks separated the purge from the brutal killing of the Austrian Chancellor by Nazi extremists. It did not suit Brecht's purpose to expose Dollfuss in turn as a dictator whose clerical-Fascist regime had much the same pedigree as Hitler's, since in the play he has to represent well-founded liberal suspicion. Still, although the annexation of Austria followed four years later than Brecht's dramatization indicates, the link epitomizes Hitler's political strategy. When asked by Roma how he proposes to extend his operations to Cicero, Ui replies:

> Mit Drohn und Betteln, Werben und Beschimpfen.
> Mit sanfter Gewalt und stählerner Umarmung*
>
> (4:1799)

which aptly describes Hitler's combination of brute force with the tactics of legality.

The role of the temporizing Schuschnigg is pre-empted by Dullfeet's wife Betty. Perhaps Brecht knew that he had attended the Chancellor's funeral. At all events Schuschnigg later recorded in his memoirs: 'As I stood at the grave of my predecessor, I knew that in order to save Austrian independence I had to embark on a course of appeasement.'[15] He did not save it. In the tragicomic meeting with Hitler at the Berghof Schuschnigg's attempt at appeasement sealed Austria's doom. This is precisely the role given to Betty Dullfeet, who, despite her moral indignation in the previous scene, meekly acquiesces in Ui's take-over as dissenters are gunned down off-stage. The open brutality of this scene ironizes Cicero's 'free choice', which represents symbolically the suspiciously unanimous result of the April plebiscite, according to which 99·75 per cent of the Austrian people were in favour of annexation.

Brecht rightly rejects Göring's insistence that the *Anschluss* was 'just a family affair'.[16] Ui more aptly calls it a dress rehearsal. The annexation of what the Nazis called the Ostmark was the fulfilment of Georg von Schönerer's Pan-German dream, which had inspired Hitler in Vienna a quarter of a century earlier. It signalled the end of the multiracial Habsburg Empire and all that the young Hitler had detested. But it was only the beginning. The seizure of Austria made Germany strong enough to call the bluff of England and France, crush Czechoslovakia and Poland, and from there move on to the unlimited *Lebensraum* of Eastern Europe. It is perhaps as well that Brecht abandoned the idea of a sequel to chronicle Hitler's anabasis in Spain, Poland, and France, for it could scarcely have added anything new to an already overburdened script, the message of which is clear enough: 'Gott schütz uns vor dem Schützer!' (4:1826).

Brecht was himself aware that he had left much unsaid and in his defence he pleaded that he had to keep the play down to manageable proportions. But the real reason for its inadequacy as a definitive explanation of the rise of Nazism is twofold. Firstly, the gangster-metaphor leaves no scope, as Brecht himself noted with regret, for the role of the proletariat, six million of whom were unemployed when Hitler came to power. The erroneous impression that results is that only the middle classes were implicated in the crisis: the industrialists by championing Hitler in the first place, and the spineless tradesmen and salariat by letting them. Nor does Brecht's parable attempt to reflect the skill with which Hitler learned to 'play like a virtuoso

[15] Shirer, *The Rise and Fall of the Third Reich*, p. 365.
[16] Ibid., p. 424.

on the well-tempered piano of middle-class hearts',[17] as Schacht put it. Resentment of the Versailles settlement and fear of Bolshevism had together enabled Hitler to unleash 'a dynamic force of incalculable proportions which had long been pent up in the German people'.[18] This was of course linked with the racial issue, which this time Brecht completely ignores.

The main reason for these omissions was not lack of space. As in *Die Rundköpfe und die Spitzköpfe*, Brecht again presents the monocausal Marxist interpretation of Fascism, and for this his allegory was plausible enough. The original Berliner Ensemble programme-cover reproduces one of John Heartfield's satirical photomontages: it depicts an anonymous bourgeois figure slipping a bundle of banknotes into Hitler's open hand from behind as he gives the Nazi salute on the speaker's rostrum. The cover design was well chosen, for it emphasizes the 'Grundgestus' of the play. The very first words are 'Verdammte Zeiten!', spoken by a representative of the shadowy but omnipotent cauliflower monopoly, which dictates every event from the bribing of Dogsborough to the capture of the Ciceronian market. It leaves Ui the illusion of power, but even the gullible Roma sees through it:

> So stammt der Plan, nach Cicero vorzustoßen
> Gar nicht von dir? 's ist nur ein Plan des Trusts?
> Arturo, jetzt versteh ich alles. Alles!
> 's ist klar, was da gespielt wird.*
>
> (4:1800)

The objections to this interpretation have been made in the previous section. Admittedly, this time we catch a fleeting glimpse of the penitent Clark, regretting like the sorcerer's apprentice that he cannot control the spirits he has invoked, but if Brecht really intended to qualify the Marxist over-simplification, this is hardly enough.

Finally, there is the question of Hitler's personality. All his biographers have been impressed by the rags-to-riches story of an Austrian malcontent who won and lost an empire in ten years. Hitler was moody, by turns lethargic and manically energetic, self-confident to the point of monomania, contemptuous of others, and untrusting, resentful, and vindictive, and

---

[17] Quoted from Alan Bullock, *Hitler: A Study in Tyranny*, 1959, p. 61.
[18] Ibid., p. 287.

according to his whim a charmer or a boor. Brecht's 'einfacher Sohn der Bronx' is all of these things, and Brecht even throws in Hitler's teetotalism and characteristic hands-before-genitals posture for good measure. But it is still not a convincing likeness. The fact remains that this neurotic misfit cajoled, bribed, swindled and manœuvred his way into the greatest concentration of power any single ruler has ever wielded. A grudging respect for Hitler's achievement characterizes nearly all the biographers, but Brecht will have none of it.

Nevertheless, Brecht devised a role that *malgré lui* has audiences spellbound. Sensing the danger, one reviewer, writing during the renaissance of interest in *Ui* in America, asked, 'How can we love a clown who murders in cold blood; who calculates, as he somersaults, the deaths of millions?'[19] But if we cannot love this clown we stand agog at his nerve and his expertise. He alone is able to take the chances the Trust offers him and weld his unruly gang into a formidable instrument of terror. Even allowing for the fact that Brecht has shorn this turbulent epoch of many of the factors that shaped it, there remains the enigma of the Führer himself. Actors almost invariably rise to the bait. Ekkehard Schall's brilliant impersonation at the Berliner Ensemble, which had the audience on the edge of its seat, has been criticized for suggesting the superman.[20] Yet it is all there in the role Brecht created, precisely because its lay figure was the Great Dictator himself, whose warped genius cannot be shrugged off with a few music-hall gags. Tadeusz Lomnicki tried a different tack in the Warsaw production of 1962. He started physically and vocally quite unrecognizable as the historical Hitler, and then gradually took on the familiar cartoon characteristics as Ui begins to realize his potential. By the time he delivered his 'Tomorrow the world' speech he was Hitler personified. A Polish reviewer wrote of his astonishing performance: 'If, at the start, Hitler lurked unseen in the petty gangster Arturo Ui, by the end of the play it is the puerile Ui who lurks in the monstrous Hitler.'[21] Paradoxically, this underscored Ui's achievement and aroused the very admiration and terror Brecht sought to inhibit.

It is difficult for a producer to convince the audience that

---

[19] P. McCoy, in *Drama at Calgary*, iii, no. 2, 1969, p. 17.
[20] Keith Hack, ibid., p. 47.   [21] E. Wysińska, ibid., p. 52.

behind the scenes the Trust still calls the odds. The obnoxious petty-bourgeois rabble-rouser dominates the stage in his own right, and in this he comes uncomfortably and unintentionally close to the historical truth. Fradkin predictably insists that the moral of the piece, which is performed in Russia under the title *The Career of Arturo Ui, who need never have been*, is that Fascism 'cannot with the aid of brute force and terror save a historically doomed system'.[22] But the only textual support for this is the implausible vaticination of Roma's ghost. The role of Hitler–Ui tells another story altogether, and Brecht's satire misfires. It is by no means clear from this ingenious but ambiguous play how history guarantees that such periodic retardations of its progress are only temporary, nor how they can be avoided.

Furcht und Elend des Dritten Reiches

Whereas *Die Rundköpfe und die Spitzköpfe* and *Arturo Ui* analyse the nature and origin of Fascism, Brecht's vivid mosaic *Furcht und Elend des Dritten Reiches*, written 1935–8, depicts the private life of the master race, as Eric Bentley aptly entitled his authorized translation. For this cycle of one-acters, based on eye-witness accounts, Brecht abandoned his familiar epic style and adopted a more realistic idiom. His aim was to counter the myth of the twentieth century with a documentary of actual conditions.

Few will agree with Fradkin, who ranks it among Brecht's finest works[23] (largely, one suspects, because its 'Aristotelian' style approximates to that of Socialist Realism), but the best of its twenty-four scenes surpass any other literary attempt to document the period. Yet Brecht shows no more interest here than elsewhere in individual psychology. Setting his scene in nineteen different parts of the Reich during the first five years of its existence, Brecht manipulates his eighty-nine speaking parts like snapshots in an illustrated guide to the reality behind Goebbels's glossy propaganda.

The proletariat and peasantry are allotted a surprisingly small role in the series. The myth of the classless society united by the national effort is debunked in *Arbeitsdienst. Die Stunde des*

---

[22] Fradkin, *Bertolt Brecht*, p. 223.　　　[23] Ibid., p. 168.

Arbeiters, in which a carefully rigged propaganda broadcast is almost ruined by factory workers speaking out of turn, deflates the streamlined image of a happy and prosperous working community. The contention, still often voiced in West Germany, that Hitler solved the unemployment problem, is countered in *Arbeitsbeschaffung*. Hjalmar Schacht and Karl Schmitt had in fact created artificial full employment by developing a *Wehrwirtschaft* geared to the economic needs of total war. In Brecht's scene it begins to dawn on the workers that they are digging their own graves, an effect further enhanced by the appearance between the scenes of an armoured tank, the occupants of which, like the soldiers in *Eduard II*, have chalk-white faces. The peasantry figures briefly in *Der Bauer füttert die Sau*, in which the virtual serfdom established by Walter Darré's radical reorganization of agriculture is ridiculed: the farmer has to let his pig starve in accordance with the Ministry's ruinous directive.

The petty bourgeoisie is represented by the tradesmen. *Zwei Bäcker* shows two victims of bureaucratic red tape, imprisoned for infringing arbitrary and contradictory regulations, in a manner anticipating the fate of Eilif in *Mutter Courage*. In *Der alte Kämpfer* a butcher, who has refused to display imitation meat supplied by the authorities, hangs himself in his own shop-window because his son, though a member of the S.A., has been arrested on a charge of black marketeering. Customers discover his body, to which is attached a placard bearing the caption 'Ich habe Hitler gewählt' (3:1169).

The professional classes are brought into sharper relief and more severely criticized as hangers-on of a regime in which they do not even believe. The impasse of the legal profession is the subject of *Rechtsfindung*, in which a typical magistrate attempts to accommodate the new conception of law. His wife naïvely supposes he can administer it simply by establishing the facts, but for him the matter is much trickier. If he finds in favour of an enemy of the regime (in this case a Jew hounded by the S.A.) he will lose his job, but two mutually antagonistic factions, both with Party connections, have irons in the fire. Whatever verdict he reaches, he will fall foul of the regime his jurisdiction serves.

The capitulation of science, which Wilhelm Roepke called 'a scene of prostitution that has stained the honourable history of

German learning',[24] is the subject of several sketches. The ignominious record of physicists such as Ludwig Bieberback, who denounced Einstein as an 'alien mountebank', provides the material for the scene *Physiker*, in which two research scientists furtively discuss the Theory of Relativity. The even more shameful betrayal of the Hippocratic oath by such outstanding physicians as Ferdinand Sauerbruch, who made no protest against the sadistic outrages of Karl Gebhardt and his accomplices, is pilloried in *Die Berufskrankheit*: a house surgeon hastily abandons his progressive theory of environmental diagnostics when faced with a battered concentration-camp victim. The pusillanimous doctor in *Die jüdische Frau*, who sacrifices his marriage to a non-Aryan to further his career, is another of the many whose failure to protest was a tacit endorsement of the regime. The same criticism is levelled at the German Churches in *Die Bergpredigt*.

The teaching profession, members of which were obliged to take an oath of personal loyalty to Hitler in 1937, comes under fire in *Der Spitzel*, in which a schoolmaster declares his readiness to teach the regime's reinterpretation of history if only someone will tell him in time what the currently orthodox version is.

Brecht's treatment of Jewish persecution is predictably less effective, despite the fact that he devotes to it the theatrically most effective scene: *Die jüdische Frau*. In a series of telephone calls which have the intensity of a Strindberg monodrama, Judith Keith covers up her traces as she prepares for voluntary exile. When she finally rehearses her speech of farewell to an inadequate husband we get closer to her as a person than to any other character in the cycle. Yet, powerful though the scene is, it gets no nearer the truth about anti-Semitism than *Die Rundköpfe und die Spitzköpfe*, since Judith Keith's case in no way differs from that of any other victim of the regime. Similarly, the racial aspect of the victimization case in *Rechtsfindung* is strictly subordinated to the theme of the magistrate's professional dilemma, and all parties act out of self-interest, not out of prejudice.

Many of the repressive effects of *Gleichschaltung* in Hitler's Germany are reflected in one or more scenes: the conformity of the censored press under Otto Dietrich, Bernhard Rust's

[24] Shirer, p. 313.

stultifying educational system, Baldur von Schirach's canalization of youthful idealism in the Hitlerjugend, and, casting its
sinister shadow across every section of German life, the elaborate
machinery of terror: the S.A., S.S., Gestapo, and concentration
camps. Though the original Heinesque title, *Deutschland: ein
Greuelmärchen*, indicated that this last aspect would be given
ample coverage, Brecht's treatment of it is characteristically
subdued. As Fradkin points out in his analysis of *Das Kreide-
kreuz*,[25] the brutality and low cunning of the storm-trooper are
products of brainwashing. Beneath this transparent defence
mechanism he is just an ordinary sort of man, with a clumsy
sense of humour, slow-witted, but polite to the cook. He pro-
fesses belief in the Nazi myth, but he acknowledges ruefully
that he has been duped into buying a new pair of jackboots out
of his own pocket. Again, the concentration-camp guard who
flogs a prisoner is no sadist. He has a job to do and he is out for
promotion. At no point does Brecht indulge the cultural
pessimism of Thomas Mann, who diagnosed Nazism as an
endemic German disease. Brecht had already endeavoured to
show that the ideology of the Third Reich was rooted in a
particular social system, not in the German soul. In *Furcht und
Elend* he demonstrates that the Germans themselves were its
first victims.

Fear is the dominant motif of the cycle. In a contemporary
poem a tourist, asked who rules Nazi Germany, replies simply:
'Die Furcht' (9:703). Fear saps the morale and disrupts normal
human relations. The camp inmates fear the brutality of the
guards, the boys in the Hitlerjugend the lascivious advances of
its organizers, the tradesmen the petty bureaucracy. Man and
wife fear that neighbours will denounce them for listening in to
foreign radio stations, or that the Blockwart has it in for them
because their New Year's gratuity was too paltry, or that even
their own child will betray them to the Gestapo for criticizing
the regime. Anti-Nazi workers fear that their ex-comrade will
betray them out of fear of retribution. The physicists fear they
will be caught discussing proscribed research, and the doctors,
lawyers and schoolteachers that they will lose their job unless
they keep on the right side of the Party.

Not only the oppressed but also their oppressors live in

[25] Fradkin, pp. 164–5.

constant fear. The S.S. men in the first sketch shoot an innocent bystander because they are afraid there will be recriminations once the victims of Nazi propaganda return to their senses. The camp guard is afraid of his commanding officer, the storm-trooper of losing face with his mates. Beneath the surface pessimism of the realistic reportage there is the optimistic belief that fear is corroding the system that generates it. A state that rules by terror is doomed from within because the man-in-the-street, who is simultaneously its dupe and its executive, cannot be permanently induced by terror into supporting it.

Furcht und Elend exposes the Nazis' brave new world as a moribund dystopia. The optimism is accentuated in such scenes as *Moorsoldaten,* in which a heterogeneous assortment of anti-Nazis, ranging from a Communist to a religious crank, find unity in suffering. It is characteristically two women, however, who articulate Brecht's optimism most effectively. In *Arbeitsbeschaffung* a woman, reproved by her husband for publicly denouncing the regime on the grounds that it will not help, exclaims: 'Then do something that will!', and in *Volksbefragung* another woman prescribes a monosyllabic reply to the Nazi plebiscite: 'NEIN!' It is the last word of the published text. Such an emphatic rejection of Nazism by the Germans themselves was still in 1938 a faint hope. *Furcht und Elend des Dritten Reiches* was an attempt, however unrealistic it may now seem in retrospect, to justify it.

Die Gesichte der Simone Machard and Schweyk im Zweiten Weltkrieg

Die Gesichte der Simone Machard and *Schweyk im Zweiten Weltkrieg* are in a sense a continuation of *Furcht und Elend* in that they extend the analysis of everyday life during the Third Reich to the newly conquered territories.

Die Gesichte der Simone Machard, begun in 1941, and originally entitled *Jeanne d'Arc 1940,* now seems a rather clumsy attempt to counter the despair of the early war years. Simone is a rather simple-minded adolescent who sabotages the petrol dump that her crafty employer has been hoarding so that he can make a bargain with the advancing Germans. She is arrested and committed to a mental hospital, but her example has already inspired refugees to burn down a gymnasium intended to billet the invaders. Resistance to Nazism is proclaimed as a crusade, but the moral lacks conviction, if only because it conflicts with the deepest instincts of an author whose most typical characters are fundamentally unheroic.

Schweyk im Zweiten Weltkrieg, on the other hand, is vintage Brecht. It advocates a very different kind of heroism, and features one of Brecht's most memorable characters. It was written in the spring of 1943 when the tide of war had already turned. On 21 January the shattered remnants of Friedrich von Paulus's beleaguered Sixth Army had surrendered to the Russians at Stalingrad and this resounding defeat signalled the beginning of the end. Although the Stalingrad disaster is only adumbrated in the last two scenes of Brecht's play it accentuates the ground bass of tempered optimism.

Brecht modelled his archetypal anti-hero on Jaroslav Hašek's comic veteran of the First World War, whose picaresque exploits had already been staged in Piscator's Berlin production of 1928, on which Brecht himself had collaborated. The kinship is unmistakable: the same indomitable little man with the inexhaustible supply of ambiguous anecdotes, tangling with a baffled bureaucracy; the same bland servility, the same mock-heroic anabasis with a doomed army on the eastern front; and above all the same irrepressible humour, which exposes the world of chauvinistic empire-builders as a pompous masquerade. 'A smiling little man demonstrates the impotence of power', wrote one reviewer of yet another stage version.[26]

When Brecht reread Hašek's novel he found the common people in it 'echt unpositiv', but he indicated that he was not going to make a hero out of Schweyk nevertheless: 'On no account may Schweyk become a crafty, cunning saboteur.'[27] Not for Brecht's Schweyk the heroics of Simone Machard. It was only a year since two Czech partisans had murdered Reinhard Heydrich, the brutal Reichsprotektor of Bohemia and Moravia, an event on which Brecht based his film-script for

---

[26] 'Ein lächelnder kleiner Mann erwies die Ohnmacht der Macht': Wolfgang Drews, *Frankfurter Allgemeine Zeitung*, 4 Jan. 1973.

[27] *Materialien zu 'Schweyk im Zweiten Weltkrieg'*, ed. H. Knust, Frankfurt, 1974, p. 290.

Fritz Lang's *Hangmen Also Die*. But the fate of Lidice, whose entire male population over the age of sixteen was butchered in reprisal, cast doubts on the wisdom of open hostility of this kind. Brecht's poem on the subject, 'Das Lidicelied', advocates readiness and solidarity but says nothing of sabotage and tyrannicide. There remains the subtler method of moral sabotage, wily manœuvring, and corrosive defeatism, which have the same effect as the constantly dripping water on stone in Brecht's poem about Lao-tzv (9:660 ff.).

Communist critics have not infrequently condemned Schweyk as an irresponsible opportunist. Hans Mayer argues that of all the subversive virtues outlined in Brecht's essay, 'Fünf Schwierigkeiten beim Schreiben der Wahrheit', Schweyk reveals only guile, and even resorts to this for his own ends.[28] This is simply not true, and in any case it misses the point. Schweyk is certainly a skilled opportunist, a trait which links him with Kragler, Galy Gay, Galilei, Mutter Courage, Azdak, and Keuner, to say nothing of Brecht himself. It is interesting to note that Brecht planned the role of Schweyk with Peter Lorre in mind, the epic actor who had made his Galy Gay such an intriguingly ambivalent figure in the Berlin days. For both of these anti-heroes survival is the highest good. In Schweyk's own words: 'Verlangens nicht zu viel von sich. Es is schon viel, wenn man überhaupt noch da is heutzutag. Da is man leicht so bescheftigt mit Ieberlebn, daß man zu nix anderm kommt'* (5:1945). But here the resemblance ends. Brecht noted of Schweyk in his diary: 'He is merely the opportunist who exploits the tiny opportunities he has left.'[29] Yet, few though they are, Schweyk makes the most of them, and there is a militancy and unassuming selflessness in his opportunism that are quite alien to his predecessors, as indeed they are to Hašek's prototype.

Schweyk's feigned enthusiasm for the New Order demoralizes all those who have climbed on its bandwagon as well as putting courage into the defeated. In the first bout of ideological shadow-boxing with Brettschneider, the ambitious Gestapo man, Schweyk reacts to the news of an attempted assassination of Hitler by expressing regret that bombs are not all they might

---

[28] Mayer, *Bertolt Brecht und die Tradition*, pp. 79 ff.
[29] *Materialien*, p. 290.

be in these days of mass production. He admits that Hitler's death would have been an irreparable loss to the Third Reich: 'Der Hitler läßt sich nicht durch jeden beliebigen Trottel ersetzen' (5:1926). Decoded, what Schweyk is actually saying is that Hitler is an egregious ass and the failure of the bomb plot an unmitigated disaster. In the course of the play Schweyk insinuates in the presence of the faithful that Hitler's eastern policy is the ruinous product of megalomania, that racial purity leads to idiocy, that sabotage is justified, that the salvation-from-Bolshevism slogan is pure charlatanism, and that the Czech 'volunteers' are helpless conscripts.

Nor is Schweyk's virtuoso performance merely verbal. Like Azdak, he would be the first to admit he is no hero, but he intervenes with a timely diversion when the vicious Bullinger is mishandling Anna Prochazka and he risks his own neck to keep his hungry friend Baloun out of harm's way. He exploits with uncanny skill the characteristic rivalry between the S.S. and the Gestapo, bamboozles a German soldier into sending an armaments truck to Bavaria and a combine harvester to Stalingrad, urges German deserters to placate their Russian captors with a machine-gun or a telescope, and finally he rescues a Russian family from a drunken German padre. None of these exploits would earn him a medal, but if his support of the Third Reich had been typical it would assuredly not have lasted as long as it did.

In the operatic interludes a monstrous Wagnerian Hitler plans Operation Barbarossa with Himmler, Göring, Goebbels, and Fedor von Bock, all larger-than-life, except for Goebbels, who according to the stage-directions is 'überlebensklein'. Hitler is obsessed not only with delusions of grandeur, but also with the question he asks in the prologue: 'Wie ... steht eigentlich der *kleine Mann* zu mir?' (1915). A seemingly casual remark made by Schweyk to Brettschneider is in reality a mock-apologetic reply to Hitler's question: 'Der kleine Mann scheißt sich was auf eine große Zeit, er will ein bißl ins Wirtshaus gehn und Gulasch auf die Nacht'* (1927). Schweyk is simply not the stuff of which great empires are made. How close Brecht came to the truth here is suggested by Hitler's own last dispatches, which hysterically reiterate the belief that he had been defeated only because he could not personally supervise every move and fire every bullet, and that the people were unworthy of his vision. As Ziffel ironically puts it in the *Flüchtlingsgespräche*: 'Alle großen Ideen scheitern an den Leuten' (14:1425). Brecht's Bohemian Eulenspiegel frustrates Hitler's grandiose ambitions not by suicidal acts of defiance like Simone, but by his calculatedly half-hearted support of a campaign that demands just the race of supermen Hitler failed to breed.

In the impressive epilogue Schweyk meets Hitler on the eastern front, and it is Hitler who despairs of the situation, not Schweyk. In the spectacular Berliner Ensemble production, first performed in 1962, a revolving stage effectively suggested the futility of Schweyk's march, and Hitler's terrifying but impotent shadow was projected on the backdrop. This gigantic silhouette lurched crazily from side to side, looking helplessly for a way of escape. Schweyk, only life-sized but three-dimensionally real, goes on marching.

The play ends with a repetition of one of the eleven interspersed songs: 'Das Lied von der Moldau', sung by full cast as they remove their make-up. The final strophe reads:

> Am Grunde der Moldau wandern die Steine
> Es liegen drei Kaiser begraben in Prag.
> Das Große bleibt groß nicht und klein nicht das Kleine.
> Die Nacht hat zwölf Stunden, dann kommt schon der Tag.*

Hanns Eisler's wistful melody demands the repetition of the last phrase: 'Dann kommt schon der Tag', which are the last words of the play and an endorsement of its basic optimism. Brecht's composer himself wrote of the song: 'And what does this song say? That after twelve hours of night, day comes— nothing more—nothing more than the simple laws of nature. Impossible at this time to offer more hope. Small comfort, but the necessary minimum. That is, our life changes just as the days and the seasons alternate—not more, but not less either . . . History has confirmed the truth of this song.'[30] In much the same spirit Ilya Fradkin maintains that Schweyk, a near relative of Brecht's indestructible 'Glücksgott', personifies the vitality and immortality of nature itself.[31] This is not an exaggerated reading. When history resumes its proper course

---

[30] *Materialien*, p. 301.
[31] Fradkin, p. 268.

the unheroic Schweyk will still be there, Brecht's most plausible guarantor of the ultimate victory of day over night.

To believe that the pen is mightier than the sword is what keeps an exiled writer's faith in the future alive, and certainly it is this faith, however illusory, that sustained Brecht's writing after 1933. His campaign was not, however, in his view terminated by the military defeat of Nazi Germany. He believed that the ideology of National Socialism, which Ernst Nolte called 'the most desperate assault ever made upon the human being and the transcendence within him',[32] was a possible mutation of the political superstructure of any pre-revolutionary society.

When Brecht revised the text of *Arturo Ui* for the Suhrkamp edition of his plays in 1953, he added an epilogue, spoken in the Berliner Ensemble production by Ekkehard Schall as he removed his make-up:

> Ihr aber lernet, wie man sieht statt stiert
> Und handelt, statt zu reden noch und noch.
> So was hätt einmal fast die Welt regiert!
> Die Völker wurden seiner Herr, jedoch
> Daß keiner uns zu früh da triumphiert—
> Der Schoß ist fruchtbar noch, aus dem das kroch!*
>
> (4:1835)

There is no doubt that at the time Brecht had the Adenauer regime in mind, which accorded with the Soviet interpretation of Bonn's anti-Communist foreign policy. Brecht failed to see that this was in large measure a tactical exigency of the Cold War, especially since Soviet Russia had openly antagonized the West with the Berlin blockade and with its brutal handling of the East German uprising of 1953. But beneath the bluster and the calculated exaggeration there was enough truth in the accusation to give Brecht's anti-Fascist writing a more permanent relevance.

It is too often argued by modern historians that radical changes in the economic and constitutional conditions that brought Hitler to power in 1933 preclude a resurgence of Fascism in Germany. The collapse of the Nationaldemokratische Partei Deutschlands in the elections of 1966–8 was due

[32] Nolte, op. cit., p. 425.

more to a schism in the leadership than to a change of heart in the electorate. The Neo-Nazis polled over 16 per cent of the votes in a local Bavarian election in November 1966, and in the general election of September 1969, nearly a quarter of a century after the end of the war, they only just failed to secure proportional representation in the Bundestag. The wide circulation of the extreme right-wing press (*Nation, Europa, Deutsche Wochenzeitung*, and *Deutsche Soldatenzeitung*) indicates Fascist sympathies that survived denazification. Nor are they confined to the older generation. In an opinion poll held in the year of Brecht's death a third of the younger generation thought there was much to be said for the Nazi point of view, and—perhaps even more sinister—another third had no opinion at all. True as it is that Fascism thrives on economic crisis, it is equally true that it breeds in the sort of intellectual climate that has persistently inhibited democratic thought in German politics. One recent historian has asserted: 'The survival of prefascist and authoritarian conditions and modes of behaviour is closely connected with the refusal to accept historical evidence.'[33] The value of Brecht's anti-Fascist writing, whether or not we agree with his diagnosis, is that it preserves this historical experience and demands a verdict on it.

Above all, however, if it is true that Fascism is as much a state of mind as a historical phenomenon, then the permanent threat it constitutes is by no means restricted to Germany, nor for that matter to any of the dozen other European countries where it took root in the twenties and thirties. Keith Hack and Michael Blackmore made this the moral of their Glasgow Festival production of *Arturo Ui* in 1967, which was an indictment of American foreign policy in Vietnam and a year later at the Edinburgh Festival provided equally apt comment on Russian intervention in Czechoslovakia. Brecht's parable was more versatile than he could have realized.

It is not necessary to share Robert Brady's Marxist convictions to agree with his pre-war evaluation of what he called the 'spectre on the Brocken'. Denying that he had in any way interpreted it as an exclusively German phenomenon, he wrote: 'Far more vital for the future of all the nations and civilizations of the world is realization that exactly the same

[33] K. D. Bracher, *The German Dictatorship*, trans. J. Steinberg, 1971, p. 499.

forces which hoisted the Nazis to the helm in Germany are at work in all other countries at the present time and that, for better or for worse, there is no possibility of avoiding the issue which those forces present for decision to every man and woman who votes, or thinks, or acts.'[34] 'History teaches', writes Bracher optimistically in his masterly anatomy of the Hitler era.[35] If the history of that era taught Brecht anything with which Marxist and non-Marxist alike can still agree, it is that the founding fathers of Utopia will have to write a foolproof safeguard against Fascism into its constitution.

[34] R. A. Brady, *The Spirit and Structure of German Fascism,* 1937, p. 35.
[35] Op. cit., p. 488.

5. Literature: Harnessing the Classics

Introduction

LITERATURE constitutes for the Marxist an integral part of the ideological superstructure. The question of the role it plays and the problem of transforming it were of particular interest to Brecht. Right from the start he was keenly aware of the influence of literary tradition. His theoretical essays on literature refer to over 250 writers from Homer to Heidegger, and Reinhold Grimm has noted over eighty direct influences on his work.[1] Paolo Chiarini observes that Brecht's imagination was not kindled by spontaneous combustion but on contact with the work of others.[2] From *Baal* to *Coriolan* Brecht's magpie method of composition borders at times on plagiarism. Alfred Kerr sarcastically described Brecht's greatest pre-war success, the *Dreigroschenoper*, as a work of Brecht's written two hundred years earlier by John Gay, and the additional pilfering of some twenty-five lines of K. L. Ammer's translation of Villon helped to make it the *pièce de scandale* of the twenties. Brecht nonchalantly ascribed this to his 'fundamental laxity in matters of intellectual property' (18:100). In a Keuner-anecdote of the same period Brecht's *alter ego* cites the example of the Chinese philosopher Chuang-tzu whose works consisted largely of quotations, and he derides critics who demand originality: 'Größere Gebäude kennen sie nicht als solche, die ein einziger zu bauen imstande ist' (12:380). It was for Brecht not the source of a work that counts, but its effect.

This is the key problem for the Marxist literary critic. What exactly *is* the effect of a work that outlives its own era and is widely acclaimed as a classic? According to Marxist criteria no

[1] R. Grimm, *Bertolt Brecht und die Weltliteratur*, Nuremberg, 1961.
[2] P. Chiarini, *L'Avanguardia e la Poetica del Realismo*, Bari, 1961, p. 5.

poetic artefact can be adequately evaluated in a historical vacuum. It must be systematically referred to the historical process which gave rise to it in the first place. The very word 'classical' suggests timeless values, which a dialectical reading of history entirely rejects. Characteristically, the only works that Brecht unreservedly referred to as classics are those of Marx, Engels, and Lenin, the prophets and executors of change, and his abortive attempt to recast *The Communist Manifesto* in hexameters represents a tribute to their revolutionary brand of classicism. The only eternal truth for Brecht as a Marxist is that all is change and that therefore all truth is relative.

The classics do not lie easy on the Procrustean bed of Marxist interpretation, though Marx himself had rather conservative literary tastes. Georg Lukács, for instance, includes *Aus dem Leben eines Taugenichts* in his survey of nineteenth-century German Realism, on the grounds that Eichendorff's immortal layabout is the projection of a moribund aristocracy's guilty conscience.[3] Taugenichts emerges from Lukács's fascinating analysis as a victim of the Industrial Revolution. He wanders aimlessly about playing his fiddle and chasing the girls because an emergent capitalism leaves him with nothing better to do. The imagination boggles at the idea of a post-revolutionary Taugenichts slaving away on a collective farm somewhere in Silesia, but if the book is judged solely as a historical document, then Lukács's argument is very persuasive. Though Brecht took issue with the Hungarian critic on other scores, his attitude to the classics as historical documents was fundamentally the same.

Brecht's particular problem as an adapter and producer of the classics was how to teach his audiences historical perspective, not by reproducing authentic detail of costume and locale in the manner of the Naturalists, but by disclosing the historical process of which both the play and its audience are part. 'The main thing', he wrote in the *Messingkauf*, 'is to stage these old works historically, and that means presenting them in stark contrast with our own age' (16:593). As early as 1926 he had quoted with approval a remark made by Piscator after his iconoclastic production of Schiller's *Die Räuber*, to the effect that he had deliberately set out to make the audience realize that the passage of 150 years is no small matter (18:112).

[3] G. Lukács, *Deutsche Realisten des 19. Jahrhunderts*, Berne, 1951, pp. 58 ff.

Brecht's adaptations and productions of the classics were based on the same principle. It was not a question of modernizing them. Granville-Barker's realistic production of *As You Like It*, complete with live rabbits, the Zulu *Macbeth* at the Aldwych Theatre in 1972, and student productions of *Henry V* in modern battledress are hardly more than a desperate rearguard action to prevent the classics from degenerating into theatrical cliché. Brecht sometimes wrote as though this were all he was trying to do himself. In 1954, criticizing producers who falsify the classics, he wrote: 'We must bring out the work's original thought-content' (17:1276), and again: 'The old works have their own values, their own nuances, their own scale of truths and beauties. These are what we must try to discover' (17:1260). But the content, truth and beauty Brecht had in mind were the relationship of the work to the dialectical process of history and the pleasure it can still give in making us aware of it.

To achieve this effect Brecht was prepared to resort to drastic adaptation if need be. The metamorphoses of *Measure for Measure* have already been discussed. John Synge's *Riders to the Sea*, though still acknowledged on the title-page, is barely discernible as the model for *Die Gewehre der Frau Carrar*, and its relationship to *Mutter Courage* is still more tenuous. No text is regarded as sacrosanct and unchangeable: 'The words of a poet are only sacred in so far as they are true', wrote Brecht with reference to Sophocles' *Antigone* (17:1218). While working on his adaptation of *Coriolanus*, he was asked whether it was permissible to alter Shakespeare's text and he gave the interesting reply: 'I think we can change Shakespeare if we can change him' (16:879). That is to say, if changes can be made in an allegedly immortal and immutable classic and a coherent text emerges which speaks more relevantly to our condition, then such changes are not only permissible but imperative.

Brecht's instinctive suspicion of the classics, perhaps the result of a stodgy school curriculum in Augsburg, found a philosophical justification in Marxism, like so many of his earlier attitudes and interests, but it affected his approach to production long before his political commitment. Brecht's first full-scale professional production of a classic was to have been Marlowe's *Edward II* for Otto Falckenberg at the Munich Kammerspiele in 1924. When he had embarked on the project

the previous year with Lion Feuchtwanger he had quickly
discovered that even a heavily revamped production would be
out of the question. He rewrote it, he explained, 'because I
wanted to produce Marlowe and he was inadequate' (15:69).

For one thing, he found that the 'oily smoothness' of Marlowe's
blank verse tended to swamp the meaning. 'I needed rhythm,'
he later wrote, 'but not the conventional jingle' (19:396). So
with Feuchtwanger's help he 'roughed it up', and the new
rhythms, though quite as distinct in their way, are much more
syncopated and what Brecht was later to call 'gestisch',[4]
ostensibly in order to bring out underlying contradictions in
the speaker. Marlowe's Isabella, for instance, utters the following lament after Edward has rejected her:

> O miserable and distressed queen!
> Would, when I left sweet France, and was embarked,
> That charming Circe, walking on the waves,
> Had changed my shape! or at the marriage-day
> The cup of Hymen had been full of poison!
> Or with those arms, that twin'd about my neck
> I had been stifled, and not liv'd to see
> The king my lord thus to abandon me!
> Like frantic Juno, will I fill the earth
> With ghastly murmur of my sighs and cries;
> For never doted Jove on Ganymede
> So much as he on cursed Gaveston.

Not only did Brecht shorten this passage by a third, omitting
the classical allusions, he also ensured that no two lines scan
alike:

> O höchst armselige Königin!
> Oh, wären, als ich das holde Frankreich ließ
> Und eingeschifft ward, die Wasser worden Stein!
> Oder jene Arme, die um meinen Nacken waren
> Hätten mich erwürgt in der Nacht der Hochzeit.
> Weh, jetzt muß ich nachjagen dem König Eduard.
> Denn er zog, mich verwitwend, in diese Schlacht
> Von Killingworth für den Teufel Gaveston.
>
> (1:224)

The characters themselves were scaled down, so that
Edward's aristocratic lover Gaveston became a butcher's boy

[4] See below, p. 290 f. and n. 8.

with a chip on his shoulder, and Edward himself, a slave to his perverted sexual appetite, forfeited his tragic-heroic stature. Mortimer, on the other hand, lost his status as an autonomous villain and became a mouthpiece for subdued social criticism. Brecht's adaptation became a creative criticism of the hero-cult. For the actual production in March 1924 Brecht abandoned the flamboyant style of traditional Tudor productions, and his bare, strictly functional stage was in itself a comment on current theatrical taste. In addition, the chronicle style of the original gave him the idea of introducing a historical distancing-effect which anticipates *Mutter Courage* and *Arturo Ui*, using scene-titles with dates. Even minor details of the production served the same fundamentally critical purpose: the strong pacifist element in the adaptation was underscored by giving the soldiers chalk-white faces, apparently at the suggestion of Karl Valentin, who had said to Brecht laconically: 'Weiß sans, Angst hams' (16: 599).

The result of all this was in effect a new play. Marlowe is still audible, but it is as though the speeches of his characters stand in quotation marks, like the Rimbaud passages in *Im Dickicht der Städte*, Brecht's previous play. It is neither an adaptation nor an original work in the usual sense of these words, but rather a practical criticism of its model, the outmoded values it represents, and the traditional attitude towards it as a classic.

Nothing offers such a striking link between the supposedly anarchical world of the angry young Brecht and that of the committed apologist for Marxism, as his productions of the classics. In the post-war period, first at Chur in Switzerland and then as founder-director of what was to become one of Europe's leading theatre companies, the Berliner Ensemble, Brecht devoted his energies more and more exclusively to the question he had raised in 1926: 'Wie soll man heute Klassiker spielen?' (15:111). Compared with the mutilation of *Edward II* and *Measure for Measure*, the script with which Brecht presented his epic actors in Chur and at the Theater am Schiffbauerdamm showed a good deal more respect for the original, but the basic attitude remained unchanged. A few cuts, one or two seemingly unobtrusive interpolations, a barely perceptible shift of emphasis at key points, and the models became so radically *umfunktioniert* that Elisabeth Hauptmann and Rosemary Hill had no hesitation in including six of Brecht's post-war adaptations in the collected edition of his published works in 1967. Of these, five are adaptations of the classics: the *Antigone* of Sophocles, Lenz's Sturm-und-Drang masterpiece *Der Hofmeister*, Shakespeare's *Coriolanus*, Molière's *Don Juan*, and George Farquhar's Restoration comedy *The Recruiting Officer* (*Pauken und Trompeten*).

In the sections to follow a detailed analysis of Brecht's adaptations of *Antigone* and *Coriolanus*, indubitably his best and at the same time his most problematic attempts to harness the classics, will suggest the virtues and limitations of his method.

Antigone

The *Antigone* of Sophocles was a natural target for Brecht's practical criticism of the classics. It has become a corner-stone of Aristotelian tragedy, and in the Hölderlin translation on which Brecht based his adaptation it forms a link with German Classicism. It is, moreover, one of the most politically orientated plays in the classical repertoire, and for good measure it was the favourite play of Brecht's favourite philosopher, Hegel.

What makes *Antigone* just as exciting and just as relevant today as when it was first produced in Athens in 441 B.C. is the head-on collision of two irreconcilable absolutes: the flagrant humanity of Antigone, who sees intuitively what is eternally right, and Creon's argument from political expediency, backed by the coercive power of the state.

Hegel saw in this conflict the dialectical process of history. For him the absolute *Weltgeist*, incarnate in Creon as ruler and in Antigone as individual conscience, is divided against itself, and thus what Sophocles had unconsciously dramatized was not the conflict of good with evil, but of one kind of good with another, in Bradley's paraphrase 'the intestinal warfare of the ethical substance'.[5] Creon was right in Hegel's view to maintain the integrity of the state at all costs, but Antigone was equally right to oppose it in the interests of individuation. Both of them are the tragic victims of historical necessity.

Hegel overrated the sympathy that Sophocles elicits for his

[5] A. C. Bradley, *Oxford Lectures on Poetry*, 1909, p. 71.

clumsy despot. Maurice Bowra has argued persuasively that the rhythm of the play ensures a gradual swing of sympathy away from Creon towards Antigone.[6] The subordinate status of women in ancient society, concern for the stability of the city-state, and a deeply rooted respect for authority must have made Creon's condemnation of Antigone's headstrong individualism seem very plausible to a Greek audience. On the other hand, an equally deep-rooted reverence for the dead—the Athenians buried even their inveterate enemies at Marathon—and unquestioning recognition of the unwritten laws which Antigone invokes in defence of her actions must also have fostered a growing suspicion that she is right after all. Creon's inflexibility is not, however, the product of wilful despotism. It is the result of inexperience and insecurity. As he ironically says himself in his opening speech it is only in office that a man shows his true mettle, and he has been in office less than a day when he is required to make his first and last political decision: how to control the warring factions that have just rent Thebes. In refusing burial to Polynices he makes the wrong decision and he is too unsure of himself to risk revoking it. Creon forfeits more and more of our sympathy as he allows personal acrimony to cloud his judgement and turns a bad mistake into a tragic ἁμαρτία in condemning Antigone to a barbarous death. By punishing her instinctive piety so cruelly and by misinterpreting his son's response to it as wanton defiance of his authority, Creon has flouted an immutable law of nature which exacts a terrible vengeance. This law, stronger than any of Creon's decrees, impels Antigone, Haemon, and Eurydice to their untimely deaths, and Creon is left to live with his guilt. As Creon's world shatters about him and his pride breaks, the pendulum of sympathy swings back the other way. Antigone and Creon are both tragic figures in their own right, but it is Creon who dominates the stage despite the title of the play. Antigone's tragedy is the measure of his own. The Chorus pronounce Sophocles' own gloomy verdict in their final summing-up:

> Wisdom is the first prerequisite
> Of happiness. No man may neglect

---

[6] C. M. Bowra, *Sophoclean Tragedy*, Oxford, 1944, pp. 65 ff.

Due reverence towards the gods. Great blows
Require the great speeches of the proud
And in old age teach wisdom.[7]

Man is educable, it seems, but all too often the experience by which he learns crushes him.

Such was the temper of Sophocles' finest work. Brecht's adaptation of it, like Anouilh's, was consciously a product of the Second World War. Although it was written (in less than a fortnight) for a provincial Swiss theatre in Chur at the end of 1947, it looks back to the recent war mainly for the benefit of a German public.

Brecht made it abundantly clear that he had turned to the ancient myth not in order to recreate the spirit of antiquity, but 'because its subject-matter facilitated a certain degree of topicality' (17:1212). If the Chur production retained many features of antique theatrical practice—a chorus, masks, more or less authentic costumes, even a sense of amphitheatrical breadth and depth in the staging—Brecht was aiming largely at alienation, not authenticity. To the bewilderment of the Swiss audience, who had seen nothing of Brecht's Epic Theatre in their provincial backwater, he amplified the antique *Verfrem-dungseffekte* with some of his own: a gong, a gramophone with music recorded from a specially doctored piano, a table for incidental props, a bench for the actors to sit on between entrances, and all this in full view of the audience. A brightly lit curtainless stage which exposed the scene-shifting, together with the then unfamiliar 'epic' style of acting, which involved addressing many of the lines directly to the audience, completes the tally of devices introduced 'to prevent the audience from feeling transported to the scene of the action' (17:1216). The beauty of ancient myth was not to be allowed to induce oblivion of the recent past, 'Memories of the late war beguiling / Into slumber sound',[8] as the Sophoclean Chorus sing in their exultant parodos. On the contrary, the production was designed specifically to challenge audiences to come to terms with 'die unbewältigte Vergangenheit'. For a production in

---

[7] *Antigone*, ll. 1347–52. All translations are my own unless otherwise indicated.
[8] ll. 150–1 in Sir George Young's translation in the Everyman edition of Sophocles' plays.

Greiz three years later Brecht wrote a new prologue which contains the express exhortation:

> Wir bitten euch
> Nachzusuchen in euren Gemütern nach ähnlichen Taten
> Näherer Vergangenheit oder dem Ausbleiben
> Ähnlicher Taten.
>
> (6:2328)

The Chur production had begun with what Brecht described as an 'Aktualitätspunkt' (17:1213), namely a rather banal prologue in rhymed doggerel, acted out on a skeletal set in front of the already visible classical stage. A placard lowered from the flies announced that the date is March 1945 and the place Berlin. Two sisters await the now inevitable defeat of Germany as the Russians close in on Berlin. A brother has deserted the army and is hanged by the S.S. Thinking he may still be alive, one of the sisters goes to cut him down, risking arrest for complicity. At the sound of a gong the two actresses, Helene Weigel and Marita Glenck, handed their coats to an assistant and returned as Antigone and Ismene respectively to play their opening scene.

Although Brecht's *Antigone* is not primarily an anti-war play, the war-theme was amplified into a major issue in order to accentuate the topical relevance. In Sophocles' version it merely serves to motivate Creon's act of terrorism. Polynices, raising an army in Argos against his brother Eteocles, has attacked his native Thebes, and the hostile brothers have killed each other in battle the night before the action begins. Creon feels justified in taking drastic measures to suppress anarchy, anticipating opposition to his succession as next of kin. He finds himself in the invidious position of having to victimize a kinsman to deter other would-be rebels, and his discomfiture is further increased when another member of his ill-fated family is the first to call his bluff. Memory of the recent war forces Creon to abide by his rash decision, but from this point on the war-theme has outlived its usefulness and is dropped.

In Brecht's adaptation war is the ground bass of the entire action, and the Chur production emphasized this by replacing the traditional fluted pillars with four totem-poles bearing the skulls of horses, which marked off the acting area of the stage. Kreon's campaign against Argos, which has obvious parallels with Germany's invasion of Russia, is no longer a defensive war, but an act of aggression against a powerful rival. But even the economic motive is little more than a pretext for Kreon. He needs Argive ore to boost his sagging economy, but he also needs the war as such to distract the attention of his subjects from the gross mismanagement responsible for the crisis. Just as historians often refer to the Second World War as Hitler's war, so Antigone, Hämon, and eventually even the Theban elders speak of this war as Kreon's. At one point, seeking to justify repressive measures really designed to shore up a corrupt regime, Kreon asks Antigone, 'Is there no war?', and Antigone replies simply, 'Yes, yours' (6:2294).

This shift in emphasis, seemingly unimportant in itself, has a disastrous effect on the characterization and ultimately also on the scale of values by which the basic issues of the play are judged. In the traditional version Polynices is a traitor to a cause with which the audience is encouraged to identify itself. No audience questions Creon's right to captain the ship of state of which he speaks in his famous opening speech. It merely learns to criticize his faulty navigation. In this light Creon's notorious edict does not at first appear unduly repressive. On the contrary, it is Antigone's defiance of it that is intended to seem wilful. In Brecht's version, however, Polyneikes was not killed by his war-hero of a brother but by the fanatical Kreon himself, ostensibly for cowardly desertion, but in fact for having realized the insanity of a war in which his own brother has just died so pointlessly. Whereas Sophocles' audience is Theban in its loyalties, Brecht's is against Kreon's Thebes from the start. This makes the outraged Polyneikes a hero of the resistance, and Antigone's symbolic burial of him is no longer an act of stubborn personal loyalty to a traitor, but a political demonstration. As a member of the ruling classes, Antigone has been brought by the course of the war to realize that this power-crazed tyrant has set the ship of state, in which both she and the Elders have a vested interest, on a course that is bound to end in disaster. When Kreon questions her motives she does not reply with her classical predecessor's plea of divinely inspired piety, nor even with the existentialist 'pour moi' of Anouilh's obstinate heroine:

> *Kreon* So sag, warum du störrig bist.
> *Antigone* Halt für ein Beispiel.
>
> (6:2293)

The rightness of Antigone's stand against tyranny no longer needs divine endorsement from the mouth of Teiresias, the blind seer. It is borne out by the military defeat of Kreon's creaking war-machine. Instead of the Messenger's moving account of the deaths of Antigone, Haemon, and Eurydice, we have a dying war-correspondent's eyewitness report on the enemy's heroic defence of Argos—at this point a transparent cipher for Stalingrad—in the face of which Kreon's army, led by his other son Megareus (whom Sophocles only mentioned in passing), has lost heart and suffered a crushing defeat. Kreon now faces the inevitable counter-attack, his striking-power on the home front paralysed by the desertion of Hämon. The play ends with the doomed Kreon anticipating an orgy of destruction.

Ronald Gray has aptly described Brecht's Kreon as 'a flatly rapacious caricature of Hitler'.[9] The character defects of Sophocles' tyrant are many and obvious, but they are the weaknesses of mediocrity, not the vices of a criminal superman. A sympathetic bungler becomes in Brecht's version a seasoned bully and a frenzied monomaniac, 'the public figure and bloody clown', as Brecht himself put it.[10] Even with his political ambitions in ruins he is not an object of tragic pity. In Brecht's notes on the play the question: 'Is Kreon to win the sympathy of the audience in his misfortune?' receives the monosyllabic answer, 'No.'[11]

Brecht's treatment of Hämon was dictated by the same principle. The Sophoclean youth is headstrong and impulsive, passionately in love with Antigone and gradually roused to open defiance of his father. The Chorus notes that his actions are controlled by Aphrodite, and this should have given pause to Creon. But by now Creon is blinded by anger and is only brought to his senses by the intervention of Teiresias. When he arrives at the tomb too late to save Antigone, his son spits in his face and attacks him with his sword before killing himself in despair. This terrible experience and the subsequent death of his wife, Eurydice, bring Creon tragic insight. There are few scenes in ancient drama more moving than our final glimpse

[9] Gray, *Brecht*, p. 95.
[10] *Materialien zur 'Antigone'*, ed. W. Hecht, Frankfurt, 1967, p. 97.
[11] Ibid., p. 95.

of the broken and contrite Creon as he mourns his dead son:

> Lead me away, a worthless wretch,
> Who unwittingly slew you, my son,
> And her too. Unhappy that I am, I know not
> Which way to turn. All paths lead astray.
> Upon my head a crushing fate has fallen. (ll. 1339–46)

By contrast, Brecht's Kreon mourns the death of Hämon only because it follows hard upon the death of Megareus, leaving him with no hope of organizing a final stand against the advancing Argives. The thwarted architect of a millennial empire, like Hitler, he braces himself for the end. Looking down at his son's tunic, he declaims:

> Seht, was ich da hab. 's ist der Rock. Ich hab geglaubt
> Es könnt ein Schwert sein, was ich holen ging. Früh ist's
> Mir verstorben, das Kind. Noch eine Schlacht
> Und Argos läg am Boden! Aber was da aufkam
> An Mut and Äußerstem, das ging nur gegen mich.
> So fällt jetzt Thebe.*
>
> $$(6:2326–7)$$

Add to this the fact that Eurydice has been omitted from the cast-list altogether, and it will be seen that Brecht has eliminated the human dimension of Creon's tragic error, which dominates the action of Sophocles' play.

This is the most serious fault of Brecht's adaptation. Though he furnished no evidence in support of his claim, Brecht maintained that he had reconstructed the pre-Sophoclean folk-legend and that, in the foreseeable future, audiences which have learned to read both history and literature dialectically would be able to see in Sophocles' original play all that his adaptation had made of it.[12] Despite this ambitious claim it is safe to predict that the sophisticated audiences of Utopia are more likely to condemn Brecht's rationalized *Antigone* as an evisceration of Sophocles' myth.

Sophocles' *Antigone* is a profoundly religious play. This is not to say that it concedes to the gods any prescriptive right to intervene in human affairs, for the supernatural as such has no part in it. It is just that in moments of crisis the noblest of men

---

[12] Ibid., pp. 109, 117.

apprehend another dimension of their mutual relationship, inexplicable in terms of reason and expediency. No rational argument can explain away human reverence for the dead, and Antigone's deepest instincts tell her to give her brother the burial that Creon has denied him. She is not a martyr to an abstract rational principle. One commentator has said: 'Antigone has no reason; she has only her instinct',[13] and another, writing at the same time as Brecht: 'her resolve sprang from an impulse of pure love, not from a calculation or a sense of duty to the family or even a religious scruple'.[14] Antigone herself says simply to Creon: 'I was born for fellowship in love, not fellowship in hate' (l. 523). A deep awareness of human kinship and human dignity motivate Antigone's defiance of Creon, and it is in this sense that her motives can be described as religious. H. D. F. Kitto has written of them: 'The religious and the human or instinctive motives are not sharply distinguished by Sophocles, indeed they are fused—and for a very good reason: he saw no distinction between them; the fundamental laws of humanity and the Dikê of the gods are the same thing.'[15]

If there is a sense of the numinous about Sophocles' *Antigone* it is not because Teiresias, whom Brecht reduces to a crafty amateur politician, is the spokesman of the gods. Teiresias merely confirms what Antigone and Haemon already know and what Creon and the Elders find out through bitter experience: Nature itself has laws with which Creon's conflict. Creon's basic failure, the commonest fault of all doctrinaire politicians, is ἀσέβεια, technically irreverence towards the gods, but in the final analysis a fatal disregard for the ultimate claims of humanity. A line from Sophocles' other great study in tyranny aptly describes the laws which govern Antigone's actions: 'There is a great god in them, who grows not old'.[16]

The universality of Sophocles' drama rests on just this sense of the numinous. Despite the studied topicality of his adaptation, Brecht also strove for universality, and he too would have claimed that he had exposed the underlying laws of nature, only

---

[13] G. Norwood, *Greek Tragedy*, 1920, p. 139.
[14] J. T. Sheppard, *The Wisdom of Sophocles*, 1947, p. 53.
[15] H. D. F. Kitto, *Form and Meaning in Drama*, 1964, p. 176.
[16] *Oedipus Rex*, l. 872.

he sought them not in human response but in economic causality. He realized himself that his *Antigone* comes perilously close to a kind of morality play, illustrating the banal maxim 'Crime does not pay.'[17] Unlike the original, it is basically optimistic, showing, he believed, 'that political enterprises demanding excessive violence are likely to founder'. Kreon's lust for power has, like Hitler's, overtaxed the resources of the state and so precipitated its internal decay. There are no 'unwritten laws' in Brecht's version, which discreetly omits the passage in which Antigone refers to them.[18] The politically far-sighted Antigone, Teiresias, and Hämon demonstrate against what amounts to a strategic blunder in the class war rather than an outrage against humanity. Oddly enough, Brecht retained Hölderlin's pithy translation of the line quoted above, in which Antigone protests her love: 'Zum Hasse nicht, zur Liebe leb ich' (6:2298). But it rings very oddly in the mouth of Brecht's political convert and fails to convince.

According to Caspar Neher, who designed the set for the Chur production, Brecht's intention had been to strip Sophocles' *Antigone* of its mythological veneer.[19] But Brecht has gone much further than this and stripped the classical masterpiece of its humanity. Just once Brecht's version rises to greatness, in a snatch of dialogue that owes nothing either to Sophocles or to Hölderlin:

> *Kreon* Immer nur die Nase neben dir siehst du, aber des Staats
> Ordnung, die göttliche, siehst du wohl nicht.
> *Ant.* Göttlich mag sie wohl sein, aber ich wollte doch
> Lieber sie menschlich, Kreon, Sohn des Menökeus.*
> (6:2298)

This is pure Brecht, but it is swamped by the dehumanized politics of the rest of the play.

Brecht was quite wrong to suppose that Sophocles' play was apolitical. Indeed it was political in the original sense, for it was an essay on the nature of the πόλις and the dangers that beset it:

> *Creon* Am I to rule this land by any other will than mine?
> *Haemon* A city that belongs to one man only is no city at all.
> (ll. 736-7)

---

[17] *Materialien*, p. 112.   [18] *Antigone*, ll. 540 ff.
[19] *Materialien*, p. 126.

Even Marx could not have improved on that. Greek audiences will certainly have seen something of Pericles in Creon's self-conscious attitudinizing, just as Brecht's are expected to see Hitler. Brecht says in his notes that he wanted his audiences to feel they were themselves Kreon's subjects.[20] There would have been more point in this identification if they could have felt the original force of Sophocles' basic political argument, namely that administrative expertise is not enough to ensure the health of the body politic, which requires a high regard for the common humanity of its citizens.

Kitto has written of Sophocles: 'His political experiences and judgments passed through his mind and when they came out, they were transmuted into something else—into that highest form of art which has contemplated and then can illuminate, human experience.'[21] This is precisely where Brecht's adaptation so signally fails, despite its ingenuity. Brecht's *Antigone* is not about human experience at all, but about political abstractions, from which no society, least of all Utopia, can be constructed.

At one remove from the hurly-burly of production, Brecht dedicated to Helene Weigel a poem, which penetrates more deeply than anything in his adaptation into the human core of the Antigone myth:

Komm aus dem Dämmer und geh
Vor uns her eine Zeit
Freundliche, mit dem leichten Schritt
Der ganz Bestimmten, schrecklich
Den Schrecklichen.

Abgewandte, ich weiß
Wie du den Tod gefürchtet hast, aber
Mehr noch fürchtetest du
Unwürdig Leben.

Und ließest den Mächtigen
Nichts durch, und glichst dich
Mit den Verwirrern nicht aus, noch je
Vergaßest du Schimpf und über der Untat wuchs
Ihnen kein Gras.*

(10:954)

---

[20] *Materialien*, p. 88. [21] Kitto, op. cit., p. 177.

Sophocles would have agreed with this, but he would not have recognized the play of which it claims to be the gist.

Coriolan

Brecht's preoccupation with Shakespeare amounts to a lifelong love–hate relationship with the father of modern drama, who still runs Brecht into second place in the German repertoire. On the one hand, Shakespeare's robust realism and his disregard for the unities have much in common with Brecht's Epic Theatre. On the other hand, the almost idolatrous reverence for Shakespeare was deeply abhorrent to the iconoclast whose greatest fear was of becoming a classic. The old lady who complained that *Hamlet* was full of quotations was a critic after Brecht's own heart. Perhaps this is why he refused to produce *Macbeth* during his Munich apprenticeship under Falckenberg. Yet there are over two hundred references to Shakespeare in his theoretical writings, and he turned to Shakespeare for inspiration again and again. *Measure for Measure* became *Die Rundköpfe und die Spitzköpfe*, *Richard III* and *Julius Caesar* were parodied in *Arturo Ui*, and there were radio adaptations of *Hamlet* and *Macbeth*. In his preface to the latter, which was broadcast in 1927, Brecht claimed that whereas most of the classics are irrelevant unless they are subjected to a radical revaluation, Shakespeare still offered 'absolute material', full of contradictions which reflect the contradictory nature of reality (15:119).

Coriolanus, the adaptation of which occupied a great deal of Brecht's time during his last five years, and after his death became one of the Berliner Ensemble's most spectacular successes,[22] presented a special challenge. To start with, it is the least popular of Shakespeare's great tragedies, which means that audiences come to it much fresher than to the established favourites. At the same time, it is the most political of all Shakespeare's plays and one reviewer, after seeing Brecht's adaptation at the Berliner Ensemble, noted with surprise that the most outspoken political comment in it was still Shakespeare's.[23]

---

[22] It was produced by Manfred Wekwerth and Joachim Tenschert in 1964 to mark the quatercentenary of Shakespeare's birth.

[23] John Mortimer in a review of Trevor Nunn's Stratford production, in the *Observer*, 16 Apr. 1972.

Again, Erich Engel's production in Berlin in 1925 had convinced Brecht that the play's construction was fundamentally epic, not dramatic, a view encouraged by the lack of act-divisions in the First Folio edition. Finally, Coriolanus himself stands alone amongst Shakespeare's tragic heroes as one with whom it is extraordinarily difficult to feel much sympathy. A recent editor has said that he is 'presented in a way that inhibits the normal spectator from identifying himself with him'.[24] Such a character clearly appealed to the non-Aristotelian who even in his later years tolerated only a strictly controlled empathy in his dialectical theatre.

What fascinated Shakespeare when he came to study the career of Caius Martius Coriolanus in Sir Thomas North's lively translation of Plutarch's *Lives*, was what had fascinated Plutarch in the first instance: the enigmatic personality of Rome's most ambiguous hero. Plutarch, a moralist as well as a historian, praised his 'natural wit and great heart' but severely censured the choleric impatience that made him 'churlish, uncivil, and altogether unfit for any man's conversation'.[25] Shakespeare retained this basic ambivalence. Coriolanus emerges from his dramatization as a man of impeccable integrity, impulsively generous, courageous, unselfish, ambitious, the personification of Roman *virtus*. Yet he also typifies Renaissance *sprezzatura*, that haughty independence embodied in Machiavelli's Prince. He does not suffer fools gladly, and is openly contemptuous of all cowardice, double-dealing, and mediocrity, and friend and foe alike are the butts of his caustic wit. So well drawn is this side of his nature that he has been a favourite of the political Right, and in 1945 a German production was banned by the Americans as a 'glorification of dictatorship'.[26] But Shakespeare in fact strikes a fine balance between praise and censure.

As both Volumnia and Aufidius observe, Coriolanus is too absolute and this isolates him not merely from the Commoners, but also from his colleagues of the right-hand file. In the first

[24] G. R. Hibbard in his introduction to the Penguin edition, 1967, p. 9.

[25] Quoted from Sir Thomas North's translation of 1579 (known to Shakespeare): Penguin edition, ed. T. J. B. Spencer, 1964, p. 296.

[26] Bernhard Kytzler, *William Shakespeare: Coriolan*, Frankfurt and Berlin, 1965, p. 157.

flurry of angry slogans Coriolanus is denounced as 'chief enemy to the people' and 'a very dog to the commonalty'. Quite apart from his scornful bearing, which some of the plebeians are prepared to condone as a harmless idiosyncrasy, his political persuasions constitute a real threat to their well-being. He calls upon his fellow patricians to overthrow the tribunes, the people's only defence against gross exploitation. He refuses to accept the fact that the people are starving and is ready to veto the free distribution of corn. Despite their unfeigned respect for Caius Martius as a warrior the commoners have good cause to fear his politics. Yet Coriolanus is equally alienated from those of his own class. Their best representative is the sane and tactful Menenius, and even in their ugliest mood the plebeians regard him as 'one that hath always loved the people' (i. i). The fact is that Menenius is just as contemptuous of these 'apron-men' and 'garlic-eaters' as Coriolanus, but he has the political good sense not to air his views in their presence. His celebrated parable of the body politic is specious bluff, expressly concocted to pacify a desperate rabble, but it works, whereas only the outbreak of war prevents Coriolanus from goading the 'worshipful mutineers' to open rebellion. Menenius rather charitably describes Coriolanus as 'too noble for the world' (iii. i) and certainly there is no place for a statesman of his calibre in the world of Roman politics.

The one activity in which Coriolanus seems to find a legitimate outlet for his talents, and a point of contact with his fellow Romans, is war. Shakespeare follows North in spelling his patronymic with a *t* to stress his affinity with the Roman god of war. The generous quota of battle-scenes is introduced not to relieve the political argument, but to show in detail the circumstances in which the hero 'proved himself a man' (i. iii). On the field of battle this 'flower of warriors' (i. vi) braves every danger in hand-to-hand combat, turns defeat into victory, and captures a strategically important city almost single-handed. 'Foolhardiness', comments a realist in his army, and the reluctance of the rank and file to follow their officer unleashes one of his most searing tirades. This does much more than emphasize Coriolanus' undisputed courage. It underscores his isolation in a situation where men commonly experience a heightened sense of comradeship. There is a marked contrast here between Coriolanus and his commander-in-chief, Cominius, who addresses his exhausted men quite sincerely as 'my friends' and gently rouses their flagging spirits in defeat. His lieutenant's flashy virtuosity steals the show, but he lacks the instinctive sympathy and tact of the born leader.

In the field Coriolanus undoubtedly has his uses despite his shortcomings. In the context of practical politics, however, they are catastrophic. Aufidius, though hardly his rival's most reliable critic, is right when he says that Coriolanus lacks flexibility,

> not moving
> From th'casque to th'cushion, but commanding peace
> Even with the same austerity and garb
> As he controlled the war.
>
> (IV. vii)

Coriolanus' trenchant criticism of the fickle populace, like that of his troops, is justified to some extent, but his stubborn refusal to demean himself by petitioning their support for his candidature in the 'gown of humility' defies the cardinal principle of democratic statesmanship, so eloquently stressed by Richard Hooker in Shakespeare's own lifetime, namely that the ruler must obtain 'the assent of them who are governed'.[27] As they say themselves, with a little prompting from Sicinius, 'The people are the city' (III. i). Coriolanus commits the beginner's error of confusing careerist hypocrisy with the studied diplomacy demanded by all practical politics. He has been described as 'a man without a mask in a world where hypocrisy and double-dealing hold sway',[28] but both Menenius and the tribunes, while admittedly lining their own pockets, do at least contrive to keep the ship of state on an even keel. Coriolanus' honour, which allegedly prevents him from meeting his political opponents half-way, is in fact a grossly inhuman abstraction divorced from all meaningful social relations. It makes him, as Wilson Knight has emphasized, 'an idiot robot, a creaking clockwork giant',[29] a man incapable of love and for this very reason a danger to both himself and Rome.

In a moment of truth Coriolanus characterizes himself as a 'lonely dragon' (IV. i), and despite the element of self-flattery

[27] Quoted from Hibbard, op. cit., p. 34.   [28] Hibbard, p. 20.
[29] G. Wilson Knight, *The Imperial Theme*, 1951, p. 190.

behind the metaphor it emphasizes his 'solitarinesse', which Shakespeare, following North's Plutarch, made the dominant tragic motif of the play. Banishment is the public recognition of the hero's total alienation. Moreover, exile in turn exposes his professed patriotism as another form of the pride that isolates him. He derides the unpatriotic attitude of lesser men when he is able to identify his own ambitions with those of Rome, but the moment Rome rejects him, Caius Martius Coriolanus, veteran of seventeen patriotic battles, defects to Rome's most implacable enemy and is prepared to reduce his native city to ashes.

Shakespeare accepted and developed Plutarch's interpretation of the hero's 'solitarinesse' as the product of a mother-fixation. In North's translation Shakespeare read that 'touching Martius, the only thing that made him to love honour was the joy he saw his mother did take of him.'[30] In Shakespeare's opening scene the garrulous First Citizen, who fancies himself as an amateur psychologist, says of Coriolanus' heroic achievements: 'Though soft-conscienced men can be content to say it was for his country, he did it to please his mother and to be partly proud, which he is, even to the altitude of his virtue.' Both his vices and his virtues are in large measure his mother's doing. It was she who taught her son his Spartan hardness, his physical courage, and his moral integrity, but also the inhuman inflexibility and the destructive pride that make him such a lonely dragon. For all his manly qualities, Coriolanus remains a perpetual adolescent, and it is revealing how he over-reacts to the taunts of Aufidius, who in the final scene calls him a 'boy of tears'.

Volumnia is the only person who can persuade Coriolanus to forget all she has taught him and temper honesty with tact. In the climactic scene her eloquent appeal, taken almost verbatim from North's Plutarch, arouses in her son a sense of integrity, no longer a form of adolescent arrogance, but based on genuine personal loyalties. It is Coriolanus' tragedy that his newly matured humanity is treason to his Volscian hosts and serves his rival as a pretext for the conspiracy that leads to his brutal assassination. In the first scene the citizens of Rome angrily demand his death, and in the last Rome's enemies carry

[30] North, Penguin edn., p. 300.

out the sentence. In death as in life, the Coriolanus of Plutarch and Shakespeare is a pariah, exiled from his fellow men by his own intransigent personality.

The sense of tragic waste in the play led one critic to call it 'the tragedy of Rome',[31] which was also Brecht's reading, though for different reasons. To be sure, Rome will be the poorer without Coriolanus, like Scotland without Macbeth, but infinitely safer to live in. The patricians and tribunes are able to make common cause only in his absence. The last time we see Rome, its rulers are preparing to 'make triumphant fires', and the concluding flourish of drums and trumpets indicates a universal joy facilitated as much by Coriolanus' departure as by his magnanimity. Characteristically, it is left to Rome's enemies to pay Coriolanus the final homage.

Brecht's adaptation appears at first sight to deviate only in inessential particulars. It is in fact unique amongst Brecht's classical adaptations in achieving the highest degree of originality with the fewest changes in the text. Brecht's treatment of his classical model was predictably most cavalier on one important count: the role played by the plebeians and their professional representatives, the tribunes.

Shakespeare's political conservatism has been much exaggerated, and to speak without reservations of his antidemocratic attitude, as Günter Grass does,[32] is extremely shortsighted. At the turn of the century Beerbohm Tree, after delivering a lecture on *Coriolanus* to a predominantly working-class audience, is said to have been embarrassed by hecklers, one of whom protested: 'You wouldn't believe the nasty things Shakespeare says in that there play.'[33] The fact is, of course, that Shakespeare does not say anything. It is the characters who make sweeping judgements of their opponents, not their creator. It is Coriolanus, not Shakespeare, who derides the 'mutable, rank-scented meiny' (III. i). If Coriolanus seems justified in jeering at its cowardliness in the battle-scenes, what price his criticism when we see him later slinking off to the enemy 'in mean apparel, disguised and muffled', despite his

---

31 D. J. Enright, '*Coriolanus*: Tragedy or Debate?', *Essays in Criticism*, 4, 1954, p. 15.

32 Günter Grass, *Über meinen Lehrer Döblin und andere Vorträge*, Berlin, 1968, p. 28.

33 K. Muir, 'In Defence of the Tribunes', *Essays in Criticism*, 4, 1954, p. 330.

horror of all forms of dissembling? If their 'vulgar wisdoms' seem to change with every shift of the political climate, so do his, with far more disastrous results. The point is that Shakespeare was able to differentiate between the *rabble*, as his own stage-directions call the citizens collectively, and the individuals who comprise it. Individually they appear reasonable, good-humoured, flexible, and surprisingly generous to their political opponents. After Menenius has pacified them in the opening scene, even the class-conscious First Citizen, whom Brecht tentatively identified with Sicinius (17:1254), only reacts to Coriolanus' blistering invective with a mildly sarcastic 'We have ever your good word'. The opening stage-directions introduce them as *a company of mutinous Citizens, with staves, clubs, and other weapons*, but they are hungry, disillusioned, and desperate, and even so do not need much persuasion from Menenius to simmer down and adopt a more reasonable attitude. Menenius uncharitably puts this down to cowardice, but it must strike less biased observers as common sense. Again, they give Coriolanus their votes despite the latter's insulting attitude, because they respect him for his nobler qualities. When they are roused against him by the skilful demagogy of the tribunes, it is unjust to call them gullible: their consul elect has after all openly defied their chosen representatives, mishandled the officers of the law, and rejected the constitution. Coriolanus calls the mob a Hydra, but it is he who is the monster, and the characteristic images associated with him are all of predatory creatures: bear, dragon, tiger, eagle, and osprey. In view of this it is hardly vindictive of the people if they come to agree with Sicinius that Coriolanus 'deserves th'extremest death' (III. iii).

And what of the much-maligned tribunes? Historically they represent the most democratic institution in the ancient world, yet Plutarch wrote them off as 'busy prattlers'.[34] Dr. Johnson spoke of the 'plebeian malignity and tribunitian insolence'[35] of their Shakespearian counterparts, and since then hardly any critic has had a good word for them. Granville-Barker describes them as 'comic villains',[36] Kytzler as 'more or less black-

---

[34] North, p. 314.

[35] John Palmer, *Political Characters of Shakespeare*, 1945, p. 259. This sound study, like Muir's, is much more generous than most towards the tribunes.

[36] H. Granville-Barker, *Prefaces to Shakespeare*, no. 5: *Coriolanus*, 1947, p. 47.

guards',[37] and Hibbard says their characteristic weapons are 'words and chicanery'.[38] But here again, Shakespeare's skill in dramatic portraiture is being sadly underrated. Of course, as newcomers to the political arena the tribunes are no match for Coriolanus in rhetoric, and their diplomacy is clumsy compared with that of Menenius, but they do their appointed task well enough. Coriolanus is undoubtedly 'chief enemy to the people' and if the people themselves are momentarily too generous towards him they must be persuaded to act in their own interests while there is time. To achieve this end glib demagogy is an indispensable trick of the trade and the tribunes are justified in resorting to it. Moreover, when they finally win their case against Coriolanus, it is they who plead extenuating circumstances and succeed in getting the death-sentence commuted to banishment. As things turn out, their humanity is ill rewarded. A dead Coriolanus could not have raised an army against them, but they clearly thought him above such petty vindictiveness. All this is not to idealize the tribunes. Shakespeare accepts the fact that they are in this game for the money like everyone else, and fleeting references hint they have done pretty well out of the democratic cause, but at least they have earned their keep. In this, as in so many other respects, Shakespeare's distribution of light and shade is superbly balanced and Coleridge rightly admired 'the wonderfully philosophic impartiality of Shakespeare's politics'.[39]

Whether Brecht saw more than most, it is difficult to say, but in any case he was not going to take chances. The portraits of both the populace and the tribunes are touched up to eliminate any doubt that theirs is the historic mission of transforming society in such a way that it is no longer at the mercy of a Coriolanus. A few judicious cuts and interpolations and Shakespeare's colourful crowd-scenes become mass demonstrations of proletarian solidarity, particularly towards the end, by which time Shakespeare's rabble has become a class-conscious revolutionary collective.

The opening scene reveals some subtle but important shifts of emphasis. Shakespeare's 'company of mutinous Citizens, with staves, clubs and other weapons' becomes *ein Haufe*

---

[37] Kytzler, op. cit., p. 151.   [38] Hibbard, p. 17.
[39] Quoted from Hibbard, p. 22.

aufrührerischer Bürger, an die Knüppel, Messer und andere Waffen verteilt werden, which introduces an element of conscious organization. The First Citizen is just as articulate and still denounces Cajus Marcius as a class-enemy, but where Shakespeare made him say: 'Let us kill him and we'll have corn at our own price', Brecht substitutes a question: '*Ihr seid bereit, nicht eher umzukehren als bis der Senat zugestanden hat, daß den Brotpreis wir Bürger bestimmen?*' (6:2397). Only when the citizens have agreed does he mention Cajus Marcius, who will be struck down if he opposes them. Instead of the spontaneous and rather aimless violence of a hungry rebel we have a determined revolutionary's demand for political rights. He no longer diagnoses the hero's mother-fixation, the Second Citizen's conciliatory remarks about his redeeming features are cut, and the description of Menenius as 'one that hath always loved the people' becomes a grudging '*Nicht der Allerschlimmste!—Er hat eine Schwäche für das Volk!*' (6:2398). The people are no longer taken in by Menenius' specious parable. Menenius himself admits it was not his rhetoric, but the timely appearance of Coriolanus (earlier than in Shakespeare) with an armed escort, that pacified the mob. Nor do the citizens 'steal away', when news of war arrives, as one of Shakespeare's revealing stage-directions indicates. Brecht found Shakespeare's depiction of the effects of the war 'wonderfully realistic' (16:873), but he could not countenance the realism that exposes their reluctance to fight. A Czech critic has sought to interpret Brecht's *Coriolan* as an essay in pacifism,[40] but the matter is more complicated than this. For Brecht the war against the Volscians was historically a necessary war which Rome had to win in order that its nascent democracy might spread to other regions. He had just read in Mao Tse-tung's *On Contradiction* that in times of crisis one dominant contradiction takes precedence over others. Consequently, Brecht makes his citizens accept the advice of their tribunes to fight for Rome against a common enemy, while the tribunes themselves undertake to continue the class struggle on their behalf. The new stage-direction reads simply *Bürger ab.* Later, whereas Shakespeare's citizens give Coriolanus their votes and must

[40] L. Moníková, 'Brechtovo prepracování Shakespearova *Koriolana*', *Časopis pro moderní filologii*, 52, 1970, pp. 180–8.

then be persuaded by the tribunes to protest against his candidature, Brecht fuses the two scenes into one. After a clumsy attempt at diplomacy Coriolanus alienates the voters' sympathies with his undisguised hostility and they properly reject him. In this way Brecht exonerates them of the charge of fickleness and political immaturity.

Brecht's idealized depiction of the commonalty makes only two minor concessions to realism. Drawing on Plutarch, Brecht adds to his cast a man with a child, who in the opening scene prefers to wait and see what will come of the revolt before throwing in his lot with the rebels. If the worst comes to the worst he can still join those who are leaving the city in protest. Similarly, in the election-scene Brecht, perhaps with *Julius Caesar* in mind, introduces a cobbler who relishes the prospect of a proven militarist becoming consul since he gets a better price for his shoes in wartime. But these are the exceptions that prove the rule, and they serve more to illustrate social conditions than to tone down the idealization of the plebs.

Brecht's treatment of the tribunes is comparable. Shakespeare's subtly shaded characterization is abandoned in favour of a pair of idealized trade-unionists, staunchly upholding the popular cause and ultimately re-educating the masses towards collective responsibility. When Coriolanus turns on Rome, neither they nor their clients panic as they do in Shakespeare, and Brutus no longer says he would give half his wealth for the news that it was all a false alarm. Sicinius, carefully distinguishing between the real plebeians and the disorganized lumpenproletariat, calmly instructs the citizenry in its new duties. Asked whether in retrospect it was wise to banish Coriolanus, he replies simply: 'Ja. Zum Kapitol!' (6:2478), and the commoners leave in an orderly manner to organize the defence of their city.

In all this Brecht has introduced fewer innovations than is commonly believed, rather accentuating certain features of the original. But the resulting imbalance robs the play of the rich *tessitura* that makes every new production such an unpredictable experience. With Brecht we know what to expect and are given no more than is good for us. Hazlitt once said of *Coriolanus* that anyone who read it could save himself the trouble of reading Burke's *Reflections*, Paine's *Rights of Man*, and every political debate since the French Revolution,[41] an eloquent tribute to the political wisdom of Shakespeare's last tragedy. Brecht's Shakespeare, however, enters the lists in the class war and forfeits the philosophic impartiality that Coleridge and Heine admired.

Despite this it is in the revamping of the character of Coriolanus himself that Brecht has made his most sweeping changes. At first sight it is all there: the valiant warrior, the rampant individualist, the unholy braggart whose heart's his mouth, and the boy of tears still emotionally tied to his mother's apron-strings. He is equally generous in victory, still interceding for a poor man who once gave him hospitality—and still characteristically forgetting his name; and he is equally petulant in defeat. He is still insufferably arrogant to all except his mother, still magnanimously humble in the climactic scene, and still superbly defiant in the presence of his assassins. But almost imperceptibly the focus has shifted, and every motif takes on a subtly new colouring which alters the total pattern of the play.

Brecht saw Coriolanus not merely as the inveterate class-enemy of the exploited plebeians, but above all as the gifted specialist who deliberately blackmails society with his own indispensability as a technician. Rome is at war with a belligerent rival and Coriolanus' indisputable talent as a fighting-machine, so far victorious in seventeen battles, seems their only hope. This is the main reason why the second half of Act 1 survived completely intact in the Berliner Ensemble production and was reproduced unchanged in the 1967 edition. Brecht intended to adapt these scenes during rehearsal, but it seems unlikely that he would have made many changes. Working on Brecht's conception of the play, which he had discussed with his collaborators in detail, Manfred Wekwerth and Joachim Tenschert put a special co-producer, Ruth Berghaus, in charge of the battle-scenes, and her inspired choreography emphasized the gist of Brecht's adaptation as a whole. In a kind of ritual mime of great visual beauty, somewhere between judo and modern ballet, Ekkehard Schall's Coriolan, in whom significantly one reviewer detected 'a blond fascist brute',[42]

---

[41] Palmer, op. cit., p. 308.
[42] Ronald Bryden, *Observer Review*, 9 May 1971.

demonstrated his consummate mastery of the war-game. His belief in his indispensability seemed well founded. In July 1952 Brecht recorded the following impression of the new Coriolanus:

The individual blackmails society with his indispensability. That is a tragedy for society. 1. It loses the individual, 2. it has to spend vast sums on self-defence. But in the first instance it is tragedy for the individual, who wrongly considered himself indispensable. The apparent indispensability of the individual from ancient times to the present day is an immense subject that is by no means exhausted. The solution will have to be positive for society, that is to say, it has no need to let itself be blackmailed by an individual.[43]

This is the solution adumbrated by Brecht's *Coriolan*. In Shakespeare's version the people had declared they were the city, but only in anger and only because the tribunes put them up to it. Nothing came of their boast. Instead of panicking as the tribunes wince under Menenius' taunts, the citizens of Brecht's Rome begin to realize their own potential. Brecht may have taken his cue from an interesting speech Shakespeare gives to Sicinius, in which, speaking of the absent Coriolanus, he says:

We hear not of him, neither need we fear him.
His remedies are tame—the present peace
And quietness of the people, which before
Were in wild hurry. Here do we make his friends
Blush that the world goes well, who rather had,
Though they themselves did suffer by't, behold
Dissentious numbers pestering streets than see
Our tradesmen singing in their shops and going
About their functions friendly.

(IV. vi)

This needed little refurbishing to become the full-blown Marxist theme of Brecht's version, in which the people learn to usurp Coriolanus' function. This virtually robs the hero of his sup-

---

[43] 'Das Individuum erpresst die Gesellschaft mit seiner Unentbehrlichkeit. Das ist eine Tragödie für die Gesellschaft. Sie verliert 1) das Individuum, 2) muss sie grosse Mittel aufwenden, um sich zu verteidigen. Aber in erster Linie ist es die Tragödie für das Individuum, das sich zu Unrecht für unentbehrlich hielt. Die scheinbare Unentbehrlichkeit des Individuums ist ein Riesenthema noch auf lange Zeit, von der Antike bis zu uns führend. Die Lösung muss positiv für die Gesellschaft sein, das heisst, sie hat es nicht notwendig, sich von einem Individuum erpressen zu lassen.' (Published in the Berliner Ensemble's *Programmheft*, 1964; cf. also 16:886.)

posedly unique identity, like the hapless Jeraiah Jip in *Mann ist Mann*. As we have seen, Brecht did not hesitate to describe as tragic the hero's discovery that the revivified Rome has no place for him, which adds, rather surprisingly, an entirely new 'Aristotelian' dimension to the play: 'In our adaptation the tragedy of the individual modulates into the tragedy of the hero's belief in his own indispensability.'[44]

This theme reaches its climax in the final meeting between Coriolan and Volumnia, still the climax of the whole play, but now fundamentally reorientated. Instead of her eloquent appeal to her son's sense of *pietas*, the new Volumnia, who has accepted with resignation the defeat of her class in the struggle against the plebeian order, simply presents Coriolan with the *fait accompli* of a social revolution that has made him redundant. Volumnia still makes her legendary attempt to avert bloodshed, but what really decides Coriolan is his realization that he cannot put the clock back. Volumnia points out that the Rome on which he now marches is very different from the one he left:

> Unersetzlich
> Bist du nicht mehr, nur noch die tödliche
> Gefahr für alle.
>
> (6:2492)

If Coriolan sees smoke rising from the roof-tops, it will not be the agreed signal of submission, but the sign that weapons are being forged for the final struggle against him. There is no room here for that most eloquent of all Shakespeare's stage-directions *Holds her by the hand silent*, nor for the hero's moving valediction and his premonition of personal disaster, nor for the threats of Aufidius, who will bring it about.

And so to the assassination: again the furious exchange of invective between the rival champions, again the angry cries of the Volscians as they smart beneath their new ally's last defiant outburst, and again the call to arms. But here the scene ends, and Coriolan is dispatched with an almost perfunctory 'Durchbohrt ihn!' which contrasts with the hysterical 'Kill, kill, kill, kill, kill him!' of Shakespeare's text, after which Aufidius stands on the mangled corpse. Moreover, Shakespeare's interest

---

[44] 'In unserer Bearbeitung verschiebt sich die Tragödie des Individuums zu der Tragödie des Glaubens an die eigene Unentbehrlichkeit' (Brecht-Archiv, 173/02), quoted from Kytzler, p. 158.

in Rome ends with the death of his hero, and the conventional apotheosis is pronounced, somewhat incongruously, by Aufidius in Corioli:

> My rage is gone,
> And I am struck with sorrow. Take him up.
> Help three o'th'chiefest soldiers; I'll be one.
> Beat thou the drum, that it speak mournfully.
> Trail your steel pikes. Though in this city he
> Hath widowed and unchilded many a one,
> Which to this hour bewail the injury,
> Yet he shall have a noble memory.
> Assist.
>
> *Exeunt, bearing the body of Martius. A dead march sounded.*

Since Rome is its new hero, Brecht's play closes with a new scene in a deliberately low key. The democratically reconstituted Senate, in which the tribunes now play a major role, busies itself with routine affairs of state: the restitution of confiscated territory, a new water-conduit. News of the death of Coriolan interrupts the agenda, but only momentarily:

Konsul Eine Frage:
> Die Marcier bitten, daß, nach der Verordnung
> Numa Pompilius' für die Hinterbliebenen
> Von Vätern, Söhnen, Brüdern, doch den Frauen
> Erlaubt werd öffentliches Tragen
> Von Trauer für zehn Monde.

Brutus Abgeschlagen.
> *Der Senat setzt seine Beratungen fort.* *
> (6:2497)

Brecht's democratic Rome has no time to mourn a tragic hero who merely served as the catalyst of revolution. History has sloughed off this war-mongering individualist as a superfluous anachronism.

There is scarcely a scene from Brecht's entire dramatic *œuvre* that more clearly reveals his rooted antipathy to traditional dramaturgy and to the ideal of heroism it commonly subserves. Although Brecht repeatedly used the word 'tragisch' to describe his *Coriolan*, the epithet is quite out of place in this optimistic drama of social conflict. Little enough sympathy is evoked by Shakespeare's hero, yet at the last there is that same sense of waste which Bradley noted in all Shakespeare's maturer work and which so rarely finds a place in Brecht. As Brecht's Rome rejects the irritant that unwittingly impelled it towards socialism, there is only that same sigh of relief that Frederick the Great said the world would utter at the news of his death.

Ronald Bryden, reviewing the 1971 National Theatre production (supervised by Wekwerth and Tenschert), wrote: 'Brecht's reworking of Shakespeare is not just Marxist travesty, but a serious, compelling criticism of its faith in the ultimate humanity of tyrants in the light of Hitler and Auschwitz.'[45] This misses the point. Brecht's *Coriolan* is hardly a study in tyranny on a par with *Arturo Ui* or the novel on Caesar, and certainly not allegorical. But two world wars taught Brecht that the brilliant individualist was a luxury neither society nor its drama can afford. In Shakespeare's tragedy of the individual, to which the skilfully articulated political themes are strictly subordinated, the hero's disconcerting greatness is measured against the mediocrity of his social environment. Brecht substitutes for this the confident self-assertion of a society that has come of age and learned to dispense with the heroic individual as a dangerous parasite. Coriolan is a life-size portrait of the 'indispensable man', satirized in a Keuner-anecdote (12:396) and again in a poem of 1944:

> Wenn der unentbehrliche Mann die Stirn runzelt
> Wanken zwei Weltreiche.
> Wenn der unentbehrliche Mann stirbt
> Schaut die Welt sich um wie eine Mutter, die keine Milch
> für ihr Kind hat.
> Wenn der unentbehrliche Mann eine Woche nach seinem
> Tod zurückkehrte
> Fände man im ganzen Reich für ihn nicht mehr die Stelle
> eines Portiers.*
>
> (10:881)

Brecht was himself aware that he had perhaps read as much into Shakespeare's text as he had read out of it. The reason he gave was that he had attempted much more than the updating of a classic whose impact has been blunted by time. He claimed he had tried to X-ray the dialectical process of history (16:888).

[45] Bryden, *Observer Review*, 9 May 1971.

His Rome is not that of the historical past any more than it is Shakespeare's. It takes its place alongside the ill-fated Paris of *Die Tage der Commune* and the triumphant Georgia of *Der kaukasische Kreidekreis* as one of those rare projections of unrealized social potential. Shakespeare's romantic tragedy has thus become a historical drama of a new and revolutionary kind. It X-rays the past in a way that transcends Shakespeare's limited historical imagination, and it projects the future as Shakespeare's political realism could never have envisaged it.

Yet Brecht was convinced that if Shakespeare had still been alive, he would have rewritten his *Coriolanus* in much the same way, 'presumably with less conviction, but with more talent' (17:1253). He was humble enough to regret the loss of artistry that his adaptation necessarily involved, and while at work on it he made the same interesting prediction that he had made with regard to his *Antigone* eight years earlier, namely that the time would come when the 'feeling for history' of the class-conscious masses would be so well developed that the original text could be left to speak its own dialectical message without the mediation of an adapter.[46] Utopia's producers will, it seems, no longer be faced like Brecht with the choice of either black-listing the classics or harnessing them by main force to the revolutionary cause. On the contrary, Brecht believed that social revolution will open up entirely new perspectives on our cultural heritage, which, freed from the ideological super-structure of a society based on exploitation, will for the first time come into its own.

[46] 'bei stärkerer entwicklung des gefühls für geschichte—und wenn das selbstbewusstein der massen grösser sein wird, kann man alles so ziemlich belassen, wie es ist' (*Arbeitsjournal*, entry for 12 Dec. 1952), Suhrkamp edn., p. 1002.

PART III:

IN SEARCH OF FORM

1. Introduction

THE problem of form was one of exceptional interest to Brecht. His preoccupation with seemingly bizarre techniques in the drama, and to a lesser extent in the novel and the lyric, earned him severe reprimands from the official interpreters of Socialist Realism, including Georg Lukács, who denounced him as a formalist. It must be emphasized that from Stalin's cultural reforms of 1934 onwards, the word 'formalist' denotes the worst kind of heretic. The *Great Soviet Encyclopedia* describes formalism as 'an artistic method that is inimical to reality', making form into a self-sufficient and autonomous entity 'to the detriment of content'. Historically the term refers to the dominant literary trend of the twenties in Soviet Russia and is associated with writers such as Jakobson, Eichenbaum, Tynianov, and, not least, Viktor Shklovski, to whom Brecht may owe some of his ideas on alienation (see below, p. 241). After Stalin had subjected Russian culture to a rigorous *Gleichschaltung* comparable to that of Nazi Germany during the same period, the term 'formalism' was used as a convenient label for all forms of art inconsistent with the principles established at the Congress of the Union of Soviet Writers in 1934. The *Encyclopedia* applies it indiscriminately to French Decadence, German Expressionism, Futurism, Surrealism, and Cubism. Brecht understandably resented being lumped together with adherents of conceptions of art very far removed from his own. In articles written at the end of the thirties, and again in the post-war period, his reply to this accusation took the form of a spirited *et tu quoque*. He objected that dogmatic insistence on formal orthodoxy is itself the worst kind of formalism.[1] In his view the problem cannot be reduced to the simplistic slogan 'formalism versus "contentism" (*Inhaltismus*)' (19:301), as though socialist writers are committed to content

---

[1] Cf. 19:287–382, 523 ff., 540 ff., 547 ff.

at the expense of form, for in reality writers who follow the authorized prescriptions are committed to a fundamentally reactionary conception of form, in the case of the novel that of Balzac and Tolstoy, in the case of the drama that of Stanislavski's neo-Aristotelianism. It made no sense to Brecht to prescribe one form as realistic and condemn all others, without first carefully defining the conception of reality that is supposedly inhibited by the one and promoted by the others. In his view a novel cannot be deemed realistic today simply because it bears a superficial resemblance to Balzac and Tolstoy, nor a theatrical work because it apes Stanislavski's productions of Chekhov. Such forms of realism were the product of specific historical factors that no longer obtain, and thus a slavish imitation of them would no longer be realistic (19:327). Conversely, even though in reality knights never fought with windmills and horses never talked, Brecht has no hesitation in calling Cervantes and Swift realists, because both in their different ways grasped imaginatively the social forces that shaped their age (19:348). Shelley resorts to grotesque distortion in his ballad *The Mask of Anarchy*, but Brecht counts him amongst the realists of the nineteenth century on the grounds that in this poem he shows himself a friend of the oppressed and thus affords insight into the social reality of his age. 'Anyone who is not the victim of formal prejudice', writes Brecht with Lukács in mind, 'knows that the truth can be concealed in many ways and must be expressed in many ways' (19:327).

There may be no truth in the apocryphal story that Brecht rejected Socialist Realism on the grounds that he was both a socialist and a realist,[2] but in one of his last essays on literature he cautions: 'The criterion should be not whether a particular work or depiction resembles other works and depictions that go under the heading of Socialist Realism, but whether it is socialist and realistic' (19:547). Brecht paraphrases the term 'realistic' as 'revealing the complex of causal factors in society / unmasking the ruling points of view as the points of view of the rulers / writing from the standpoint of the class that offers the broadest solutions for the most urgent problems of human society / emphasizing the factor of development / concrete, and facilitating abstraction' (19:326). This definition leaves

---

[2] *Geschichten vom Herrn B.*, ed. A. Müller and G. Semmer, Munich, 1968.

plenty of room for Cervantes, Swift, and Shelley, and of course, by implication, plenty of room for Brecht.

Brecht's preoccupation with the problem of form was not exclusively the product of his conversion to the Marxist rationale. He showed an iconoclastic attitude towards conventional ideas of form in both history and practice in the early twenties. But this is not to say, as many of his critics still do, that the artistic rebel and the social revolutionary are two different Brechts. The rejection of traditional form even in the early work is the result of a rejection of traditional content. Brecht had already developed a new conception of social and psychological reality during the Augsburg period, and for this conception traditional forms were totally inadequate. It was when this conception modulated into a Marxist world-view, however, that the problem of form came to a head. If, as the epitaph on Karl Marx's tomb proclaims, it is no longer a matter of interpreting the world, but of changing it, then a writer must be aware that forms conducive to mere interpretation are unlikely to prove conducive to political agitation and may even militate against it. In Hegel's words: 'True works of art are only those in which form and content prove to be completely identical.'[3] The relationship between form and content in a given work of art is so intimate that any change in the one immediately affects the other. If Brecht had ignored this basic Hegelian principle, forcing his revolutionary message into traditional moulds, it would not have the ring of truth about it that so many have discerned.

Brecht's versatility as a creative writer brought him up against problems of form in all three major fields of literary activity. The ensuing chapters particularize the problems of form presented by each of them and indicate Brecht's attempts at a solution.

---

[3] Hegel, *Sämtl. Werke* (Jubiläumsausgabe), ed. H. Glockner, Stuttgart, 1927 ff., vol. 8, p. 303.

2. Drama and Theatre

'MODERN theatre is epic theatre' (17:1008–9), proclaimed Brecht at the height of his enthusiasm for a new philosophy and the new dramatic form he thought best adapted to express it. A few years later he was calling himself the Einstein of modern drama[1] and though during the post-war era he adopted a somewhat humbler tone, recognizing that in an age of theatrical experimentation his attempt to solve the problem of form was only one of many, he was still prepared to claim that it had been the most successful.

Brecht's first works, albeit a far cry from what he was later to call Epic Theatre, already mark a clean break with theatrical tradition. Neither the text of *Trommeln in der Nacht* nor Otto Falckenberg's production of it at the Kammerspiele in Munich in 1922 owed anything to the *trompe-l'œil* of Naturalism, and little remained of the hectic symbolism and lyricism of the Expressionists. The anti-illusionistic effect of the paper moon that Kragler knocks into an empty river was enhanced, at Brecht's suggestion, by the display of placards in the auditorium, on which were inscribed sobering captions from the play, such as 'Glotzt nicht so romantisch'. Erich Engel's production of *Im Dickicht der Städte* and Alwin Kronacher's *Baal* the following year resorted to relatively few technical innovations, but the absurd, unmotivated conflict in the former and the episodic structure of the latter, and the unrealistic dialogue of both, nevertheless resulted in sensational premières that introduced bewildered audiences to an entirely new theatrical idiom. In Brecht's own production of his and Feuchtwanger's adaptation of *Edward II* at the Kammerspiele in 1924 the chronicle style of the original was emphasized by means of dated scene-headings, while the austerely furnished stage and the restrained acting showed disregard for

---

[1] Mordecai Gorelik, 'Brecht: I am the Einstein of the New Stage Form', *Theatre Arts* Mar. 1957, pp. 72–3.

the hallowed tradition of classical production in the German theatre.

It was *Mann ist Mann*, however, in many ways a transitional piece, that Brecht first described as an 'epic drama', a term that the theatrical *avant-garde* had introduced about 1924 and that Brecht probably inherited from Döblin and Piscator. In its context the term refers to the consciously anti-romantic subject matter and its quasi-scientific treatment: the behaviouristic conception of character and the studiedly undramatic, unemotional nature of the plot and dialogue (15:150). Brecht had in fact used the term before this. In an interview with Bernard Guillemin in July 1926 he spoke of the necessity in the modern theatre to outlaw feeling, on the grounds that this is a purely private affair, whereas reason is a reliable assessor of the objective truth. He demanded a style of production that brings out the events in a completely sober and matter-of-fact way, eschewing the bombast of much contemporary theatre and seeking to present the characters to the audience dispassionately. 'Ich bin für das epische Theater!', he exclaimed enthusiastically.[2] *Mann ist Mann* was produced by Jacob Geis in Darmstadt two months later, and the projected scene-titles, interspersed songs, anti-illusionistic props and décor, and the way in which the actors addressed the audience directly, all contributed to the effect of 'cool' theatre demanded by Brecht in his interview with Guillemin.

The basic ingredients of Epic Theatre were all plainly visible in the Darmstadt production of *Mann ist Mann*, many of them the direct result of a text written many years earlier, yet it was not until the autumn of 1926 that Brecht embarked on the intensive study of Marxism that was to prove the great turning-point of his life. It has been fashionable among non-Marxist critics to deduce from this that although Brecht saw a close connection between Marxism and Epic Theatre, such an alignment is quite arbitrary and we are therefore dealing with a purely aesthetic revolution, quite independent of the ideology on which Brecht grafted it. Yet the theatrical rebel who demanded an unemotional, anti-illusionistic kind of

---

[2] *Schriften zum Theater*, ed. W. Hecht, Frankfurt, 1963, p. 269. Hecht has not included this dialogue in the 1967 edition, presumably because Guillemin admitted to having bowdlerized the text.

theatre is quite consistent with the rationalist to whom Marxism appealed so strongly; conversely, the kind of experimental theatre he had already developed proved eminently conducive to the propagation of Marxism as he understood it. There were for Brecht three essential points of contact between the two: a materialist conception of man, the primacy of reason, and an unshakeable belief in the possibility of changing the world.

Brecht's rejection of individualism, analysed earlier, provides the closest link between his pre-Marxist search for a new form of drama and the conceptual world of Communism. In a discussion broadcast from Cologne in January 1929, Fritz Sternberg, the sociologist to whom Brecht owed most in his study of Marxism, defined drama from Shakespeare onwards as the product of individualism. He found it significant that Shakespeare himself, standing at the watershed between the Middle Ages and the modern era, showed no interest in the most characteristic period of Roman Republican history, preferring instead themes from Rome's remoter past, when the individual could still assert himself against the masses (*Coriolanus*), or from the period of its decline when the great individual re-emerged (*Julius Caesar* and *Antony and Cleopatra*). At this point Brecht took up the argument:

Oh, yes, the great individuals! The great individuals were the subject-matter, and the subject-matter dictated the form of these dramas. It was the so-called dramatic form, and in this context 'dramatic' means agitated, passionate, contradictory, dynamic. What was the nature of this dramatic form? What was its purpose? You can see it exactly in Shakespeare. In the course of four acts Shakespeare cuts off the great individual, Lear, Othello, Macbeth, from all human ties with the family and the state, driving him out on the heath, into total isolation, where he is required to show his greatness in defeat (15:149).

He went on to say that future generations would call such drama cannibalistic, on the grounds that the great individual is 'consumed' by the audience. Sternberg maintained that the whole conception of the individual in the literal sense of an indivisible and sovereign entity was now outdated. Collective man was the dominant idea of the age. Brecht accepted this and argued that 'epic drama' was the only form adequate to such a conception. His notes on the *Dreigroschenoper*, which was his first fully fledged epic production, are more explicit, claiming that wherever materialism predominates epic forms emerge in dramatic writing. 'Today, when the human being must be understood as the "total nexus of social relations" the epic form is the only one capable of grasping those processes that furnish a comprehensive world-view as the raw material of drama' (17:999).

Thus, on Brecht's reading, traditional drama from Shakespeare to Hauptmann glorifies the individual. Whereas in Shakespeare's time this was a progressive sign of the emancipation of Renaissance man from feudal bondage, in the capitalist era it has fulfilled a reactionary function, 'teaching people to see the world the way the ruling classes wanted it seen' (15:358). If in his theoretical essays Brecht frequently inveighs against the 'culinary' tradition of dramatic writing and theatrical production, this is not simply because such a tradition is unpolitical, but, on the contrary, because any form of theatre that allows its audience to wallow in individualistic emotion shores up a moribund social order that relies on an illusory sense of the worth and power of the individual.

It is this factor, rather than the inherent rationalism of the Marxist system, that explains Brecht's tendency to over-emphasize the primacy of reason in his early writing on theatre. If feeling is unfavourably contrasted with reason, it is not so much that Brecht rejects emotion as an improper response, but rather that he believes that the emotion stimulated by traditional drama has been put to the wrong use. Brecht argues that audiences are made to identify with the great heroes of traditional drama in order that they may indulge the illusion of power, whereas in reality they are at the mercy of economic and political forces beyond their immediate control. To ensure the success of this confidence trick it is necessary that the spectator should feel exactly what the character on the stage feels, no more and no less. Brecht objects, for instance, that King Lear's anger is contagious and that in the traditional theatre the audience's response can only be anger (15:299). In the discussion with Sternberg he compares this with the way an epileptic fit tends to induce the symptoms of epilepsy in anyone who has a latent susceptibility to the disease (15:152). On a more popular level Brecht claims to have experienced for himself the insidious effect of an appeal to the emotions that entirely bypasses reason. On watching a film loosely based on Kipling's famous ballad of Gunga Din, he found himself admiring the heroism of the British, despising the primitiveness of the Indian natives, and applauding Gunga Din's loyalty to his superiors; whereas his reason told him that the British were imperialist exploiters, that the Indians had attained a high level of civilization, and that Gunga Din was a quisling (15:430 f.). Brecht repeatedly describes traditional theatre as a form of intellectual drug-traffic[3] because, like the opium to which Marx likened religion, it paralyses the reason and induces a false sense of security in a chaotic world.

Another persistent metaphor in Brecht's theoretical writing on theatre is hypnosis. Brecht argues that traditional theatre affects the senses by means of a process akin to hypnotic suggestion. One wonders if Brecht had read Strindberg's request that his *Miss Julie* should be performed without an interval so that the audience has no chance to escape 'the suggestive influence of the author-hypnotist'.[4] The implication is again that theatre induces a condition over which the audience has no rational control. In his *Kleines Organon für das Theater* Brecht describes an imaginary visit to a theatre run on traditional lines:

Let us go into one of these theatres and observe the effect it has on the audience. Looking around one sees almost motionless figures in a peculiar state: they seem to be strenuously tensing up all their muscles, in so far as these are not already flabby from exhaustion. They take hardly any notice of each other, their attitude being solely that of people asleep, but restlessly dreaming because they are lying on their backs, as it is said people having nightmares do. They have their eyes open, but they are not looking, they are staring, just as they do not simply hear what is said but listen in like eavesdroppers. They look at the stage spellbound, an expression that has come down to us from the Middle Ages, the period of witches and clerics. Looking and listening are activities, sometimes entertaining, but these people seem absolved from all activity and resemble people to whom something is being done. (16:673–4)

In the *Mahagonny* notes he demands that the theatre abandon

---

[3] Cf. 15:305; 16:514, 661.
[4] Quoted from *Six Plays of Strindberg*, trans. E. Sprigge, New York, 1955, p. 69.

'all attempts at hypnosis, undignified intoxication and be-fuddling of the senses' (17:1011).

This is why Brecht characterizes his own form of drama as non-Aristotelian. The term as he uses it has little or nothing to do with the unities (in which Aristotle in any case showed much less interest than his neo-classical apologists). His entire polemic is directed against the psychological effect of a form of theatre that dupes its audience into a temporary suspension of dis-belief. It has been argued that empathy is not in itself an Aristotelian category and that no audience is capable of total identification.[5] Certainly, the yokel who warned Caesar against his stage assassins is not a representative theatre-goer, but it will not be denied that empathy and illusion have figured prominently in dramatic theory and practice since the Renaissance. Sir Laurence Olivier has admitted that as an actor he is 'selling an illusion all the time',[6] and Ronald Hayman says of a typical dramatic situation: 'It must almost seem possible that this Othello will not kill this Desdemona at this performance.'[7] This is precisely the illusionistic effect, a synthetic product of script, décor, acting, and artistic direction, that Brecht consistently rejects. He maintains that empathy is a *sine qua non* of traditional dramatic theory and on one occasion he paraphrases his term 'non-Aristotelian' as 'not aiming at empathy' (15:282). Empathy seems so essential to one of the disputants in the *Messingkauf* dialogues that his antagonist playfully suggests the neologism *thaëter* to designate any form of theatre that dispenses with it (16:508).

Brecht might have regarded empathy merely as an expend-able luxury, had it not been for its correlative, catharsis, to which he devotes more space in his critical writings than to any other single aspect of traditional theatre. Although, strictly speaking, this critical term applies only to tragedy, so much serious European drama has taken that form that Brecht came to regard it as the cardinal principle of dramatic tradition. In one of the *Messingkauf* dialogues he renders Aristotle's famous definition of tragedy as 'an imitative depiction of a morally serious, complete action, of such and such a length, in embellished

---

[5] Gray, *Brecht*, pp. 62–3.
[6] In an interview with Kenneth Harris for the *Observer*, 2 Jan. 1969.
[7] R. Hayman, *Techniques of Acting*, 1969, p. 2.

diction, the several kinds of which are applied separately in different parts of the work, not narrated but performed directly by characters, effecting by means of the stimulation of pity and fear the purification of such emotions' (16:507). Brecht nowhere argues a case for either of the main views on Aristotle's term κάθαρσις: the medical interpretation (now generally accepted), according to which Aristotle envisaged tragedy working on the emotional system in the same way as a purgative drug, to cleanse it of unwanted elements; or the moral interpretation, according to which tragedy accustoms us to ennobling sentiments. Nor does he explore that other moot point, whether it is a catharsis *by* or *from* pity and fear (he translates it both ways in the *Organon*). For him this is a purely academic point, since either way potentially valuable emotion is being wasted. According to the *Mahagonny* notes dramatic theatre 'consumes the spectator's activity'. This suggests that Brecht had in mind that liberating sense of reconciliation with which nearly all Shakespeare's great tragedies end, whether it is Malcolm, the lawful heir to Duncan's usurped throne, inviting us to see him crowned at Scone, or Fortinbras restoring law and order at Elsinore, or the Prince of Verona reconciling the Capulets and Montagues over the dead bodies of their children. Bradley was no doubt right to include a sense of waste amongst the essential ingredients of tragedy, but it is not the only emotion the audience is made to feel as the final curtain falls. Faced with a fundamentally ambiguous world, in which even the noblest perish, we are encouraged nevertheless to leave the theatre in that state of mind described by the final chorus of Milton's *Samson Agonistes* as 'calm of mind, all passion spent', and again in our own day by T. S. Eliot as a 'condition of serenity, stillness and reconciliation.'[8] According to Schiller such an effect justifies the description of the stage as a moral institution, since it teaches audiences the great art of enduring fate.[9] If this is catharsis, Brecht will have none of it. The pity and fear and kindred emotions aroused and purged by the tragic experience have better uses.

[8] T. S. Eliot, 'Poetry and Drama', *Selected Prose*, ed. J. Hayward, Harmondsworth, 1963, p. 81.

[9] Schiller, 'Die Schaubühne als eine moralische Anstalt betrachtet', *Werke* (Nationalausgabe), Weimar, 1943 ff., vol. 20, p. 96.

The comparative list of 'shifts of emphasis' tabulated by Brecht in his notes† on the opera *Aufstieg und Fall der Stadt Mahagonny*:

Dramatic Form of the Theatre	*Epic Form of the Theatre*
direct action	narrative
involves the audience in the action on stage	makes the audience into observers, but
uses up their activity	awakens their activity
facilitates emotions	enforces decisions
experience	image of the world
the audience is projected into an action	the audience is confronted with it
hypnotic suggestion	argument
the feelings are conserved	are impelled to the point of recognition
man is taken for granted	man is the object of inquiry
unchangeable man	man as both the subject and object of change
suspense as to the outcome	suspense as to the process
one scene leads to another	each scene a separate unit
linear development	in a series of curves
evolutionary necessity	leaps
the world as it is	the world in the process of development
man as a fixed entity	man as a process
thought determines existence	social existence determines thought
feeling	reason

† This is the list of *Akzentverschiebungen* as it was first published in the second issue of the *Versuche* in 1930. It differs considerably from that of the *Gesammelte Werke*, which is the revised version of 1938.

This raises a point of Brecht's dramatic theory that has given rise to much misunderstanding: the relationship between reason and feeling. Misled by Brecht's cryptic notes on *Mahagonny*, in which reason and feeling are held to be the dominant characteristics of the epic and dramatic forms of theatre respectively, critics and theatre-goers have concluded that he was out to rob them of their legitimate right to emotion in the theatre. He never in fact intended any such thing, even during the relatively austere period of the Lehrstücke. Such a misinterpretation of his theoretical writings ignores the caveat that accompanied his *Mahagonny* notes, in which he specifically states that his list of comparative values is not intended to represent 'absolute antitheses', but merely 'shifts of emphasis' (17:1009). Generations of students have been misled by an annotated edition of *Mutter Courage*, in which the editors mistakenly attribute to Brecht the assertion: 'Most of all we want people to think in the theatre.'[10] This much-quoted statement was actually made in a discussion of popular misconceptions about the aims and principles of the Berliner Ensemble, held in 1955, and the speaker (not Brecht) is quoting an unfavourable review. This discussion goes on to stress the importance of emotion in Epic Theatre (16:901 ff.). In one of his earliest attempts to define his form of theatre Brecht says: 'The essential thing about Epic Theatre is perhaps that it appeals more to the spectator's reason than to his feeling. The spectator is not supposed to share the experience, but to come to terms with it. It would, however, be completely wrong to deny the role played by feeling in this form of theatre'(15:132).

Brecht seems nevertheless to have realized that he over-emphasized his point in the early days, and when he revised his *Mahagonny* notes for the Malik edition of his works in 1938 he deleted the final antithesis: 'Gefühl—Ratio'. His later essays abound in statements that concede an important function to the emotions evoked by good theatre. In exile he began to compile a list of the commonest misunderstandings to which the Epic Theatre had given rise, and the notion that it is opposed to emotion was one of the first: 'Epic Theatre does not combat the emotions, but it does not stop at merely

[10] 'Wir wollen hauptsächlich, dass man denkt im Theater': see *Mutter Courage und ihre Kinder*, ed. H. F. Brookes and C. E. Fraenkel, 1960, p. 5.

producing them, it investigates them' (15:277). He goes on to accuse traditional theatre of divorcing feeling and reason by virtually eliminating the latter, which recalls an earlier dialogue in which he objects that the traditional theatre-goer is expected to hand in his reason at the cloakroom along with his hat and coat (15:189). The *Messingkauf* philosopher, who consistently represents Brecht's point of view, counters the actor's objection that his art is basically an emotional business, with the words: 'Oh, I've nothing against feelings. I agree that feelings are necessary so that representations, imitations o events can take place, and I agree that the imitations must evoke feelings' (16:506). Brecht begins to make a distinction between empathy and emotion: 'Rejection of empathy is neither the result nor the cause of a rejection of the emotions.' (15:242).

In his later writings on theatre Brecht concedes that emotional participation is a vital component of any kind of thought-process, particularly one that involves human relations. In a characteristic dialogue, Thomas, whose views largely coincide with Brecht's, rejects the contention that in Epic Theatre the rational is amplified at the expense of the emotional: 'Quite the contrary. How can you think without emotions? But just as there are erroneous thoughts, not merely imprecise ones, so there are also erroneous feelings and not merely imprecise ones. These ought to be inhibited' (15:313). Conversely, there are legitimate emotions from Brecht's point of view. In an interview with the much more orthodox Communist dramatist, Friedrich Wolf, Brecht stated:

It is not the case—although this has sometimes been alleged—that Epic Theatre ... raises the battle-cry 'Reason versus feeling'. It does not in any way renounce emotion. Least of all the sense of justice, the urge for freedom and righteous indignation. Far from renouncing them, it does not even rely on their presence, but seeks to strengthen or create them. The 'critical attitude' it strives to inculcate in its audience can never be passionate enough. (17:1144)

The Soviet producer Boris Zakhava reports that Russian audiences were moved to tears by a performance of *Mutter Courage* and he claims that this contradicts Brecht's theory.[11]

[11] B. Zakhava, 'Sila i slabost teatra Brechta', *Znamya*, no. 8, Aug. 1957, p. 162.

It can be seen from what has been said so far that this is simply not true. Epic Theatre is intended to evoke an emotional response. The emotions are, however, to be different from those stimulated by older forms of drama, and above all an effort has been made to eliminate the subconscious factor in their production. Among the emotions Brecht is fully prepared to concede are pity for Grusche and Kattrin as the victims of injustice, a different kind of pity for the ignorant workers who fail to seize their chances in *Die Mutter*, and as for the exploiter, not only anger but even pity for those such as Mother Courage who are blind to the fact that they are in turn exploited. The collaborator who describes pity for Anna Fierling's incapacity to learn from experience as a 'very noble and useful feeling' meets with no opposition from Brecht, the more especially as he points out that such a complex form of pity would have been impossible in a theatre that relies entirely on empathy (16:904). This sort of response is no doubt what Brecht had in mind when in his diary for 1938 he mentions 'a legitimate kind of empathy'.[12]

Far from conflicting with this kind of empathy, the rational process fostered by Brecht's theatre is held to amplify it so that the result is a 'natural unity of thought and feeling' (16:905). Brecht goes so far as to speak of a catharsis of the emotions that his form of theatre alone facilitates, and he describes it in this sense as 'a school of the emotions' (16:927). The interplay of feeling and reason is emphasized in the 1955 discussion of common misconceptions, which ends with the sentence: 'Feelings impel us to the utmost exertion of the reason, and reason purges our feelings' (16:919).

It will generally be agreed that whereas a sense of urgency and involvement facilitates an emotional response to the dramatic situation, a sense of detachment is more conducive to rational judgement on it, and it is essentially in this sense that Brecht uses the term 'epic' to denote his form of theatre. Current Anglo-American usage misleads some theatre-goers into expecting an element of the spectacular and panoramic in the style of Cecil B. DeMille's cinematic extravaganzas. Although Brecht does claim that his form of theatre creates an

---

[12] *Arbeitsjournal*, i, p. 35 (entry for 23 Nov. 1938).

image of the world as a whole (*Weltbild*), as distinct from the restricted segment of reality analysed by Ibsen, Chekhov, and Hauptmann, this is one of its many by-products rather than an essential distinguishing feature. Brecht's use of the word 'epic' corresponds to that of Goethe and Schiller in their famous exchange of letters in 1797, and theirs in turn looks back to Aristotle.

It is a commonplace of dramatic criticism that drama is etymologically a 'doing', a derivation to which Aristotle alludes in his definition of tragedy as 'the direct imitation of men in action (δρῶντων)'. The word epic, on the other hand, implies the use of a narrator as mediator between the events depicted and the addressee. If in classical or neo-classical tragedy the spectacular death of Hippolytus, which could in any case hardly have been depicted on the stage, is reported by the conventional messenger, this does not constitute a breach of Aristotle's ruling that tragedy must not resort to narration, since the focal point is not the death of Hippolytus but its effect on Theseus, and in both Euripides and Racine this has all the emotive immediacy of great theatre. In a famous essay on tragedy Schiller distinguishes between the two genres with reference to their dominant tense: 'All narrative forms make the present past; all dramatic forms make the past present'[13] and this distinction is recognized by Goethe in their correspondence of 1797, from which Brecht quotes in the *Organon* and again in his notes on *Antigone* (16:684; 17:1213).

This is why the list of 'shifts of emphasis' in the *Mahagonny* notes begins by contrasting the direct action of the dramatic theatre (*handelnd*) with the indirect narration of Brecht's own (*erzählend*). Brecht alters the basic tense of drama, as it were, from present continuous to past historic. His form of theatre is calculated to get the best of both worlds. Theatrical immediacy ensures emotional involvement—one thinks of Kattrin shot down by soldiers, or Grusche crossing a dangerous ravine. On the other hand, the sense of pastness created by the now familiar epic devices—narrators, choruses and songs, projected texts and captions, the brightly lit, curtainless stage that reveals not only the scene-shifting but also the sources of

[13] Schiller, 'Über die tragische Kunst', *Werke*, Nationalausgabe, vol. 20, p. 165.

lighting and music, the anti-illusionistic props and décor, and above all the anti-Stanislavski style of acting—all this strictly limits the degree of identification and is calculated to activate the spectator's rational faculties. In this way Brecht seeks to enable the audience to see emotion itself, which is 'not by any means universally human and timeless' (15:242), in historical perspective. This is one of the things Brecht means when he speaks of a 'historicizing' theatre (16:629) and elsewhere says his aim is to turn his audience into social historians (15:420).

Much of what has so far been said appears to rank Brecht alongside such dramatists as George Bernard Shaw, whom Brecht greatly admired and whose *Saint Joan* also appeals to the intellect and seeks to provide insight into a particular period of history. Brecht, however, makes much more ambitious claims for his form of drama than Shaw. He seeks not only to provide insight into the mechanics of history, but also to stimulate the desire to change its course. This is in fact the root meaning of his famous 'alienation-effect', which, although he does not appear to have used the word before 1936, has rightly been called the key concept of his whole theory of literature.[14]

No example of Brecht's sometimes irritating jargon has given rise to more discussion and more misunderstanding than *Verfremdung*. The commonest Anglo-American equivalent has misled theatre-goers into speaking of the way Brecht 'alienates the audience', a sense in which Brecht never used the term himself because it would have contradicted the very purpose of his theatre, which aims to activate the audience. Russian and Italian translators, rendering the term with *ochuzhdenie* and *straniamento* respectively, have suggested something nearer to the Theatre of the Absurd than to Brecht's Epic Theatre. The French *distanciation* and *éloignement*, favoured by Sartre, are less misleading but hardly say more than is covered by the term 'epic'. Perhaps the alternative French translation *dépaysement* best expresses Brecht's meaning, since the most important function of the technique is to transpose the stalely familiar into a new and unexpected context. Although the word 'alienation' is probably too firmly entrenched to be abandoned by

[14] Reinhold Grimm, *Bertolt Brecht: die Struktur seines Werkes*, Nuremberg, 1959, p. 14.

English critics, a recent translator has attempted to catch this sense by coining the neologism 'defamiliarization'.[15]

Taken out of context Brecht's most frequently quoted definition of *Verfremdung* does not reveal its full scope. 'An alienating (*verfremdend*) depiction', he writes in the *Organon*, 'is one that enables the object to be clearly recognized but at the same time to appear alien (*fremd*)' (16:681). This hardly distinguishes his technique from that of dramatists such as Ionesco, who insists that he has nothing in common with Brecht. The word made its first appearance at the end of 1936, however, in a discussion of the Danish première of *Die Rundköpfe und die Spitzköpfe*, and in this context its meaning is clearer. Here Brecht paraphrases *verfremdet* as 'removed from the sphere of the everyday, the self-evident, and the expected' (17:1087). A few years later Brecht amplifies this into a working definition: 'Alienating an event or a character means first of all simply stripping the event or character of its self-evident, familiar, obvious quality, and creating a sense of astonishment and curiosity about them' (15:301), and an article in the *Messingkauf* contains the statement: 'Everyday things are removed by means of this art from the realm of the self-evident' (16:621). In other words, Brecht's alienation-effect seeks to break down what Coleridge long before him called the 'lethargy of custom',[16] which inhibits true perception. As Hegel put it: 'What is familiar (*bekannt*) is not recognized (*erkannt*) precisely because it is familiar.'[17]

John Willett was the first to surmise that *Verfremdung* is a loan-translation of the Russian word *ostranenie*, coined just after the First World War by Viktor Shklovski, leader of the Formalists, though this view has met with vigorous opposition on both sides of the ideological fence.[18] Brecht visited Moscow in 1932 and again in 1935, and though he nowhere mentions Shklovski's work, he certainly knew of it from Sergei Tretyakov, and the resemblance between Shklovski's conception of artistic

---

[15] Martin Nikolaus in his translation of an article by Manfred Wekwerth: 'Brecht Today', *Tulane Drama Review*, 12, 1967–8, p. 119.

[16] Coleridge, *Biographia Literaria*, Ch. 14; *Select Poetry and Prose*, ed. S. Potter, 1950, p. 248.

[17] Hegel, Preface to *Phänomenologie des Geistes*, in *Werke*, Berlin, 1832 ff., vol. 2, p. 24.

[18] J. Willett, *The Theatre of Bertolt Brecht*, pp. 208–9; but see Hultberg, *Die ästhetischen Anschauungen Bertolt Brechts*, p. 136, and Fradkin, *Bertolt Brecht*, pp. 132–6.

'alienation' and his own is superficially very striking. In his essay 'Art as method' Shklovski defines *ostranenie* as 'not calling a thing by its usual name, but describing it as though it were being seen for the first time'[19] and he cites as a good example of it a story by Tolstoy in which all the events are seen through the eyes of a horse. A Russian dictionary of modern literary usage defines *ostranenie* as 'the accentuation of a particular element in a literary text, with the aim of stimulating a perception of it that is free from its customary associations so that it appears as something unfamiliar, something not encountered before'.[20] If this were also a satisfactory definition of *Verfremdung*, then the charge of formalism so often brought against Brecht by earlier Soviet critics would be thoroughly justified. Brecht's world would be all of a piece with that of T. S. Eliot, who claimed that the function of poetry is to 'make people see the world afresh'[21] and who cast the famous knights' scene in *Murder in the Cathedral* in prose in order to 'shock the audience out of their complacency'.[22] Marcel Duchamp, who 'defamiliarized' household utensils by exhibiting them as *objets d'art*, and Chirico, who transposed an egg to the desert in one of his paintings on the grounds that such things are otherwise so stalely familiar that they pass unnoticed, would be kindred spirits.

It is true that Brecht sometimes writes as though this were the case. His examples of the *V-Effekt* in everyday life certainly suggests such an affinity. He says that in order to see his mother as a woman and his schoolteacher as an ordinary human being a boy needs a step-father and a bailiff respectively, that driving a T-type Ford 'alienates' the modern motor car by revealing the true nature of a combustion-engine, and that the Eskimos alienate it for us in a different way by defining it as a wingless creeping aeroplane (15:356–7). Brecht applies the term *Verfremdung* to the shock-tactics of Dada and Surrealism and even to the work of Matthias Grünewald, who includes himself amongst the bystanders in his famous painting of the Crucifixion (ibid.). He repeatedly compares his own *V-*

[19] Viktor Shklovski, *Iskusstvo kak priëm*, in *O Teorii Prozy*, Moscow, 1929, p. 14.
[20] *Slovar sovremennogo russkogo literaturnogo yazyka*, Moscow, 1959.
[21] T. S. Eliot, *The Use of Poetry and the Use of Philosophy*, Cambridge, 1933, p. 149.
[22] T. S. Eliot, *Selected Prose*, 1963, p. 74.

Effekte with those of oriental theatre, which makes liberal use of anti-illusionistic décor, props, and masks, and in which the actors, who demonstrate their roles rather than impersonate them, often address the audience directly. In all these cases the subject undergoes the 'semantic shift' in which Victor Erlich discerns the essence of Shklovski's *ostranenie*.[23] Brecht is, however, usually careful to stress that the use to which such effects are put by art other than his own is very different. In the *Messingkauf*, for instance, he particularly warns the reader interested in theatrical technique that oriental *V-Effekte* cannot simply be grafted on the European stage in the name of Epic Theatre (16:626). His principal objection to them is that they tend to operate on the same level of hypnotic suggestion as traditional Western theatre and that 'the social aims of these old alienation-effects were completely different from our own' (16:681).

The point is that whereas for Shklovski, and the many others with whom Brecht is so often compared, the alienation-effect is essentially an aesthetic device that removes art still further from the world of reality, for Brecht it is not, strictly speaking, an aesthetic category at all, but an instrument of social change. 'The alienation-effect is a social device', he cautions in an appendix to the *Messingkauf*, written in 1940 (16:655), and in a 1954 addition to the *Organon*: 'Genuine alienation-effects are combative in character'(16:706). The socio-political significance Brecht attached to his idea of alienation can be seen by comparing the definitions of it quoted earlier with the passage in the *Organon* in which he explains why his own technique is so different from that of the Asiatic theatre, despite the striking resemblance: 'The function of the modern alienation-effects is to remove from events susceptible to social influence the stamp of familiarity that at present renders them immune from interference' (16:681). This immunity is the result of what Engels calls the *vis inertiae* of history.[24] As Marx puts it: 'The tradition of all past generations weighs like an Alp upon the brain of the living',[25] and in Brecht's own words: 'What has long remained unchanged seems unchangeable' (16:681). Brecht's alienation-effect is intended to break the force of inertia by showing what

---

[23] V. Erlich, *Russian Formalism*, The Hague, 1955, p.3 8; cf. *The Double Image*, Baltimore, 1964, p. 137.

[24] Dietz, vol. 22, p. 310.   [25] Ibid., vol. 8, p. 115.

we otherwise take for granted not only as remarkable, but also as capable of being changed.

Brecht anticipates this dimension of his alienation-effect in the epilogue at the end of *Die Ausnahme und die Regel*, written at least five years before his first recorded use of the term, which, as Fradkin points out,[26] shows that it is irrelevant whether or not Brecht borrowed it from Shklovski:

> So endet
> Die Geschichte einer Reise.
> Ihr habt gehört und ihr habt gesehen.
> Ihr saht das Übliche, das immerfort Vorkommende.
> Wir bitten euch aber:
> Was nicht fremd ist, findet befremdlich!
> Was gewöhnlich ist, findet unerklärlich!
> Was da üblich ist, das soll euch erstaunen.
> Was die Regel ist, das erkennt als Mißbrauch
> Und wo ihr den Mißbrauch erkannt habt
> Da schafft Abhilfe!*
>
> (2:822)

The call to arms is less strident in the major works, but it is implicit wherever the alienation-effect is in evidence: 'The purpose of the effect is to enable the spectator to exercise fruitful criticism from a social point of view' (16:553). This critical attitude, of which Brecht repeatedly speaks in connection with Epic Theatre, is not so much a balanced armchair assessment as rather a reasoned commitment to purposeful intervention. By 'fruitful' (one of his favourite words) he means 'active' and 'positive', as another context reveals (15:378). He defines criticism in this way in the *Organon*: 'In the case of a river it consists in regulating its course; in the case of a fruit-tree in the process of grafting; in the case of locomotion in the construction of vehicles and aircraft, in the case of society it consists in revolution' (16:671). (See p. 27.)

Verfremdung is a correlate of the term *Entfremdung*, which Marx took over from Hegel's philosophical vocabulary, and it seems significant that Brecht himself in one early essay on Epic Theatre uses the term *Entfremdung* to describe its function (15:265). 'The immediate task is to unmask human alienation (*Entfremdung*)', wrote Marx in 1844. Men are temporarily unfree

26 Fradkin, *Bertolt Brecht*, p. 135.

because they do not recognise the nature of the forces that determine their existence; once they have gained this insight the desire to bring them under control and so achieve freedom is held to be an instinctive response, and this is the response Brecht's alienation-effect seeks to elicit. *Verfremdung* reveals and challenges *Entfremdung*.

Brecht's idea of *Verfremdung* explains why problems of form assumed such a significance for him. In narrowing the gap between art and life the Naturalists had introduced a quasi-scientific element, to which Brecht traced the origins of Epic Theatre.[27] But they had largely ignored the question of form. Despite the furore that Hauptmann's *Die Weber* caused at the time, and despite Lenin's admiration of it as a drama of revolution, Brecht claims that its illusionistic appeal to the sympathy of the audience restricts its practical effect to superficial reforms, which not only leave the basic problem unsolved but actually facilitate a more thorough exploitation of the masses (19:364). Brecht recalls that Friedrich Wolf's *Cyankali* and Paul Credé's *Paragraph 218*, both realistic *pièces à thèse* that attacked the inhumanity of the law on abortion during the Weimar period, resulted in the free distribution of contraceptives; but in his opinion the Aristotelian form of such plays severely limits their social usefulness,[28] making them incapable of questioning the structure of society as a whole. They are too preoccupied with the minutiae of a particular environment to create the wider perspective that Brecht claimed for his Epic Theatre. 'What are the events behind the events?', is the question Epic Theatre is supposed to raise (15:258), which explains his inclusion of the word *Weltbild* on his list of its distinguishing features in the *Mahagonny* notes. One of the most interesting essays in the *Messingkauf* collection contrasts what he calls the P-type and K-type of theatrical experience. 'K' stands for roundabout (*Karussell*) and Brecht compares the artificially induced excitement of the illusionistic theatre with the thrill of being whirled past a painted landscape on imaginary horses or aeroplanes to the hypnotic blare of a fairground organ. 'P' stands for planetarium and Brecht likens the effect of his own form of theatre to the scientific experience of studying

---

[27] Cf. 15:151 and 358; 16:545 and 780.
[28] Cf. 15:248; 16:545 and 780.

the simulated movements of real constellations (16:540 ff.). Brecht acknowledges the limitations of his analogy, but its general applicability is clear enough. By dispensing with illusionism Epic Theatre seeks to provide a scientifically accurate working model of social reality that will encourage large-scale revolutionary intervention. If, like Tennessee Williams, Brecht rejects 'the exhausted theatre of realistic convention',[29] it is not in his case because literary realism is artistically inadequate, but because it is not realistic enough. For Brecht the only truly realistic form is one that elicits a dialectical response, since he sees reality itself as a dialectical process.

In the post-war period Brecht began to entertain serious doubts about the efficacy of the term 'epic' as a label for his kind of theatre, especially since in the meantime theatrical criticism had begun to apply it almost indiscriminately to the work of writers as different as Pirandello, Paul Claudel, Thornton Wilder, Tennessee Williams, Arthur Miller, Jean Anouilh, and Max Frisch, none of whom has very much to do with Epic Theatre as Brecht understood it. As early as 1929, in an essay that almost entirely avoids the word 'epic' he described his theatre as dialectical (15:211). The epic tag is again rejected as inadequate in the *Coriolan* dialogue of 1953 (16:869) and in the *Organon* appendices a year later (16:701), and although no alternative is offered, the word 'dialectic' abounds in the text; in another late and fragmentary essay the term *dialektisches Theater* actually occurs (16:923).

The embryo of this idea, as of so many others, appears in the *Mahagonny* notes, in which 'argument', as a dominant characteristic of Epic Theatre, is contrasted with the 'suggestiveness' of the traditional stage. At first sight this appears to justify a drama of ideas in which debate replaces action, as it tends to do in Shaw and in Georg Kaiser. Brecht had in fact something quite different in mind. Whereas the argument of traditional theatre is confined to the stage and the audience merely enjoys the cut-and-thrust of its dialectic, in Brecht's case the technique of *Verfremdung* is intended to make the audience an accredited partner in the debate.

[29] Quoted from the Penguin edition of *Sweet Bird of Youth, A Streetcar Named Desire*, and *The Glass Menagerie*, 1963, p. 229.

In a fragmentary but revealing note Brecht relates the effect of his Epic Theatre to the Marxist dialectic as follows:

1. Alienation (*Verfremdung*) as understanding (understanding—not understanding—understanding), negation of the negation.
2. Accumulation of incomprehensible factors until understanding occurs (conversion of quantity into quality) (15:360).

By negation of the negation, a term used rather vaguely by Marx and elucidated by Engels, Marxists usually mean the resolution of a conflict of opposing forces, at which point the antithesis suddenly passes over into the higher state of synthesis; the quantitative accumulation of internal contradictions in a given system precipitates a revolutionary development that results in a qualitatively new state. Engels discerned this dialectic at work in the natural order of things and cited the example of water turning into steam and seeds into plants. Brecht applied this to the process of audience-response in the theatre. What theoretically takes place is that *Verfremdung* accentuates the condition of unfreedom in which men live and to which they have become so inured that they take it for granted; in the perspective of Epic Theatre this familiar condition is made to appear incomprehensible; finally, as the true state of alienation is grasped, there is understanding on a higher plane. In one of his many essays on the art of acting Brecht writes: 'The self-evident is to some extent rendered unintelligible, but this is only to make it all the more intelligible' (15:355).

In the *Flüchtlingsgespräche* Brecht's exiled physicist, Ziffel, refers to Heisenberg's assertion that the scientific observation of physical objects actually changes them, and he applies the same principle to society: 'The investigation of social processes does not leave these processes untouched; it has a considerable, indeed a revolutionary effect on them' (14:1420). Wolfdietrich Rasch, to whom we owe our knowledge of the extent of the influence exerted by Karl Korsch on Brecht's thinking, has drawn attention to the overwhelming importance accorded by Korsch and his pupil to critical awareness as a factor in the revolutionary process, and he has stressed Brecht's belief that stimulating such awareness is the fundamental purpose of literature. 'If a change of consciousness takes place in literature', says Rasch, summing up Brecht's theory, 'then reality itself has been changed.'[30] In this way Brecht has sought to translate into theatrical practice a prediction of the younger Marx. 'Theory too will become a material force as soon as it seizes the masses.'[31]

Brecht's theory of literature coincides at this point with the notion of 'blik' that has enjoyed a certain vogue in post-war moral philosophy in America and that one of its exponents defines as the result of 'a situation which is seen suddenly in a new way demanding a commitment of the viewer'.[32] What is important for a full understanding of Brecht is to grasp that for him such a 'blik', though facilitated by the simulation of reality on stage, is not a derivative of it, but an independent and spontaneous reaction against it, a negation of the negation. His work has often been misunderstood for this reason. The 'message' of *Mutter Courage* or *Der gute Mensch von Sezuan* has been sought in the text of the play itself: audiences have accepted Mother Courage's defiant gesture in the final scene as an affirmation of human courage in the face of over-whelming odds, or they have seen in Shen Te's tragic dilemma an insoluble existential problem. But the technique of *Verfremdung* is intended to elicit a dialectical response: the audience is supposed to reject both the blind courage of the one and the defeatism of the other and in imagination reconstruct their respective worlds in such a way that the tragic issue is no longer necessary. The famous epilogue in *Der gute Mensch von Sezuan* explicitly challenges the audience to look for a solution:

> Verehrtes Publikum, los, such dir selbst den Schluß!
> Es muß ein guter da sein, muß, muß, muß!*
>
> (4:1607)

Brecht maintains that the spectators' conditioned response to the tragic experience is to say in effect: 'This character's suffering moves me because there is no way out for him'; confronted with a comparable situation in the Epic Theatre he is supposed to say: 'This character's suffering moves me because there *is* a way out for him' (15:265). If there is anagnorisis in Brecht's non-Aristotelian form of drama, it is experienced by the audience, not by the tragic hero. In 1949

---

[30] Rasch, p. 996 (see p. 66 n. 10).   [31] Dietz, vol. 1, p. 385.
[32] Paul van Buren, *The Secular Meaning of the Gospel*, Penguin edn., 1963, p. 147.

Friedrich Wolf, author of such Communist classics as *Die Matrosen von Cattaro* and *Tai Yang erwacht*, had a conversation with Brecht, later published in *Theaterarbeit* under the significant title 'Formprobleme des Theaters aus neuem Inhalt', in the course of which he queried the wisdom of leaving Mother Courage in the error of her ways. Surely it would be more effective, he suggested, if her words 'Verflucht sei der Krieg', uttered after the assault on Kattrin half-way through the play, came right at the end. Brecht objected that he was too much of a realist for this: 'But even if Courage fails to learn anything—the audience can in my opinion nevertheless learn something by watching her' (17:1147). Later Brecht said that his heroine learns no more from the catastrophe that overwhelms her than a guinea-pig learns of biology: 'It is not the playwright's job to open Mother Courage's eyes to the truth at the end—he is concerned to make the audience see it' (17:1150).

Even the failure of the Zurich audience to suppress its sympathy for Mother Courage in 1941 did not lead to sweeping changes in the text. Brecht put it down partly to Therese Giehse's emotive performance, but mainly to the fact that audiences have been brainwashed into empathy. In a publicity handout for *Theaterarbeit* which was published in 1952, Brecht wrote: 'Two arts need to be developed: the art of acting and the art of watching' (16:710). Only a mature audience-response makes Epic Theatre in Brecht's sense possible.

The independent function of the audience in such a conception of theatre explains why Brecht was less preoccupied with the question of drama as a literary form than with the theatre as a social institution. Whereas Lessing, who himself had a lively interest in the practical side of theatre, published his reviews under the title *Hamburgische Dramaturgie*, Brecht's most systematic attempt to formulate a coherent theory of drama is entitled *Kleines Organon für das Theater*, and although the term *episches Drama* occurs in the early essays it was quickly abandoned in favour of *episches Theater*. Even the spirited reviews Brecht wrote for the left-wing Augsburg daily, *Der Volkswille*, during his student days show much more interest in the practicalities of theatre than in the literary aspects of the Augsburg repertoire. His principal objection to fourth-wall theatre as a whole is that the audience is virtually redundant.

'A theatre that fails to make contact with the audience is a nonsense', he wrote even before his decisive reading of Marx (15:83). Sir Laurence Olivier has defined the essential quality of the theatre as 'the participation of a watching group in the group which it watches' and he claims that of all the arts only the theatre can provide 'this peculiar reciprocal experience'.[33] Brecht goes even further and describes the function of the audience as 'co-authorship' (*Ko-fabulieren*) (16:924).

For Brecht Epic Theatre is more realistic than even the most illusionistic products of Naturalism, and this includes the variant developed by Stanislavski into the authorized vehicle of Socialist Realism in Russia. In one of the *Messingkauf* dialogues a worker demands realistic acting, to which the philosopher representing Brecht's views replies: 'But the fact that one is sitting in the theatre and not in front of a keyhole is surely also a reality! How can it be realistic to conceal this fact behind grease-paint? No, we must pull down the fourth wall' (16:579). The removal of the fourth wall and the operation of *Verfremdung* in Brecht's form of theatre transfers the centre of gravity of the piece from the stage to the auditorium. The dialectical interplay between mimesis and observation, drama and audience, was for Brecht a true image of social reality. Exposed to his form of dramatic art in the theatre, the audience participates in the revolutionary process of history.

The foregoing analysis sheds some light on one of the most remarkable paradoxes in Brecht's writing. What is presented often seems to reflect a predominantly tragic vision, yet the intention behind it, and the response aimed at, are essentially optimistic and are based on a belief in progress through contradiction. In an obituary one of Brecht's French admirers called him 'l'homme incapable de tragédie'.[34] If Brecht's theatre is judged by its intention rather than its effect then this is certainly true. Brecht does not eliminate the term 'tragic' from his aesthetic vocabulary and he uses it liberally of *Die Tage der Commune* and *Coriolan*, but certainly he felt that tragedy as an art-form reflects an obsolescent civilization. 'Tragedy', he wrote as early as 1921, 'is based on bourgeois virtues, draws its strength from them, and will perish along with them' (15:57).

[33] See p. 233 n. 6.
[34] D. Fernandez, *La nouvelle Nouvelle Revue Française*, July–Dec. 1956, p. 726.

Modern man is no longer ready to learn humility in the face of inscrutable powers because he no longer believes in them. George Steiner, in his diagnosis of the decay of the tragic form, has argued that whereas true tragedy is 'irreparable', the typical crises of modern drama can be solved 'by saner economic relations or better plumbing'.[35] It would admittedly take much more than this to solve the problems of Johanna Dark, the Young Comrade, Shen Te, Mother Courage, Galilei and Coriolan, to say nothing of the Paris Communards, and even Grusche is only saved by a fluke, but Brecht can envisage a distant Utopia in which their individual tragedies need not take place. Ultimately all catastrophes are, like the rise of Arturo Ui, resistible.

Friedrich Dürrenmatt, who for very different reasons shares Brecht's scepticism about the viability of the tragic form, writes that whereas tragedy is the product of an ordered society, the dramatic form in which the grotesque disorder of our own civilization can best be reflected is comedy. Although *Trommeln in der Nacht* and *Mann ist Mann* are the only plays Brecht calls comedies on the title-page, his work as a whole abounds in comic invention. Eric Bentley, comparing Brecht with Aristophanes, has rightly described his whole dramatic theory as a theory of comedy.[36]

Brecht acknowledged that many of his *V-Effekte* belong to the stock-in-trade of traditional comedy (15:309) and he told the Milan producer, Giorgio Strehler, that if he wanted to achieve a truly epic dimension in a play it would have to be directed along the lines of a comedy, on the grounds that in a comedy there is *Verfremdung* to start with.[37] 'Humor ist Distanzgefühl', he wrote in one of his earliest essays on literature, (18:3). Thus the comic effects in his plays are calculated to set the audience at that one vital remove from reality that enables them to judge it impartially and, in Brecht's special sense of the word, critically.

At the same time comedy is an end in itself. The Marxist dialectic has been dubbed 'the cult of contradiction' and, since comedy and contradiction are very closely related, it follows

[35] George Steiner, *The Death of Tragedy*, 1963, p. 8.
[36] Quoted from *Seven Plays by Bertolt Brecht*, p. xvii.
[37] Quoted from the *Dreigroschenbuch*, Frankfurt, 1960, p. 134.

that any art-form designed to reflect the basic contradictions of which reality is compounded will tend to be comic. Brecht himself relates humour and dialectics. In the *Flüchtlingsgespräche* Ziffel declares that he has never met anyone capable of understanding Hegel, the father of the dialectical method of analysis, without a sense of humour (14:1462), and he describes Hegel's great treatise on logic as one of the most comical works in world literature. It may well be doubted whether many readers share Ziffel's sophisticated sense of humour, but his point is clear. Hegel's entire philosophical system, like that of Marx after him, is based on the notion of inherent contradiction, 'the interpenetration of opposites', as Engels later called it, and inasmuch as the sudden revelation of a basic contradiction tends to have a comic effect, a dialectical philosophy is in this sense intrinsically 'comic'.

Herr Puntila und sein Knecht Matti provides the best illustration of the tendency of Brecht's most characteristic work to assume the guise of comedy. The contradiction between the harassed mother and the calculating opportunist in Anna Fierling, the irresponsible gourmet and the revolutionary scientist in Galileo Galilei, the kindly prostitute and the ruthless exploiter in Shen Te-Shui Ta, have tragic implications (at least in a limited sense), but the contradiction between the hail-fellow-well-met in the drunken Puntila and the joyless grasping landowner who dominates him during his occasional 'attacks of sobriety', is uninhibitedly comic. The prologue reveals the function comedy is intended to have in this work, which was written in Finland during the first year of the war under conditions that scarcely fostered the spirit of comedy. Spoken by the actress taking the part of the milkmaid, it begins:

> Geehrtes Publikum, der Kampf ist hart
> Doch lichtet sich bereits die Gegenwart.
> Nur ist nicht überm Berg, wer noch nicht lacht
> Drum haben wir ein komisches Spiel gemacht.*
>
> (4:1613)

This indicates that the comedy will be neither the *humour noir* of a chaotic world beyond redemption that one finds so often in Adamov and Beckett, nor the escapist buffoonery of a Whitehall farce. The corollary of the third line is that anyone capable of laughing at the contradiction Brecht held to be characteristic of all society, including Nazi society, is already 'out of the wood' because he has already notionally solved the contradiction. This is why the prologue presents Puntila as a prehistoric monster, *estatium possessor*. Laughter makes him obsolescent and projects the spectator into a future society, in which both the landowner and the schizophrenic condition he suffers from will be regarded as truly 'prehistoric', in Marx's special sense of the word (see p. 128).

Puntila offers an interesting perspective on the kind of theatre one might expect to survive the advent of the socialist Utopia. Lunacharski, the first Soviet Commissar of Education, maintained that Communist culture would dispense with tragedy, and in *Language and Silence* George Steiner ventures to predict that instead of the *lacrimae rerum* the theatre of Utopia will evoke 'the laughter of intelligence': 'If future society assumes the contours foretold by Marxism, if the jungle of our cities turns to the polis of man and the dreams of anger are made real, the representative art will be high comedy.'[38] Brecht is less dogmatic. While engaged on the adaptation of both *Antigone* and *Coriolanus*, as we have seen, he anticipated an age of emancipation in which sophisticated audiences will again be able to enjoy tragedy, because it will no longer subserve a moribund ideology, and because in the meantime they will have learned the art of dialectical analysis. But it is certain that he did not envisage the tragic emotion remaining a constituent element of post-revolutionary theatre, which would more probably be characterized by the urbane serenity that Schiller called 'Gemütsfreiheit' and that is most often associated with high comedy. Of Brecht's early works perhaps *Mann ist Mann*, of his later works *Puntila*, come nearest to establishing a prototype. Brecht has been quoted as saying that God spends all day laughing at himself.[39] In a world where all contradiction is seen as soluble the theatre will encourage utopian man to do the same.

---

[38] *Language and Silence*, p. 424.   [39] See Willett, p. 84.

3. Fiction

AN interest in fiction came naturally to a dramatist who consciously introduced a narrative dimension into his form of drama. Yet the novel and the short story are the poor relations in Brecht's literary career. He theorizes about these forms much less than he does about the drama, and he seems to have tried his hand at them largely because they promised quicker returns than other genres, or, in exile, because a reading public was the only one he could still reach if he continued to write in German. Nevertheless his narrative prose as a whole constitutes a fifth of his total *œuvre* and includes three large-scale novels in varying stages of completeness, together with a considerable number of short stories.

The novel was of special interest to Brecht. He was a voracious reader and in his critical writings he shows a detailed knowledge of most of the major European novelists, from Cervantes and Swift to Thomas Mann and Hemingway, as well as a large number of more popular writers such as G. K. Chesterton and Dorothy L. Sayers. In the late thirties Brecht found himself increasingly obliged to come to terms with the novel as a literary form, and with the nineteenth-century novel in particular, since it was largely to novelists such as Balzac and Tolstoy that Georg Lukács looked when he sought to establish the critical norms of Socialist Realism. As the introduction to this section indicated, Brecht took issue with Lukács on the definition of such terms as 'realism' and 'formalism', and he insisted that the adjective 'realistic' could not meaningfully be defined as 'written in the style of realistic bourgeois novels of the previous century' (19:340).

Although Brecht's major concern was the charge of heresy brought against him as a dramatist by fanatical adherents of Socialist Realism at the end of the thirties, the dispute must have been exacerbated by the fact that he had already published a full-length novel of his own, which flouts most of the conventions observed by the nineteenth-century novelists, and he was engaged on an even more revolutionary successor.

Der Dreigroschenroman, like both of Brecht's later attempts at the novel-form, is essentially a by-product of his work as a dramatist, It is in effect a revision of *Die Dreigroschenoper*, which in 1928 established his international reputation almost overnight. No doubt Brecht, whose financial situation was always precarious, was anxious to cash in on the popularity of the musical, especially since his hopes for a film on the same subject had been dashed. Moreover, the advent of National Socialism rendered the German theatres inaccessible. But the sequel cannot be dismissed as a mere pot-boiler. If the Nero Film Company rejected the script from which the novel later emerged, it was not because the Dreigroschen theme was no longer a marketable product (Pabst's film, of which Brecht washed his hands in the summer of 1931, was a box-office success), but because Brecht had materially altered his conception of it. He had faced the fact that the muted social criticism underlying the stage-version passed unnoticed even by the militant Left and therefore needed amplification. And in the meantime the Wall Street crisis and the rise of Fascism had added two new factors that had to be absorbed into any comprehensive analysis of contemporary society. These factors, already apparent in the abortive film-script that Brecht submitted in 1930, were still further accentuated in the novel. Brecht began work on it in Denmark early in 1934 and by the summer he was reading the proofs.

In view of its origins it is hardly suprising if, at first sight, the *Dreigroschenroman* seems to fit into Edwin Muir's category of the dramatic novel. Its four hundred pages relate the events of a mere six months during the Second Boer War, and with the exceptions of Coax's trips to inspect potential troop-carriers in Southampton and Polly's secret honeymoon in Liverpool, its scene never shifts away from London's commercial and banking centre and its insalubrious dockland. Muir argues that such a severely restricted stage is an essential feature of the dramatic novel and constitutes 'the framework within which the logic of the action can develop unimpeded, and shut off from the arbitrary influence of the external world'.[1] Certainly, the action of Brecht's novel is remorselessly logical, and if the outside world is mentioned at all it is only to register the influence exerted on it by the action—in this case the impact of Peachum's coffin-ship swindle and the frustrated dock-strike on the war in South Africa.

The unity of place commonly observed by dramatic novelists usually compensates for the lack of panoramic breadth by intensifying local colour. Dickens's Coketown, Hardy's Casterbridge, Balzac's Saumur, and the anonymous estate in Goethe's *Die Wahlverwandtschaften* attain a vivid reality that vies with that of the characters. Brecht's London seems comparable at first. The arena is authentically staked out with familiar landmarks: the City, St. Paul's, the Old Bailey, the West India Docks, Scotland Yard, Smithfield Market, and Covent Garden; Kensington, Whitechapel, Limehouse, Poplar, Lambeth, Chelsea, Battersea, and Hampstead. All this builds up impressively, but for all that the contours of Brecht's London seem hazy and blurred, as though they were obscured by the symbolic fog that continually drifts through its streets. Little or no attempt is made to squeeze any local colour out of these topographical details, which remain conventional tags like Shakespeare's Bohemia or the Forest near Arden. Brecht shows his customary indifference to authenticity, identifying Newgate as a working-class district of Victorian London, and writing Coventgarden and Turnbridge. The topography did not interest Brecht, and it is not intended to interest the reader. The Turkish Baths, in which Peachum meets his fellow directors of the Marine Shipping Company, are very precisely located at the corner of Fourney Street and Dean Street, but the realistic effect is attenuated by prefacing the chapter in which the Baths are first mentioned (Chapter 6) with a lengthy quotation from the Book of Job, and then stressing the comically symbolic overtones of the scene: as Coax embarks on his extortionate scheme his partners are both literally and metaphorically sweating it out. In this novel Brecht's London is interchangeable with the Chicago of his earlier work as a symbolic megalopolis, the urban jungle where Peachum and Macheath are embroiled in much the same existential struggle as Shlink and

[1] Edwin Muir, *The Structure of the Novel*, London, 1967, p. 59.

Garga. As a geographical symbol, however, London has the advantage of being at the time the world's largest city, so that the reader, like the unfortunate Fewcoombey, finds himself 'in einer großen und geordneten Stadt, der Hauptstadt der Welt' (13:734). The cover of a popular English translation proclaims that it is 'a sordid Dickensian town',[2] but any attempt on Brecht's part to vie with Dickens in his depiction of Victorian London would have invalidated his novel as a symbolic statement about world capitalism.

For the same reason little or no attempt is made to give the novel the period flavour captured so nostalgically by such writers as Galsworthy and Arnold Bennett. The early Victorian background of the *Dreigroschenoper* has been updated to allow for the rampant jingoism at the time of the Second Boer War. In Brecht's London the traveller has the choice of tram, hackney carriage, and train, and he may read *The Times* by gaslight, but these are almost the only concessions to popular expectations of period flavour. The elaborate machinery of finance and big business, and the problems of an economy beset by strikes, lock-outs, and mass demonstrations, are essentially those of any industrial society of the last hundred years. Brecht did not even bother to look up the dates of the Boer War (he postdates the siege of Mafeking by two years and antedates the death of Lord Kitchener by fourteen). For Brecht there are much bigger issues at stake than those accessible to conventional realism. Victorian England is a transparent metaphor for Weimar Germany. Its cash-value is particularly apparent at the point where Peachum visualizes the burning-down of Westminster Abbey by a cabinet minister, or when left-wing agitators are made the scapegoats for the sinking of a coffin-ship, or when the narrator stresses Macheath's abstemiousness, vegetarianism, and humble origins. Not that the *Dreigroschenroman* is a simple *roman à clef* any more than the Caesar-novel, but a liberal sprinkling of allegorical features is intended to impress upon the reader the contemporary relevance of its basic theme, just as the mock-heroic comparison of Macheath with Napoleon, and Peachum's reference to Neanderthal man, ironize and universalize the struggle at one and

---

[2] *Threepenny Novel* (originally *A Penny for the Poor*), trans. Desmond Vesey and Christopher Isherwood, Penguin Books, 1965.

the same time. Ilya Fradkin is understandably disturbed by the tendency to schematization in this novel, since it conflicts with the principles of Socialist Realism, but he aptly states the case when he says that Brecht 'sees his task as helping the reader to turn aside from the narrow local-historical situation, reach conclusions of a more general nature and pass sentence on capitalist society as a whole'.[3] In other words, the dominant principle of Brecht's theatre, *Verfremdung*, also operates behind the imaginative world of his fiction.

The principle of *Verfremdung* has a significant effect on the structure. Despite the tightly knit plot, this 'dramatic' novel cannot end with the sense of equilibrium that Edwin Muir finds in typical examples of that genre. Muir sees in the death of Heathcliff and Catherine on the inhospitable Yorkshire Moors, or in the death of Ahab after his titanic struggle with the white whale, a 'catastrophe which cannot be pursued further'.[4] Brecht's novel ends with the execution of George Fewcoombey, a one-legged veteran of the Boer War, for the murder of Mary Swayer. The reader knows he is completely innocent of the crime, but, unlike the *Dreigroschenoper* with its cynically conventional happy ending, the novel permits no last-minute reprieve. Macheath and Peachum join forces to enjoy their ill-gotten gains, for which an insignificant go-between pays with his life. The ending is as provocatively untidy as that of most of Brecht's plays. If there is drama in the *Dreigroschenroman* it has essentially the same 'non-Aristotelian' character as Epic Theatre (Brecht had in fact applied the term 'non-Aristotelian' to the novel at the end of the twenties, several years before he adopted it to describe his form of theatre; 15:17).

Closely linked with this is Brecht's almost total renunciation of suspense, which, as E. M. Forster has observed, is the most atavistic and persistent element in narrative art.[5] The reader is warned of the impending death of George Fewcoombey in the first chapter, reminded of it half-way through, and then casually informed of it in the final paragraph with almost the identical words used hundreds of pages earlier. As in Brecht's drama, so in his fiction it is 'suspense as to the process' (*Spannung*

[3] Fradkin, *Bertolt Brecht*, p. 149.
[4] Muir, *Structure of the Novel*, p. 58.
[5] E. M. Forster, *Aspects of the Novel*, Penguin edn., 1962, p. 34.

auf den Gang) not 'suspense as to the outcome' (*Spannung auf den Ausgang*)[6] that commands the reader's interest. This may be why the plot of the *Dreigroschenoper* is plainly discernible. The reader knows in advance what will happen and can bring to the novel that same detached attitude that he is expected to bring with him into Brecht's theatre.

Brecht's rejection of empathy as a wasteful anachronism of the Aristotelian theatre has its exact counterpart in the novel. 'The whole technique of empathy in the bourgeois novel has reached a fatal crisis', he writes in the aftermath of the controversy with Lukács (19:377), and he relates this crisis in particular to the predominance of a single central character in so much traditional fiction. Repeating the argument he had already applied to drama, he argues that individualism is dead and therefore any formal technique devoted to the characterization of a dominant individual is fundamentally reactionary. Elsewhere he accuses Lukács of being unrealistic (*wirklichkeitsfremd*) in his demand for individual characterization in the novel. A writer cannot put the clock back, he argues: 'The human being will not become human again by emerging from the masses, but by becoming part of the masses' (19:298). He objects that Lukács is continually harking back to Balzac, whose technique of characterization typifies the age for which he wrote, the 'jungle era of capitalism' in which individualism was rife (311). Brecht must certainly have been thinking of his own first novel when he wrote these essays, for his *Dreigroschenroman* renounces heroes as emphatically as his plays. Macheath does not attain the stature of a conventional villain, much less that of a hero. The few sympathetic traits that survived from *The Beggar's Opera* in Brecht's stage-version have disappeared, and yet even as a *picaro* Macheath is never allowed to dominate the reader's interest in the same way as he dominates his underlings. Peachum, Polly, and Coax enjoy still less of the limelight, and even George Fewcoombey, despite his importance as a kind of chorus-figure, never looks like developing into a hero.

The elimination of empathy is assisted by the paucity of physical description, which is all the more surprising in a novel based on a film-scenario. George Cruikshank and 'Phiz' had no difficulty in accumulating visual detail for the sketches

---

[6] See above, p. 235.

that still embellish editions of Dickens's novels, for the narrator himself supplies them in abundance. By contrast, Brecht's narrator is very niggardly. Peachum is 'a small man' with 'a fleshy and brutal appearance' when roused, but the reader is specifically informed that he would scarcely have attracted attention in a crowd; Polly has 'a very beautiful skin'; Macheath is 'a short stocky forty-year-old with a head like a radish'; Coax, the crooked broker, wears gloves to avoid handling dirt; Mary Swayer is 'a pretty, buxom blonde in her late twenties' (a fact so unimportant that the narrator later changes her age).

Physical description of the habitat was the nineteenth-century novelist's commonest method of indirect characterization—one thinks of Balzac's leisurely introduction to *Eugénie Grandet*—but Brecht's narrator assiduously avoids it. By contrast with the copious details we are given of Fagin's malodorous den, Peachum's instrument shop (in reality a factory for the production of the gear needed by his sham beggars) is simply described as narrow, having two windows and 'a rambling interior'; Fanny Crysler, Macheath's agent and mistress, inhabits 'a small apartment in Lambeth with attractive old furniture and a spare bedroom', a milieu that adequately reflects Macheath's taste and requirements; Brown has pictures of Queen Victoria and the Duke of Wellington by turns on his wall to illustrate the bogus patriotism that characterizes nearly everyone in the book. Perhaps the most revealing descriptive comment is the observation that Coax works 'in one of the City's innumerable small, bare, yellow-furnished offices'. If there is nothing in them to attract the well-trained eye of the nineteenth-century novelist it is because, like the characters themselves, they resemble too closely the countless others that they are intended to represent.

'Life escapes', complained Virginia Woolf of the realistic novelist's obesssion with physical detail.[7] Similarly, during the debate with Lukács, Brecht insists that realism should not be confused with sensualism, which he links with empathy (19:326 and 371). Enabling the reader to smell, taste and feel everything a character does, in no way pins down the social reality to which he contributes. If in Chapter 15 Brecht's

---

[7] Virginia Woolf, 'Modern Fiction', *Collected Essays*, vol. 2, 1966, p. 105.

narrator indulges in a graphic description of Macheath tackling his breakfast egg in his prison cell, from which, like Al Capone, he still rules his empire, it is because it impresses on Polly the ruthlessness that marks this racketeer of genius. The passage suggests a parody of the bourgeois realist's technique. Brecht has no time for 'long detailed scenes with *intérieur*' (19:299).

Brecht's use of the term *intérieur* in this context indicates that his affinity with Virginia Woolf is restricted to an aversion for physical detail. The life that Virginia Woolf saw escaping from the conventional novel was the inner life of the characters. Brecht, on the other hand, evinces no more interest in this in his fiction than he does in his plays, and the 'stream of consciousness' that had established a seemingly irreversible trend in the European novel within Brecht's own lifetime plays no part in it. In a later essay on realism in literature he writes: 'Novelists who replace the description of the character by a description of his psychological reactions and thus resolve him into a mere complex of psychological reactions fail to do justice to reality' (19:321). Such reactions are from Brecht's point of view merely the epiphenomena of economic forces, and it is with these forces that the realistic novelist must concern himself, not with 'psyches, artificially separated from their environment' (358). Brecht guards against the common assertion that as a Marxist he is 'against the individual' as such(309), but to reduce the individual to a bundle of nervous reactions is putting the cart before the horse. Despite his admiration of James Joyce in general and of his *Ulysses* in particular, the concluding *monologue intérieur* that tips out the unedited contents of Marion Bloom's mind onto the last fifty pages of Joyce's masterpiece would be quite unthinkable in Brecht's fiction.

Here and there Brecht parodies the psychological novel in his *Dreigroschenroman*. The narrative is interspersed by italicized passages, most of which purport to convey the unspoken thoughts of one of the characters. The following passage is typical:

'Sie warten nur darauf, Verträge machen zu können', dachte Macheath angewidert. 'Dabei ekelt mich, den einstigen Straßenräuber, dieses Gefeilsche wirklich an! Da sitze ich dann und schlage mich um Prozente herum. Warum nehme ich nicht einfach mein

Messer und renne es ihnen in den Leib, wenn sie mir nicht das ab-
lassen wollen, was ich haben will? Was für eine unwürdige Art, so
an den Zigarren zu ziehen und Verträge aufzusetzen! Sätzchen soll
ich einschmuggeln und Andeutungen soll ich fallen lassen! Warum
dann nicht gleich lieber: das Geld her, oder ich schieße? Wozu
einen Vertrag machen, wenn man mit Holzsplitterunterdiefinger-
nägeltreiben das Gleiche erreicht? Immer dieses unwürdige
Sichverschanzen hinter Richtern und Gerichtsvollziehern! Das
erniedrigt einen doch vor sich selber. Freilich ist mit der einfachen,
schlichten und natürlichen Straßenräuberei heute nichts mehr zu
machen. Sie verhält sich zu der Kaufmannspraxis wie die Segel-
schiffahrt zur Dampfschiffahrt. Ja, aber die alten Zeiten waren
menschlicher.'* (13:1129)

The chapter from which this passage is taken is ironically
entitled 'Fog', but Macheath's thoughts are far from nebulous.
He articulates with complete lucidity a cynical world-view that
affects to find the good old days of open banditry more human
than the disguised exploitation practised by modern capitalism.
It is clear that Macheath himself could never have entertained
such thoughts. They are ascribed to him by a narrator who has
chosen this typically oblique method of social criticism. In the
same way Peachum hypocritically consoles himself with the
thought that catastrophes such as the sinking of his coffin-ship
are natural and inevitable hazards, and he goes on to diagnose
the problem of unemployment in the same way: 'Da sind zum
Beispiel meine Angestellten. Ich profitiere davon, daß sie nicht
wissen, wo sie hingehen sollen, wenn ich sie auf die Straße
werfe. Ich bedrücke sie so gut ich kann und ziehe meinen
Gewinn heraus. Sie müssen, das kann ich annehmen, ein
starkes Bedürfnis nach Hilfe haben. Vielleicht wäre also auch
noch ein Gewinn daraus zu ziehen, ihnen zu helfen?'* (13:1103).
He contemplates the introduction of a compulsory health
insurance scheme, from which few but himself would benefit,
since the workers mostly die off anyway or cannot prove they
are ill; the state might be induced to curb the 'criminal optimism' of those who think they can get by without insurance.
Integrity is not one of Peachum's virtues, but even he is
incapable of such shameless reasoning, since he cannot understand his social situation as clearly as this stream of consciousness indicates. On another occasion George Fewcoombey

passionately denounces the system that punishes girls who refuse to bring their illegitimate children into 'these over-crowded stinking hovels, filled with the cries of the starving'. But his remarks are sharply ironized by the narrator, who comments that this is what Fewcoombey would have been thinking if he had been thinking at all: 'Aber er dachte nicht: er war zur Disziplin erzogen' (805). It is not Few-coombey but his creator who is thinking aloud, and such monologues, far from illuminating the individual psyche of the character concerned, function in much the same way as the interpolated songs in the plays, interrupting the action and provoking thought. The italics replace the special lighting that Brecht asked for in his staging of the songs in the *Drei-groschenoper*.

At the end of Chapter 13 the narrator tells the reader what Fewcoombey is *probably* thinking as he finishes off the dying Coax with his wooden leg. This pretence of ignorance is a playful indication that Brecht has entirely abandoned the convention of an omniscient narrator. His narrator is not above the occasional outburst of caustic humour at his characters' expense: thus we are informed that Coax's uncontrollable attacks of sensuality are the result of constipation, and that Peachum, a formidable adversary in his own sphere, is as harmless in his dealings with Coax as a crocodile in Trafalgar Square. But in general the narrator keeps himself aloof from both characters and events and confines himself to the 'cine-matic method' that Brecht admired in R. L. Stevenson (18:24 ff.). He relays what he can see and hear as an impartial observer and affects to know little more than his characters. Although the author himself avowedly knows better, his narra-tor makes no attempt to contradict Coax when the latter accuses the socialists of crude materialism or the right-wing press when it denounces their hypocrisy. Indeed, he tacitly assents to the view that the attack on Macheath's illicit chain-store business by the left-wing press cannot be taken seriously on the grounds that it is unsporting and in any case aims at the forcible overthrow of the existing social order.

The sham monologues, however, in themselves show that the reader is not to be left entirely to his own devices. Revolu-tionary conviction bursts through the pose of impartiality at

significant points. The two apocalyptic glimpses of the wrath
to come, vouchsafed to Brown and Fewcoombey, are an additional clue to the way in which the novel is to be read.
Peering down into the murky waters of the Thames, Brown has
a hysterical vision of the irresistible rise of the downtrodden;
Fewcoombey presides over a nightmarish tribunal in which
he condemns Christ for encouraging the illusion that everyone
receives a talent, and condemns himself for believing it.
Neither of these dreams, in which the voice of prophecy
momentarily relieves the sordid reality of the present, emerges
logically from the characters as Brecht has portrayed them.
They are inserted to compensate for the loss of clarity that
results from Brecht's renunciation of both traditional and more
modern narrative techniques.

The usual alternative to the omniscient narrator in the
modern novel is the carefully controlled perspective which has so
consistently been termed 'point of view' since Henry James
that Brecht himself quotes the term in English (19:299). In the
opening chapter of his *Dreigroschenroman* it looks as though
Brecht has opted for this alternative. George Fewcoombey has
no counterpart in the *Dreigroschenoper* (though his role is fore-
shadowed to some extent by that of Filch). In the novel he is a
wounded veteran of the Boer War, recruited in Peachum's
fraudulent organization. He dominates the first chapter and
the epilogue, but apart from intermittent appearances as
general factotum, and even as an unsuccessful assassin, he is
largely ignored in between. And his is assuredly not the 'fine
central intelligence' that Henry James looked for in a good
novel. Yet, paradoxically, if James's 'commanding centre' is
sought in the *Dreigroschenroman* it can only be found in the
figure of Fewcoombey, despite his neglect by the fast-moving
plot. That the novel is in a very real sense his, is indicated by
its title and endorsed by the apocalyptic dream with which it
closes. Of the latter Fradkin writes: 'Brecht's impatient anger
is directed not only against the crimes of the ruling class in the
form of open violence, but also against the corrupting influence
of bourgeois ideology on the consciousness of the backward
workers.'[8] But Brecht has gone much further than this. In
making George Fewcoombey condemn himself to death in his

[8] Fradkin, *Bertolt Brecht*, p. 150.

dream he indirectly accuses the working classes of unwitting complicity in the crimes committed against them by their exploiters. Fewcoombey's execution for a crime of which he is innocent is a kind of poetic justice by which he is punished for retarding the Revolution.

It is significant that of the novelists Brecht most admired, Swift, Cervantes, Joyce, Döblin and Hašek are all grouped together in his mind as satirists, for Brecht's approach to the craft of fiction is essentially that of a satirist. His *Dreigroschenoper* was already an elaboration of the satirical tone set by the opening song of *The Beggar's Opera*:

> Through all the Employments of Life
>> Each Neighbour abuses his Brother;
> Whore and Rogue they call Husband and Wife;
>> All Professions be-rogue one another:
> The Priest calls the Lawyer a Cheat,
>> The Lawyer be-knaves the Divine:
> And the Statesman, because he's so great,
>> Thinks his Trade as honest as mine.

John Gay had intended his theatre-goers to see Peachum as an amalgam of Jonathan Wild, the notorious fence executed in 1725, and Sir Robert Walpole, the Whig Prime Minister, to whose misguided policies the author ascribed his own failure to obtain preferment. But Brecht was not interested in the specific social abuses of Weimar Germany. *Die Dreigroschenoper* and its sequels satirize the whole structure of bourgeois society. They are dominated by a single metaphor, that of the bourgeois criminal. Gay's dashing highwayman becomes a crafty entrepreneur with an impeccable taste in clothes and furniture; the fence and informer becomes an equally resourceful exploiter of human misery, but he has an eminently respectable position as a poor-relief officer and business man. In his notes on the opera Brecht writes: 'The predilection of the bourgeoisie for robbers can be traced to the fallacy that a robber is no bourgeois gentleman. This fallacy is the child of another: that a bourgeois gentleman is no robber'(17:994). If property is theft, it follows that all existing society is basically criminal, in the sense that it promotes the exploitation of one class by another. In the *Dreigroschenoper* Macheath plans to give up his dangerous position in London's criminal underworld and put his crimes on a legal footing by opening a bank. 'Was ist ein Dietrich gegen eine Aktie?', he asks, 'Was ist ein Einbruch in eine Bank gegen die Gründung einer Bank? Was ist die Ermordung eines Mannes gegen die Anstellung eines Mannes?' (2:482). His namesake repeats the speech verbatim in the novel (13:998), in which the crimes of both Macheath and Peachum are now identical with the legalized banditry of big business.

The satirical possibilities of this metaphor are what gave Brecht, parodist extraordinary, the idea of couching his oblique *exposé* of Weimar Germany in the form of a detective story. In an early essay on the popularity of the genre he argues that whereas in everyday life the nexus of cause and effect is usually inaccessible to analysis, the good detective story has the advantage of offering a self-contained world where every effect has its cause, and where the 'inside story' (Brecht uses the English cliché) can be deduced from the available evidence (19:454–6).

Brecht's purpose in his *Dreigroschenroman* is to enable the reader to deduce the 'inside story' of the criminal workings of capitalism. The one essential ingredient omitted from his parody of the detective story is the detective himself. There is no Sherlock Holmes or Father Brown to intervene in the final chapter, disentangle all the threads, and denounce the miscreant. The one man professionally concerned with the detection of crime, the police chief, has a vested interest in its continuation. One of the features Brecht particularly admired in the conventional detective story is that it has the logic of a crossword puzzle (19:450), but his parody deliberately leaves the syllogism incomplete. Percy Lubbock has suggested one point in which the serious novel resembles the detective story, when he describes its subject-matter as 'life liberated from the tangle of cross-purposes, saved from arbitrary distortion'.[9] Brecht's aim in his novel is similarly to liberate life from the complex subterfuge that masks injustice, and to expose arbitrary distortion. But whereas the conventional detective story sublimates the desire for social justice, Brecht's parody calls for redress in the real world. The crime remains unsolved since its solution is the reader's prerogative.

[9] P. Lubbock, *The Craft of Fiction*, 1926, p. 19.

Interwoven with the detective story is another parodied form, that of the traditional novel of family life. The *Drei-groschenroman* contains all the familiar ingredients of a family novel of the more popular variety: an authoritarian father, a wayward daughter and her doting mother, a rich suitor, a gay seducer, and an elopement. But each of these ingredients is strongly ironized. The puritanical father is a swindler who needs his daughter as a decoy; the doting mother is a sexually frustrated alcoholic; the wayward daughter is a randy adolescent with no real affection for any of her suitors, least of all for Macheath, whom she cuckolds with his star burglar; there are two rich suitors and both of them are crooks; the young seducer is an unprepossessing solicitor's clerk whom the pregnant Polly soon abandons in favour of her chain-store proprietor; and as for the elopement, Macheath thoughtfully combines it with a business trip. The contrast with the respectable families of the nineteenth-century novel could hardly be more pointed. One of the wilder predictions of *The Communist Manifesto* is the abolition of the bourgeois family, in which it sees the same principle of exploitation at work as in capitalist society at large. In his novel Brecht draws the same parallel between family and society, and beneath the buffoonery he urges the same radical reform.

In his pompous speech at the amalgamation ceremony of the A.B.C. Syndicate, Peachum recommends that Messrs. Aaron, Chreston, and Macheath, the new barons of trade and commerce, should use their influence to bring culture to the common man, on whom they depend for their livelihood: ' "Sie müssen ihm auch *Bildung* verkaufen, ich meine Bücher, ich denke an billige Romane, solche Sachen, die das Leben nicht grau in grau, sondern in lichteren Farben malen, die dem Alltagsmenschen eine höhere Welt vermitteln, ihn mit den feineren Sitten der höheren Schichten bekannt machen, der so erstrebenswerten Lebensweise der gesellschaftlich Bevorzugten" '* (13:1146). Brecht here indirectly articulates his view that the traditional family novel is a reactionary form, which for him is equally true of its more serious relative, the social novel. At the beginning of the nineteenth century Jane Austen's novels expose the foibles of bourgeois society, but also extol its sense and sensibility; at the end of the century Thomas Mann's *Budden-*

brooks laments its decay, while admiring its cultural refinement. Brecht's threepenny novel, on the other hand, documents the *mores* of the socially privileged in order to expedite the end of their era.

Brecht's second attempt at the novel form, *Die Geschäfte des Herrn Julius Caesar*, has already been analysed as an essay in historiography. This present section will confine itself to formal issues that reveal new aspects of Brecht's approach to fiction, and in particular to the historical novel.

The historical novel has on the whole been cultivated much less by German than by English writers, though there has always been interest in the genre and Sir Walter Scott has perhaps been more widely admired in Germany than in Britain. Georg Lukács, whose classic study of the genre appeared at the very time Brecht was engaged on background research for his Caesar-novel, makes the point that the historical novel is not a separate category at all; it is rather the legitimate heir of the social novel of the eighteenth century, applying to the past the meticulous analysis of contemporary society found in the work of Defoe, Fielding, Richardson, and Sterne.[10] Alfred Döblin goes even further in claiming that every good novel is a historical novel.[11]

Lukács describes the past as 'the concrete precondition of the present'.[12] Brecht's aim as a historical novelist is to interpret present social conditions as the product of a historical process in which it is the reader's duty to intervene. This gives rise to a number of formal problems.

The novelist must first decide to what extent to allegorize the historical material. The temptation to over-allegorize was one to which many historical novelists with left-wing sympathies, such as Neumann and Feuchtwanger, succumbed during the thirties, and, as we saw before, Brecht, while on his guard against overdoing it, also brought out the obvious parallels between the Nazi era and the period of the Roman Revolution (see p. 65 f.).

[10] Georg Lukács, *The Historical Novel*, trans. H. S. Mitchell, Penguin edn., 1969, p. 200 ff.

[11] Quoted from *Theorie und Technik des Romans im 20. Jahrhundert*, ed. H. Steinecke, Tübingen, 1972, p. 31.

[12] Lukács, *The Historical Novel*, p. 118.

The second problem is more serious. Having decided to let history speak for itself as the precondition of the present, the novelist is faced with the difficulty of maintaining a consistent narrative tone. In order to articulate the past for the benefit of a readership that inevitably approaches it with a mentality very different from that of any of the characters portrayed, he finds himself forced to resort to what Lukács, invoking the authority of Goethe and Hegel, calls 'necessary anachronism'.[13] If he were to attempt an accurate reconstruction of the mode of thought of any of his historical characters his novel would only be fully intelligible to his readers if their historical awareness were considerably greater than any novelist can reasonably expect. At the same time, systematically to update the mentality of his characters is likely to result in a travesty of the historical material.

Despite the criticism of a friend who objected that Brecht expects far too much from his readers, *Die Geschäfte des Herrn Julius Caesar* makes surprisingly few concessions. Spicer, the banker who financed Caesar's career, and his guest, Afranius Carbo, an industrial tycoon, both reveal much greater insight into the dialectic of history than any contemporary could have had. In their case this entails a conscious grasp of the part they allegedly played in the establishment of Caesar's dictatorship. Yet the Marxist propagandist shows remarkable restraint. Carbo, for instance, boasts of the achievements of the equestrian order under Caesar's regime, and his glib interpretation of the victory of the City over the Senate as the victory of the little man over the aristocratic cliques can be read as specious bluff. Between the lines the reader is expected to infer what no member of the equestrian order could ever have realized at the time (even supposing it to be a historical fact), namely that their victory was purchased at the expense of the peasants, the urban proletariat, and the slaves.

In this respect the treatment of the anonymous historian in the framework and of Rarus, Caesar's private secretary, is particularly interesting. Their first-person accounts provide the dual focus that gives the novel its unique perspective. (Brecht may have been inspired by R. L. Stevenson's novel *The Master*

---

[13] Ibid., p. 68.

of Ballantrae, which he greatly admired.) This might well have tempted Brecht to exploit 'necessary anachronism' to the full in the interests of a revolutionary interpretation of history, but he resists the temptation. The harsh reality of a slave-economy is everywhere in evidence, yet neither of the narrators shows the least trace of anachronistic compassion for the oppressed. The young historian witnesses entirely unmoved the brutalizing conditions under which the slaves live on Spicer's estate, which he describes as exemplary. He refers to their quarters as stables and manifests no surprise when Spicer uses the still more degrading word 'pound' (*Zwinger*). Spicer's callous account of breeding experiments, or the torturing of one slave to discover the whereabouts of another, who escapes during their discussion, evokes no more response from his guest than the melancholy songs he hears the Celtic slaves singing as he walks down to the lake on his way home. The reason for his indifference is clear from the first page of the novel, on which we learn that the young historian has a slave of his own, to whom he refers throughout as 'mein Sempronius'. Brecht's aim is to shock the reader not merely with the unsavoury details of the conditions under which slaves lived during this period, but even more by the total indifference of the average Roman citizen.

If this perspective is important in the framework, it is even more important in the case of Rarus' memoirs. Since all Caesar's affairs are seen exclusively through the eyes of an educated slave, Brecht has every opportunity to reveal at first hand the subhuman standard of living of the Roman slave population. But Rarus is a privileged slave, enjoying, as the Roman proletariat notes with resentment, a higher standard of living than many Roman citizens. He is much better off, for instance, than Caebio, his homosexual partner, to say nothing of the slaves employed in rough manual labour. He guards his privileges jealously, and this is what binds him to Caesar, for he stands to lose or gain in accordance with his master's fluctuating fortunes. Thus, although the *Kammerdienerblick* ironizes Caesar's historical situation, it is not allowed to usurp the reader's prerogative of judging a slave-economy from a historical vantage-point not vouchsafed to those who gained by it. Much the same might be said of the eyewitness account of the carnage that followed the defeat of Catiline's army. Though more graphic than most, the description of the battle-field is chary of detail. Rarus notes that there are no slaves among the dead (Catiline having dismissed them before the battle because of the resentment of the others), and that friend and foe are now indistinguishable, but there is no pathos. He records that he vomited when news of the defeat arrived, but this was because his lover, forced by unemployment to throw in his lot with the Catilinarians, is amongst the fallen. To register more protest than this would have been an anachronism, for he is far too accustomed to brutality and bloodshed to pay it much attention unless it affects him personally. The main point of the novel is that neither the slaves nor the urban proletariat of Rome had any understanding of the role they played in the dialectic of history and so they failed to seize their opportunities. Any sign of such an awareness would have invalidated the point, and it is arguable that the restraint Brecht shows in his treatment of 'necessary anachronism' is more effective than moral indignation.

The question of perspective also touches on a point of narrative technique that Brecht appears to have learned from Dos Passos, namely the skilful use of montage. Just as Dos Passos introduces documentary material—newsreel items, newspaper headlines, snatches of popular song, and the like—into the fabric of his monumental novel *U.S.A.* (1930–6), so Brecht supplements the impression of Ancient Rome received from the historian's conversations with Spicer, Carbo, Alder, and the anonymous legionary, with lengthy excerpts from a supposedly authentic private journal. Actually Brecht follows the example of Dos Passos less closely than does Thornton Wilder, who gives his pseudo-authentic documents a catalogue number in his Caesar-novel. Brecht restricts his editorial activity to the dating of the journal entries according to the Roman reckoning (where Wilder incongruously dates them B.C.). The inclusion of the journal is, however, essential to his purpose, which is to ensure that Caesar nowhere appears in his own person. As a character Caesar is entirely dependent on the mediation of his contemporaries, a technical subordination that exactly matches his contribution to history as Brecht understood it.

Lukács notes that Scott eschewed all 'romantically decorative hero-worship'[14] and favoured mediocre heroes who emerge as 'maintaining individuals'—Hegel's term for the anonymous personnel of history through which the *Weltgeist* works out its purpose. Brecht's maintaining individuals are Caesar's sponsors and Rarus. The reader starts on equal terms with the young Roman historian, searching for a traditional hero, and finding instead a mediocre speculator, seen through the eyes of a private secretary, whose memoirs are disconcertingly frank because they were not intended for publication. If Brecht in this novel again refrains from detailed topographical description on the one hand and interior monologue on the other, his restraint is satisfactorily grounded in the adoption of a severely restricted point of view. The net result is that Brecht reverses the process by which writers such as Scott and Conrad Ferdinand Meyer imply the greatness of a historical figure by devoting the foreground to imaginary characters who have no pretensions to heroic stature. He forces his reader to share the young historian's disappointment that the 'real' Caesar fails to emerge either from the interviews with contemporaries or from Rarus' journal.

The way in which the framework figure, and through him the reader, is educated into an entirely new appraisal of Caesar's role in history, suggests a serious parody of the traditional German *Bildungsroman*. There the hero is subjected to a process of purification through experience that either fits him for his place in the world of social reality, like Wilhelm Meister or Hans Castorp, or enables him to opt out of it, like Grimmelshausen's Simplicissimus. Brecht's mediocre narrator-hero learns nothing that he can put to any use, for Caesar's sponsors have already reaped the benefits of his revolution and consolidated its political achievements (Spicer and Alder, although of humble origin, are senators). As in the *Dreigroschenroman*, only the reader can make full use of the novel's social perspective.

Hans Winge saw in his friend's fragmentary Caesar-novel 'the beginnings of a completely new literary genre'.[15] Certainly this parody of the traditional historical novel and the *Bildungs-*

---

[14] Lukács, *The Historical Novel*, p. 38.   [15] Brecht-Archiv, 189/95.

roman breaks new ground and it has even been considered an early example of the anti-novel.[16] Perhaps the fact that Brecht left it unfinished indicates that he nevertheless realized he had bitten off more than he could chew, and that to submit the whole of Caesar's era to a radical and consistent revision that satisfies the requirements of a novel demands a greater control of the medium than he had acquired. This view is supported by Brecht's subsequent failure to organize the plethora of detail he had begun to accumulate from about 1930 for his so-called *Tui-Roman*, which was to have been a semi-allegorical exposure of the role of intellectualism in Weimar Germany.

Brecht's preoccupation with fiction was not confined to intermittent experimentation with the novel. Indeed, in some ways his shorter fiction is more impressive and more satisfying, if only because of its completeness and its diversity, and it comprises a whole volume of his collected works. He began writing short stories at school, continued experimenting with the genre throughout his early career, and in 1928 won first prize in a competition organized by the *Berliner Illustrierte Zeitung*, for a story entitled *Die Bestie*. It was the stories he wrote during his exile in Scandinavia and America, however, to which Brecht himself attached the most importance and in which he reveals a consummate mastery of a form that unites two separate traditions of German fiction. He included seven of them in an anthology of prose and verse to which he gave the title *Kalendergeschichten*, first published in 1949, and certainly these are among his best.

The title Brecht adopted for his anthology indicates his principal source of inspiration. Almanacs had become popular with the lower classes during the Reformation, when they constituted their only reading-matter beyond the Bible. They flourished throughout the sixteenth and seventeenth centuries and served a dual pupose of entertainment and the dissemination of useful information. Edifying tales were interspersed with titbits of popular astronomy, medicine, meteorology, and agriculture. The peasant was not only given practical hints on farming, but supplied with diagrams showing how to let blood in accordance with the zodiac and told the most propitious

[16] H. Dahlke, *Cäsar bei Brecht*, Berlin, 1968, p. 116.

times for taking sweat-baths and eating salads. It was the practicality of these publications that made them so popular until well into the nineteenth centruy. Even the astrological tips and moral injunctions were intended to serve a practical purpose, and Grimmelshausen, now remembered as the author of the powerful anti-war novel *Simplicissimus*, described an almanac, of which he was the editor in 1670, as a 'gospel of hope' for the hard-pressed peasant who had otherwise nowhere to turn for advice and consolation.

During the eighteenth century the popular almanac became an instrument of the Enlightenment. Its elevation to the level of serious literature, however, was the work of Johann Peter Hebel at the beginning of the nineteenth century. By turns a schoolmaster and preacher, Hebel combined both of these functions as the editor of a popular almanac, *Der Rheinländische Hausfreund*. He contributed many items to it personally, for the most part didactic but pithy and unpretentious anecdotes. A digest appeared in 1811 under the title *Das Schatzkästlein des Rheinischen Hausfreundes*, which eventually reached a readership far wider than the peasantry for which Hebel had originally written and earned the approval of many eminent men of letters, including Goethe. One example will serve to illustrate Hebel's approach to this form of fiction. In *Kaiser Napoleon und die Obstfrau in Brienne*, Hebel tells the apocryphal story of the young Napoleon's visit to Brienne, where a kindly fruit-vendor lets him have some of her wares on credit. Many years later Napoleon, now the Emperor of France, returns. He remembers the old woman and not only honours his long-standing debt but builds her a new house and educates her son at his own expense. A famous historical figure is thus juxtaposed with a member of the humble class for which Hebel wrote. The peasant-woman's generosity stimulates Napoleon's equally generous response, and his spectacular political and military achievements pale into insignificance compared with the gratitude he shows to a social inferior to whom he is linked by bonds of common humanity. Despite the sharp social contrast the political attitude underlying the narrative remains fundamentally conservative. The old woman acknowledges Napoleon's divine right to rule when she falls at his feet in astonishment that he should have remembered her. Napoleon's rise to power seems in retrospect the result of a kind of natural selection, a privilege for which his humanity uniquely qualified him.

Though Brecht nowhere mentions Hebel, there can be little doubt that he was directly influenced by him. One of his own *Kalendergeschichten* bears a particularly close resemblance to the tale described above. *Das Experiment*, written in 1939, was originally entitled *Der Stalljunge*. This is significant, for the main character is in a sense not Francis Bacon, the famous philosopher, but his fictitious stable-boy, Dick. In Brecht's account of Bacon's last days Dick's unprejudiced, inquiring mind is the guarantee of the ultimate victory of empiricism and reason over reactionary superstition. At first sight this imaginary figure seems to function in much the same way as that of the old peasant-woman in Hebel's story. Francis Bacon's true greatness is revealed through his relationship with the boy, who after his master's death verifies Bacon's hypothesis about the effects of refrigeration by eating the chicken he buried in the snow. Unlike the curate, who can see no good reason why a stable-boy should want to learn Latin, and the grandmother, who assumes that a chicken that has been dead for a week must be poisonous, Bacon has learned to question accepted habits of thought and perception and he teaches Dick to do the same. But whereas Hebel's peasant accepts the divinely appointed order of her world, the open-mindedness and scientific curiosity that Dick has inherited from his illustrious teacher mark the beginning of a long process of attrition which threatens the very social order that allows corrupt politicians such as Bacon to enjoy a life of affluence. Bacon himself embodies a contradiction comparable to that found in Brecht's Galilei. His scientific outlook is at odds with the role he played in politics. Although for him science is more or less a hobby, the scientific world-view of which he is the pioneer will lead not only to the Industrial Revolution, but eventually to the scientific socialism of Marx and Engels, whose heirs will end the injustice that makes Dick the slave of his social environment.

Das Experiment begins with a moralizing statement that seems to fit well into the pattern of a traditional *Kalendergeschichte*: 'Die öffentliche Laufbahn des grossen Francis Bacon endete wie eine billige Parabel über den trügerischen Spruch "Unrecht macht sich nicht bezahlt".'* But Brecht's narrator is teasing his readers, for this is not at all the moral of his story. It focuses on the revolutionary implications of a seemingly fortuitous discovery made by a frustrated political intriguer during his enforced retirement. The account closes with a brief description of Bacon's funeral. His sonorous titles— Baron of Verulam, Viscount St. Albans, Lord Chancellor of England—and the shots fired over his grave pay ironic tribute to a man whose true greatness has nothing to do with the privileged position he so shamelessly exploited. The faith he has inspired in his stable-boy is the true measure of his historical greatness.

It can readily be seen from this that Brecht has submitted the traditional *Kalendergeschichte* to the same process of alienation that characterizes his theatre. Although it remains a didactic form, the chief aim of which is to bring enlightenment to the masses, it has undergone a fundamental ideological shift. The traditional form taught its reader 'zufrieden zu sein mit seinem Schicksal, wenn auch nicht viele gebratene Tauben für ihn in der Luft herumfliegen', as Hebel himself puts it in the opening sentence of *Kannitverstan*, one of his most popular tales. Brecht's adaptation of the genre, on the other hand, seeks to inculcate in his reader a sense of righteous indignation at the arbitrary treatment he has received from fate.

Der Mantel des Ketzers, written in 1939, relates an apocryphal story about Giordano Bruno along similar lines. The opening sentence affects to tell us how the hero fell foul of the Inquisition on account of his unorthodox views on astronomy. The epithet *groß* has a less ironical ring to it here than it did when applied to Bacon. Brecht has no quarrel with the historical foundations of Giordano Bruno's fame in the age of discovery. Yet it is none of Bruno's discoveries that makes him a revolutionary figure comparable with Copernicus and Galileo, but the man's dignified bearing in the hands of the Inquisition. And it is again an encounter with a fictitious character, Frau Zunto, a tailor's wife, that puts the doomed philosopher's fame in its true perspective. Frau Zunto demands that the Inquisition's illustrious, but by now penniless, prisoner should pay up the 32 scudi he still owes her husband, despite the fact

that he is engaged in a life-and-death struggle with the Holy
Office. He goes to considerable trouble to have the coat returned
in lieu of payment, and at the end of the tale he is led off to
Rome in the depths of winter to endure the final stage of his
martyrdom. Again, at first sight the humanitarian level of the
story seems to accord with the spirit of the traditional almanac.
But Bruno's attitude represents more than Christian forbearance
in the face of adversity. He accepts Frau Zunto's apparent
pettiness as the natural consequence of poverty. The 32 scudi
are equally a life-and-death issue for the poor. In this way the
heresy of which Bruno stands indicted is sharply ironized. It
has ultimately nothing to do with the trumped up charges
brought against him by the vindictive Mocenigo. It consists in
his acceptance of the fact that the poor have rights and that to
preach Christian indulgence to them would be hypocrisy.
Certainly Bruno's saintly forbearance is a Christian virtue, of
which the mantle is a transparent symbol, but it also exemplifies a revolutionary attitude of great historical potential.

One further example of Brecht's shorter fiction will serve to
show his ingenuity in harnessing an essentially reactionary
form to a revolutionary purpose. *Cäsar und sein Legionär* is an
offshoot of the Caesar-novel.[17] It seems to have been written
in America in 1942 in an attempt to work out ideas for a film,
the title of which, *Die Iden des März*, indicates that Brecht is here
concerned with the last phase of Caesar's career. Many of the
narrative features of the novel reappear: the dry, unemotional
tone, the paucity of visual description, and the refusal to
characterize the figures from within. In addition, the allegorical
overtones of the novel are here amplified to evoke à strong sense
of historical parallel. It is the demythologization of Caesar
himself, however, that provides the clearest link with the novel
and the other short stories. Just as the introduction of fictitious
characters puts an entirely new construction on the careers of

---

[17] Dahlke maintains that the story antedates the novel (op. cit., p. 39), but
Herta Ramthun and Klaus Völker give the date as 1942 in their notes to Volume 11
of the *Gesammelte Werke*. Müller, on the other hand (op. cit., p. 131), asserts that
the death of Caesar was part of Brecht's original plan for the novel, but the brief
synopsis in the Archiv (187/90) clearly indicates that the climactic event was to
have been the crossing of the Rubicon. It seems more likely, as Völker has suggested
(*Brecht-Chronik*, Munich, 1971, p. 93), that the short story was based on the abortive film-scenario of 1942 and has nothing to do with the novel as such.

Bruno and Bacon, so Caesar's death, the subject of so much literary idealization, is ironized by showing it in dual focus. The story is divided into two synchronized sections of equal length, which exercise a reciprocal alienation-effect. The first section reviews the last three days of Caesar's life from Caesar's own point of view; the second covers the same events from the point of view of a minor character, not the private secretary of the novel, but one of Caesar's veterans.

At the height of his career Caesar has no illusions about his vulnerability. Realizing that he has outlived his usefulness to the forces that brought him to power, he knows that the days of his dictatorship are numbered. He does not panic, but wearily and without real conviction seeks a way out of his dilemma. He is too resigned to his fate even to read the dossier containing the names of his future assassins. After an abortive attempt to kindle enthusiasm for a democratic revolution, Caesar's palace is raided and his secretary is murdered. The Ides of March arrive and the conspirators close in on Caesar as he enters the Senate. 'Sie fallen über ihn her', is the narrator's laconic and dispassionate description of the most celebrated assassination in history. The second section follows the fortunes of Terentius Scaper, the veteran of Caesar's victorious campaigns, who has been evicted from his farm because he is in arrears with the rent. His attempt to scrape together the 300 sesterces that would save him from ruin coincides with Caesar's equally abortive attempt to extricate himself from the political impasse. After the veteran's daughter has made the money by accommodating an elderly admirer, it is lost on bribes in an unsuccessful endeavour to smuggle Caesar out of the city. Caesar dies, unwittingly owing 300 sesterces to an unknown veteran, a debt that 'alienates' the political power he has just lost.

Another German literary tradition appears to have influenced Brecht's short stories, which have not infrequently been referred to by German critics as *Novellen*. The German *Novelle* is perhaps the most disciplined form of fiction. Goethe emphasized its stringent economy when in his much-quoted conversation with Eckermann he called it 'eine sich ereignete, unerhörte Begebenheit'.[18] In Brecht's own lifetime Georg

18 Conversation with Eckermann, 25 Jan. 1827.

Lukács defined it as 'a human life expressed through the infinite sensual force of a fateful hour'.[19] Whereas David Copperfield tells his whole life-story at a leisurely pace with many interludes of varying degrees of relevance to its main strands, Droste-Hülshoff's *Die Judenbuche* and Storm's *Der Schimmelreiter* concentrate on carefully selected episodes that illustrate one specific trait and culminate in a single sensational event. The narrative economy of such fiction encourages its critics to speak of the unities, since the time-span, the locale and the number of characters are severely limited in the interests of dramatic concentration, which was perhaps what Storm had in mind when he called the *Novelle* 'the sister of drama'.[20] In addition to this, writers of *Novellen* not infrequently resort to symbolism in order to enrich the texture of their narrative. Paul Heyse's insistence on a 'falcon'—he had a famous tale from Boccaccio's *Decameron* in mind—has found little favour, yet *Die Judenbuche* is unthinkable without the dominant central image indicated by the title; in Kleist's *Michael Kohlhaas* a pair of horses, in Mörike's *Mozart auf der Reise nach Prag* an orange-tree, and in Gerhart Hauptmann's *Bahnwärter Thiel* a railway train greatly increase the poetic power of the narrative.

Brecht's narrative economy is equally striking in his shorter fiction. The lives of Bruno, Bacon, Caesar, Socrates (in *Der verwundete Sokrates*), Dollinger and Anna (in *Der Augsburger Kreidekreis*) are all skilfully compressed into a single outstanding event, involving a restricted number of characters and in most cases observing a limitation of place and time that certainly recalls classical drama. Matching this there is an economy of language and a stylistic restraint that suggested to one reviewer 'a texture like that of good strong cloth'.[21] Moreover, the concrete symbol supplies the focal point of a number of the stories: the dead chicken in *Das Experiment*, the disputed coat in *Der Mantel des Ketzers*, the embarrassing thorn in the philosopher's foot in *Der verwundete Sokrates*, and the chalk circle in *Der Augsburger Kreidekreis*. In each case the dominant characteristics of the central figure—Bacon's empiricism, Bruno's forbearance, Socrates' wit and wisdom, Dollinger's cunning, and

---

[19] Quoted from Benno von Wiese, *Novelle*, Stuttgart, 1963, p. 19.

[20] Storm, *Werke*, ed. A. Köster, Leipzig, 1919–20, viii, p. 122.

[21] F. Hope (in a review of the Methuen translation), *Spectator*, 24 Nov. 1961.

Anna's stubbornness—are all vividly associated with the central image. There is, however, one essential difference between Brecht's symbolism and that of many writers of *Novellen*. Whereas Droste-Hülshoff intended her symbolism to evoke a sense of the irrational and the numinous that could not be conveyed directly without breaking the spell, Brecht's imagery is totally accessible to reason, acting merely as a kind of shorthand that can readily be translated into the 'social equivalent'. There is no suggestion of mysticism, for instance, about Bruno's coat, though the religious overtones are audible enough. It simply brings into sharper focus the revolutionary nature of the martyr's heresy: his attitude to its loss vindicates Frau Zunto, condemns the Inquisition, and raises its unassuming owner to the level of true greatness. The concrete symbols of the other tales are likewise decipherable. In short, whereas the most characteristic German *Novellen* offer a self-contained world of poetry and symbolism that is often a surrogate for the increasingly prosaic world in which their writers found themselves, Brecht's short stories have their centre of gravity outside the work in the contradictory world of social reality. In this respect there is no essential difference between Brecht's shorter fiction and his novels, nor for that matter does his narrative fiction as a whole differ fundamentally from his theatre.

Traditional fiction has often exercised a dual function. The tightly organized world it conjures up is at once a protest against the incoherence of the real world and a consolation for those who are forced to live in it. E. M. Forster, like Brecht both a theorist and a practitioner, asserts categorically that it is the function of narrative to solace the reader by suggesting 'a more comprehensible and thus a more manageable human race', and by giving him 'the illusion of perspicacity and power'.[22] This view offers an illuminating contrast with Brecht, who in one of his essays on realism insists that Balzac's narrative technique can no longer be adopted by the modern writer, but goes on to contrast him favourably with Dickens in that he presents a more manageable (*handhabbar*) view of the human condition (19:362). Despite the verbal similarity of their argu-

[22] Op. cit., p. 71.

ments, Brecht and Forster are poles apart. Forster is referring to the carefully insulated, autonomous world of fiction, which is demonstrably more comprehensible and manageable, even in its most tragic moments in Hardy, Tolstoy, or Dostoevski, than reality. Brecht, on the other hand, is asserting that the essential funtion of narrative is to point away from itself to the chaos and contradictions of the real world, of which it is an abstract and brief chronicle. The sense of perspicacity and power that the imaginative world of Brecht's fiction is intended to evoke is no illusion, but a revelation of the latent energies with which reality might be transformed.

4. The Lyric

COMPARED with Brecht the dramatist or even Brecht the novelist, Brecht the poet is still virtually unknown outside Germany, although in his own country he is commonly regarded as one of the best poets of the century. From his school-days onwards he ranked poetry amongst his artistic priorities, and his verses comprise three of the twenty volumes of his collected works.

At first sight this seems paradoxical. Brecht was not in the least concerned with art as self-revelation, and the lyric is potentially the most intimate of all literary forms. In drama the writer's ego, even a Strindberg's, has to don a mask in order to speak to us, and in fiction the narrator constitutes another kind of intermediary. In the lyric, on the other hand, the poet is free to speak with his own voice, and since the advent of Romanticism he has frequently exercised this freedom in order to express his innermost thoughts and feelings. The phenomenal world, which is made to seem objectively real in drama and fiction, is also powerfully present in the lyric, but only as an image refracted by the poetic consciousness. Moreover, whereas it is axiomatic for Brecht that art is communication, the existence of a real or imaginary addressee affects the writer's orientation towards his subject-matter much less in the lyric than it does in the other literary forms. With few exceptions the reader is given the impression of eavesdropping on a private monologue. Otto Ludwig, though himself no poet, spoke for most poets from Romanticism onwards when he wrote: 'The lyric poet sings of himself and for himself, that is to say, *to* himself, like someone singing hymns in church.'[1]

In Goethe's 'Mailied', to take a familiar example, the

---

[1] Otto Ludwig, *Gesammelte Schriften*, ed. A. Stern and J. Schmidt, Leipzig, 1891, vi, 30.

distinguishing features of the lyric mode are clear in the very first stanza:

> Wie herrlich leuchtet
> Mir die Natur!
> Wie glänzt die Sonne!
> Wie lacht die Flur!

Nature, the sun and the meadows are differentiated from their counterparts in any other form of communication by the dynamic rhythm of the lines, the punctuation, the use of the repetitive 'wie', and above all by the accentuated dative pronoun in the second line. The itemized phenomena have no independent life outside the poet's awareness of them: their proper referent is a private inner landscape. Again, the exclamatory punctuation is not directly concerned with the business of communication as it would be on a hoarding or a notice-board: it belongs to the first-person stratum of the poem, evoking a strong sense of the intensity of feelings that demand an outlet but not necessarily a hearing. If the reader is able to identify with such feelings, that is his affair.

Any conception of poetry as a form of soliloquy was abhorrent to Brecht from the start. In his essay 'Die Lyrik als Ausdruck', written about 1927, he points out that the term 'expression' is ambiguous. It is used of a patient who expresses his pain with a cry or a groan in order to summon help, but also of poets who supposedly 'render only pure expression, in such a way that their activity consists solely in expressing and their intention can only be to express themselves' (18:59). Brecht advocates a form of poetry in which the presence of the addressee is implicit in the actual structure of the poem, just as it is the precondition of his theatre. It will 'express' the poet's feelings only inasmuch as such feelings are of direct concern to the reader and must on that account be communicated, not merely externalized. This, more than anything else, is what makes Brecht's lyric voice so unmistakable. Walter Jens has Brecht's later poetry in mind when he writes: 'Jede Zeile sucht ihr Du',[2] but the reader's active participation is in fact demanded by nearly all his verse.

It may seem unfair to cite a little-known poem that Brecht

---

[2] Nachwort to the *Ausgewählte Gedichte*, Frankfurt, 1964, p. 86.

wrote for children, but the basic shift in emphasis is all the clearer because its context is relatively unsophisticated, and the title 'Mailied' seems a deliberate provocation:

> Am Ersten Mai
> Gehn Vater und Mutter in einer Reih
> Kämpfen fur ein beßres Leben.
> Fron und Armut darf's nicht geben:
> > Grün sind die Zweige
> > Die Fahne ist rot.
> > Nur der Feige
> > Duldet Not.
>
> 's ist Monat Mai
> Im Acker die Hälmchen stehn Reih an Reih.
> Gute Ernte—gutes Leben!
> Lasset uns die Hand drauf geben
> Daß es die unsere sei.
> > Grün sind die Fluren
> > Die Fahne ist rot.
> > Unser die Arbeit
> > Unser das Brot!*

(10:974)

In these lines, written in 1950, the poet identifies his own feel, ings—the lyric *ich* becomes the *wir* of socialist solidarity—with the young community for which he writes. For once Brecht could have agreed with his fellow Communist Becher, who wrote in 1952: 'Das lyrische Ich ist immer ein Wir'.[3] The poets' traditional merry month of May has, since the Second International of 1889, begun with Labour Day, on which in this song a fully secularized Pan is jointly celebrated by poet and addressee in jubilant anticipation of harvest home. Goethe's exclamation marks reappear: 'Gute Ernte—gutes Leben!', 'Unser das Brot!', but they punctuate collective determination, not the self-indulgence of a lover. Goethe's impassioned synthesis of love-song and nature-panegyric has become the marching-song of Utopia's future citizens. A comparable sense of urgency and collective concern informs the 'Solidaritätslied', 'Lob der Dialektik', 'Einheitsfrontlied', and scores of other later poems.

This tendency in Brecht's poetry is by no means confined to

---

[3] J. R. Becher, *Bemühungen*, Berlin, 1972, vol. ii, p. 55.

the period after his conversion. Even in the anarchical period of
Baal we encounter the stark but strictly controlled despair of
'Der Nachgeborene':

> Ich gestehe es: ich
> Habe keine Hoffnung.
> Die Blinden reden von einem Ausweg. Ich
> Sehe.
> Wenn die Irrtümer verbraucht sind
> Sitzt als letzter Gesellschafter
> Uns das Nichts gegenüber.*
>
> (8:99)

The early Brecht had no compunction about the use of the
first-person pronoun, and it is here strongly accentuated three
times in as many lines. But it modulates into the plural in the
second strophe, as though the nihilist were anxious to share with
others his insight into the human predicament. There is
solidarity in despair. From the same period the complementary
poems 'Vom Klettern in Bäumen' and 'Vom Schwimmen in
Seen und Flüssen', which are amongst Brecht's finest, only once
use the first person. The first of these poems restricts itself
exclusively to the second-person plural, while in the second the
impersonal *man* occurs eleven times, together with three
appearances of the first-person plural. In this way vividly
personal *Erlebnisdichtung*, which this still is, is universalized and
its general tone resembles that of the instructions on an unfamiliar gadget. Brecht's feeling of oneness with nature is
ostensibly one that his readers can learn to imitate. Again, the
famous autobiographical poem 'Vom armen B.B.', despite the
personal orientation of its opening line

> Ich, Bertolt Brecht, bin aus den schwarzen Wäldern

is imbued with a cynical resignation which is offered as an
experience the reader will readily recognize:

> Wir wissen, daß wir Vorläufige sind
> Und nach uns wird kommen: nichts Nennenswertes.
>
> (8:261–2)

Brecht's attitude as a poet diverges very strikingly from that of
his immediate predecessors. Rilke, whom Brecht patronizingly
describes as 'an otherwise really good man' (18:55), does not

invite us to follow the labyrinthine ramifications of his thought in the *Duino Elegies*, where he is too preoccupied with his angels to notice the bewildered reader. Stefan George, the arch-priest of German aestheticism, in whom Brecht saw only a smug, opinionated egotist, begins an arcane incantation with a characteristic Horatian flourish

des sehers wort ist wenigen gemeinsam

Such an attitude of *odi profanum vulgus* was anathema to the Brecht of all periods. As he puts it in a later essay: 'These poems tell ordinary people nothing, sometimes comprehensibly, sometimes incomprehensibly' (19:334).

George's hieratic aloofness represents in intensified form another familiar aspect of the mainstream lyric that Brecht rejects. As the *musarum sacerdos* the poet has often felt he is under a special dispensation and able to mediate between inscrutable higher powers and the uninitiated common herd. At its finest the notion appears in Shelley's statement: 'Poetry redeems from decay visitations of the divinity in Man.'[4] Enthusiasm in its etymological sense of a divinely induced trance is a hallmark of much lyric writing, and the awesome *hwyl* with which it is often read aloud marks it off as a hallowed utterance that the ear could distinguish from prose even in an unknown language. Although Brecht enjoyed reading his own poetry aloud, his manner of delivery characterized his whole approach to the lyric. In his youth he had sung his verses to the guitar with his flat tuneless voice in the taverns of Augsburg. Max Frisch, who describes Brecht as 'a poet without incense',[5] gives us a vivid impression of his relaxed 'secular' style three decades later in Zurich:

The way Brecht read us his poem, in a shy but relaxed manner, he is no different from before and after, his voice is quiet, retaining the accent of his native dialect, almost lisping and yet clear and precise especially as regards rhythm, seemingly without emphasis, matter-of-fact, showing words as one shows pebbles, pieces of cloth or anything else that has to speak for itself; the attitude of a man who, smoking his cigar, is obliged to read out a text for the simple reason that not

---

[4] Shelley, in 'A Defence of Poetry', *The Complete Works*, ed. R. Ingpen and E. Peck, 1930, vii, p. 137.

[5] Max Frisch, *Tagebuch 1946–1949*, Frankfurt, 1971, p. 292.

everyone has a copy of it in front of him; roughly the way one reads out a letter: with the aim of communicating. And it creates no disturbance if the bell goes when someone else arrives or if Brecht's daughter crosses the room because there is no way round. 'I'm just reading a poem,' he says to the new arrival, 'it is called "To Posterity".' He just says this so that the newcomer will postpone his conversation for a while, and then goes on reading, communicating the rest of what he wants to say to posterity.... The interval customarily observed after the recitation of a poem because, on leaving the church, as it were, and suddenly finding the organ out of earshot, we are dazzled and have to make our own way back to the ordinary world, which is of course very different from poetry—such an interval is not necessary; the poem that is itself real has no need to shun the real world; it can hold its own, even when the bell goes and an unexpected guest arrives, who, whilst we are still holding the same cup of coffee, tells us of his four years' imprisonment . . .

'Truly, I live in a dark age!'[6]

We are not here dealing with a mere idiosyncrasy of recitation. Brecht's conception of the lyric as a highly controlled but relaxed communication is something that affects the warp and woof of his poetry.

When asked to judge a poetry competition for *Die literarische Welt* early in 1927, Brecht rejected several hundred entries— 'poems consisting entirely of pretty imagery and aromatic words'—mainly on the grounds that they were of no demonstrable use: 'And lyric poetry in particular must certainly be capable of being scrutinized for its utility-value' (18:55). Following the esoteric tradition of Rilke, George, and Werfel, the contributors had paraded their sentimentality and *Weltfremdheit*, and Brecht found their poetry phoney because it failed to communicate anything. In his opinion Hannes Küpper's 'He, He! The Iron Man' (not submitted) deserved the prize because it at least dealt intelligibly with a common interest (a six-day cycling champion of the twenties called Reggie MacNamara). Many years later he praised the poetry of Po Chü-i and noted with approval that he is said to have read all his poems to an old peasant-woman to see how intelligible they were.

The revolt against an 'aromatic' aestheticism resulted in a calculated demythologization of the very language of poetry.

[6] Ibid., p. 227.

Brecht's early verse reeks of brandy and tobacco, excrement and putrefaction, the unashamedly mortal sacraments of a doomed megalopolis ('Vom armen B.B.') and decaying flotsam on storm-tossed seas of absinth. There is a wilful rejection of the respectable motifs of the drawing-room lyric:

Gegen Morgen in der grauen Frühe pissen die Tannen
Und ihr Ungeziefer, die Vögel, fängt an zu schrein.
Um die Stunde trink ich mein Glas in der Stadt aus und schmeiße
Den Tabakstummel weg und schlafe beunruhigt ein.*

(8:263)

Villon, Verlaine, Rimbaud and Wedekind had handed on the tattered mantle of the *poète maudit* to Brecht.

Brecht's poetry, like his drama and prose, shifted its ground after his conversion, and cynical resignation gave way to a passionate *engagement*, but it was still audibly the same Brecht. In his poem 'Ausschließlich wegen der zunehmenden Unordnung', written about 1934, Brecht again rejects the conventional motifs of lyric poetry: harbours, snow on the roofs, women, the smell of ripe apples in the cellar, sensual feeling, in short

All dem, was den Menschen rund macht und menschlich

and turns instead to the bitter class struggle with its drab technical jargon as a necessary evil that a poet of integrity can no longer neglect:

verstrickt in die Geschäfte
Der Politik und das trockene 'unwürdige' Vokabular
Der dialektischen Ökonomie*

(9:519)

Some see Brecht making a virtue of necessity. According to them, lacking the finer feelings of a born lyric poet, he takes up cudgels on behalf of an austere ideology that camouflages his sterility. It is after all easier to write a protest-song than a love-sonnet. Clearly, such critics have never read the *Hauspostille*, which teems with daring imagery, wild rhythms, and experimental vocabulary, and in which romantic mythopoeia is not entirely swamped by cynical rationalism. Nor have they noticed the extreme reluctance with which the Marxist convert rejects traditional lyricism, nor yet the subtle way in which he still dwells nostalgically on what he is rejecting:

Die grünen Boote und die lustigen Segel des Sundes
Sehe ich nicht

(9:743)

he claims in 'Schlechte Zeit für Lyrik', but the reader still sees
them, isolated by the versification of the strophe before the
negative erases the image to make room for 'der Fischer rissiges
Garnnetz'. Why speak only of the prematurely aged cotter's
wife, asks the poem, when the breasts of young girls are still as
warm as ever they were?

In mir streiten sich
Die Begeisterung über den blühenden Apfelbaum
Und das Entsetzen über die Reden des Anstreichers.
Aber nur das zweite
Drängt mich zum Schreibtisch.*

The harsh juxtaposition of the tree in blossom and the cartoon-
ist's caricature of Hitler leaves us in no doubt what Brecht
would rather be writing about, but in the poetry of the dark
ages nature must give way to politics. It is, as the elegiac title
indicates, a bad time for poetry.

This is only a politically orientated and rationalized form of
the scepticism Brecht showed in his earlier poetry. If we find
there an occasional love-poem it perpetuates a passion for a
woman whose name Brecht can no longer recall and who by
now probably has seven children ('Erinnerung an die Marie
A.'), or it is spoken antiphonally by the inmates of a Mahagonny
brothel ('Die Liebenden'). The lyricism is still unmistakably
present in these poems, now popular anthology-pieces, but
Brecht was half ashamed of it since its very existence is an
indictment of an unjust world in which, as he put it later in the
poem quoted by Max Frisch, to speak of trees is almost a
crime.[7]

Not only are the lyric voice of poetry, its themes and vocabulary subject to a stringent revision. Rhyme becomes a
debatable luxury, and the accent falls differently. Of the former
Brecht complains in 'Schlechte Zeit für Lyrik':

In meinem Lied ein Reim
Käme mir fast vor wie Übermut.

[7] See above, p. 25.

There were plenty of them in the early verse: of the *Hauspostille*'s forty-six poems only five are rhymeless, and of these three are secularized psalms in rhythmic prose. But later Brecht felt they were an encumbrance and could too easily degenerate into cliché. In his essay 'Über reimlose Lyrik mit unregelmäßigen Rhythmen', written in 1938, he explains: 'Rhyme seemed to me inappropriate, since it gives the poem a self-contained quality, something that slips past the ear' (19:403). But Brecht is not dogmatic. Of the eighty-two poems in the *Svendborger Gedichte*, which were published in Copenhagen in 1939, sixteen still rhyme, one of them ('Der Gottseibeiuns') quite elaborately. In the post-war period, too, there are many rhymed poems, especially those such as 'Aufbaulied' and the numerous children's poems intended primarily to be sung. Even the long didactic poem *Die Erziehung der Hirse*, Brecht's most pious tribute to Socialist Realism, rhymes conventionally.

The question of rhythm was of much greater importance to Brecht and most of the essay quoted above is concerned with it. The early verse often lurches drunkenly along in imitation of the syncopated rhythms of jazz, but just as often it affects an anti-literary simplicity in adopting the metre of folk-song, the Protestant hymn, and Kipling's barrack-room ballads. Brecht's early habit of accompanying his own songs to the guitar helps to explain the relatively conventional versification of the early poetry.

Brecht still resorts to the artless jingle or the heavy, regular accentuation of the Protestant hymn in his middle period, but usually by way of parody, as in the *Hitler-Choräle*, which mock the reader for his blindly 'religious' devotion to this bogus Messiah. In the more personal lyrics, however, the versification, no less disciplined for being 'free', adopts a new principle. In 'Über reimlose Lyrik' Brecht notes, with obvious satisfaction, that some readers have questioned his right to call such verse 'poetry', on the grounds that it not only fails to rhyme, but has no clearly definable rhythms. Nevertheless, Brecht insists that the term 'lyric' is still applicable: 'My reply to the question why I call it lyrical is that although it has no *regular* rhythm it still has a rhythm (alternating, syncopated, *gestisch*)' (19:395).[8] He

---

[8] Brecht's term 'Gestus' and its derivatives defy translation. John Willett notes

recalls the lessons he learned from studying the poetic prose of Arthur Rimbaud for his play *Im Dickicht der Städte* and from his decision to avoid 'the oily smoothness of the conventional iambic pentameter' for his adaptation of Marlowe's *Edward II*. It was not a question of cramming the ideas into an iambic strait-jacket, but of making the accentuation follow natural speech-rhythms, at the same time focusing attention on the dominant idea of the line.

At first sight Brecht seems to be exaggerating the revolutionary nature of his approach. Were the free rhythms of Walt Whitman or the sprung rhythms of Gerard Manley Hopkins very different? Or for that matter, what about the odes of Klopstock, Goethe, and Hölderlin? Even a famous anthology-piece such as 'Über allen Gipfeln', which Brecht parodies in his 'Liturgie vom Hauch', imposes a different metrical pattern on each of its eight deceptively simple lines. But Brecht would have argued that the rhythms of such poetry, though clearly freer than those of a sonnet or a folk-ballad, are still a law unto themselves. His scathing comments on Ludwig Hardt's attempt to bring out the symbolic flow of Goethe's 'Mahomets Gesang' when he read it aloud, are typical: 'det Janze stelltn Strom dar, hastenichjemerktwa?', gibed Brecht, mimicking his friend's Berlin accent. As in his form of theatre, he is anxious to avoid any suggestion of the hypnotic trance. The versification of Hopkins's famous 'Windhover' is extremely irregular, but the words are nevertheless subordinated to the unmistakable lilt of the line, which follows the flight of the bird.

Brecht's conception of what he called the 'gestische Formulierung' of lyric poetry is quite different. He borrowed the term from the language of his own essays on theatre. In one of those essays he offers a homely illustration by describing the nod as a 'Grundgestus' of everyday communication. The speaker may have complex reasons for his agreement and some important reservations, but a nod of the head expresses the fundamental attitude. Every play and every individual scene has its own 'Grundgestus' according to Brecht, and this can be summed up in a pithy sub-title that will reveal a character's basic social

---

that they subsume the ideas of 'gesture and gist, attitude and point' (p. 175). It refers above all to the concrete, physical manifestation of underlying social attitudes.

attitude and the 'social point' of the play (16:694). Brecht reduces the basic 'Gestus' of a scene from Georg Büchner's *Woyzeck* to the caption 'Woyzeck buys a cheap knife to kill his wife'. Woyzeck, like Othello, is driven by powers apparently beyond his control to kill the thing he loves, but his penury forces him to do it with a cheap knife instead of a tastefully embroidered pillow. What is more, the profiteer is ready to exploit the hero's tragic *hamartia*. Thus the social gist of the play is condensed into a single brief episode. Applying this to the question of prosody in the lyric, Brecht draws attention to the 'gestisch' choruses of popular demonstrations. Rhythm is the servant, not the master, of the idea in the mouths of demonstrators during a hunger-march. Their strident protest against social injustice scans differently from the love-sonnet or the folk-ballad:

$$\overline{\text{Wir}} \quad \overline{\text{ha}} \quad \overline{\text{ben}} \quad \underset{\text{Hun}}{\overline{\smile}} \quad \underset{\text{ger}}{\smile}$$

(19:399, Brecht's own scansion)

Even the newspaper boy and the market cheapjack observe a form of 'gestisch' versification as they advertise their wares. Brecht admits that this principle could lead to sloppy writing, but at its best it opens up new possibilities in the lyric, which need no longer be ashamed of its antisocial aloofness. Moreover, given such freedom in the scansion, and observing a strict caesura at the end of each line, even rhyme can resume its function of imposing an over-all sense of symmetry and balance.

'Finnische Landschaft', one of the most moving poems of exile, illustrates how Brecht has avoided traditional rhythms, yet still preserves the lyric mode in giving the individual word an accentuation and value it could not have in prose:

> Fischreiche Wässer! Schönbaumige Wälder!
> Birken- und Beerenduft!
> Vieltöniger Wind, durchschaukelnd eine Luft
> So mild, als stünden jene eisernen Milchbehälter
> Die dort vom weißen Gute rollen, offen!
> Geruch und Ton und Bild und Sinn verschwimmt.
> Der Flüchtling sitzt im Erlengrund und nimmt
> Sein schwieriges Handwerk wieder auf: das Hoffen.*
>
> (9:822)

So runs the first part. There can be no question of a seductive rhythm swamping the sense, for every line scans differently and there must be readers who have failed to notice that the form of the poem is that of a Petrarchan sonnet. At the same time, the great beauty of the Finnish landscape, far from being denied by the socially orientated poet, is rhythmically linked with the imagery evoked by freely moving dactyls ('Fischreiche', 'schwieriges', 'eisernen', 'Birken und') and iambics ('Die dort vom weißen Gute rollen, offen!'). The synaesthesia of the line 'Geruch und Ton und Bild und Sinn verschwimmt' is all the more effective because the flow of iambics comes so unexpectedly, and the dactylic 'schwieriges' is nicely timed to break up the iambic climax of this first section. The heavy caesura in the first line, caused by the two strong stresses that follow the so-called Adonian opening (dactyl and trochee: 'Fischreiche Wässer') forces the two images apart and creates an exhilarating sense of space; this is reinforced by the second caesura at the end of the line and further emphasized by a shortened second line that refuses to scan regularly despite the rhyme. One sees from this the point of Herr Keuner's remark that, just as Roman senators were obliged to wear pocketless robes to discourage bribery, so poets should wear garments without sleeves 'damit sie keine Verse aus ihnen schütteln können' (12:397).

In this poem Brecht feels he can now afford the luxury of a rhyme that is prevented from 'slipping past the ear' by the irregularity of the lines it unites. The rhyme-scheme has sufficient variety to avoid the jingle-effect, and the folk-rhyme 'Wälder—behälter' adds a popular touch. The clash between pure evocation and social challenge, momentary enjoyment and sad awareness of exile, stands out all the more starkly against the harmony of its linguistic vehicle. T. S. Eliot has written: 'It is a function of all art to give us some perception of an order in life, by imposing an order upon it',[9] and rhyme and rhythm are the tools of the lyric poet's craft in achieving this end. Brecht's position is fundamentally different. For him it is a function of all art to expose the chaos in life, and until it has been overcome rhyme and rhythm must not obstruct the view.

'Gestus' is not the only link between Brecht's dramatic theory and his poetry. *Verfremdung*, the basic principle behind

[9] *Selected Prose*, 1963, p. 80.

all his later drama, also has its counterpart in the poetry. The children's ballad 'Der Schneider von Ulm', which Brecht included in his *Kalendergeschichten*, tells the story of an over-ambitious artisan who killed himself trying to fly from the tower of Ulm Minster. As in *Leben des Galilei*, the Church represents the reactionary forces of an Establishment that has a vested interest in curbing human endeavour. The Bishop apparently has the last word:

> Die Glocken sollen läuten
> Es waren nichts als Lügen
> Der Mensch ist kein Vogel
> Es wird nie ein Mensch fliegen
> Sagte der Bischof den Leuten.*
> (9:646)

Mention has already been made of a seminar in which several students discussed the 'strophe' that relates how history proves the Bishop wrong (see p. 61). This furnishes a good example of *Verfremdung*. Just as we are expected to oppose the opportunism of Mother Courage, although the text of the play seems to support it, so we superimpose on the ballad our knowledge of subsequent developments in technology. Our independent and unsolicited contribution to the poem is more important than the words on the page. As Brecht puts it in his poem 'Der Gedanke in den Werken der Klassiker', thought is impotent without an audience. Brecht's poetry, like his drama, asks urgent questions, to which his reader is to provide the relevant answers. The poem 'Fragen eines lesenden Arbeiters' closes bluntly with:

> So viele Berichte
> So viele Fragen.
> (9:657)

The poem itself asks who built seven-gated Thebes, who rebuilt Babylon, where the builders of Golden Lima and the Great Wall of China and Byzantium lived, who erected the triumphal arches of Rome, and over whom the Caesars conquered. No less than fourteen question marks punctuate the text, but the answers are the reader's responsibility. The sixth of eight fine elegies later grouped under the heading *1940* originally bore the misleading title 'Die Antwort'. Brecht's young son receives in fact three negative answers to his inquiry whether he should study mathematics, French, and history. In the dark days of 1940 there seemed little point in perpetuating the anachronistic farce of a liberal education in the face of the Nazis' seemingly invincible barbarism. But the repeated formula 'möchte ich sagen' indicates that the despair is hypothetical, for the poet has once again resumed his 'schwieriges Handwerk', hope. Suddenly the poem changes direction and concludes with a threefold imperative, separated from the rest of the text by a gap:

> Ja, lerne Mathematik, sage ich
> Lerne Französisch, lerne Geschichte!
>
> (9:818)

No reason is given for the abrupt change of mood. The reader is left to supply the argument that to go on learning is a symbolic gesture of defiance.

All the features discussed above are those of a kind of poetry expressly designed as a weapon with which to combat a corrupt world, and Brecht never writes as though he regarded them as anything more than a temporary and regrettable expedient. The tension created by the conflict between the poet's desire to write about the apple-tree in blossom and the propagandist's political mission constitutes an indictment of the dark age in which he lives, an age that has made pure lyric poetry an illicit pastime. The poem 'An die Nachgeborenen' is addressed to the citizens of that distant Utopia where lyric poetry will come into its own:

> Dabei wissen wir doch:
> Auch der Haß gegen die Niedrigkeit
> Verzerrt die Züge.
> Auch der Zorn über das Unrecht
> Macht die Stimme heiser.*
>
> (9:725)

During the era for which Brecht writes, the features of lyric poetry are likewise distorted by hatred of baseness, and its voice also becomes hoarse with anger against injustice. Happy the post-revolutionary poet, whose energies will not be sapped by the struggle against exploitation, for he will be free to develop his art along lines Brecht can only wistfully anticipate.

Though Brecht can scarcely have been tempted to believe that the contours of his Utopia were more than faintly adumbrated by Ulbricht's Germany, its tentative foundations had at least been laid, and there is a noticeable mellowing of Brecht's poetry in the final period as a result. He gives us a foretaste of the future of poetry as he envisaged it.

Protest-songs and satirical poems still constitute a generous proportion of the post-war lyrics and one of them is significantly entitled 'Schlechte Zeiten', but in some poems there is a new note of reconciliation that reduces conflict and strain to a scarcely audible discord. The twenty-one short poems published in 1953 under the title *Buckower Elegien*, barely 150 lines in all, are amongst the finest in the language and certainly give the lie to the common assertion that Brecht wrote nothing of merit after making his final 'choice of evils'. Under the influence of the pithy oriental verse that Brecht admired so much, he achieves an astonishing simplicity of diction and rhythm that runs counter to the general trend of modern verse and forms a fitting epilogue to Brecht's own. There is still a satirical ring in 'Die Lösung', which asks the Pankow government, in view of its protested loss of faith in the people after the abortive uprising of 17 June 1953, why it does not simply dissolve the people and elect another; there is still a call for solidarity beneath the socialist banner in 'Die Wahrheit einigt'; rhyme is still absent and there is still a marked irregularity in the versification. But there is an autumnal tranquillity about much of it, which is due more to Brecht's state of mind in his last years than to any formal technique.

'Der Rauch', already discussed in another context (see p. 28) is perhaps the best:

> Das kleine Haus unter Bäumen am See.
> Vom Dach steigt Rauch.
> Fehlte er
> Wie trostlos dann wären
> Haus, Bäume und See.
>
> (10:1012)

Three impressionistic motifs are isolated from the landscape in the first line. The roof has a line to itself and the emphasis on the rising smoke gives the idyll the same sense of movement as the breath of wind in Goethe's 'Über allen Gipfeln'. Then comes a dramatic but characteristically laconic change of mood. After a heavy caesura the smoke-motif is removed from the canvas and the second part of the diptych is moved into position alongside the first, the versification pointing the contrast. The title of the second picture, as it were, 'Trostlos', indicates that the lyric observer, though a good deal less obtrusive than his counterpart in the Romantic tradition, is still present, comparing and contrasting the two images. The hypothetical subjunctive that connects the one with the other has much the same force as the 'möchte ich sagen' in 'Die Antwort'. It is the anthropocentric idyll that is real. Its dehumanized counterpart may well appeal to a world-shy Stifter or Mörike, but not to Brecht. In the well-earned peace of his week-end retreat in Buckow, where he spent more and more of his time in 1953, Brecht can describe the landscape with an easier conscience than he did in Svendborg before the war, but only because its social context has begun to make sense. What the poem does not need to say is that social justice, even if it is only in its infancy, has liberated the energies of the committed poet for other tasks.

'Tannen' is a companion piece from the same anthology:

> In der Frühe
> Sind die Tannen kupfern.
> So sah ich sie
> Vor einem halben Jahrhundert
> Vor zwei Weltkriegen
> Mit jungen Augen.*
>
> (10:1013)

The coppery glow of the firs in the early morning sun is, like the features of Goethe's incandescent landscape in 'Mailied', much more than an objective visual motif. The poet's eye is no camera. There is in Brecht's poem a retinal after-image that makes a double exposure of what is essentially an inner landscape. 'Thus I saw them', it claims, shifting the tense ominously in the third line. Visually the firs—incidentally no longer urinating or harbouring vermin—remain the same, but the resemblance is superficial and deceptive. Half a century of bitter conflict, the two most destructive wars in the history of civilization, dark ages during which to speak of trees had seemed criminal irresponsibility, have left their indelible imprint. As useless for Brecht as for Wordsworth to attempt to recapture 'the glory and the freshness of a dream'. Social reality powerfully affects memory and perception. But in this final period of Brecht's creative activity the poet can reflect on life without bitterness and above all without a sense of shame.

It is not for the commentator to explode the political myth on which this conciliatory mood is based. The logic of poetry is beyond the reach of such criticism. What makes the elegiac strain of this late verse so moving is that same Olympian serenity found on Brecht's death-mask, which is strangely at odds with the care-lined, prematurely aged Brecht who smiles wanly from most of the post-war photographs. It is only one side of what must have been a very complex post-war Brecht if the truth were fully known, but it is plainly the image of himself he valued most. Brecht saw himself as a poet born not out of his time as the title of 'Der Nachgeborene' had proclaimed during the period of *Baal*, but, as the later title 'An die Nachgeborenen' indicates, born just soon enough to envisage a happier future for society and its poetry, albeit too soon to enjoy it himself.

Brief Chronology of Brecht's Life and Works

1898   Birth of Berthold Eugen Friedrich Brecht in Augsburg (10 February)

1904–8   Elementary school in Augsburg.

1908–17   Realgymnasium, Augsburg (1914, *Die Bibel* published in school magazine; 1915, Brecht threatened with dismissal for writing a pacifist essay).

1917   Matriculation at the University of Munich.

1918   Military service as medical orderly in a V.D. ward in Augsburg. First version of *Baal*.

1919   *Trommeln in der Nacht.*

1921   *Im Dickicht der Städte.*

1922   First performance of *Trommeln in der Nacht*, in Munich (29 September). Brecht awarded the Kleist Prize. Marries Marianne Zoff (3 November).

1923   First performance of *Im Dickicht der Städte*, in Munich (9 May). First performance of *Baal*, in Leipzig (8 December).

1924   First performance of *Leben Eduards des Zweiten von England*, in Munich (18 March). In September Brecht moves to Berlin to work at the Deutsches Theater under Max Reinhardt.

1926   First performance of *Mann ist Mann*, in Darmstadt (26 September). During the summer Brecht begins intensive study of economics and Marxism.

1927   *Bertolt Brechts Hauspostille* published. Divorce.

1928   First performance of *Die Dreigroschenoper* at the Theater am Schiffbauerdamm in Berlin (31 August).

1929   Brecht marries Helene Weigel (10 April). First performance of *Der Flug der Lindberghs* (later renamed *Der Ozeanflug*) and *Das Badener Lehrstück vom Einverständnis* at the Baden-Baden Music Festival in July. *Die Ausnahme und die Regel.*

1930   First performance of *Aufstieg und Fall der Stadt Mahagonny*, in Leipzig (9 March). First performance of *Der Jasager*, in Berlin (23 June). Brecht sues the Nero Film Company in connection with their screen version of the *Dreigroschenoper*.

First performance of *Die Maßnahme*, in Berlin (10 December). First two issues of *Versuche* appear.

1931   *Die heilige Johanna der Schlachthöfe.*

1932   First performance of *Die Mutter*, in Berlin (17 January). Brecht attends first showing of film *Kuhle Wampe* in Moscow in May. *Die Spitzköpfe und die Rundköpfe.*

1933   Brecht leaves Germany for Paris via Prague, Vienna, and Lugano (28 February). First performance of *Die Sieben Todsünden der Kleinbürger*, in Paris (7 June). Brecht settles in Skovbostrand, near Svendborg, Denmark, in December.

1934   *Die Horatier und die Kuriatier. Der Dreigroschenroman* published in Amsterdam and *Lieder Gedichte Chöre* in Paris.

1935   Brecht visits Moscow in the spring and New York in the autumn.

1936   First performance of *Die Rundköpfe und die Spitzköpfe*, in Copenhagen (4 November).

1937   First performance of *Die Gewehre der Frau Carrar*, in Paris (17 October).

1938   First performance of eight scenes from *Furcht und Elend des Dritten Reiches*, in Paris (21 May). Brecht works on *Die Geschäfte des Herrn Julius Caesar*, and completes the first version of *Leben des Galilei*.

1939   *Das Verhör des Lukullus. Mutter Courage und ihre Kinder. Svendborger Gedichte* published in Copenhagen. Brecht leaves Denmark for Sweden.

1940   Brecht moves to Finland in April as the guest of Hella Wuolijoki. *Herr Puntila und sein Knecht Matti.*

1941   *Der gute Mensch von Sezuan. Der aufhaltsame Aufstieg des Arturo Ui.* First performance of *Mutter Courage*, in Zurich (19 April). May–July, Brecht moves to California, via Moscow and Vladivostok, and settles in Santa Monica, near Hollywood.

1942   Film-script for *Hangmen Also Die.*

1943   *Die Gesichte der Simone Machard.* First performance of *Der gute Mensch von Sezuan*, in Zurich (4 February). First performance of *Leben des Galilei*, in Zurich (9 September). *Schweyk im Zweiten Weltkrieg.*

1945   *Der kaukasische Kreidekreis.* Brecht works with Charles Laughton on American version of *Leben des Galilei*.

1947   First performance of the American *Galileo*, in Hollywood (31 July). Brecht appears before the Un-American Activities Committee in Washington (30 October) and leaves for Zurich, via Paris, the next day.

1948   First performance of *Antigone*, at Chur (15 February). First performance of *Puntila*, in Zurich (5 June). Brecht returns to Berlin (22 October).

1949 First performance of the revised version of *Mutter Courage* at the Deutsches Theater in Berlin (11 January). *Die Tage der Commune*. The Berliner Ensemble opens with *Puntila* (8 November). *Kalendergeschichten* published.

1950 Brecht gains Austrian nationality. First performance of his adaptation of *Der Hofmeister* (15 April) by the Berliner Ensemble.

1951 First stage performance of *Das Verhör des Lukullus* (later modified and renamed *Die Verurteilung des Lukullus*) (17 March) by the Berliner Ensemble.

1952 Brecht works on his adaptation of *Coriolanus*. Publication of *Theaterarbeit* (containing some 500 photographs of six productions by the Berliner Ensemble).

1953 *Buckower Elegien. Turandot oder Der Kongreß der Weißwäscher.*

1954 Berliner Ensemble moves into the Theater am Schiffbauerdamm and opens with Brecht's adaptation of Molière's *Don Juan* (19 March). Brecht appointed Vice-President of the Deutsche Akademie der Künste. First performance of Brecht's adaptation of Farquhar's *The Recruiting Officer* (*Pauken und Trompeten*) (19 September). German première of *Der kaukasische Kreidekreis* at the Berliner Ensemble (7 October). Brecht receives the Stalin Peace Prize in Moscow (21 December). Work begins on rehearsals of *Galilei* at the Berliner Ensemble. *Die Kriegsfibel* published.

1956 Brecht dies of coronary thrombosis (14 August).

Select Bibliography

The prodigious output of secondary literature on Brecht over the last two decades—the far from exhaustive Soviet bibliography of 1969 alone lists over sixteen hundred items—precludes any possibility of comprehensiveness in a bibliography of this kind. The following list is restricted to works exclusively or mainly on Brecht and of particular relevance to the present study.

Bibliographies

NUBEL, W., 'Bertolt Brecht-Bibliographie', *Sinn und Form*, 9, 1957, pp. 485–623.

PETERSEN, K.-D., *Bertolt-Brecht-Bibliographie*, Bad Homburg, 1968.

SEIDEL, G., *Bibliographie Bertolt Brecht*, Berlin, 1975 ff.

VOLGINA, A. A., *Bertolt Brecht: Bibliograficheskii ukazatel'*, Moscow, 1969.

Biographical and general

ANDRES, G., *Bertolt Brecht: Gespräche und Erinnerungen*, Zurich, 1962.

ARENDT, H., 'Quod licet Jovi . . .: Reflexionen über den Dichter Bertolt Brecht und sein Verhältnis zur Politik', *Merkur*, 1969, pp. 527–42, 625–42.

BARTHES, R., 'Brecht, Marx et l'histoire', *Cahiers de la Compagnie Madeleine Renaud–Jean Louis Barrault*, Dec. 1957, pp. 21–5.

BENJAMIN, W., *Versuche über Brecht*, Frankfurt, 1966.

BRANDT, T. O., *Die Vieldeutigkeit Bertolt Brechts*, Heidelberg, 1968.

BRONNEN, A., *Tage mit Bertolt Brecht: Geschichte einer unvollendeten Freundschaft*, Vienna, 1960.

BRÜGGEMANN, H., *Literarische Technik und soziale Revolution: Versuche über das Verhältnis von Kunstproduktion, Marxismus und literarischer Tradition in den theoretischen Schriften Bertolt Brechts*, Hamburg-Reinbek, 1973.

CHIARINI, P., *Bertolt Brecht*, Bari, 1959.

DEBIEL, G., *Das Prinzip der Verfremdung in der Sprachgestaltung Bertolt Brechts*, Bonn, 1960.

DEMETZ, P. (ed.), *Brecht: a Collection of Critical Essays*, Englewood Cliffs, 1962.

DESUCHÉ J., *Bertolt Brecht*, Paris, 1963.

DORT, B., *Lecture de Brecht*, Paris, 1960.

DOWNER, A. F., 'The Poetry, Drama and Theory of Bertolt Brecht', M.A. thesis, Univ. of Swansea, 1954.

DYMSHITS, A., 'Bertolt Brecht', *Zvezda*, Apr. 1957, pp. 192–9.

ESSLIN, M., *Brecht: A Choice of Evils*, London, 1959.

—— *Bertolt Brecht*, New York and London, 1969.

EWEN, F., *Bertolt Brecht: His Life, his Art and his Times*, London, 1970.

FEDIN, K., 'Vechnyi iskatel', *Literaturnaya gazeta*, 18 Aug. 1956.

FRADKIN, I., 'Bertolt Brecht: khudozhnik mysli', *Teatr*, 1956, no. 1, pp. 142–55.

—— 'Bertolt Brecht', in *Literatura novoi germanii*, Moscow, 1959, pp. 205–66.

—— *Bertolt Brecht: Put i metod*, Moscow, 1965.

FUEGI, J., *The Essential Brecht*, Los Angeles, 1972.

GRAY, R., *Brecht*, Edinburgh, 1961.

—— *Brecht, the Dramatist*, Cambridge, 1976.

GRILLET, F., *Bertolt Brecht*, Brugge and Utrecht, 1962.

GRIMM, R., *Bertolt Brecht: die Struktur seines Werkes*, Nuremberg, 1959 (rev. edn. 1968).

—— *Bertolt Brecht und die Weltliteratur*, Nuremberg, 1961.

—— *Bertolt Brecht*, Stuttgart, 1963.

HECHT, W., *Sieben Studien über Brecht*, Frankfurt, 1972.

HELLER, P., 'Nihilist into activist: two phases in the development of Bertolt Brecht', *Germanic Review*, 28, 1953, pp. 144–55.

HOFFMANN, C. W., 'Brecht's humour: laughter while the shark bites', *Germanic Review*, 38, 1963, pp. 157–66.

JENS, W., 'Poesie und Doktrin', in *Statt einer Literaturgeschichte*, Pfullingen, 1957, pp. 227–58.

KESTING, M., *Bertolt Brecht in Selbstzeugnissen und Bilddokumenten*, Hamburg-Reinbek, 1959.

KLOTZ, V., *Bertolt Brecht: Versuch über das Werk*, Darmstadt, 1957.

KNOPF, J., *Bertolt Brecht: ein kritischer Forschungsbericht*, Frankfurt, 1974.

KOPELEV, L., *Brecht*, Moscow, 1966.

MANN, O., *B.B.—Maß oder Mythos?*, Heidelberg, 1958.

MAYER, H., *Bertolt Brecht und die Tradition*, Pfullingen, 1961.

—— *Anmerkungen zu Brecht*, Frankfurt, 1965.

MELCHINGER, S. (ed.), *Das Ärgernis Brecht*, Basle and Stuttgart, 1961.

MILFULL, J., 'The development towards "optimism" in the works of Bertolt Brecht: its relation to the "pessimism" of the earlier period and to Marxist influence', Ph.D. thesis, Univ. of Sidney, 1967.

MILFULL, J., *From Baal to Keuner: the 'Second Optimism' of Bertolt Brecht*, Berne and Frankfurt, 1974.

MÜLLER, K.-D., *Die Funktion der Geschichte im Werk Bertolt Brechts*, Tübingen, 1967 (rev. edn. 1972).

MÜNSTERER, H. O., *Bertolt Brecht: Erinnerungen aus den Jahren 1917–1922*, Zurich, 1963.

PFELLING, L., 'Brecht im Spiegel sowjetischer Publikationen', *Weimarer Beiträge*, 14, 1968 (Sonderheft Brecht), pp. 155–70.

QURESHI, Q., *Pessimismus und Fortschrittsglaube bei Bertolt Brecht*, Cologne, 1971.

RASCH, W., 'Brechts Marxistischer Lehrer', *Merkur*, 17, 1963, pp. 988–1003.

REICH, B., *Brecht: ocherk tvorchestva*, Moscow, 1960.

RISCHBIETER, H., *Bertolt Brecht*, Hamburg, 1966.

ROSENBAUER, H., *Brecht und der Behaviorismus*, Bad Homburg, 1970.

SPALTER, M., *Brecht's Tradition*, Baltimore, 1967.

STERNBERG, F., *Der Dichter und die Ratio: Erinnerungen an Bertolt Brecht*, Göttingen, 1963.

VÖLKER, K., *Brecht-Chronik: Daten zu Leben und Werk*, Munich, 1971.

—— *Bertolt Brecht: eine Biographie*, Munich, 1976.

WEIDELI, W., *The Art of Bertolt Brecht*, London, 1963.

WITT, H. (ed.), *Erinnerungen an Brecht*, Leipzig, 1963.

WITZMANN, P., *Antike Tradition im Werk Bertolt Brechts*, Berlin, 1964.

Brecht's Theatre in Theory and Practice

ALTER, M. P., 'Bertolt Brecht and the Noh drama', *Modern Drama*, ii, 1968, pp. 122–31.

BECKLEY, R., 'Adaptation as a feature of Brecht's dramatic technique', *German Life & Letters*, 15, 1961–2, pp. 274–93.

BENTLEY, E., 'Die Theaterkunst Brechts', *Sinn und Form*, 9 (Sonderheft Brecht), 1957, pp. 159–77.

BÖCKMANN, P., *Provokation und Dialektik in der Dramatik Bert Brechts*, Krefeld, n.d.

CHIARINI, P., 'Lessing und Brecht', *Sinn und Form*, 9, 1957, pp. 188–203.

—— *Bertolt Brecht: Saggio sul teatro*, Bari, 1967.

DICKSON, K. A., 'Brecht: an Aristotelian malgré lui', *Modern Drama*, 1968, pp. 111–21.

—— 'Of masks and men: an aspect of Brecht's theatrical technique', *New German Studies*, i, 1973, pp. 1–14.

FERNANDEZ, D., 'Bertolt Brecht ou l'homme incapable de tragédie', *La nouvelle Nouvelle Revue Française*, July–Dec. 1956, pp. 725–6.

GLUMOVA-GLUKHAREV, E. I., *Dramaturgia Bertolta Brechta*, Moscow, 1962.

GRIMM, R., 'Verfremdung: Beiträge zu Wesen und Ursprung eines Begriffs', *Revue de la littérature comparée*, 35, 1961, pp. 207–36.

HECHT, W., *Brechts Weg zum epischen Theater*, Berlin, 1962.

HINCK, W., *Die Dramaturgie des späten Brecht*, Göttingen, 1962.

HULTBERG, H., 'Brecht und Shakespeare', *Orbis Litterarum*, 14, 1959, pp. 89–104.

—— *Die ästhetischen Anschauungen Bertolt Brechts*, Copenhagen, 1962.

JENDREIEK, H., *Bertolt Brecht: Drama der Veränderung*, Düsseldorf, 1969.

JHERING, H., *Bertolt Brecht und das Theater*, Berlin, 1959.

KLYUYEV, V. G., *Teatralno-esteticheskie vzglyady Brechta*, Moscow, 1966.

LUTHARDT, T., 'Vergleichende Studien zu Bertolt Brechts "Kleines Organon für das Theater" ', Ph.D. thesis, Univ. of Jena, 1955.

LYONS, CH. R., *Bertolt Brecht: the Despair and the Polemic*, London and Amsterdam, 1968.

MITTENZWEI, W., *Bertolt Brecht: von der 'Maßnahme' zu 'Leben des Galilei'*, Berlin, 1962.

RÜLICKE-WEILER, K., *Die Dramaturgie Brechts: Theater als Mittel der Veränderung*, Berlin, 1968.

SCHÖNE, A., 'Bertolt Brechts Theatertheorie und dramatische Dichtung', *Euphorion*, 52, 1958, pp. 272–96.

SCHRIMPF, H. J., *Lessing und Brecht: von der Aufklärung auf dem Theater*, Pfullingen, 1965.

SCHUMACHER, E., *Die dramatischen Versuche Bertolt Brechts, 1918–1933*, Berlin, 1955.

SERREAU, G. *Brecht*, Paris, 1955.

STEER, W. A. J., 'Brecht's Epic Theatre: theory and practice', *Modern Language Review*, 62, 1968, pp. 636–49.

STEINWEG, R., *Das Lehrstück: Brechts Theorie einer politisch-ästhetischen Erziehung*, Stuttgart, 1972.

SUBIOTTO, A., 'A "mathematical" note on "Verfremdung" and Brecht', *German Life & Letters*, 17, 1963–4, pp. 233–7.

SYMINGTON, R., *Brecht und Shakespeare*, Bonn, 1970.

SZYDŁOWSKI, R., *Dramaturgia Bertolta Brechta*, Warsaw, 1965.

WEKWERTH, M., *Notate über die Arbeit des Berliner Ensembles, 1956–66*, Frankfurt, 1967.

WILLETT, J., *The Theatre of Bertolt Brecht*, London, 1959.

WIRTH, A., 'Über die stereometrische Struktur der Brechtschen Stücke', *Sinn und Form*, 9, 1957, pp. 346–87.

306 *Select Bibliography*

WULBERN, J. H., *Brecht and Ionesco: Commitment in Context*, Illinois, 1971.

ZAKHAVA, B., 'Sila i slabost teatra Brechta', *Znamya*, no. 8, Aug. 1957, pp. 160–6.

ZÉRAFFA, M., 'Shakespeare, Brecht et l'histoire', *Europe*, 35, 1957, pp. 130–1.

ŽMEGAČ, V., *Kunst und Wirklichkeit: zur Literaturtheorie bei Brecht, Lukács und Broch*, Bad Homburg, 1969.

ZWERENZ, G., *Aristotelische und Brechtsche Dramatik*, Rudolstadt, 1956.

Discussion of Individual Plays

BAHR, G. (ed.), *Im Dickicht der Städte: Erstfassung und Materialien*, Frankfurt, 1968.

BECKLEY, R. J., 'Some aspects of Brecht's dramatic technique in the light of his adaptation of English plays', M.A. thesis, Univ. of London, 1961 [*Eduard II* and *Coriolan*].

DICKSON, K. A., 'History, Drama, and Brecht's chronicle of the Thirty Years War', *Forum for Modern Language Studies*, 6, 1970, pp. 255–72.

—— (ed.), *Bertolt Brecht: Fünf Lehrstücke*, London, 1969.

GARNER, G. N., 'Bertolt Brecht's use of the Bible and Christianity in representative dramatic works', Ph.D. thesis, Louisiana State Univ., 1969.

GOLDHAHN, J., *Das Parabelstück Bertolt Brechts als Beitrag zum Kampf gegen den deutschen Faschismus*, Rudolstadt, 1961 [*Arturo Ui* and *Die Rundköpfe und die Spitzköpfe*].

GRATHOFF, D., 'Dichtung versus Politik: Brechts *Coriolan* aus Günter Grassens Sicht', *Brecht Heute*, i, 1971, pp. 168–87.

GRIMM, R. (ed.), *Leben Eduards des Zweiten von England: Vorlage, Texte und Materialien*, Frankfurt, 1968.

HECHT, W. (ed.), *Materialien zu Brechts 'Leben des Galilei'*, Frankfurt, 1963.

—— *Materialien zu 'Mutter Courage und ihre Kinder'*, Frankfurt, 1964.

—— *Materialien zur 'Antigone'*, Frankfurt, 1967.

—— *Materialien zu 'Der gute Mensch von Sezuan'*, Frankfurt, 1968.

—— *Materialien zu 'Der kaukasische Kreidekreis'*, Frankfurt, 1966.

HOFFMANN, C. H. and FUEGI, J. B., 'Brecht, Schweyk and Communeism', *Festschrift D. W. Schumann*, Munich, 1970, pp. 337–49.

HOFFMEIER, D., 'Notate zu Bertolt Brechts Bearbeitung von Shakespeares *Coriolan*', *Shakespeare-Jahrbuch*, 103, 1967, pp. 177–95.

HUMMEL, E., 'Zu einigen Problemen der dramatischen Gestaltung der Pariser Kommune durch Bertolt Brecht und Nordahl

Grieg', *Wissenschaftliche Zeitschrift der Universität Greifswald*, 12, 1967, pp. 49–53.

JUSOWSKI, J., 'Bertolt Brecht und sein guter Mensch', *Sinn und Form*, 9, 1957, pp. 204–13.

KAUFMANN, H., *Bertolt Brecht: Geschichtsdrama und Parabelstück*, Berlin, 1962 [*Die Tage der Commune*].

KNUST, H. (ed.), *Materialien zu 'Schweyk im Zweiten Weltkrieg'*, Frankfurt, 1974.

LABOULLE, L. J., 'A note on Bertolt Brecht's adaptation of Marlowe's *Edward II*', *Modern Language Review*, 54, 1959, pp. 214–20.

MARE, M. (ed.), *Brecht: Der gute Mensch von Sezuan*, London, 1960.

—— (ed.), *Brecht: Herr Puntila und sein Knecht Matti*, London, 1962.

MENNEMEIER, F. N., 'Brechts *Mutter Courage und ihre Kinder*', in *Das deutsche Drama vom Barock zur Gegenwart*, ed. Benno von Wiese, Düsseldorf, 1964, vol. 2, pp. 386–404.

MONÍKOVÁ, L., 'Brechtovo prepracování Shakespearova *Koriolana*', *Časopis pro moderní filologii*, 52, 1970, pp. 180–8.

ONDERDELINDEN, J. W., 'Brechts *Mann ist Mann*: Lustspiel oder Lehrstück?', *Neophilologus*, 54, 1970, pp. 149–66.

PFRIMMER, E., 'Brecht et la parodie: *Arturo Ui*', *Études germaniques*, 26, 1971, pp. 73–88.

ROHRMOSER, G., 'Das Leben des Galilei', in *Das deutsche Drama*, ed. Benno von Wiese, Düsseldorf, 1964, vol. 2, pp. 405–19.

RÜLICKE-WEILER, K., '*Leben des Galilei*: Bemerkungen zur Schluß-szene', *Sinn und Form*, 9, 1957, pp. 269–321.

SCHMIDT, D., *Baal und der junge Brecht*, Stuttgart, 1966.

—— (ed.), '*Baal*': *drei Fassungen*, Frankfurt, 1968.

—— '*Baal*', '*Der böse Baal der asoziale*', Frankfurt, 1968.

SCHUMACHER, E., *Drama und Geschichte: Bertolt Brechts 'Leben des Galilei' und andere Stücke*, Berlin, 1968.

SPEIDEL, E., 'The mute person's voice: Mutter Courage and her daughter', *German Life & Letters*, 23, 1969–70, pp. 332–9.

—— '*Puntila*: a Marxist comedy', *Modern Language Review*, 65, 1970, p. 319–32.

STEER, W. A. J., '*Baal*: a key to Brecht's communism', *German Life & Letters*, 19, 1965–6, pp. 40–51.

—— 'The thematic unity of Brecht's *Der kaukasische Kreidekreis*', *German Life & Letters*, 21, 1967–8, pp. 1–10.

STEINWEG, R., '*Die Maßnahme*': *kritische Ausgabe mit einer Spielanleitung*, Frankfurt, 1972.

SZCZESNY, G., *Das Leben des Galilei und der Fall Bertolt Brecht*, Frankfurt, 1966.

TSCHARCHALASCHWILI, S., 'Der kaukasische Kreidekreis: seine Geschichte und Verfremdungstheorie von Bertolt Brecht', *Weimarer Beiträge*, 14, 1968 (Sonderheft Brecht), pp. 171–84.

WEISSTEIN, U., 'Two measures for one: *Die Rundköpfe und die Spitzköpfe*', *Germanic Review*, 43, 1968, pp. 24–39.

ZIMMERMANN, W., *Brechts 'Leben des Galilei': Interpretation und didaktische Analyse*, Düsseldorf, 1965.

Fiction

BUONO, F., *Zur Prosa Brechts*, Frankfurt, 1973.

DAHLKE, H., *Cäsar bei Brecht: eine vergleichende Betrachtung*, Berlin, 1968.

DAKOWA, N., 'Die erzählende Prosa Bertolt Brechts, 1913–1934', Ph.D. thesis, Univ. of Leipzig, 1961.

DICKSON, K. A. (ed.), *Bertolt Brecht: Kalendergeschichten*, London, 1971.

GOLDHAHN, J., 'Von der Kraft der Freundlichkeit: Brechts Kalendergeschichten', *Deutschunterricht*, Berlin, 1967, pp. 194–208.

SCHWIMMER, H., *Bertolt Brechts 'Kalendergeschichten': Interpretationen*, Munich, 1968.

SPAETLING, R. H., 'Zu Bertolt Brechts Cäsar-Fragment', *Neophilologus*, 45, 1961, pp. 213–18.

Poetry

BLUME, B., 'Motive der frühen Lyrik Bertolt Brechts', *Monatshefte*, 57, 1965, pp. 97–112, 273–81.

DICKSON, K. A., 'Brecht's doctrine of Nature', *Brecht Heute*, 3, 1973–4, pp. 106–21.

HAYS, H. R., 'The poetry of Bertolt Brecht', *Poetry*, 67, 1945–6, pp. 148–55.

HESELHAUS, C., 'Die Masken des Bertolt Brecht', in *Deutsche Lyrik der Moderne von Nietzsche bis Yvan Goll*, Düsseldorf, 1961, pp. 321–38.

LERG-KILL, V. C., *Dichterwort und Parteiparole: propagandistische Gedichte und Lieder Bertolt Brechts*, Bad Homburg, 1968.

McLEAN, S. K., *The 'Bänkelsang' and the Work of Bertolt Brecht*, The Hague, 1972.

MARSCH, E., *Brecht-Kommentar: zum lyrischen Werk*, Munich, 1974.

SCHLENSTEDT, S., 'Die Chroniken in den "Svendborger Gedichten": eine Untersuchung zur Lyrik Brechts', Ph.D. thesis, Berlin, 1959.

SCHUHMANN, K., *Der Lyriker Bertolt Brecht, 1913–1933*, Berlin 1964.

—— 'Themen und Formen der späten Lyrik Brechts', *Weimarer Beiträge*, 1968 (Sonderheft Brecht), pp. 39–60.

STEFFENSEN, S., 'Brecht und Rimbaud: zu den Gedichten des jungen Brecht', *Zeitschrift für deutsche Philologie*, 84 (Sonderheft), 1965, pp. 82–9.

THIEME, K., 'Des Teufels Gebetsbuch', *Hochland*, 29, 1931–2, pp. 397–413.

Translations

W/M indicates that the translation is from *Bertolt Brecht: Poems*, ed. John Willett and Ralph Manheim with the co-operation of Erich Fried, 1976 (reprinted by kind permission of the publishers, Eyre Methuen, and of Mr. Kurt Bernheim, agent for Brecht's Estate). All unsigned translations are my own.

p. 1
Our forces were slight. Our goal
Lay far in the distance
It was clearly visible, though I myself
Was unlikely to reach it.
So passed my time
Which had been given to me on earth.

(John Willett[4]
W/M, p. 319)

p. 10
I need no gravestone, but
If you need one for me
I would like it to bear these words:
He made suggestions. We
Carried them out.
Such an inscription would
Honour us all.

(Michael Hamburger[5,8]
W/M, p. 218)

p. 16
Even the sky may at times collapse
As stars fall to the ground
And it and us to dust they pound
All that will be tomorrow perhaps.

p. 16
And while she gets the hay down someone
Is milking her. Patient, without a sound
She lets his hand go tweaking at her teats.

She knows that hand, and doesn't turn around
She'd sooner not know what is going on
But takes advantage of the evening mood, and shits. (John Willett[2]
W/M, p. 115)

p. 20
A few people have a bed for the night
For a night the wind is kept from them
The snow meant for them falls on the roadway
But it won't change the world
It won't improve relations among men   (George Rapp[3]
It will not shorten the age of exploitation.   W/M, p. 181)

pp. 20–21
Now the shark has teeth like razors
And he shows them in a fight
All Macheath has is a flick-knife
And he keeps it out of sight.   (Hugh MacDiarmid)[10]

pp. 21–2
On to Mahagonny!
Of one thing we are sure:
From sy-sy-syphilization
It's there we'll find a cure.

p. 25
What kind of times are they, when
A talk about trees is almost a crime
Because it implies silence about so many horrors?   (John Willett[4]
          W/M, p. 318)

p. 27
Canalizing a river
Grafting a fruit tree
Educating a person
Transforming a state
These are instances of fruitful criticism.   (John Willett[3]
          W/M, p. 309)

p. 28
The little house among trees by the lake
From the roof smoke rises.
Without it
How dreary would be   (Derek Bowman[7]
House, trees and lake.   W/M, p. 442)

p. 29
Why then sow buckwheat for ever
In such a stony bed?
For nobody else will water
The tamarisk when I'm dead.

p. 30
Green are the meadows
The flag is red.
Ours the labour
Ours the bread!

p. 30
Peoples of the world, together
Join to serve the common cause!
So it feeds us all for ever   (John Willett[3]
See to it that it's now yours.   W/M, p. 185)

pp. 30–1
Apart from this star, I thought, there's nothing and it
Is so devastated.
It alone is our refuge and this
Is how it looks.

p. 31
Tend the fires in the boiler
Steer well and warily
That you may weather every storm
And traverse every sea!

p. 31
The voice of the October storm
Around the little house by the reeds
Comfortably
I lie on my bed and hear
Above the lake and above the city   (Humphrey Milnes[5]
My voice.   W/M, p. 432)

p. 35
As her pale body decayed in the water there
It happened (very slowly) that God gradually forgot it
First her face, then the hands, and right at the last her hair
Then she rotted in rivers where much else rotted.   (Peter Tegel)[11]

p. 41
Mr. Brecht maintains a man's a man
Which anyone could have said since life began.
But Mr. Bertolt Brecht goes on to show
How far with one man you can really go.
We're going to reassemble one right here,
And that he'll be the loser, do not fear:

We'll deal with him just like a human being
And do our level best to ensure his seeing
The need to adapt to the world without contrition
And to renounce all personal ambition.
And Mr. Bertolt Brecht hopes you'll all see
The ground on which we stand is slippery
And that you'll learn from Packer Galy Gay
How dangerous it is on earth to stay.

p. 42
Whatever we make of Packer Galy Gay
With confidence of him we all can say:
If we just let him once out of our sight
He could become our murderer overnight.

p. 47
Of course you must lie upon your back
As if by habit. And drift along.
You need not swim, no, only behave as if
It's just to the mass of gravel you belong.
You should look at the sky and act
As if a woman held you, which is right.
Quite without great upheaval as the good God does
When he swims in his rivers at evening light   (Lesley Lendrum[1]
                                                                                    W/M, p. 30)

pp. 50–1
Seven men built my machine in San Diego, often working 24 hours
at a stretch from a few yards of steel tubing. I must make do with
what they have made. They have done their work, I must continue
it, I am not alone, there are eight of us flying here.

p. 53
Then you will no longer be yourselves, no longer Karl Schmitt
from Berlin, or Anna Kyersk from Kazan or Peter Savitch from
Moscow, but all of you will be men without a name or a mother,
empty pages on which the revolution writes its instructions.

pp. 55–6
The individual has two eyes, the Party has a thousand. The party
sees seven states, the individual only one city. The individual has his
hour but the Party has many hours. The individual can be destroyed
but the Party is indestructible for it is the vanguard of the masses
and leads their struggle, adopting the methods of the classics,
which were based on a knowledge of reality.

p. 56
But who is the Party? . . . We are. You and I and all of us. It is in your clothes, comrade, and it thinks with your brain. Its house is where I live and it fights wherever you are under attack.

p. 59
Every page a victory.
Who cooked the feast for the victors?
Every ten years a great man.   (Michael Hamburger[4,8]
Who paid the bill?   W/M, p. 253)

p. 66
See how he ascends! He comes
Irresistibly, in his hands the sun
Now he rises
His name is Caesar!

See how he ascended. He came
Irresistibly, in his hands the sun
Often he rose
His name was always different.

pp. 71–2
The great Caius Julius Caesar . . . had inaugurated a new era. Before his time Rome had been a big city with a few scattered colonies, whereas he had founded the Empire. He had codified the laws, reformed the currency, even adapted the calendar in accordance with the latest scientific principles. His campaigns in Gaul, which carried the Roman standards into remote Britain, had opened up a new continent for trade and civilization. His statues stand among those of the gods; cities and a calendar month were named after him and monarchs added his illustrious name to their own. Roman history had acquired its own Alexander.

pp. 74–5
These last six months have proved one thing at any rate. C. was no great politician and never will be. Despite all his brilliant qualities! He is not what Rome now needs more than ever, the strong man, capable of going his own way unerringly and imposing his will on the world in the realization of a great idea. He lacks both the character and the idea. He dabbles in politics because there is nothing else left for him to do. But he is not a born leader. I'm far from optimistic about our future.

p. 78
And I hear you're approaching your subject from the right angle. The concept of the Empire! Democracy! The idea of progress! At

last, a book with a scientific basis, one that both the little man and the City businessman can read. His victory, their victory! Facts!

pp. 87–8

Princes will have to wax their own boots
The Emperor can bake his own bread
For orders the soldiers won't care two hoots
They'll go for a stroll instead.

p. 88

I'm not just any old creature on some tiny star gyrating somewhere in space for a short while. I walk securely on firm ground, which is at rest at the centre of the universe. I am at the centre and the eye of the Creator rests on me and on me alone. Around me, fixed to eight crystal spheres turn the planets and the mighty sun, which has been created to illuminate my environment. And me too, so that God may see me.

p. 88

There's no sense in our misery: hunger just means we haven't eaten, it's not a trial of strength; exertion is just bending and dragging, not a special merit.

pp. 88–9

Your Campagna peasants pay for the wars that the representative of gentle Jesus wages in Spain and Germany. Why does he place the earth at the centre of the universe? So that the throne of St. Peter may stand at the centre of the earth.

p. 93

Up rose Dr. Galileo (chucked away the Bible, grabbed his telescope, had a look at the universe) and said to the sun: stand still. The *creatio dei* shall now revolve the other way for a change. And so the mistress shall revolve around the maid for a change, too.

p. 95

There are little patches of shadow in it. And it's almost sweet, but just stops short at 'almost'—Andrea, clear away all this stuff, the ice, the bucket and the needle.—I have a high regard for creature comforts. I've no patience with those cowardly souls that go on about weakness. I say enjoyment is an achievement.

p. 98

To hear the big shots talk you'd think they make war for fear of God and all things bright and beautiful. But if you take a closer look, they're not so stupid. They make war for profit. And ordinary folk like me wouldn't join in for any other reason, either.

p. 104
Two years have passed. The war covers more and more territory. Pressing on without respite Mother Courage's little wagon traverses Poland, Moravia, Bavaria, Italy, and again Bavaria. 1631. Tilly's victory at Magdeburg costs Mother Courage four officers' shirts.

p. 105
I feel sorry for such a general or emperor. There he was p'raps, thinking as how he was doing something special, something people will be talking about in times to come, and thinking they'll build him a statue. He goes and conquers the world, for example, now there's an ambition worthy of a general, he can't ask for nothing better. In short, he works himself to a standstill and then it all comes to nothing because of the ordinary folk what p'raps want a mug of ale and a bit of company, nothing grander than that. The best plans have come adrift along of the pettiness of them as are supposed to carry 'em out, for of course the emperors can't do nothing for themselves, they rely on the support of their troops and the folk as happen to be around at the time, ain't I right?

p. 105
Though steel and lead are stout supporters
A war needs human beings too
Report today to your headquarters
If it's to last, this war needs you!   (Trl. Eric Bentley)[12]

pp. 119–20
This is the first night in history, my friends, in which this Paris of ours will have known no murder, no robbery, no brazen fraud and no violation. Its streets are safe for the first time, it needs no police. The bankers and the petty thieves, the tax-collectors, industrialists, ministers, cocottes and clergy have all left for Versailles: the city is inhabitable.

p. 134
Be not exploited and deceived
Fear not when drawing your last breath
From retribution you're reprieved
Since there is nothing after death.

p. 136
Many of us say you are not—and a good thing too.
But how could *that* thing not be which can play such a trick?
If so much lives by you and could not die without you—
Tell me how far does it matter that you don't exist? (John Willett[2]
W/M, p. 9)

p. 138
So anyone down here who says that there is a God, though none is visible, and that he may be invisible and still help people, he should have his head smashed against the pavement until he's done for.

p. 140
What I learned in my school, the gutter, through beatings and deception, shall now stand you in good stead, my son: I will be good to you and a tigress and a savage beast to all others if need be.

p. 143
On my wall hangs a Japanese carving
The mask of an evil demon, decorated with gold lacquer.
Sympathetically I observe
The swollen veins of the forehead, indicating   (H. R. Hays[6,9]
What a strain it is to be evil.   W/M, p. 383)

p. 147
We all abide by the law! The law serves only to exploit those who do not understand it or who cannot adhere to it out of sheer necessity. And anyone who wants to benefit from this exploitation must abide by the law.

p. 150
Unless I have the judge in my pocket by putting something in his, any policeman on the beat can shoot me down if I rob a bank.

p. 154
Let justice over all your life hold sway
For that has been the moral of our play.

p. 155
That's right. I get nothing from you miserable lot, you'd sooner see me starve. You want justice, but do you want to pay for it? When you go to the butcher's you know you have to pay up, but you go to the judge as though you were off to a lyke-wake.

p. 158
But you who have heard the story of the chalk circle, note the opinion of the ancients: that what there is belongs to those who are good for it, children to the motherly, that they may thrive, tractors to good drivers that they may be driven well, and the valley to the irrigators, that it may bear fruit.

p. 176
By threats and exhortation, wheedling and cajoling, by gentle coercion and steely embrace.

p. 178
And so the plan to move to Cicero
Was not from you. It's just the Trust's new plan?
Arturo, now I see what all this means.
It's clear what sort of game is being played.

p. 186
Don't expect too much of yourself. You're doing a good job if you're still alive these days. You're so preoccupied with survival that there's no time for anything else.

p. 187
The little man doesn't give a shit for a great era; all he wants is to go to the pub now and then and have a bowl of stew for his supper.

p. 188
The pebbles shift on the bed of the river
In Prague three emperors lie mouldering away
The great and the small do not stay thus for ever
The night lasts twelve hours, but it ends with the day.

p. 189
But you must learn to use your eyes, not stare
And act instead of talking: stay awake.
The world was almost ruled by that thing there
Successful though the final bid to break
His power, let no one prematurely swear
It's over: there are others in his wake!

p. 203
Look what I'm holding here. His coat. I thought
It was a sword I went to fetch.
My son died all too soon. Just one more battle
And Argos would collapse. But all the courage
And daring that we saw was theirs alone.
So Thebes now falls.

p. 205
K. You only see the nose before your face
   And fail to see the divinely ordered state.
A. It may be divinely ordered, Creon, but I'd rather
   See it humanely ordered, child of Menoeceus.

p. 206
Emerge from the darkness and go
Before us a while

Friendly one, with the light step
Of total certainty, a terror
To wielders of terror.

You turn your face away. I know
How much you dreaded death, and yet
Even more you dreaded
Life without dignity.

You would not let the mighty
Get away with it, nor would you
Compromise with the confusers, or ever
Forget dishonour. And over their atrocities   (Martin Esslin[5]
There grew no grass.   W/M, pp. 414–15)

p. 220
Consul   A question:
  The Marcii request ten days of mourning,
   According to the Lex Pompilia, for their sons,
   Fathers, brothers, women-folk.
Brutus   Rejected.
  (*The Senate resumes its business*)

p. 221
If the indispensable man frowns
Two empires quake.
If the indispensable man dies
The world looks around like a mother without milk for her child.
If the indispensable man were to come back after his death
In the entire country there wouldn't be a job for him as a hall-
   porter.   (Derek Bowman[6]
            W/M, pp. 398–9)

p. 244
So ends the story of a journey. You have heard and you have seen.
You saw what is usual, what continually happens, but we ask you:
whatever is not strange, find it estranging! Let what is usual astound
you. What is the rule, recognize as an abuse. And where you have
recognized abuse, make redress!

p. 248
Go! Try to solve the problem we've discussed!
There must be a solution, must, must, must!

p. 252
The struggle, as you see, is pretty tough
And yet there is already hope enough.
So long as you can laugh you're almost free
And that's why we've put on this comedy.

pp. 261–2

'They're only waiting for the chance to get contracts,' thought Macheath with revulsion. 'And if there's one thing the ex-thief in me detests, it's all this haggling! There I am, bothering about percentages. Why don't I just take my knife and stick it in them when they won't let me have what I want? What an indignity, pulling away at a cigar and drawing up contracts! I'm supposed to wangle clauses into them and drop hints! Why not simply "Your money or your life"? Why bother with a contract when you can achieve the same end by shoving splinters under their fingernails? Why all this undignified skulking behind magistrates and bailifs? It's so degrading. Of course, you don't get anywhere nowadays with good old honest-to-goodness daylight robbery. That's to commercial practice what sail is to steam in navigation. Yes, but the good old days were more essentially human.'

p. 262

'Take my employee for example. I cash in on their ignorance as to where to turn if I throw them out on the street. I squeeze them as hard as I can and I make a profit out of it. I can assume that they need help pretty badly. Perhaps I could make a profit out of helping them?'

p. 267

'You must sell him *culture*. I mean books, cheap novels, the sort of stuff that doesn't depict life drably, but in brighter colours, something to give the man-in-the-street a sense of higher values, acquaint him with the manners of high society, the desirable way of life of the socially privileged.'

pp. 275–6

The public career of the great Sir Francis Bacon ended like a cheap parable based on the fallacious proverb 'Crime does not pay'.

p. 284

On the First of May
Father and Mother march away
Fighting for prosperity.
No more grinding poverty
   Green are the branches
   The flag is red.
   Only the coward
   Lives in dread.

'T is the month of May
The corn is ripening day by day.

Fair the harvest—life is fair!
Let us all join hands and swear
That we're certain of the way.
   Green are the meadows
   The flag is red.
   Ours the labour
   Ours the bread!

p. 285
I admit it: I
Have no hope
The blind talk of a way out. I
See.

When the errors have been used up
As our last companion, facing us   (Michael Hamburger[4,8]
Sits nothingness.   W/M, p. 59)

p. 288
In the grey light before morning the pine trees piss
And their vermin, the birds, raise their twitter and cheep.
At that hour in the city I drain my glass, then throw
The cigar butt away and worriedly go to sleep.
                (Michael Hamburger[1,8]
                W/M, p. 107)

p. 288
          enmeshed in the business
Of politics and the dry, indecorous vocabulary   (Frank Jellinck[5]
Of dialectical economics.   W/M, p. 225)

p. 289
Inside me contend
Delight at the apple tree in blossom
And horror at the house-painter's speeches.
But only the second   (John Willett[3]
Drives me to my desk.   W/M, p. 331)

p. 292
Those fish-stocked waters! Lovely trees as well!
Such scents of berries and of birches there!
Thick-chorded winds that softly cradle air
As mild as though the clanking iron churns
Trundled from the white farmhouse were al lleft open!
Dizzy with sight and sound and thought and smell
The refugee beneath the alders turns   (John Willett[3]
To his laborious job: continued hoping.   W/M, p. 353)

p. 294
Let the church bells ring
It was nothing but a lie
A man is not a bird
No man will ever fly   (Michael Hamburger[4,8]
Said the bishop to the people.   W/M, p. 244)

p. 295
And yet we know:
Hatred, even of meanness
Contorts the features.
Anger, even against injustice   (John Willett[4]
Makes the voice hoarse.   W/M, p. 320)

p. 297
In the early hours
The fir-trees are copper.
That's how I saw them
Half a century ago
Two world wars ago   (Derek Bowman[7]
With two young eyes.   W/M, p. 442)

Index of Brecht's Works

General Index of Names

Abraham, P., 33
Adamov, A., 252
Adenauer, K., 189
Agranovski, A., 26n.
Alexander the Great, 58–9
Ammer, K. L., 192
Anouilh, J., 199, 201, 246
Aquinas, T., 79, 131
Aristophanes, 251
Aristotle, 45, 81, 86–7, 108, 180, 197, 219, 226, 233 ff., 245, 248, 258–9
Arnould, A., 115
Augustine, 131, 149
Austen, J., 267

Babeuf, F. N., 77
Bacon, F., 23, 49, 61, 79, 275–9
Bakunin, M., 55
Balzac, H. de, 226, 254, 256, 259–60, 280
Barberini, F., 82, 85–6, 95, 130
Bebel, A., 117
Becher, J. R., 108–9, 160, 284
Beckett, S., 252
Beethoven, L. van, 123
Bellarmino, R., 84–5
Bennett, A., 257
Bentley, E., 105, 129, 180, 251
Berblinger, A., 60
Berdyayev, N. A., 7
Berger, L., 165
Berghaus, R., 217
Beria, L., 113
Beslay, C., 112, 122
Bieberback, L., 182
Bismarck, O. Prinz von, 111, 117–18, 122
Blackmore, M., 190
Blanqui, L. A., 121
Bloch, E., 123–4
Bober, M. M., 77
Boccaccio, G., 279
Bock, F. von, 187
Bormann, M., 133
Bosch, R., 169

Bowra, C. M., 198
Brabant, F. H., 117
Bracher, K. D., 191
Bradley, A. C., 197, 221, 234
Bradley, J., 91
Brady, R., 190
Breughel, P., 87
Brontë, E., 258
Brüning, H., 174
Bruno, G., 61, 276, 278–80
Brunt, P. A., 69n.
Bryden, R., 41n., 217, 221
Büchner, G., 292
Buckwitz, H., 94
Bukharin, N. 91, 146
Buren, P. van, 248
Burke, E., 216
Burns, R., 44
Burri, E., 57
Busch, E., 57, 94, 96
Butler, S., 2

Caccini, T., 85
Čapek, K. M., 43
Capone, A., 171–2, 261
Carsten, F. L., 163
Castelli, B., 83, 91
Cervantes, M. de, 226–7, 254, 265
Chamberlain, H. S., 170
Chaplin, C., 173
Chekhov, A. P., 40, 226, 239
Chesterton, G. K., 254, 266
Chiarini, P., 192
Chirico, G. di, 242
Christian, R. F., 108
Chuang-tzu, 192
Claudel, P., 246
Clausewitz, K. von, 75
Clavius, C., 85
Coleridge, S. T., 214, 217, 241
Condorcet, M. J., marquis de, 4
Confucius, 153
Constantine the Great, 131–2
Copernicus, N., 81–3, 87–8, 276
Cortez, H., 15, 58